GW00671592

The Decline
of the
Big House in Ireland

A Study of Irish Landed Families
1860–1960

Terence Dooley

WOLFHOUND PRESS

Published in 2001 by
Wolfhound Press Ltd
68 Mountjoy Square
Dublin 1, Ireland
Tel: (353-1) 874 0354
Fax: (353-1) 872 0207

© 2001 Terence Dooley

All rights reserved. No part of this book may be reproduced or utilised in any form or by any means digital, electronic or mechanical including photography, filming, video recording, photocopying, or by any information storage and retrieval system or shall not, by way of trade or otherwise, be lent, resold or otherwise circulated in any form of binding or cover other than that in which it is published without prior permission in writing from the publisher.

British Library Cataloguing in Publication Data
A catalogue record for this book is available from the British Library.

The author and publishers have made every reasonable effort to contact the copyright holders of photographs and texts reproduced in this book. If any involuntary infringement of copyright has occurred, sincere apologies are offered and the owners of such copyright are requested to contact the publishers.

ISBN 0-86327-850-7

5 4 3 2

Cover design: Wolfhound Press
Front-cover image: 'Fête Day at Castle Bernard. Bessie, Evie, Vera and Rika the dog. 29 July 1904.' Spine image: 'Castle Bernard, King's County, 29 July 1904'. Both Magan Collection, courtesy Offaly Historical and Archaeological Society
Typesetting and book design: Wolfhound Press
Printed and bound by MPG Books Ltd., Bodmin, Cornwall

CONTENTS

ACKNOWLEDGEMENTS

The writing of this book would not have been possible without the support, encouragement and advice which I have received from Professor R.V. Comerford. I am particularly grateful for his friendship and the innumerable kindnesses which he has shown me over many years. I would also like to take this opportunity to thank the academic and executive staff of the Department of Modern History, NUI Maynooth, for their help. A special word of thanks to Monsignor P.J. Corish who, as then Professor of Modern History, was very supportive of me when I first contemplated post-graduate study.

I wish to thank the directors, governing bodies and staffs of the following for allowing me to use collections of manuscripts in their keeping: the National Archives, Dublin; the National Library of Ireland; the Public Record Office of Northern Ireland; the Irish Architectural Archives, Dublin; the Public Record Office, London; the Library of Trinity College, Dublin; Russell Library, Maynooth; Church of Ireland Library; Monaghan County Museum; Offaly Historical and Archaeological Society; Valuation Office, Dublin; Registry of Deeds, Dublin; Monaghan County Council Offices; Monaghan County Museum; Cavan County Library; and University College Dublin, Archives Department.

I am also especially grateful to the many individuals who have helped me along the way. While apologising to any whose names I may have omitted inadvertently, I wish to record my indebtedness to the following: Dr W.E. Vaughan who most generously read an earlier draft; Professor P.J. Duffy, Hon. Desmond Guinness, Catriona Crowe, Aideen Ireland, Jim O'Shea, Dr Niamh Brennan, Michael Byrne, John Kenny, Brian Connolly, Oliver Dunne and Padraig Clerkin, all of whom gave me valuable assistance in finding sources and selecting illustrations. Gerard Morgan has always been available, not only as a friend, but also as photographer and computer guru (!); Jim King spent many late nights and early mornings listening to this author attempting to unravel his thoughts and helping immeasurably in the process; thanks to Michael McMahon, Pat McKelvey and

Pat Mulvihill for long years of friendship and encouragement. The staff of St Laurence College provided a friendly and supportive environment in which to work during the progress of this book. Catherine Heslin typed an earlier draft with the speed that only she can, saving me an immense amount of time; Dermot and Janet Beaumont-Nesbitt most generously provided me with access to their family archive and went to great trouble to locate photographic material.

I would like to thank Seamus Cashman of Wolfhound Press for taking on this project and Emer Ryan and the staff of Wolfhound for guiding it through the various stages.

Finally, the completion of this work would not have been possible without the support, encouragement and friendship of those closest to me. To my parents I owe a debt of gratitude that goes deeper than words. Thanks also to my brothers, sisters and their respective families who throughout each year continue to provide such wonderful and generous hospitality to one who still finds it difficult to resist the allure of Monaghan. Unfortunately, neither Paddy nor Nan Dolan lived to see this work completed but their memories are cherished.

Above all I wish to thank my wife, Annette, and my son, Conor, both of whom have had to live with this project as long as they have had to live with me. Annette has been a wonderful source of strength and encouragement for many years. Conor has lit up both our lives in the last three years. In partial recompense for all the sacrifices they have had to make, this work is dedicated to them with love.

1
INTRODUCTION

Is it height — in this country of otherwise low buildings — that got these Anglo-Irish houses their 'big' name? Or have they been called 'big' with a slight inflection — that of hostility, irony? One may call a man 'big' with just that inflection because he seems to think the hell of himself.

ELIZABETH BOWEN, 'THE BIG HOUSE' IN HERMIONE LEE (ED.), *THE MULBERRY TREE* (1986), P. 26

In Ireland, the country homes of Irish landlords were traditionally referred to as 'big houses' by the wider community (but very seldom, it seems, by landlords themselves)[1]. Much of the explanation for the use of this terminology lies in the above quotation from Elizabeth Bowen. Even the houses of the lesser gentry were big in comparison to those of the largest Irish tenant farmers and in pre-Famine Ireland huge in comparison to cottiers' mud cabins and labourers' cottages. One can only imagine a tenant's reaction on seeing for the first time (if the opportunity arose) a palatial mansion such as Carton or Castletown. Of course, these houses were built to inspire awe in social equals and, indeed, deference in the lower social classes. But deference in Ireland was also tinged with a sense of resentment primarily because they were built on what most tenant farmers would deem to have been confiscated land. So they were called 'big' with more than a slight inflection for, above all, and particularly from the 1880s, they inspired hostility.

In England such open hostility towards landlords' homes did not exist, at least not in the same virulent nature that it did in Ireland following the period of the land war. Undoubtedly, the political monopoly and economic wealth of English landowners were the targets of a growing commercial and urban class that was clamouring for a commensurate share in both from the nineteenth century onwards. But there the fall of the landed class took place much more slowly and much more peacefully than in Ireland. Country houses did not come under physical attack from social and political revolutionaries as big houses did in Ireland, most notably during the revolutionary period from 1919 to 1923. In fact, as Peter Mandler has recently written:

> ... the older stately homes were popularised as symbols of the common national history shared by all classes.... The older houses were viewed ... not as private homes but as common property; they were the 'mansions of England', not merely of their aristocratic owners. The owners, as befitted a progressive, adaptive elite, accommodated themselves to this view. They indulged a rapidly growing audience for national history in its desire to write about, read about and indeed to visit the mansions of England: the mid-nineteenth century was the first great age of country house visiting.[2]

Not so in Ireland. Few cultural bonds existed between the vast majority of Irish landlords and tenants. Big houses were not popularised as symbols of a common national history shared by all classes. And, above all, in Ireland they remained private homes until the late twentieth century, unopened to a public that was not as curious as the one in Britain to view their lavish surroundings or as appreciative of them as public repositories of works of fine art.

* * *

This book is a study of big house life from around 1870 to 1950 in the twenty-six counties that now constitute the Irish Republic. It was felt necessary to confine the study geographically because of the different socio-economic and political conditions which existed in the six north-eastern counties of Ulster as much before 1920 as after the passing of the Government of Ireland Act of that year which established the state of Northern Ireland. Big houses there require and deserve a separate treatment.

For the purposes of this work a big house is defined as the primary country residence of a landlord who held more than 500 acres, part of which was rented to tenant farmers. The Irish landed class was not a homogeneous socio-economic grouping. At the upper end of the scale there were the landed magnates who owned tens of thousands of acres sometimes spread throughout the length and breadth of the country and who were almost invariably peers — dukes, earls, marquises, viscounts and barons[3] — or land-owning baronets and knights. At the lower end of the scale were the lesser gentry whose estates might be confined to a few townlands in one parish. While landlords were predominantly Protestant, there were a number of significant Catholic landlords by the 1870s including the Earl of

Granard who owned around 15,000 acres in Longford and Leitrim. Nevertheless, regardless of religion, social standing or estate size all landlords shared the same cultural values, and to varying extents they exercised the same social, political and economic powers that were conferred by landownership in their respective localities.

In almost all cases the size of the landed estate dictated the physical size of the big house. A titled magnate such as the Duke of Leinster resided in a palatial mansion at Carton; the houses of the lesser gentry were often no larger than glebe houses. However, all big houses could claim to have a variety of functions. Simultaneously, it could be a home, the economic nerve-centre of a large estate, a political gathering place, and a social arena capable of facilitating dinner parties, concerts, and balls. It had a multitude of rooms, a large dining area, sometimes a concert hall (if not one of the drawing rooms sufficed), and often a ballroom. Elaborate reception rooms, such as the hall and saloon in Powerscourt or the picture gallery in Kilkenny Castle, were designed as display areas for collections of fine art. A big house doubled as a theatre, a school, and a gathering place for huntsmen and huntswomen. Its demesne and parkland provided the facilities for shooting and other outdoor pursuits popular in the late-nineteenth century such as cricket, tennis, croquet, or ice-skating on ponds and lakes during the winter. Inside the demesne walls was a hive of industry where gardeners, gamekeepers, farm labourers, masons, carpenters, grooms and a variety of other craftsmen and servants kept house and surroundings going thereby making the big house a major employment centre in rural Ireland.

While every big house was unique, as was every individual family that lived in one, generalisations need to be made and they can be made in order to understand big house life and Irish landlordism. At the time this study begins, there were probably around 4,000 big houses in the twenty-six counties under study. To record in any detail the history of them all would be impossible primarily because of the lack of primary source material. However, in order to acquire an in-depth understanding of big house life during what was essentially a period of great economic, social and political change, this writer decided upon a sample of 100 big houses and 100 landlord families who lived in them. The houses chosen for study were not chosen on the basis of their architectural design, but rather on the basis of the size of the estates owned by the 100 landlords in an attempt to make the sample representative of all the socio-economic strata of the landed class. By the 1870s, twenty-two of the landlords in the sample owned less than 5,000 acres; twenty-one owned between 5,001 and 10,000 acres; twenty-two owned between 10,001 and 20,000 acres, while thirty-five owned over 20,000 acres (see Appendix II). Choosing this cross-section enabled this writer to examine aspects of landed class life which up to now have received inadequate treatment from historians.[4]

To make the sample geographically representative, at least two houses were chosen from each of the twenty-six counties under study. Choosing houses on this basis highlighted the fact that while landlords throughout Ireland shared much in common, the geographical location of their estates influenced the extent to which they were, for example, intimidated during periods of crisis: during the revolutionary period 1919–23, landlords in a relatively peaceful county such as Kildare were much less likely to have their houses burned than landlords in a county such as Cork where IRA activity was extremely pronounced and much more violent. (It should be pointed out here that for some topics, particularly the burning of big houses from 1919 to 1923, a slightly different methodology was used. To deal with houses within the sample alone would not have created the full picture as to what happened during these turbulent years and so an attempt was made to estimate the total number of big houses burned in the twenty-six counties.)

The choice of houses was further determined by the existence of primary source material.[5] The most important sources in a study such as this are estate rentals and accounts simply because so much is based on the economics of the landed estate. Where a series of estate rentals and accounts is available for the entire period under study, they provide a reliable guide to a landlord's changing financial situation. They illustrate, for example, how changes in rental income from year to year impacted upon big house expenditure. Ideally, a series of estate accounts should be available for the entire period under study and, of course, they should be legible and organised in a systematic manner to give details of such things as the changes of rents from year to year. Unfortunately, with regard to Irish estate records, the ideal is too often unattainable. Many series of estate rentals used were unfortunately broken — some covered the early years; some the later years; some covered both but were broken in between. Few collections exist to cover the entire period under study as comprehensively as the Ormonde, Clonbrock and Headfort papers (all on deposit in the National Library of Ireland) and those that tend to belong to larger estates such as these. Nevertheless, all of the estate collections used, comprehensive or otherwise, helped piece together the jigsaw of economic decline that characterised Irish landlord life from the late nineteenth century. The mortgage papers of the Representative Church Body and of

Maynooth College provided important information on the extent of indebtedness amongst the sample owners and on the changing relations between landlords and mortgagees from the 1880s. Annual reports of various landlord bodies such as the Irish Landowners' Convention provided further insight into landlords' reactions to economic and, indeed, socio-political changes, from the end of the nineteenth century.

Of equal importance were parliamentary papers. This is particularly true of the return of advances under the various land acts (continued in the *Iris Oifigiúil* after 1923) which allowed this writer to trace the acreage sold by the sample owners under each land act from 1881 and the amount of money received by them. In the past the ending of landlordism in Ireland has been largely associated with the passing of the Land Act of 1903. However, these returns showed that the majority of the 100 sample owners were still substantial landowners up to the 1920s and that with the exception of two of them they had retained their big houses. It was the 1930s before most of the sample owners sold, demolished or vacated their big houses coinciding with a worldwide economic depression that decimated their share portfolios and the reduction of the land they had retained below a viable level by compulsory acquisition under the Free State land acts.[6]

Considering the fact that accounts and figures alone do not tell the history of the big house, the choice of a number of those in the sample was determined by the existence of personal papers that might tell something of the social life within an individual big house or something of the political life and opinions of its owners. Therefore, houses such as Currygrane, the County Longford home of J.M. Wilson, and Charleville, the County Wicklow home of Viscount Monck, were chosen not because of the richness of estate accounts but because of the existence of personal correspondence that shed light on areas that accounts could not. While sources such as diaries and memoirs may have their limitations, they should not be easily dismissed. For example, diaries such as those of Lady Alice Howard of Shelton record in some detail her own social life and that of her peers. In autobiographies and published memoirs writers also provide an insight into such areas as their upbringing and education and record their reaction to events as they unfolded.

Quantitative data on landlord families and the servants they employed was drawn from the household schedule returns of the 1901 and 1911 censuses. Further information on servants was gleaned from wage books and newspaper columns. Inventories and sales catalogues (published and unpublished) were invaluable in reconstructing what the typical big house looked like inside.

From a political point of view, material on deposit in the Public Records Office of Northern Ireland (PRONI) relating to the Unionist movement in Ireland proved very informative. Pamphlets and colonial office papers, particularly the monthly police reports from the mid-1880s to 1921 (available on microfilm in the NLI) supplemented these sources. These police reports helped to gauge the extent to which landlords were exposed to agrarian agitation during the extended land war and to estimate the number of big houses burned during the revolutionary period. This estimate could not be completed without a comprehensive study of the daily editions of *The Irish Times* and the compensation files in both the National Archives and the Public Record Office in London. Files from various departments especially those of the Taoiseach, Justice and Finance helped to sort out the chaos of this period and what followed as the embryonic Free State government began to assert its authority. Newspapers proved to be a very valuable source for the entire study and along with *The Irish Times*, the *Freeman's Journal* was used extensively to give a balanced view of national events. For more regional issues it was found necessary to supplement the national newspapers with a wide range of provincial ones, a full list of which appears in the bibliography. To formulate the overall picture, minutes of evidence of select committees and inquiries, official publications, guides, works of reference, contemporary works, and works of fiction, which had the big house as their theme or setting did the rest.

* * *

There is no doubting the fact that the big house has exuded a certain mystique which has attracted Irish writers from the beginning of the nineteenth century and which has resulted in an outpouring of works of fiction. (More recently it has inspired critical analyses of the genre such as Jacqueline Genet (ed.) *The Big House in Ireland: Reality and Representation* (1991) and Vera Kreilkamp, *The Anglo-Irish Novel and the Big House* (1998).) One of the simplest reasons for this is that many nineteenth and early twentieth century writers who used the big house as a backdrop to their works were themselves born into landed families including Maria Edgeworth, George Moore, Somerville and Ross, Lennox Robinson and Elizabeth Bowen. Modern writers such as John McGahern and John Banville continue to use the big house as a setting for some of their works. Their cultural and class backgrounds are not the same as the aforementioned writers but they have continued to find the romantic qualities of the big house alluring (and probably financially rewarding). Indeed, one critic has pointed out that the genre 'seems to have flourished in direct proportion to the historical demise of the culture it seeks to portray'.[7] However, while works of fiction can offer interesting side-lights on changing aspects of big house life, especially those written by the landlord class who actually witnessed the demise of the big house firsthand, they cannot substitute for an historical study of the factual reasons for decline. The dictates of publishing, the impor-tance of characterisation (which too often has given us the disreputable, dissipative heir who propels an estate and big house into financial crisis by his improvidence) and the necessity of provid-ing an audience with a lighter form of entertainment mean that a writer of fiction might not necessarily draw inspiration or back-ground for his or her work from items such as estate accounts, mortgage papers and such tools of statistical evidence — the logical sources of reference for an historian.

Since the early 1970s, the big house has also drawn much atten-tion from specialists in art and architecture such as Desmond Guinness and William Ryan,[8] Mark Bence-Jones,[9] Peter Somerville-Large[10] and Maurice Craig.[11] These writers have all made an invaluable contribution to recreating in print the former splendour of Irish big houses and their surroundings and, indeed, their efforts to awaken large sections of the public and public bodies to the impor-tance of the preservation of big houses have been highly commendable. It was, in fact, Mark Bence-Jones's tremendous efforts to catalogue the big houses of Ireland in his *A Guide to Irish Country Houses*, which largely inspired the idea to undertake this study. His *Guide* proved invaluable as a reference for such information as dates of con-struction and architectural design of the sample houses.

And what of historians? In recent years the landed class has attracted a great deal of attention from scholars such as B.L Solow,[12] J.S. Donnelly Jr.,[13] and W.E. Vaughan.[14] They have contributed to a major re-interpretation of Irish landlordism which saw the predatory Irish landlord as the central figure in nineteenth century Irish life which from an historiographical point of view owed much to J.E. Pomfret's *The Struggle for Land in Ireland, 1800–1923* (Princeton, NJ, 1930). However, their works concentrate on certain aspects of landlord–tenant relations, in Dr Vaughan's case to 'evictions, rents, tenant right, estate management, agrarian outrages, and conflicts between landlords and tenants' in mid-nineteenth century Ireland.[15] Similarly, little has been written about the social lives of Irish land-lords, the most scholarly work to date on this aspect of the subject being an essay by L.P. Curtis Jr.[16]

This book provides a new dimension on Irish landlords by providing a perspective from within the big house and carrying the history of their demise as a socio-economic class through to the 1950s. Besides analysing how the great social and political upheavals from the late 1870s impinged upon big house life, it explores such themes as the consequences of the revolutionary transfer of landowner-ship post-1903 under the terms of the Wyndham Land Act; the effects of a new phase of land agitation from 1917 to 1923 and the final break up of landed estates under the Free State Land Acts from 1923. Finally, it shows how the coincidence of the break up of estates, increased taxation and the economic depression in the 1920s and 1930s, sounded the death knell for so many Irish big houses.

The political decline of Irish landlords has been well documented by historians such as K.T. Hoppen[17] and Alvin Jackson.[18] Patrick Buckland has examined Unionist politics in both Northern Ireland and the twenty-six counties.[19] However the history of Unionism (and specifically from this work's perspective the role of landlords in the movement) in the three northern counties of Monaghan, Cavan and Donegal, has largely got caught, and lost, between two stools, again something this work attempts to rectify.[20] It also takes an in-depth look at the effects of the revolutionary period 1919–23 on the big house in Ireland. Michael Hopkinson's authoritative work on the Civil War devotes just over two pages to southern landlords during these traumatic years. This is quite surprising, considering his own assertion that 'in the long term, the part of the population which suf-fered most from the revolutionary period were the southern Unionists, particularly those of them who were large landowners'.[21] Indeed, until now no attempt has been made to investigate in detail the actual number of big houses which were burned during the War of Independence and the Civil War, or to examine the motivation behind their burnings.

This book does not claim to be the 'astonishing tome' that Sir Shane Leslie once claimed would be necessary to relate the 'achieve-ments' and 'delinquencies' of the Irish landed class.[22] This author is only too aware that some aspects of big house life are merely touched upon and will in future require much more detailed examination, if not by him then hopefully by others. The role of women in big house life, for example, is largely glossed over. But rather than this being in any way intentional it is merely a reflection of the non-status of women at the time. As David Cannadine pointed out in his *The Decline and Fall of the British Aristocracy* (1990), the 'wealth, sta-tus, power, class consciousness' of the landed class in Britain as a whole by the 1880s 'were preponderantly masculine assets and attributes'.[23] In fact each of the chapters herein could form the basis of a complete volume in its own right. Indeed, having completed this work this writer is conscious of the fact that separate studies of the lesser gentry, middling-sized landowners and the titled landed magnates might very well be a good idea at a later stage.

2

BIG HOUSE SPLENDOUR IN POST-FAMINE IRELAND

'HOUSES OF PLENTY AND BOUNTY'

Each of these family homes, with its stables and farm and gardens deep in trees at the end of long avenues is an island — and, like an island, a world.

ELIZABETH BOWEN,
BOWEN'S COURT, P. 19

INTRODUCTION

Long before the 1870s, the typical Irish big house had become akin to an artificially created island. By reasons of wealth, social standing, religion, cultural upbringing and political power, landlords and their families had become psychologically distanced from the vast majority of the people. By locating their houses amidst hundreds of acres of parkland and gardens, by building high demesne walls or surrounding their houses with woodland (or doing both) landlords had physically distanced themselves from the local community. A buffer of employees made up of agents, stewards, bailiffs and so on maintained this distance and most landlords, when residing in the country, were happy thus to insulate themselves and confine themselves within the geographical boundaries of their demesnes.

Unfortunately, few landlords (or members of their families) have left behind descriptions of their houses and demesnes as complete as those of Elizabeth Bowen and Mervyn Wingfield, seventh Viscount Powerscourt. One can of course reconstruct the architectural shape of a house, enumerate its rooms and describe its furnishings from plans, photographs, published or unpublished auction catalogues and inventories. However, in doing so one loses something of the sense of what the house, its contents and its surroundings meant to its owner, an impression that can be more readily gleaned from memoirs.

POWERSCOURT AND BOWEN'S COURT IN ALL THEIR SPLENDOUR

Powerscourt is amongst the most famous of all Irish big houses, built between 1731 and 1740 to the design of Richard Castle. Architecturally, it basically consisted of a three-storey centre block joined by single-storey links to two storey wings in the Palladian manner.[1] As in the case of most great houses, its location was chosen to take maximum advantage of the natural scenery available to the estate owner. Located about two miles from reputedly the highest waterfall in Ireland and Britain, the southern façade of the house faced across a wide valley and had a panoramic view of the Sugarloaf Mountain.

In 1844, Mervyn Wingfield, succeeded to the family estate of 49,000 acres (36,700 of which were in Wicklow[2]) but did not reach his majority until 1857 by which time, he tells us: 'the place had been somewhat neglected ... so that I found thrown upon myself the work of restoring and adding to the various buildings, and also of completing and ornamenting the terraces and gardens....'[3] In 1857, the Irish economy was quickly improving and so Lord Powerscourt raised the rents on his Wicklow estate by 23 per cent, thereby increasing the annual rental income accruing from it to £18,550.[4] He used his considerable wealth to redesign and embellish his home over the next twenty years or so. Had he been able to foresee the events that would unfold from the late 1870s, he would perhaps have been more frugal. In 1903, he wrote: 'I have often felt since that if one had only known what a depression of agriculture there was to be, I ought never to have embarked in all that expense.'[5]

Powerscourt had at least sixty-eight rooms.[6] The principal interior architectural features were the main entrance hall and the saloon directly above it. The entrance hall was sixty feet long by forty feet wide by fourteen feet high. Its ceiling was divided into square compartments, each division enclosed in shell work of stucco. The hall, as was fashionable at the time with the grandees, was effectively an exhibition centre, where arriving guests were immediately and rather dramatically exposed to curios and works of art collected by successive generations. It was decorated with rare suits of armour and weapons of all types, some of which had been purchased by his father in Italy, the remainder by himself at Christie's and Manson's in London.[7] There was a very large collection of antlers fixed either on the walls or hanging from the ceilings as chandeliers. These antler-type chandeliers, which were enhanced with wood carvings, were known as Lusterweiblen and were of sixteenth and seventeenth century Austrian and Tyrolean craftsmanship. The hall also contained souvenirs of Lord Powerscourt's hunting expedition to India from November 1860 to June 1861, including two elephant skulls. Off the hall were an armoury, gun-room, morning-room and two libraries (one a small octagonal room essentially used as a study, and the other the main library, which had originally been the dining-room.) The main library contained a fine collection of family and other portraits including Walter Osborne's *Mervyn Wingfield, seventh Viscount Powerscourt* and Sir Thomas Lawrence's *Frederick, Viscount Castlereagh.*[8]

His mother's bedroom and bathroom had originally been on the same floor but Lord Powerscourt had both of these rooms merged and converted into a new dining room. The conversion was necessary:

> owing to the great inconvenience which formerly existed, as in almost all old houses, that the dining-room was at one side of the houses and the kitchen and still-room and offices, cellars etc. was as far removed from the dining-room as it was possible for them to be. It is curious that our fore-fathers never seem to have thought of the great inconvenience to themselves, as well as to servants, of this old arrangement.... Whenever guests came to dine they used to meet the soup in the entrance hall. The only way for service was through the passage into the entrance hall and the services of every meal, breakfast, luncheon or dinner had to be carried on actually in the entrance hall. The consequence was a constant attempt to screen the service from the arriving guests and as the preparation for dinner had to go on, there was a cross stream of servants, necessarily in undress, carrying buckets of ice for champagne, dishes, plate etc., through this part of the house.... It may be imagined the bad temper into which servants got, as having to do all the service in this way it became intolerable in the working of the house, the servants were always leaving and made complaints that 'there was nowhere to do anything in' which was perfectly true. After I married in 1864 [Julia Coke, daughter of the Earl of Leicester] I found the state of things so disagreeable that we considered what should be done.[9]

The focal point of the dining-room was a chimney-piece of red Verona marble that had come out of a Venetian palace. There were two very rare alabaster columns on each side of the sideboard recess, which Lord Powerscourt had bought in Christies' and which had originally come from a church in Italy. There was a marble wine cooler, which had come from the collection of the dowager, Lady Carrington, after Carrington House in London had been demolished. A sideboard from Hamilton Palace in London; a pair of ormolu mounted ebony and

Pietra Dura pedestals; and a collection of portraits by Duchatel, Coello, Zuccaro as well as Cornelius Jansen's *Richard Wingfield, first Viscount Powerscourt* also adorned the dining-room.[10]

On the first floor were the main reception rooms (which was unusual for an Irish big house as they were more often located on the ground floor.) The largest of these was the saloon or ballroom, which measured sixty feet long by forty feet wide and forty feet high. Here, in August 1821, George IV had been entertained to dinner by Richard Wingfield, fifth Viscount Powerscourt. The floor was made of walnut parquetry, its design as ornate as the elaborately moulded and gilded ceiling above it from which hung huge Baroque chandeliers which came from a palace in Bologna. The room was heavily ornamented with statues and marble busts on consoles of Homer, Aesop, Cicero, Wellington, Napoleon and Pitt. On the east-side of the room was a fireplace of Verona stone and over it hung a mirror also brought from a palace in Bologna. The two huge chandeliers, partly of carved wood, which hung from the ceiling came from the same palace. On the walls was a series of paintings on panels of gilt canvas representing scenes from the poems of Thomas Moore.

There had originally been three rooms adjacent to the saloon, used as nurseries for Lord Powerscourt and his brothers during their childhood. But he believed that 'for nurseries to open direct out of the saloon was rather inappropriate'. So he had one long room made out of them which presumably was then used for theatricals and such amusements in the evenings, while the nurseries were moved to rooms above the servants' hall. There were two drawing-rooms on the same floor. Amongst the furnishings of the main room were two large Chippendale mirrors (sold by accident out of Tyrone House in Marlborough Street, the former Dublin home of the Marquis of Waterford!) and a Waterford chandelier. There was a further impressive collection of paintings including Brueghel's *St John in the Island of Patmos* and *A view of a Dutch town, 1610*; Cuyp's *Aetatis Suae 24*; Tintoretto's *St Mark Preaching at Venice* and Fra Filipo Lippi's *The Adoration of the Holy Child*.

There were many more valuable paintings and works of art in the house. These included Claude Joseph Vernet's *A Mediterranean Seaport with Figures in Foreground*; Charles Grey's *Merry Days in Glenisla*; Bassano's *Nativity* and Dürer's *Adoration of the Magi*, the latter a bas-relief in terracotta believed to have been brought from a church in Germany by the sixth Viscount.[11] The main reception rooms also contained a wealth of valuable curios such as a William IV silver-gilt circular shaped salver by James Fray; a pair of large Victorian four-light candelabra; an Ormolu-mounted rosewood bureau of Louis XV design; Ormolu-mounted ebony and Pietra Dura pedestals; and Florentine Pietra Dura table tops. Lord Powerscourt and his father bought many of these works of art and curios as 'bargains', it seems, during their various tours of the continent at a time when the British and Irish landed classes were the main purchasers and collectors of such artefacts from the more impoverished European aristocracy. By 1903, Lord Powerscourt was lamenting that such bargains were no longer available:

> I am afraid the days of collecting works of art by amateurs are nearly over; what comes into the market now is often of very doubtful origin, and where genuine old curios are offered for sale the price has risen so as to be within the reach only of the very wealthy, and bargains are seldom to be met with; so many works of art have been purchased for museums and public collections. Also that the number of those which come to auctions is now very much less than was formerly the case.[12]

The fact that the principal reception rooms were located on the first floor and the secondary reception rooms on the ground floor left little space for bedrooms. There were only three bedrooms, a schoolroom, Lady Powerscourt's sitting-room and Lord Powerscourt's dressing-room on the east wing of the upper floor. In the mid 1860s, bedrooms were built in the former stable wing to the east and in the 1880s more were built in wings that were added to the west side.

When reconstruction of the house began in 1859, the old servants' hall was converted into a stewards' room. The original hall had been too small and 'the very cramped and insufficient accommodation thus afforded used to make constant disputes in the house among the servants' and so Lord Powerscourt built 'commodious and proper offices' including a new servants' hall, pantry, plate-room, butler's room, shoe-room, brushing-room and larders. New apartments were built for the female servants and beyond the servants' hall were bedrooms for the male servants.[13] (By 1911, there were at least nineteen household servants living-in. The butler, Sherwood, was married and lived in a house on the demesne.)[14]

Prior to 1859, the local Protestant population of Enniskerry and the surrounding area used the church on the demesne grounds for Sunday service. This the Powerscourts found obtrusive. Lord Powerscourt wrote:

> ... in consequence of the demesne being on Sundays filled with people attending Divine Service, who used to tie their horses to the trees in the avenues, and whose carriages filled the old stable-yard, destroying all privacy, my mother and her [second] husband, fourth Marquis

of Londonderry, determined as my guardians to build a new parish church outside the demesne [in 1857] and more conveniently situated for the parishioners, and also to make the demesne more private.[15]

The new church was completed two years later. A clause in the Disestablishment of the Irish Church Act of 1869 stated that any church and graveyard situated within a demesne could be claimed by the landowner and become vested in him and his heirs. Lord Powerscourt, therefore, claimed the old church and only those parishioners who had rights to burial in the old graveyard prior to 1869 could claim them thereafter, the remainder had to use the new churchyard in Enniskerry. There was also a Catholic graveyard in the demesne, which Lord Powerscourt had closed with the consent of the parish priest, Fr Thomas O'Dwyer, on condition that he gave two acres for a new graveyard at Curtlestown.[16]

The demesne itself was approximately 850 acres in size. In 1911 it contained at least forty-four out-offices for labourers and tradesmen engaged in farming, gardening, carpentry, masonry and so on.[17] The demesne and the home farm at Luggala provided a great deal of employment. In the early 1870s, the number of workmen on the estate, a good many of whom were gardeners, varied from twenty to fifty depending on the season.[18] There are no farm account books available for this time but those for the early 1890s show that Luggala farm was stocked with fifty cattle and over 1,000 sheep.[19]

The gardens were very much the show-piece of the demesne. They were originally designed by Daniel Robertson who, in 1842, began converting Richard Castle's eighteenth century unadorned grass terraces into an Italian-type garden, supposedly inspired by the gardens at the Villa Butera in Sicily.[20] The terracing was still in progress in 1844 when the sixth Viscount Powerscourt died at the early age of thirty. From then until his son succeeded thirteen years later, the work was suspended and the variety of garden statuary collected by the sixth Viscount on the continent remained in their boxes.

For inspiration on how to redesign the gardens, the seventh Viscount Powerscourt travelled to Versailles, the gardens of Schönbrunn in Vienna and Schweitzingen near Mannheim. He consulted a wide variety of gardening experts in Britain and the continent including James Howe and Brodrick Thomas. However, he himself claims much credit for the final design (with the help of his gardener, Alexander Robertson, whom he describes as being 'a very clever man' with 'more taste than any man of his class' that he had ever met.)[21] The gardens were not fully completed until 1880, much of the cheap labour being provided by 'a quantity of poor people on the estate up at Glencree'.[22] By then broad terraces stretched from the house, dotted here and there with statues, and dropped to a large pond a few hundred yards away. In the middle of the pond was a Triton fountain that spewed water 100 feet into the air. A platform made up of different coloured pebbles woven into intricate designs, and five lesser terraces with flights of steps led to a grille at the pool's edge. Two winged-figures of Fame and Victory, made for Lord Powerscourt by Hugo Hagen of Berlin in 1866, stood sentinel either side of the terraces. The pleasure-grounds where family members and guests strolled for relaxation were filled with many kinds of rare shrubs and plants. Powerscourt later wrote: 'The planting of all the choice plants and shrubs, and seeing them increase year by year in size and beauty, has been one of the greatest pleasures of my life.'[23] Rare conifers and deciduous trees were planted throughout the grounds and the arboretum at Powerscourt was to become one of 'the finest in Ireland'.[24] The splendour of these gardens as they then were (and as they remain) is, perhaps, best captured by Edward Malins and the Knight of Glin:

> The whole garden is possibly the last example of the aristocratic tra- dition of gardening in Europe, made at a time when fashionable horticulturists usually had more influence than artists or architects. The unique attraction of this garden is the unity of objects like foun- tains, wrought-iron gates, pebble-paved floors and classical statuary, complementing the careful placing of trees according to their shape, size, outline, colour and foliage. It is a work of art, set below the sky- line back-drop of the Sugar Loaf Mountain. In fact it is a perfect example of what Alberti, the Italian Renaissance architect, meant when he said that 'familiar mountains' should be seen beyond 'the delicacy of gardens'. In this union of architect and horticulturist, Powerscourt equals any of the existing great gardens of Europe.[25]

Such palatial mansions as Powerscourt were owned by landed magnates; the houses of the middling and small landowners were much less imposing. In the 1870s, Bowen's Court was the home of Robert Cole Bowen whose ancestors had come to Ireland with Cromwell in the seventeenth century. It was located on what could be described as a small- to middling-sized estate of 6,740 acres, the bulk of which (5,060 acres) was situated in County Tipperary.[26] The family preferred to live on the Cork estate and it was here in the north-east corner of the county, about a mile from Kildorrery and at the foot of the Ballyhoura mountains, that Bowen's Court was completed in 1776

having taken some ten years to build. Physically, the house was relatively isolated, lying between seven and thirteen miles from any of
the larger towns of Doneraile, Mitchelstown, Fermoy and Mallow. For
Elizabeth Bowen, its final owner, this physical isolation mirrored
something of an emotional isolation which she felt pervaded most big
house families: 'Each of these houses, with its intense, centripetal
life, is isolated by something very much more lasting than the physical fact of space: the isolation is innate; it is an affair of origin.'[27]

Architecturally, the house, reputedly designed by Isaac Rothery,
was a classic example of the tall, square eighteenth-century Irish
house of three storeys over a basement.[28] Originally, it was intended
to form a complete square, with both sides of the house being constructed of six bays, but when money ran out the north-east corner
was sacrificed. The house remained a 'great bare block' untouched by
creepers of any kind. Excluding the basement, it had fifty windows,
twenty of these in the south facade. Indoors the plan was simple; the
rooms were large, 'lofty and few'.[29] There were four rooms down-
stairs — a hall, drawing-room, dining-room and library. They were
all decorated with 'friezes of Italian plaster-work, and moulded patterns
appear[ed] on the hall and the staircase ceilings'.[30] In the long, lofty
hall hung portraits of members of the Bowen family; in the drawing-
room hung huge Victorian mirrors and in the library glass-fronted
bookcases stood between or opposite the windows. In the early 1940s,
the library looked very much as it had been for generations:

> The library, with its bookcases and four windows, is an airy, everyday
> sort of room, only sombre in the worst weather. The arrangement of its
> tables, armchairs and sofas conforms, more or less, to the modern pat-
> tern of living — the only unexpected factor is height. At the south-east
> corner the room receives morning, often still misty, sun. The library is
> pleasant, too, in the evenings, when an afterglow comes in from the
> country round and the log fire, newly made up, blazes away. It smells
> of dry calf bindings, polish, plaster, worn carpet and wood smoke.[31]

Inside the front door was a Victorian glass porch with a glass
inner door, built to exclude draughts. The dining-room was situated
behind the drawing-room while the service door to it opened off the
end of the hall, at the foot of the staircase. The dining-room was
'crowded — with massive reddish Victorian furniture' bought by
Elizabeth's grandfather. The walls of the drawing-room were decorated
with white, grey and gold scrolled wallpaper put up when Elizabeth's
grandmother first came to Bowen's Court. A grand piano formed the
centre-piece of the room.

At the back of the hall, there was a swing door, which led to the
back stairs used by the servants. They worked from the kitchen,
pantry, larder, laundry, wine and coal cellars and boot-room in the
basement. There was also a servants' hall where they ate and
socialised. The main staircase, lit by a Venetian window, was made
of oak. It led to a large upper hall, known as 'the lobby', off which
were three bedrooms. Above the lobby, on the third floor, was a
larger room running the length of the house. It was originally
intended to be the ballroom but 'shortage of money' and 'the hurry in
which the house was finished' meant it was never completed and
rarely if ever used for its original purpose.[32] Balls were held instead
in the drawing-room, while the ballroom was used for a playroom
during wet days and for theatricals in the evenings. On the same
floor, there were six further bedrooms. Each of these bedrooms and
those on the lower floor took their names from the colours of their
wallpapers — the green room, the yellow room, the blue room and so
on. Access to or exit from the house could only be made through the
front door, opening on to the front steps, or through the back door,
leading down to the yard. Elizabeth Bowen wrote:

> The few large living-rooms at Bowen's Court are, thus, a curious para-
> dox — a great part of their walls being window-glass, they are
> charged with the light, smell and colour of the prevailing weather; at
> the same time they are very indoor, urbane, hypnotic, not easily
> left.[33]

The house was surrounded by plantations, with 'belts of wood'
running out from each side of it. The two avenues leading up to the
house met 'in a bow of gravel under the front steps'. Beyond the
gravel was an expansive lawn, set halfway with a grove of trees, that
was used for tennis and croquet during the summer months. The out-
offices were located to the north of the house, overlooking the yard.
They included the stone-cut stables, harness rooms, coach houses,
dairy and cart sheds. Beyond the out-offices lay a quadrangle of farm
buildings and beyond those the haggard.[34] A walled-garden of three
acres lay some distance away, approached by walks between laurels
and rockeries. Bowen described it as follows:

> Inside its walls this far-off garden is a world in itself. The continuous
> rustle of trees round it only makes its own silence more intense. A
> box-edged path runs all the way round, and two paths cross at the
> sundial in the middle; inside the flower borders, backed by espaliers,
> are the plots of fruit trees and vegetables, and the glasshouse backs
> on the sunniest wall.... Inside the bottom wall runs a nursery for

conifers, to be drafted to the plantations as they grow up.... In this garden planned to feed twenty people or more we raise more fruit and vegetables than we can eat, so we sell to anyone who will come and buy. The flowers are, on the whole, old-fashioned — jonquils, polyanthus, parrot tulips, lily o' the valley ... voluminous white and crimson peonies, moss roses, mauve-pink celestial roses, borage, sweet pea, snapdragon, sweet william, red and yellow dahlias, Michaelmas daisies of none of your fancy kinds and small dark-bronze and yellow chrysanthemums see the different flowering seasons through.[35]

This then was Bowen's Court, 'an isolated, partly unfinished house, grandly conceived and plainly and strongly built', like so many other big houses of its type throughout Ireland. Loved by its owners, it was regarded with a great deal of ambiguity by those who lived outside its demesne walls, a fact not lost on Elizabeth Bowen herself. She wrote: 'Imposed on seized land, built in the ruler's ruling tradition, the house is, all the same, of the local rock, and sheds the same grey gleam you see over the countryside'.[36]

THE BUILDING OF IRISH BIG HOUSES

It is difficult to estimate with certainty the number of big houses in existence in Ireland by the 1870s. Mark Bence-Jones's excellent guide to Irish country houses lists approximately 2,000 but he admits himself that his book 'is a single-handed effort produced in a very limited time; so that although it has some 2,000 entries it is not complete'.[37] Moreover, some of the houses listed therein would not strictly come within the definition of big house used in this work including, for example, Ballyknockane in County Tipperary which was used by the Ormondes as a hunting lodge rather than the primary seat of their country estate. There are obviously many omissions in the *Guide* primarily 'due to complete lack of information'.[38] While, for example, Bence-Jones lists only nineteen big houses for County Monaghan, research by this author has found that there were at least forty in the county in the 1870s. This number does not correspond to the number of owners of landed estates of over 500 acres in Monaghan. Officially there were ninety-eight, although some of these were permanent absentees who lived outside of Ireland, such as the Marquis of Bath while even more, such as Lord Clonmell, William Brownlow and Sir William Verner lived on estates elsewhere in the country. It does, however, correspond closely to the number of justices of the peace resident in the county of whom there were forty-seven.[39] The number of justices of the peace resident in a county may therefore be taken as a fairly reliable indicator of the number of big houses in it for, as W.E. Vaughan rightly pointed out, these JPs were after all the 'established, potentially active gentry in the country'.[40]

However, one must also take into consideration that there were landlords throughout Ireland who built big houses on outlying estates as well as on their core estate. The Rossmores owned both Rossmore Park and Camla Vale in Monaghan. The Headforts owned both Headfort in Kells, County Meath and Virginia Park in County Cavan. The Dukes of Leinster owned Kilkea Castle as well as Carton in Kildare. The Powerscourts owned Wingfield in Bray as well as Powerscourt in Enniskerry, County Wicklow. Houses such as Camla Vale, Wingfield and Kilkea were usually used as dowager houses, houses to which a landlord's widow moved when her son succeeded to the family estate and married.

The evidence that exists, points to the fact that the vast majority of big houses in existence by the 1870s had been built before 1850.[41] The core structures of some of these dated back to the Middle Ages including Kilkenny, Dunsany and Killeen Castles. But the high point of big house construction in Ireland was from the beginning of the eighteenth century to the middle of the nineteenth century.[42] The beginning of this building boom coincided with a period of landlord enterprise and investment as their financial prosperity increased greatly, due to a sharp rise in rental income from 1710 to 1730. This was largely the result of the falling in of long-term leases, which gave many landlords the opportunity to increase their rents for the first time in perhaps generations. From the mid-1740s rent levels doubled again and in the last quarter of the eighteenth century there was another noticeable 'sustained boom in rent levels'.[43]

As their prosperity increased, the larger Irish landowners attempted to emulate their counterparts in England by building extravagant houses that would symbolise their economic and social positions in local communities. Landed magnates such as Thomas Conolly and the Duke of Leinster built huge palaces at Castletown and Carton between 1720 and 1750. Castletown was described by Arthur Young at the end of the eighteenth century 'as the finest house in Ireland and not exceeded by many in England'.[44] It was the earliest and largest of the great Irish Palladian houses, designed in part by Alessandro Galilei and Sir Edward Lovett Pearce.[45] Around the same time, Lady Caroline Dawson wrote of Carton:

> Everything seems to go on in great state here, the Duchess appears in a sack and hoop and diamonds in an afternoon. French horns playing at every meal; and such quantities of plate etc. that one would imagine oneself in a palace.[46]

This palatial lifestyle continued at Carton up to the end of the nineteenth century. Writing sometime towards the end of the 1880s, a rather awe-struck Rev Charles Ganly attempted to capture the splendour of the ducal residence, both inside and outside. He enthused:

> Among the many lovely spots that adorn our land Carton stands in the front rank — surrounded by all the accessories that comprise the beau ideal of an Irish noble-man's seat. Here one might wander beneath the shade of ancestral trees that spread their luxuriance over the green sward, or take a boat and float dreamily over the placid lake, or stroll through the gardens loitering awhile to admire some rare exotic, or traverse the spacious halls and saloons of the mansion, or visiting the library, pore over many of the rare and choice volumes of the great writers of old, or passing through the picture gallery, revel in the splendid collections, delighted to find an Irish collection, the work of the greatest painter England has produced, Sir Joshua Reynolds, or astonished to meet so many pictures by Albert Cuyp.... The collection of objections of vertu, especially of old china, attract attention.[47]

Building continued apace in the first half of the nineteenth century. If houses were not built from scratch landlords used their wealth to renovate extensively or modify existing ones. Killeen, for example, was enlarged and altered both at the beginning of the nineteenth century and again in 1841 by the eight and ninth Earls of Fingall. The 1841 renovations gave it a Gothic appearance, a style very popular with Irish landlords at this time.[48] In two stages from 1801 to 1806 and from 1839 to 1842, Tullynally (also known as Pakenham Hall) was transformed from a plain Georgian house into 'a small fortified town: a Camelot of the Gothic revival.'[49] When John Evans Freke inherited Castlefreke in the 1780s he 'found the castle in such a neglected and dilapidated state that but a small part of it could be preserved'.[50] He chose a site in the parkland and constructed a new house. In the 1820s he employed Richard Morrison to carry out further alterations. When they were finished the principal storey consisted of a drawing-room in the gallery style measuring fifty feet by twenty feet; a library of thirty-six feet by twenty-two feet; a dining-room of the same dimensions; a breakfast-room and two other apartments. There was also 'a magnificent hall and staircase', a bed chamber storey of twelve rooms and a basement storey.[51]

The Great Famine effectively brought the building boom to an end. Dartrey Castle was one of the very few big houses built in the late 1840s and was actually finished in 'Black '47', the worst year of

the Famine. It could be argued that those landlords who survived the
Famine already had their big houses; there was no need to build new
ones when they could satisfactorily modify existing ones to suit the
change in fashions. There were exceptional cases, such as the philan-
thropic Oliver-Gascoigne sisters who built Castleoliver in Limerick
in order to provide employment after the Famine. The rich brewing
family of Guinness, obviously not dependent upon agricultural rents,
built big houses such as St Anne's and Farmleigh in Dublin and
Ashford on the Mayo–Galway border. Gurteen de la Poer was built
for Edmond, first Count de la Poer in 1866. There were also the likes
of Sir John Leslie, who came through the Famine relatively
unscathed. He built Glaslough in the 1870s to mark his elevation to
the baronetcy, to have a house worthy of 'holding his Italian pictures'
and, perhaps, as his son suggested because 'his English wife disliked
the rats and the damp' of the original house.[52]

Unfortunately very little evidence exists to establish how much
landlords spent on the building or modification of their houses in the
second half of the nineteenth century. One source suggests that
the Dawsons spent around £30,000 on the building of Dartrey in the
late 1840s.[53] Lord Devonshire spent £48,000 on rebuilding Lismore
Castle from 1851 to 1858.[54] In 1861, Lord Clanricarde spent at least
£12,000 on the rebuilding of Portumna after the old house had been
gutted by fire.[55] Kylemore Abbey, set in the picturesque surroundings
of Connemara, and completed in 1868 for Mitchell Henry MP,
an English manufacturer, cost almost £24,700.[56] In July 1874,
Palmerstown, the home of Lord Mayo in Kildare, was completed for
almost £21,300.[57] Quite recently an article in the *Sunday Tribune* has
estimated that the cost of building such houses today could be £30
million.[58] When one takes into consideration that some of the great
houses took anything up to a decade to build; that scores of labourers
and craftsmen had to be employed; that special teams of stucco workers were often taken in from Italy to spend up to three years
intricately decorating each room; and that they were furnished in the
most extravagant fashion, this estimate is probably quite realistic.

LANDLORD ECONOMIC POWER IN MID-VICTORIAN IRELAND

It was on the basis of their economic strength, derived from the
rental income accruing from their tenanted estates, that landlords
first constructed their big houses. Economic growth from the mid-
1850s (with the exception of a temporary interruption in the early
1860s) facilitated the continuance in expenditure on big houses. By
the mid 1850s, rents were better paid than they had been for a

decade before. More significantly arrears accumulated during the Famine were also paid off, ensuring that many landlords were receiving more than their projected rents in any given year which, in turn, allowed them perhaps a larger share of the economic boom than has been thought. From the early 1850s to the mid 1870s rent receipts on the Ashtown, Clonbrock, Crofton, Inchiquin, Ormonde and Cloncurry estates, for example, did not fall below 95 per cent of projected rentals.

From the early 1860s, rent increases on estates, while not excessive, also put more money into landlords' pockets (although they do seem to have had some difficulty in keeping it there.) Recent findings by historians have put typical rent increases in post-Famine Ireland at between 20 and 30 per cent which findings for estates in the sample verify.[59] Rents on the Crofton estate in Roscommon, for example, were increased by 26.5 per cent from 1852 to 1880. Rents on the Butler estate in Clare were increased by 28 per cent from 1848 to 1880. On the Pratt estate in Cavan, there were general rent increases in 1855 and again in 1866 resulting in an aggregated increase of just over 29 per cent. On the Ormonde estates in Kilkenny and Tipperary rents increased by 26 per cent from 1850 to 1880 (see Table 2.1, p. 281); while on the expansive Fitzwilliam estate in Wicklow rents increased by only 15 per cent from 1859 to 1880.[60] The conclusion of the Bessborough Commission in 1881, for all the scepticism that one might attach to the evidence supplied to it by landlords and their representatives, now seems quite a valid one; only under 'special circumstances' did Irish landlords regard land as a commercial commodity to be let to the highest bidder'.[61] W.E. Vaughan quotes William Wann who claimed in 1857 that it was better for a landlord 'to set his lands at a moderate rent than to subject them to [a] sharper figure and render the payment uncertain'.[62] Similarly, John La Touche informed the Bessborough Commission in 1881:

> I don't think that landlords in general have the land let at the highest rental they could obtain for it. I was offered double the rent a few months ago for a farm that I let at exactly one half the rent I was offered for it.... I would rather have those that I have known holding farms about me than a stranger coming in.[63]

Landlords such as Wann and La Touche, and there were many more like them, considered a regular income to be preferable to any long term economic plan. The latter might maximise profits but it would simultaneously irk a prospering tenantry who were becoming used to a widening profit margin that was raising them above subsistence level, and who would perhaps react negatively to any diminution of it. Furthermore, the economic climate of post-Famine Ireland saw an increase in property values and Irish land became safe collateral, thus creating an intricate web of relationships based on borrowing. Even the economic depression of the early 1860s was seen to be only a temporary interruption such was the mood of optimism created by the previous seven or eight years of economic growth. Tenant farmers used the credit facilities available to them from shopkeepers, publicans and 'gombeen' men. But landlords used each other as well as financial and even Church institutions to borrow heavily in order to better their standards of living, at the same time presuming that the economic boom would last well into the future.

The period from the 1860s to the mid-1870s was important in this respect. By the 1880s, Sir Richard Griffith calculated that British insurance companies alone had lent £12 million out in Ireland.[64] Under the Disestablishment Act of 1869, the Church of Ireland had received compensation of almost £8.5 million; by 1877 it had lent £3.5 million to around 120 Irish landlords. Similarly under the same act Maynooth College received a capital sum of £369,000 and during the early 1870s lent around £315,000 of this to seven Irish landlords.[65] In many cases it would seem that landlords wanted to simplify their financial obligations by securing one large loan to pay off a number of smaller debts they had accumulated or inherited. In 1873, when Lord Cloncurry, for example, entered into agreement with Maynooth College for a loan of £70,000 it was to pay off three loans and a number of family charges, which amounted to £61,500.[66] Around the same time Alexander Stewart of Dunfanaghy, County Donegal, acquired a loan of £55,000 from the college to pay off a loan of £5,000 to a Mr Mackey, and six separate loans of £5,000 each acquired from the Scottish National Insurance Company between 1862 and 1867.[67]

Even though landlords may not have exploited the rental capacity of their estates to the maximum commercial capacity during the economic boom, the regular and full payment of rents (and arrears from previous years) gave them a cushion of profit. This allowed them to meet estate expenditure and still have perhaps up to 40 per cent of gross rental income available to them to remit to their personal accounts. The estate of Robert Dillon, third Baron Clonbrock, in County Galway provides a fairly typical example of a well-managed large estate (approximately 27,650 acres) in post-Famine Ireland. Clonbrock was rather exceptional in the sense that he was one of the few landed magnates who was permanently resident on his estate; he rarely ventured outside Galway and was 'utterly unknown to the society throngs in London'.[68] On the other hand, he was like an increasing number of his fellow landowners who kept a more watchful eye on the day to day running of their estates. In 1848, at the height of the Famine, arrears on the estate had stood at £2,340 (26.5 per cent of projected rental) but by 1860 this figure had dropped to only £57 (0.6 per cent of projected rental). In the interim Clonbrock had evicted tenants hopelessly in arrears (and for no other reason) on an individual rather than a clearance basis, and used a system of assisted emigration to get his estate back on a sound footing.[69] He consolidated many of the vacated small farms, turning them into larger more viable holdings so that by the mid-1850s he had at least twenty tenants who were paying in excess of £100 rent per annum and between them accounting for 40 per cent of total rents paid.[70] Amongst these was Charles Filgate, his agent, who paid a yearly rental of around £320 for two holdings in Doon and Killupaun.

Clonbrock's hands-on approach to estate management was a definite advantage. His ability and that of his agent to judge the mood of the tenants — to cajole where necessary or threaten where necessary — meant that even during the economic slump of the early 1860s, the arrears figure as a percentage of projected rental did not rise above 5.5 per cent.[71] It obviously helped that his larger tenants, if Clonbrock's own farm accounts are anything to judge by, were relatively unaffected by the agricultural depression of the early 1860s.[72] However, Clonbrock also seems to have made a significant pre-emptive strike in 1861 when he allowed his smaller tenants a temporary but full abatement of either a year's or a half-year's rent. His own gross income for 1861 was unaffected. His large tenant farmers and the payment of previous arrears saw to that. Then in the following year most of those who had been granted abatements doubled up on their rents with the result that Clonbrock received something of a windfall of over £14,000. Nor did Clonbrock use the economic boom as a pretext to exploit the rent levels of his estate; rents were increased by only 13 per cent from 1854 to 1869 (with a further increase of 11 per cent from 1869 to 1880.)[73] By 1864, he was in the position to borrow £9,000 from Lord Ashtown to add a further 600 acres to his estate bringing his total acreage to 28,250 acres and raising his annual rental income by approximately 5 per cent.[74] If tenants' addresses are in any way a reliable indicator of their attitude towards their landlords, Lord Clonbrock's efforts on his estate during the post-Famine period were appreciated, for in April 1867, on the marriage of his son, Hon Luke Gerald Dillon, to Augusta Crofton, the Clonbrock tenants proclaimed:

The alliance which you, the son of one of the best landlords in Ireland have contracted with the daughter of a neighbouring nobleman [Lord Crofton], who rivals him in excellence, both resident on their estates, and discharging every duty of their exalted stations in a manner that has ensured to them the love and respect of all.... [Lord Clonbrock's] judicious management of landed property ... has rendered us a happy and prosperous tenantry.[75]

(It is interesting to note that for the nine years for which estate rentals are available for the Crofton estate between 1867 and 1878, they show that Lord Crofton collected aggregate rents of £52,008, a mere 0.5 per cent below his projected rental. Arrears as a percentage of rents due averaged only 3.4 per cent over the period.[76])

For the years 1860 to 1869 inclusively, Lord Clonbrock collected £104,413 in rents, an average of £10,441 per annum, which each year was well above his projected annual rental of around £9,900.[77] During the same period, outlay on estate expenditure aggregated £48,741 or 47 per cent of gross income. For each of the ten years, Clonbrock had between 49 and 62 per cent of gross rental income remitted to his personal bank account in Ballinasloe, receiving in total £58,962 over the period.

BIG HOUSE EXPENDITURE IN MID-VICTORIAN IRELAND

Even though they did not spend lavishly on the building of big houses in the post-Famine period, landlords did continue to spend lavishly on renovating, updating, or remodelling those in existence. In 1855, a single-storey two bay bow-ended wing was added to Clonbrock and the interior of the house redecorated. As the economy began to reinvigorate itself, the Ormondes undertook extensive work on Kilkenny Castle from 1854. The earlier *porte cochère* was extended to become the front hall linking the two wings of the castle and a Moorish staircase was built adjoining the picture gallery.[78] The gallery became the main focal point of the house and, according to a catalogue of 1875, at least 184 paintings were displayed there alone (as well as almost forty in other rooms.) There were works by Van Dyck, Holbein, Zucchero, Canaletto, Murillo, Tintoretto, Kneller, Romney and Lely. The centre-piece of the gallery was a white Carrara marble chimney-piece, designed by J. Hungerford Pollen in 1862, which had seven panels depicting significant incidents in the history of the Butler family. The extensive pleasure grounds and woodlands reserved for hunting, fishing and shooting and the private gardens, furnished with wrought iron gates, statues and fountains, were further embellished around this time. A tennis court and summerhouses were built and an artificial lake was constructed at the far end of the park.[79] In 1874, the building of a porch at Burnham for Lord Ventry cost £1,200; in 1880, additions to Tullyra in Galway cost £6,700; in 1885 the restoration of Killashee in Kildare cost £3,650; while in 1886 the building of kitchens at St Anne's in Clontarf cost £6,300.[80]

While such renovations represented once off payments, landlords had to spend a very significant proportion of their rental income on the annual upkeep of their houses, probably varying from around 20 per cent in the case of small landowners to around 40 per cent in the case of large landowners. At Clonbrock, the annual upkeep of the big house and its surrounding features — gardens, demesne, woods and game — was a major drain on financial resources, accounting for around 35 per cent of aggregated rental income during the period 1860–69 (see Table 2.2, p. 281). (The percentage for 1862 is noticeably lower at 27.9 per cent only because rents collected that year were higher than average; the amount spent on the house and estate maintenance was actually higher that year than any other year during the 1860s.) It is also noticeable that from 1864, when agricultural depression ended and Clonbrock's rental income rose, expenditure on the big house also rose from an average of 4.9 per cent of income per annum for the years 1860–64 to 6.2 per cent for the years 1865–69.

Thus, from the 1850s to the late 1870s landlords in general seem to have had few qualms in paying out a significant proportion of rental income on the running of their houses and surroundings. This was particularly true of aristocratic landowners such as the Ormondes who had to spend in order to maintain their status position. As Table 2.3 (p. 282) indicates, the Ormondes spent 37.7 per cent of aggregated rental income from 1870 to 1877 on the upkeep of Kilkenny Castle and gardens, and in individual years that percentage could be as high as 62.6 per cent as was the case in 1876.[81]

The confidence of landlords to spend on their houses during the 1850s and 1860s may also have been related to the fact that many of them became profit-making farmers in their own right for the first time or else greatly expanded existing farming practices on their demesnes. Increasingly from the 1850s they had retained large tracts of untenanted land which they had not re-let following Famine evictions, clearances or simply disappearances, or which they had appropriated as leases fell in.[82] Lord Clonbrock was an extensive farmer. His net farming profits do not reflect the benefit of farming to him during the 1860s. If accounts are taken at face value, the farm ran at a net loss of £464 over the ten-year period from 1860 to 1869. However, when one scrutinises livestock sales, one sees that

average annual gross profits were almost 250 per cent and were
disrupted only in 1862 by the depression when they fell to a very
respectable 97 per cent (see Table 2.4, p. 282). What one must consider is that the demesne farm was the big house's main supplier. It
could supply to it in one month alone almost 500 gallons of milk, over
100 pounds of butter, twenty pints of cream, twenty dozen of eggs,
eight turkeys, three geese, twenty-five fowl, sixty-five sheep, and one
pig which were then written off against farm expenditure.[83]

By the 1850s, Willoughby Bond of Farragh farmed about one
third of his 6,000-acre estate in Longford. He was, according to his
granddaughter, 'a born farmer [who] loved cattle and considered
them the safest of investments'.[84] From 1855 to 1890, William Ross
Mahon of Castlegar in Galway appropriated over 2,000 acres from
large graziers on his estate as their leases fell in, thus using one
third of his estate for farming purposes. While his predecessor,
James Ross Mahon, had farmed a mere 250 acres in 1850 on which
he reared 48 heifers and 160 lambs, William was rearing 1,000 cattle
and 2,000 sheep on a farm over ten times that size by 1890.[85] In 1887,
Lord Cloncurry, who specialised in buying store cattle, fattening
them and exporting them to England, told the Cowper Commission
that he farmed 2,300 acres of his own land in Kildare, Dublin and
Meath as well as 300 acres, which he rented from the court of
chancery, and 1,300 acres of mountain land in Galway.[86] In Wicklow,
Earl Fitzwilliam reclaimed an extensive farm from a bog at a cost of
nearly £40,000 and by the 1880s he was annually distributing
'several score' of well-bred shorthorn bulls, Leicester rams and
Shropshires to his tenants in an attempt to improve their rent-
paying stock.[87] In 1907, Lord Ashtown described himself as: 'a resident landlord in County Galway, a farmer on a large scale and a
large employer of labour'. He retained 1,200 acres for grazing stock
he reared himself and farmed 4,500 acres of demesne farm and out-
farms.[88] In 1913, the Leslies of Glaslough farmed 950 acres of their
1,500-acre demesne. 100 acres of this was 'fine cropping land' under
tillage, which yielded 'a good weight of grain'. In the summer, the
stock was made up of 140 store cattle, fourteen shorthorns, fifteen
dairy cows, 300 sheep — 'The Glaslough flock of Border Leicesters is
well known and the ram lambs are in great request both for crossing
purposes and pedigree breeding' — and fifteen pigs.[89]

If large tenant farmers were reaping significant profits from a
reinvigorated agricultural economy from the 1850s to the late 1870s,
then so too were the even larger landlord-farmers. As farmers they
were now aware of the profits accruing to their tenants; as landlords
this made them less apprehensive about the possible loss of their

own rental income and more adventurous, if rather too cavalier, in their borrowing and spending. While the decline of the big house was largely initiated by the decline in rental income from the late 1870s, landlord diversification into farming over the previous twenty to thirty years became significant. While landlords sold the majority of their tenanted holdings under the Land Acts from 1881 to 1909, many retained enough untenanted land to continue farming as a viable commercial enterprise. As we shall see, there was certainly a correlation between the reduction of retained land below a viable level under the compulsory terms of the Free State Land Acts from 1923 and the sale, demolition and abandonment of big houses from the 1920s.

INTERIOR SPLENDOUR

The type of expenditure outlined above is merely that spent on the day to day maintenance of the big house. It takes no account of the money spent on furnishing them or on decorating them with works of art. The great houses such as Powerscourt were in many ways purposely built to meet the requirements of housing great collections of paintings, books and curios often bought on the continent during the grand tour. Sometimes, as at Powerscourt the effect spilled over outdoors with gardens and terraces dotted with statuary. Big houses became repositories; rooms in them such as the hall at Powerscourt or the picture gallery in Kilkenny Castle were exhibition areas for owners to show off their collections. Thus in 1820, J. P. Neale wrote of houses in Great Britain and Ireland:

> The mansions of our nobility and gentry, completed at a vast expense, and manifesting a corresponding magnificence of appearance, are many of them the depositories of the choicest specimens of art in the collections of pictures or galleries of sculpture. Natural history in all its branches is also elucidated in the cabinets formed within their walls by their respective patrons; the libraries too are rich in curious and rare examples.

By the 1870s this was still very much the case. Landlords continued to have a basic desire to spend, and particularly to collect fine art, in order to create an environment or lifestyle that formed an outward expression of their perceived status in the society in which they lived. From 1871 to 1880, Sir John Leslie travelled the continent 'collecting treasures from pictures at Florence to books at Sothebys' with which to furnish the newly built Glaslough.[90] Anita Leslie described the house as it looked afterwards:

Within Tudor and Georgian fireplaces had been salvaged [from the old house] and placed in fresh settings, fine plaster work covered the ceilings, marble columns were set up as in Italian palazzos, one bedroom was completely furnished with dark carved oak from a demolished Perugia castello and the drawing room was embellished by a unique fireplace made by the Della Robbia brothers for the sacristy of Santa Maria Novella in Florence.[91]

On the drawing-room walls hung pictures by early Italian masters collected during the tours.

As in the case of Powerscourt and Glaslough most Irish big houses had benefited from the continental tours undertaken by successive heirs. W.B. Yeats wrote of Coole Park, the home of the Gregorys in County Galway:

> Every generation had left its memorial.... Eldest sons had done the grand tour, returning with statues and pictures.... Mogul or Persian paintings had been brought from the Far East by a Gregory chairman of the East India Company, great earthenware ewers and basins, great silver bowls by Lady Gregory's husband.... [Richard Gregory] had brought in bullock carts through Italy the marble copy of the Venus De Medici in the drawing room, added to the library the Greek and Roman classics bound by famous French and English binders... [Those paintings] that I keep most in memory are a Canaletto, a Guardia, a Zurbaran.[92]

Three of the original granite stones in Lord Cloncurry's home at Lyons in County Kildare came from the Golden House of Nero in Rome. Originally they had been placed in the banqueting hall of the Farnesine Palace by Raphael but the second Lord Cloncurry later bought them from the King of Naples. The fourth column was taken from the Baths of Titus in Rome. The hall at Lyons contained a sarcophagus of white marble from the gardens of Venus at Tivoli.[93]

Irish houses subsequently became the repositories of many fine art collections. Amongst the works of art at Glaslough were Giacomo de Campagna's *Venetian Madonna* (later deposited in the Victoria and Albert museum) and Poussin's *The Marriage of Thetes and Peleuz* (later sold to Sir Hugh Lane and now in Dublin's National Gallery.) In 1902, 140 paintings were sold from Carton including works by Van Der Hayden, Brueghel and Gainsborough.[94] In 1937, paintings sold from Dartrey included works by El Greco, Zoffany, Reubens and Coates.[95] In 1910, there were two paintings by Caravaggio in Ballynastragh, the Wexford home of Sir Thomas Esmonde.[96] There were two more Caravaggios in Killua Castle —

The Death of Seneca and Alexander and Diogenes — and one attributed to Rembrandt, *Samson Threatening his Father-in-Law*. In published sales catalogues from the 1880s it is the names of Reynolds, Romney, Lawrence, Holbein, Kneller, Cuyp, Van Dyck, Rubens, Tintoretto, Canaletto, Turner and Gainsborough that appear most often.

In the same way, Irish landlords created huge libraries, often at great expense, as an expression of what they held important and essential to maintaining a certain standard of life. In fact, books were not always bought to be read, but instead to project an image that their owners were aware of what was fashionable reading at the time of purchase or essential reading at any time. Shane Leslie wrote:

> For centuries the printed book was the perquisite of the clergy or the hobby of the big house. Notable were the great libraries which were collected in the specious days. Only wealthy bibliophiles could have collected the Acheson Library at Gosford, the Percy Library at Caledon, the Shirley Library at Lough Fea.... By present values [1930s], a quarter of a million dollars would not have covered those three wonderful hoards.[98]

In the 1880s, there were at least 2,000 books in the Glaslough library.[99] In the nineteenth century the library of Shelton Abbey was 'adorned with a valuable collection of paintings of the Italian, French and Flemish schools' and contained 'an extensive collection of scarce and valuable books, medals, drawings and engravings'.[100] In 1937, over 5,000 books were sold from the library at Dartrey.[101] The collection in the library at Ballynastragh dated back to the eighteenth century. As well as valuable books, the library contained archival material relating to the 1641 rebellion, manuscripts of Henry Grattan's speeches, correspondence of Charles J. Fox, Daniel O'Connell, William Smith O'Brien, W.E. Gladstone, Charles Stewart Parnell, Pope Leo XII and Pope Pius X.[102]

DEMESNES

Moving out from the residence, the demesne played an important role in the day to day life of the big house — it was essentially the focal point of the estate and like big houses themselves could be designed and redesigned to suit changing fashions. Demesnes varied greatly in size and often bore no proportional relationship to the size of the estate. Of the 100 demesnes in the sample, seventy-three were below 600 acres in size while the remaining twenty-seven were over 600 acres. Lord Ventry's huge estate of 93,600 acres in Kerry had a

demesne of only 170 acres. On the other hand, Lord Drogheda's
19,300 acre estate at Moore Abbey in Kildare had a demesne of 1,300
acres.[103] However, all demesnes had much in common: demesne walls
stretching for miles such as those around Lough Fea, home of the
Shirleys in Carrickmacross; gate lodges; plantations; open parkland;
ornate gardens and expanses of lawns for recreational purposes; and
kitchen gardens for the more practical purpose of keeping the big
house self-sufficient.

The big house itself was primarily located so as to take maximum
advantage of the natural scenery available to a landlord, although
the choice of location could sometimes lead to conflict between an
owner and a renowned architect such as William Vitruvius Morrison.
In 1824 Morrison suggested one location for Rossmore Park in
Monaghan but Henry Westenra, Lord Rossmore's eldest son and
heir, disagreed:

> I have received Morrison's answer to my observations. He adheres
> rigidly to his own idea on the subject. I certainly cannot actually dis-
> approve of his plans, but I do think he might have made them upon a
> better arrangement, to suit the situation and the aspect. He writes in
> a rage, I think, at being found fault with, and huffily declares he
> finds it impossible for him to alter or amend his plan, and that it
> gives him more complete satisfaction than any he ever produced....
>
> [The location preferred by Westenra] is a very uncommon and a
> very beautiful place unlike every other. The house should therefore
> be constructed in an uncommon, but picturesque manner, unlike
> every other and in accordance with the place.[104]

Plantations and woodland were extensively created (if not already
present) not only to provide shelter and privacy, but also to cater for
landlords' interests in sports such as hunting and shooting. Landlords
reared their own game and provided fox coverts for the hunting
season. There was approximately 120 acres of plantations around
Castlefreke where the evergreens were said to be 'remarkably fine,
particularly the arbutus which thrives with unusual richness'.[105] At
Shelton Abbey, the woods were composed mainly of oak, beech and
chestnut, the beech trees near the house reputedly being amongst the
first to have been planted in Ireland.[106] Arthur Young described
Castletown as being 'quite surrounded with fine plantations disposed
to the best advantage to the north ... through which many winding
walks lead, with the convenience of many ornamented seats....'[107] At
Glaslough there was a wonderful variety of oak, ash, sycamore, beech,
larch, pine and 'rows of limes in alignment with leafy horse-chestnuts

and Irish yew'.[108] If plantations gave an aesthetic beauty to a big house's surroundings, they also had a more practical function. All estates required a considerable portion of timber for estate purposes such as fencing or the repair of roofs and so on and because of this many demesnes also had their own saw mills. Likewise, timber was a commercial commodity to be sold at profit. From 1895 to 1903 inclusively, the Ormonde estate received £3,800 from timber sales.[109] In 1913, the Leslie estate received £8.10s. per oak tree, £10. 10s. per ash tree, £16.10s. per sycamore tree 'and a plantation of 400 larch poles brought in £250'.[110]

In front of the house was open parkland where cattle and horses grazed. While these animals were visible from the house, they were usually kept away from them by fences or ha-has.[111] Ha-has were sunk ditches, which created an illusion of continuity between the lawns and gardens in front of the house and the open parkland. While they could not be seen from the house they fulfilled the practical function of preventing livestock from invading the ornamental gardens. Close to the house were gardens formally laid out in borders, carpet beds, paths and clipped hedges.[113] The style and grandeur of a large landowner's gardens usually distinguished his residence from that of a smaller landowner. Nowhere was this more obvious than at Powerscourt.

Demesnes were also characterised by the existence of out-offices. Sometimes, as in the case of Castletown, utilitarian farm buildings formed an extension of the house. Generally, however, out-offices were arranged around the sides of a cobbled courtyard, which was entered by an archway. They were not necessarily constructed adjacent to the house. In the case of Dartrey, they were built about a mile from the house, a short distance from one of the main avenues. They were of cut stone and red brick built in a circle around a cobbled yard which one entered through high iron gates. The steward's house was directly across the avenue, a large two-storied red brick residence, of a much higher standard than most farmers' houses. Above the stables were living quarters for the grooms while a short distance away was a row of houses in Foster Place built for estate labourers. (In the 1880s these labourers were paid five shillings per week, out of which one shilling per week was stopped as rent for their houses.)

The number of out-offices usually varied according to the size of the estate. According to the 1911 household schedule returns Clonbrock, Woodlawn and Slane had more than seventy out-offices. Slane had forty stables, four coach houses, six sheds, three cow houses, two harness houses, two fowl houses, two boiling houses, and one calf shed, dairy, barn, workshop, potato shed, store, forge, laundry, sawmill, and motor shed. At the other extreme, a house situated on a much smaller estate such as Beaulieu in Louth (1,400 acres) returned only eight out-offices. Generally, the existence of out-offices contributed to the self-sufficiency of each estate. All employees were provided with workshops or storage areas for their needs. Out-offices of all types were available for animals — dairies, piggeries, calf sheds, cow houses and particularly stables. The predominance of stables — houses such as Woodlawn, Slane, Curraghmore and Summerhill all returned between sixteen and forty stables — reflected the importance of horses in farm work and transport. They also indicated their importance to the social lives of landed families who spent much of their leisure time hunting and racing.

CONCLUSION

The houses of Irish landlords were architecturally as varied as the personalities of those who resided in them. Indeed, the same house may have been architecturally altered several times by successive generations, constructed and reconstructed to suit changing fashions, so that the house in existence in the 1870s bore little resemblance to the one first built perhaps a century or more before. The one thing that they all had in common was their size and even the more modest houses of the lesser gentry were magnified by the wide, open spaces that surrounded them. Their size was the most obvious statement of the economic and social strength of their owners in their localities and as a class as a whole.

As a starting point to measuring decline one must begin with a high water mark from which big houses ebbed. It would be foolish to consider the post-Famine period as the ultimate high water mark. That had come in the late eighteenth and early nineteenth centuries. But after the Famine there was some rejuvenation in big house fortunes and a return to the type of high living that had been temporarily interrupted by the economic and social upheavals of the 1840s. There was no need for landlords who survived the Famine to embark on a further spree of big house building from the 1850s to emphasise their change in fortunes. Big houses were already in existence. So what they did instead was embark on a further stage of embellishment or remodelling of existing houses.

By the 1860s big house life for most landlords had returned to one of splendour and plenty. Most owners spent lavishly on maintaining them as they had done in the past. Their magpie-like owners continued to scour the continent during their grand tours, as their ancestors had done before them, seeking bargains from the palaces and great houses of the more impoverished continental aristocracy that would provide symbolic expressions of the lifestyle that they deemed appropriate to their class. Ironically, it would not be long until they themselves would become impoverished and the works of art with which they had filled their houses would become the targets of the wealthy plutocrats of America.

3

BIG HOUSE SOCIAL LIFE
c. 1860–1914

'AND NO ONE CERTAINLY WILL EVER LIVE LIKE THAT AGAIN'

Country life was entirely organised to give nobility and gentry and
demi-gentry a good time.

SHANE LESLIE (NLI, LESLIE PAPERS, MS 22,885)

INTRODUCTION

For Irish landlords and their families, wealth and social standing went hand in hand with a leisured lifestyle. In the years before socio-political change imposed restrictions on their social lives and before economic necessity curtailed expenditure, landlords' big houses were central to entertainment. In one of her non-fictional essays, Elizabeth Bowen claimed that big houses 'were planned for spacious living — for hospitality above all.... The idea that begot them was a purely social one'. She wrote: 'The getting together of people was meant to be at once a high pleasure and a willing discipline.... The big or big seeming rooms in the big house [were] meant for just such pleasures of intercourse.'[1] T.R.R. Henn, formerly of Paradise in County Clare, described a typical big house as 'a centre of hospitality, of country life and society'.[2] In the 1930s, a former resident magistrate reminisced on the days that he had spent at Lord Kenmare's home in Killarney with 'its hospitable doors always opened and its owners always ready to welcome their numerous and devoted friends'.[3]

But to whom were the 'hospitable doors' of big houses 'always opened'? Who could be included amongst Lord Kenmare's 'numerous and devoted friends'? The aim of this chapter is to survey aspects of the social life of the Irish landed class, in particular to examine the content of it, to examine who landlords and their children married, where they were educated and whom they deemed it proper to entertain.

THE LESLIES OF GLASLOUGH

The Leslies of Glaslough were amongst the largest landowners living in South Ulster during the nineteenth century. By the 1870s, they owned almost 50,000 acres located in the seven counties of Monaghan, Cavan, Donegal, Down, Fermanagh, Meath and Tyrone. Their largest estate was in County Donegal (28,827 acres) and included St Patrick's Purgatory, Lough Derg, from which the Leslies ironically derived significant income from Catholic pilgrims during the Penal Era. Their most valuable estate was in Monaghan (13,674 acres with a valuation of £11,540 compared to £3,473 in Donegal) and it was here in that triangle of the county that borders both Tyrone and Armagh that Glaslough was built in the 1870s. The social life of Sir John Leslie I (1822–1916), his eldest son, Sir John II (1857–1914) and their respective families during the second half of the nineteenth century provides a microcosmic insight to the social life of the Irish landed class, particularly the higher echelons of it.

From the 1840s, the Leslies had become related through marriage to some of the most influential landed families in Ireland and Britain. One of Sir John I's sisters, Christiana, had married the fourth Marquis of Waterford in 1843. Another sister, Prudentia, had married George Augustus Cavendish-Bentinck MP in 1850. Sir John himself married Lady Constance Dawson-Damer, sister of the fourth Earl of Portarlington in 1856. Of his daughters, Mary married Robert Crawshaw of Cyfartha Castle in Glamorgan; Constance married Sir Edward Stanley Hope KCB; Theodosia married Josceline Fitzroy Bagot MP of Levens Hall, Westmoreland and Olive married Walter Murray Guthrie MP of Torosay Castle, Isle of Mull.[4] Although *Burke's Peerage and Baronetage* makes no reference to it, the surviving memoirs of family members and even publicity material circulated by the present owners of Glaslough claim that Sir John's wife, Lady Constance, was the daughter of Minnie Seymour, reputedly the illegitimate daughter of George IV and Mrs Fitzherbert.[5]

Sir John II married Leonie Jerome, the daughter of a wealthy American newspaper tycoon, in 1884. This marriage meant that the Leslies became related through marriage to the Dukes of Marlborough as Leonie's sister was Lady Jennie Churchill, wife of Sir Randolph and mother of Sir Winston. Both marriages were frowned upon in landed circles. Sir Shane Leslie (Sir John II's eldest son and godson of Sir Randolph) later wrote of Sir Randolph's marriage to Jennie Jerome: 'He had married an American in days when such an alliance was considered as experimental as mating with a Martian'.[6] When Sir John married Leonie Jerome it was: 'with the active dis-approval of both sides ... though the American press pointed out that he was heir to Irish estates with twenty thousand gold sovereigns a year virtually tax free'. Mrs Leonard Jerome thought that 'these Irish squireens were poor fish after the magnificent Churchills. A visit to Blenheim and then one to Castle Leslie, Glaslough, decided her!'[7]

At home the Leslies do not seem to have entertained on a lavish scale. Perhaps that northern part of Monaghan was perceived to be too isolated or inaccessible, at a time when travel within the county was still extremely cumbersome. Sir Shane wrote:

> In the county the Rossmores, Dartreys and Shirleys were too far to be easily reached. Lucas-Scudamores were the nearest but all travel entailed hours on a jaunting car or trailed behind heavy black horses in a barouche or sociable with a liveried footman to open gates or to pick stones out of a horse's hoof in days before macadam.[8]

After the rebuilding of Glaslough, the first house party was held in the new house in 1878.[9] Those that were held thereafter were relatively modest affairs. However, in 1896, 'Glaslough was greatly honoured' when both the Archbishop of Canterbury and the Archbishop of Armagh spent time there as guests.[10] Around the same time Queen Victoria's son, the Duke of Connaught, Horace Plunkett and Professor John Pentland Mahaffy were regular visitors to Glaslough for the shooting and 'conversation was naturally sporting and social at dinner'.[11] The raising and preservation of game on the estate was a prerequisite to shooting parties and so a pheasant aviary was erected on the demesne. The 'record bag' for a shoot on the estate (the date of which has not been found) consisted of 511 pheasants, twelve woodcock, twenty-five rabbits, twenty-seven wild duck, nineteen teal and four snipe.[12] The Leslies do not seem to have had the same interest in fox-hunting as landlords further south. Then again, fox-hunting hardly existed in Monaghan, not because landlords were not interested in it — many travelled elsewhere to partake in this sport — but rather because the topography of the county was not conducive to it.

Dinner, whether for family members alone or for family and guests, was an important social event and Sir John relished 'the sacred hour of port following dinner for which he dressed immaculately every evening. And why not since a staff of laundresses was maintained under the butler's wife'.[13] Some time before dinner, a dressing-gong announced that it was time to prepare. The housemaids emptied large brass cans of hot water into hip baths for family members and guests. Ladies' maids attended to their mistresses and valets to their masters. A second gong sounded just before 8 p.m. announcing that dinner was ready to be served. Then 'the grown ups, all dressed for the coming ritual, left the drawing room arm-in-arm for the dining room' where they sat around an enormous table. According to Seymour Leslie, etiquette was simple — initial conversation was with the lady on one's left but after the first course, one turned to converse with the person on the right. The table was laid out with an Irish linen tablecloth, old Irish silver, a Charles II fruit basket, William and Mary candlesticks, Waterford glass and 'a too-high arrangement of flowers'.[14]

Sir John I, however, 'never counted much socially' being a rather shy man who tended to avoid travelling to social events in other big houses. He was more interested in painting (as an artist he was reasonably competent having his major work, '*Peter Negat Christum*', exhibited at the Fine Arts Exhibition in 1872) and male-orientated leisure activities such as shooting and horse-racing:

> When he was dying he expressed his one regret to his physician, Sir James Reid, not that he had lost Irish elections or been rejected at the academy — only that very long ago he had lost a famous steeple-chase in Ireland.[15]

While big house entertainment at Glaslough was reserved for members of the landed class or those associated with it, academics and politicians (providing they shared the family's anti-Home Rule stance from the 1870s), the demesne was opened at certain times to the tenantry and people of Glaslough village. During the 1890s, the Monaghan militia was under the command of Sir John II and when the training period was over 'there always was a day of rough sports' on the demesne. Occasionally, tea parties or picnics were given for the tenants' children.[16] During the third Home Rule crisis, Sir John opened his demesne to allow the UVF to drill there and such drills became spectator events akin to the early days of the American civil war when southern families picnicked on hill-tops overlooking battle-fields. On 16 April 1914, the *Belfast Newsletter* carried an article on a skirmish held there the previous day:

> A fairly large crowd of spectators witnessed the operations, amongst those present being Mrs Leslie, Mrs Guthrie, Lord and Lady Kerry, Lady Caledon, Mrs Crowsley, the venerable Archdeacon Abbott.... The place chosen for the operations was ideal as timber cutting had been in progress and the fallen trees and hilly ground provided splendid cover for the attacking force.
>
> At the conclusion tea was supplied to the men by Col and Mrs Leslie who along with the members of the house party present were indefatigable in attending to their wants.

Sir John I had four daughters. The importance of securing suitable husbands for them is clear from his grandson's remark that 'four daughters required a London spring-board and it was necessary to purchase the lease of Stratford House' in 1872.[17] (The fact that the Leslies frequented London on a regular social basis also made such a purchase necessary.) London at this time was a city of great houses such as Dorchester, Lansdowne and Grosvenor. Stratford was not as grand but still very impressive. On either side of the mansion stretched colonnades behind which were the kitchen (which was out of doors) and the stables. Within the house was a Y-shaped staircase that branched to either side of the balconied landings leading into drawing-rooms. The ceilings in the drawing and dining-rooms were designed by Angelica Kauffmann 'and the chimney pieces were such as only Adams could conceive or construct for the English aristocracy'.

Glaslough held little appeal for Sir John I's wife compared to the social life of London. Sir Shane wrote:

> We moved over to London frequently — as soon as the foreign wives wearied of Ireland ... their country duties were devoted to visiting the poor, entertaining the clergy, agents and duller neighbours. It was no wonder that my grandmother and mother sat down all morning and wrote endless letters to their happy friends on the banks of the Thames deploring the state of Ireland, weather or politics, and making rainbow plans to return to London as soon as possible.[18]

When Sir Shane was a child, his parents and grandparents travelled over and back to London at least three times a year taking with them 'squads of servants, male and female'. Their parents always brought nurses for the children while their grandparents 'were accompanied by carriage horses, butler and footmen'.[19] It was a journey that took up to fifty hours to complete. In London his grandmother hosted lavish parties, sometimes for up to 500 guests, and from the 1850s had entertained not only the most notable landed families of Britain but also writers such as Dickens and Thackeray and artists such as Landseer.[20] Sir Shane remembered his first garden party at Holland House: 'the grounds set with marquees and bunting lit by sunshine.... I remember the graceful iron gates beside which [once] sat ensconced Charles James Fox and even more exciting the powdered flunkey who gave us ices.'[21] One of the highlights of Sir Shane's London childhood was seeing Buffalo Bill's Wild West Exhibition at Earl's Court in the early 1890s. At the exhibition, he watched his own grandfather (along with his cousins, Charlie and

Bill Beresford) ride around the arena 'in the battered old Deadwood coach ... each wearing top-hat and frock-coat but holding a rifle'.[22]

In 1847, at the height of the Great Famine, Sir John I had made the 'grand tour' visiting Seville, Madrid, Frankfurt, Rome, Paris and Egypt. His son and grandson were to do likewise, Shane making it as far as Russia in 1907. During holiday periods the Leslies went to Brighton and Eastbourne, while Cowes, during yacht week in the aftermath of the London season, became Leonie Leslie's 'happiest time of the year'.[23]

The education of the Leslie family began in the home where a schoolroom was set aside. From birth they were under the care of a succession of nurses, nannies and governesses. A German governess, Clara Woelke, was Shane and Norman's first teacher while their younger brother Seymour had a French governess. Indeed, the children had much more contact with servants than they had with their parents. Anita Leslie wrote of Sir John II: 'The small boy had no contact with his mother ... or his father engrossed in artistic projects'.[24] Sir Shane claimed that, as a father, John II 'took no notice of us but if we were particularly horrible he would threaten that when we were grown up he would have us made into bishops'.[25] As a parent, Shane himself seems to have learned little from his relationship with his father. His daughter Anita claimed: 'In my parent's view schools performed the same function that kennels did for dogs. They were places where pets could be conveniently deposited while their owners travelled'.[26]

On the other hand, memoirs are teeming with accounts of servants on the estate with whom the children spent much of their free time. During the late-Victorian period there were thirteen indoor servants at Glaslough and at least twenty more on the demesne. Sir Shane wrote:

> The Irish keepers were a hardy crew and brought me and my brother [Norman] up. They were untiring as they trotted us over the bogs in daily pursuit of the snipe. They whisked us over gaping drains and seemed to know where the snipe would be almost to the rush and the bush. When we suffered cuts they bound them up with cobwebs.[27]

James Vogan, the head gamekeeper on the Glaslough estate in the latter decades of the nineteenth century, came in for special commendation. This 'red-bearded Celt' was the children's 'real governess'. According to Sir Shane:

> We threw ourselves into any lessons whose accomplishment would be followed by an excursion with James Vogan. Our greatest treat was to

rise at six with the gardeners when an immense bell was clanged in
the high boughs of a lime tree by a white-bearded lacky like Time
himself ... and hurriedly dressing in green Caledonian tweeds run
across the river to the hill opposite and over into the woods and up
another hill to the gamekeeper's house for breakfast prepared by his
sister.[28]

Frank Trainor, the groom, nicknamed 'Punch' because of his
addiction to Punch and Judy shows, served three generations of
Leslies before being killed in an accident at Berkhampstead. The
Gilroys were foresters on the estate for generations. 'Old Heatley'
and his father were rat-catchers on the estate getting a penny for
every tail. George Hearst, 'the old carpenter', served the Leslies for
years, while 'Old Matty of the hundred wrinkles ... slaved at a hand-
laundry' all her life, never taking a holiday and saving all her money
'to be spent by friends at her own wake'.[29] Sir Shane claimed to have
been spoiled by maids and housekeepers and a still-room maid 'who
spent her whole life making light refreshments' in a 'house of plenty
and bounty'. However, and perhaps despite himself, he obviously still
viewed in rather condescending terms the relationship between
employer and employee to be very much a feudal-type master–
servant one:

> Servants were still Victorian: willing and respectful, ill accommo-
> dated and poorly paid, but they were more than the friends of the
> family. They were *us* as much as ours and this is a relationship which
> the present age has destroyed. I think they were happy. They gave so
> much and in our absurd feudal manner we loved them.[30]

Sir John I and Lady Constance had four daughters and one son.
The son, Sir John II, was sent to preparatory school at the age of
eight 'according to the new Victorian fashion ... in preparation for
Eton'.[31] In turn, his sons were sent to Ludgrove preparatory school
or Hoddenton preparatory school in London. None of the four
daughters, however, attended school, being educated at home by a
governess.

From there the sons moved to public school in England. While Sir
John I attended Harrow, his grandsons, Shane and Norman, both
attended Eton. Sir Shane was not at all impressed by Eton. As a lower
boy he and his room-mates occupied 'an old battered warren betwixt
the chapel cemetery and Wise's horse yard.... The food was wretched
and tasteless ... Those who had cash spent it on food.... As for the
thrashings which tyrannised rather than disciplined our house, they
were excessive'. He claimed that the standard of teaching was

appalling, that bullying was endemic and that 'Irish boys were ridiculed ... especially on St Patrick's Day'. His whole experience of public school life was, therefore, 'gruesome' in what he termed 'that house of schoolboy horrors'.[32] He could not understand the stories of old Etonians 'shedding tears on the day they left Eton. No member of our house ever wept on the day of liberty'.[33] When his own sons came to that stage of their lives, Shane insisted that neither be sent to Eton and so Jack was sent to Downside and Desmond to Ampleforth.[34]

After Eton, Sir Shane went to Cambridge while Norman went to Sandhurst to pursue an army career. Their grandfather had been a captain in the 1st Life Guards, their father a lieutenant in the Grenadier Guards serving in the Egyptian war of the early 1880s and the Boer War in 1900. Norman was to reach the rank of captain in the Rifle Brigade before being killed at Armentières in October 1914. By that time, a great deal had changed at Glaslough.

BIG HOUSE ENTERTAINMENT

There is ample evidence of tenants being entertained by the landlord on the demesne and sometimes even within the servants' quarters of the big house, particularly between the mid-1850s and the late 1870s which was a period characterised by relatively stable landlord–tenant relations. It was what today might be termed 'good PR' for the tenants to present a decorative and illuminated address to a new landlord or to express congratulations to an existing one on his son coming of age or getting married. It was traditional for the landlord, in return, to reward his tenants' support with a dinner or a luncheon. In June 1855, leaflets were distributed throughout the area of the Clonbrock estate in County Galway announcing a 'great display of fire-works, balloon ascents and artificial illuminations to be given to welcome the coming of age of the Hon. G[erald] Dillon, the heir of Clonbrock'.[35] On the day, 'a vast concourse' of people assembled on the lawns outside Clonbrock and they gave an 'enthusiastic' welcome to the Dillon family when they appeared at the window to greet their guests. A deputation of tenants (composed mainly of the larger tenants on the estate and led by Captain Kelly of Longford Lodge) read an address of congratulations. At 4 p.m. a banquet was given to the tenants and other guests (who included Lord and Lady Crofton, Lord and Lady Clanricarde, Lord Dunsandle, W.H. Gregory and Clonbrock's agent, Charles Filgate) in a huge tent erected on the demesne. Drink and food, supplied by Gill's Hotel in Ballinasloe, was provided for the estimated 600 people present while a string band entertained the guests throughout the evening.[36]

Similarly, in 1864, the tenants and farm labourers on the Crofton estate were 'hospitably regaled at a sumptuous dinner in honour of the return of the Hon. Charles Crofton and his lovely bride from their wedding tour' held in the large barn on the demesne.[37] When Reginald Brabazon (later twelfth Earl of Meath) got married in 1868, his wife recorded in her diary:

> When we neared Bray, Irish cheering in the shape of yells and screeches commenced and increased more and more. Our reception was as grand and hearty as if it had been for royalty; no less than nine arches covered with evergreens and with different inscriptions were erected, and I was presented with a lovely bridal bouquet by the Bray school children and led to make a speech of thanks. When we came to the bottom of the hill before the lodge, a mass of people seized upon the horses, took them out of the traces, and dragged us themselves right up to Kilruddery.

At noon the following day a tenant delegation presented a 'beautifully illuminated' address to the newly-wedded couple and in return they were invited to remain to luncheon.[38] On the night that the Fingalls arrived home from honeymoon in 1883: 'there was a tenants' party in the big servants' hall and it overflowed into a marquee that had been put up on the lawn'.[39]

However, social interaction between the two classes remained extremely limited. Shane Leslie and his brother Norman may have spent a great deal of time with gamekeepers, their families, and tenant families around the local village. But they did not reciprocate this hospitality within Glaslough;[40] farmers, shopkeepers and publicans may have mingled with the landed class on hunting fields, but they did not intermarry with them. In choosing guests to social functions within the big houses, landlords were as particular as they were in choosing spouses. For example, a list of people to be invited to balls and social functions at Kilkenny Castle around the turn of the century reads like a who's who of the Irish landed class. Of the county names, at least sixty-two were landlords. All forty-two names listed for the neighbouring counties were landlords. In total the guest list included twenty-four peers, thirty-four clergymen and twenty-seven army officers.[41] Within this directory, there are three loose sheets of paper which constitute a list of people to be invited to a 'house party' held in honour of the Duke and Duchess of York, later King George V and Queen Mary, who stayed at the castle for five nights in 1899. Altogether over 160 invitations were sent out. 'Honoured guests' included Lord and Lady Roberts, Lord and Lady

De Vesci, Lady Dugdale and Lord Avon. Eighteen peers from Kilkenny and neighbouring counties such as the Carricks, Castletowns and Desarts were invited. Sixty invitations went to other landlord families including the Ducketts of Duckett's Grove in Carlow, the Kavanaghs of Borris in Queen's County (Laois), and the Congreves of Mount Congreve in Waterford. Invitations were also sent to twenty-four army officers including those of the King's Royal Rifles and the fifth battalion of the Royal Irish Regiment stationed locally, and to ten district inspectors of the RIC. Invitations were also sent to twenty-six clergymen including the Bishop of Ossory and his wife, and the Dean and Archdeacon of Ossory.

The diaries of Lady Alice Howard also illustrate the narrow social circles in which landlords and their families moved and offer an insight into how they amused themselves. In January 1874, Lady Alice went to a big house ball, danced until 6 a.m. and was unable to get up for breakfast until noon the following day.[42] During that month, her evenings were taken up by theatricals and concerts and the 'conjuring tricks of Col Crichton'. For afternoon tea she visited neighbouring houses such as Powerscourt, Glenart and Kilruderry.[43] As spring approached, walks became her favourite form of afternoon activity and she was often accompanied by such as Lord and Lady Listowel, the La Touches of Harristown, Lord and Lady Powerscourt, Lady Edith Scott and Col Foster.[44] She returned the visits of her friends spending a week, for example, in Lord Listowel's home at Convamore in Cork at the end of March and beginning of April 1874, where she enjoyed the games of tennis and billiards.[45] Later in the year she attended a cricket match at the Parnell home in Avondale. She wrote: 'It was very pleasant — all the county was there — but we were nearly consumed by midgets.'[46]

Lady Crofton's diaries show that her family spent much of their time in Lord Clonbrock's and vice-versa.[47] Lord Cloncurry's diaries are full of references to shooting parties on estates and demesnes all over Ireland from neighbouring Straffan in Kildare to Castlebernard in Cork.[48] Elizabeth Bowen wrote that at Mitchelstown Castle 'there used to be tennis tournaments on the King's-Square lawns, brightened by cavalry officers from Kilworth and the Kingston's young visitors'.[49] For her, daytime pleasures during the summer included garden and croquet parties and cricket and archery matches; during the winter the highlights were dinner parties, lunch gatherings and the Duhallow Hunt meets.[50]

The houses of large landowners, in particular, extended hospitality all year round. From May 1887 to May 1888, for example, a total of 278 guests were entertained at Headfort — all seem to have been landlords, clergymen or army officers and their families.[51] For the three years 1902 to 1904 inclusive over 400 people came to stay at Sir Algernon Coote's house, Ballyfin, in Queen's County.[52] During the Punchestown race meeting, the big houses of Kildare and neighbouring counties annually extended hospitality to landlords and their families who had to travel a distance. For the meeting in April 1880, for example, the *Leinster Express* listed sixteen big houses from which approximately 400 guests left on one day to attend Punchestown. The Marquis and Marchioness of Drogheda, the Royses of Wicklow, Lord and Lady Clonmell and the Fowlers of Meath had stayed at Killashee with the Moores. The Headforts, the Earl of Bandon and Major Gregory of Coole had stayed at Straffan with the Bartons; the Marquis and Marchioness of Waterford and Lord Langford of Summerhill were amongst the guests who had stayed with Charles Bourke at Roseborough.[53]

Balls were a popular form of big house entertainment during Punchestown and would also account for many of the overnight guests at Headfort from 1887 to 1888 and at Ballyfin from 1902 to 1904. 'All the county people' were at the first ball attended by Elizabeth Fingall at Killeen.[54] She had never stayed in 'such a large house' before and was in awe of the fact that the ball:

> lasted the whole night and was magnificently done in every way. Killeen, lit up with many lamps and candles, roaring fires in the old fireplaces ... with the music in it and the tables in the great dining-room spread for supper, seemed to me more than ever like a fairy palace.[55]

Dinner, as at Glaslough, was an important formal occasion. Lady Londonderry once remarked: 'Breakfast and lunch are informal occasions, but dinner is a parade and you must not be late for it.'[56] While the Londonderrys entertained on a very grand scale, and while dinner may not have been regarded as 'a parade' in all houses, it was, nevertheless, an important social event organised in its own right or after shoots, fox-hunts and race meetings. It was probably the most popular form of big house entertainment, offering the family the opportunity to show off its collection of plate. The family plate collection at Kilkenny Castle contained over 1,000 pieces including 100 gold dinner plates.[57] Annie MacManus, who worked as a servant at the much smaller Clohamon, the Wexford home of the Kinahan family, recalled two huge black chests of silver plate, which the family used on special occasions.[58]

Organised shoots were one of the most popular forms of big house entertainment and almost invariably an expensive one. Game had to be reared on the demesne; gamekeepers had to be employed and a shooting party that could go on for a number of days meant a land-lord had to extend his hospitality and provide guests with accommodation and meals. Shooting parties were male-dominated although the ladies did often go out in brakes and joined the men for lunch, sometimes held in a tent that could be moved according to the location of the shoot.[59] One of the keenest shots of his day was Valentine Lawless, fourth Baron Cloncurry. At a shoot held at Glenart between 9 and 12 November 1886, attended by Cloncurry, Prince Edward of Saxe-Weimar, the Marquis of Drogheda, the Earl of Bandon, the Earl of Carysfort, Lord Powerscourt and Lord Inchiquin, 1,687 pheasants; sixty-eight woodcock; two hares and ninety-seven rabbits were shot.[60] In a diary entry for 4 January 1887, Cloncurry expressed his admiration at Lord Ardilaun's account of a famous shoot at Muckross in 1863. During the shoot, 800 woodcock had been shot in eight days by only six guns, and Cloncurry was impressed by the Duke of Abercorn's claim that 12,644 woodcock had been shot at Baronscourt over a period of forty years.[61] For Cloncurry, it could be said to have been a matter of 'have gun, will travel' for during 1897 alone he attended thirty-five shooting parties on estates including his own, Glenart, Lough Crew, Straffan, Moore Abbey, Ashford, Dromoland and Castlebernard. These were all the estates of fellow peers or, in the case of Straffan, large landowners.

Houses such as Kilkenny Castle and Carton hosted stately func-tions at various times. The future King Edward VII and Queen Alexandra, then Prince and Princess of Wales, visited Carton during their Irish visit of 1885.[62] Later, in 1904, a banquet was held for the same couple in the picture gallery of Kilkenny Castle on the occasion of their visit there. This is how Molly Wills, wife of a local rector, described the evening's events:

> Our carriage was in a queue with a heap of others but they were so slow in moving that Mr. Power, Mr. McElroy, and Percy [her hus-band] came to the window and advised us to walk through the courtyard which many others were doing and so save nearly twenty minutes. This we accordingly did and at last got into the outer hall where the ladies went to one room and the gentlemen did the same in another. We then met in a big square hall with a big marble affair like a square table in the middle on which I managed to get a seat, and the babble of voices for quarter of an hour or so was like nothing I ever heard. At last the word was given and we tramped up the big stairs to the picture gallery where each party was announced and was met and greeted by Lady Ormonde and her daughter....

It's very like a ballroom with a row of chairs down each side and a band playing half way up. We talked to our friends and each other till everyone had arrived, and then there was a stir and everyone got in line three or four deep down the gallery on each side. The band played the national anthem and the King and Queen entered and passed along between their subjects who humbly bowed as they passed, they doing likewise to both sides.... Then after a while their majesties passed on and out again just as they came in and we all began to make a move to get down to supper which was served down-stairs.[63]

Big houses were regularly used for wedding receptions. Lady Elizabeth Fingall's uncle, Sir Patrick Keenan, gave the wedding reception for her and Lord Fingall at his home, Delville, in County Dublin. It was attended by 'an enormous number of guests' including 'the viceroy, [Lord Spencer] and Lady Spencer and all the viceregal court'.[64] A more modest affair was the reception held for Georgiana Sidney Bond and Captain Thomas Meredith at the bride's home, Farragh, in County Longford in the mid-1850s. Eighty people sat down for the wedding breakfast, which was laid in the drawing-room. The couple sat in the middle of a horse-shoe table in the bow window while the guests sat at three long tables. Outside on the lawn, music was provided by the band of the 7th Dragoon Guards.[65] In July 1866, Luke Dillon, heir to the Clonbrock estate in Galway, married Augusta Crofton, daughter of Lord Crofton in Roscommon Church. Déjeuner was given at Mote Park attended by eighty guests, while music was provided by the band of the 59th Regiment.[66]

OUTDOOR PURSUITS

During the winter months landlords and their families indulged in what was arguably their favourite form of outdoor leisure pursuit, fox-hunting. Lady Fingall had 'little heart' for hunting but recalled that 'if you didn't hunt in Meath you might as well be dead. The whole life of the country centred round that occupation. During the hunting season no one talked of anything else.'[67] Similarly, in 1882, J.P. Mahaffy argued in an essay entitled 'The Irish landlords':

... not to hunt is the certain sign of a fool or an ass, or whatever other strong term can express human worthlessness. To shoot a fox is regarded as a far more mortal sin than any in the Decalogue.... Many gentlemen are so devoted to this sport, that they regard the summer as merely a disagreeable interruption to hunting.[68]

Almost a century before, during the high point of landlord enterprise in Ireland from the 1790s to the 1820s, fox-hunting had
developed on a grand scale. While previous to this several landlords
such as Thomas Conolly of Castletown had kept private packs of
hounds and hunted large areas of the country, the beginning of the
nineteenth century saw landlords establish regional hunts on a more
organised basis.[69] The Earl of Portarlington established the Emo
hunt; the Done20les established the Duhallow Hunt and John Beamish
established the Carbery Hunt.[70] By the 1850s, Earl Fitzwilliam had
established the Coollattin Hunt in Wicklow and Richard Levinge
of Knockdrin had established a hunt club in Westmeath.[71] Already
dominant in counties as landowners and politicians, the new title of
Master of Foxhounds further enhanced the social position of such
landlords and many more besides. Despite the fact that being MFH
in Meath from 1888 to 1891 and from 1908 to 1911 'nearly ruined'
Lord Fingall, and despite the fact that Lady Fingall took to the hunting field rather reluctantly, she 'enjoyed being "mistress" and the
position' it gave her.[72]

The initial organisation of hunt clubs was carried out at great
personal expense to landlords.[73] Early organisation involved not only
the building of kennels but also the construction of gorses and earths
to facilitate the breeding of foxes. By the 1860s, the practice of leaving everything to the MFH was replaced by a system whereby the
hunt district was divided into certain regions and other hunt members made contributions towards charges for kennels, hounds,
coverts and damages to farmers' property in their designated area.
This new-type arrangement was seen to be 'fairer to the master as
well as to the farmers and covert keepers'.[74] There remained, however, the added expense of travelling, usually with a retinue of staff
in train, for landlords did not confine themselves to hunting in their
native counties. John Congreve of Mount Congreve in Waterford, the
Earl of Howth from Dublin and Lord Drogheda from Kildare hunted
regularly with the Kilkenny Hunt.[75] Lord Castletown hunted with
the Duhallow, Waterford and Kilkenny packs as well as his own
pack, the Queen's County.[76]

Landlords did not monopolise the composition of the actual fields.
As with other aspects of their social lives, they were at first joined
by agents, army officers, RIC officers and clergymen and as the
nineteenth century drew to a close by an increasing number of
large farmers, merchants and shopkeepers. A list of subscribers
to the Limerick Hunt dated 1 May 1879 contains 112 names.[77] It
includes ten peers — Lords Ashtown, Dunraven, Clarina, Emly,
Fermoy, Guillamore, Massy, Devon, Limerick and Sandwich; sixty-one

Limerick landowners of whom nine owned less than 500 acres, fifty-two owned over 500 acres and of the latter group twenty-six owned more than 2,000 acres.[78] At least another two were land agents; two were doctors; six were army officers and two were ladies. It was not possible to determine the backgrounds of others but it is probable that they were local merchants and shopkeepers or even landed proprietors from outside the county. It was certainly true at this time that few hunts could operate without the support of all classes in the countryside. On occasion, country people called upon members of local hunts to help rid them of foxes. Thus a Mrs Cotter wrote to Edith Somerville, a member of the West Carbery Hunt, that 'the fox is making a great set on me. I am beggared with him. He have [sic] eight hens and two ducks carried [sic] and I badly in want of them'.[79] Local farmers, while undoubtedly annoyed by the damage done to their crops, nevertheless allowed access to their fields. The hunt gave employment to local huntsmen, farriers, vets and coopers. It was also a source of entertainment to country people who, if they could not take to the field, could watch proceedings from various vantage points along the route.

The hunt itself was of great importance and appearances in the field had to be maintained. Lord Fingall might not recognise a dress that his wife had been wearing for five years, but it was an entirely different matter when it came to her hunting clothes. Lady Fingall wrote:

> He would say of a dress after I had worn it for five years or so and when I was about to discard it: 'I like that thing that you are wearing. Is it new?' But my hunting clothes were another matter. If they had fallen short of his high standard he would not have allowed me to come out in them.[80]

The fact that the weather was often 'chilly and showery' or 'wet and cold' did not dampen the enthusiasm of the participants. A meeting of the Meath Hunt at Batterstown in mid-December 1883 attracted 120 members despite 'a chilly raw air and strong wind with ominous dark clouds all around betokening hail or snow'.[81]

Much emphasis was placed on the chase and the kill and sporting bravado may occasionally have added to what was already a good story. Regarding a hunt that took place on 26 November 1859, Lord Naas (whose father, the Earl of Mayo, was MFH at the time) wrote: 'Kildare men claim that not only was it the best run ever known in Kildare, but the finest of any time in any country'. The hunt met in Maynooth from where it made its way to Laragh, on to Kilcock and across the Meath border into Collestown. There the fox was 'savagely killed' but remembered as 'a brave old traveller ... [who] scorned to go to ground in any of the earths he had passed, all of which were of course open'. In all it had been a journey of some twelve miles covered in just under an hour with only fifteen out of the original 150 riders finishing.[82]

At any given hunt in Kildare at this time there was an average of 150 members present.[83] Between 1868 and 1874, the club had over 400 hounds hunting with which they found 970 foxes of which 152 were killed, 273 were run to ground, and 543 were lost.[84] *The Irish Times* described the Kildare Hunt country in the 1860s as being 'one of the best in Ireland.' It went on to describe the eastern and northern districts as 'being the cream, a large portion of which is not surpassed by any country in the United Kingdom as regards scent and good going in all seasons'.[85]

There were close links between fox-hunting and steeplechasing. In their early days steeplechases took the form of what today would be described as point to point races. They were limited to hunters who had hunted regularly with established packs of foxhounds and who had to be ridden by gentlemen in fox-hunting costume. It was very much a natural progression for landlords who were enthusiasts of fox-hunting to become involved in national hunt racing. In 1842, the Marquis of Waterford developed a three mile race track with thirty-two fences on his estate at Ronscar near Cahir for the running of the 'New Melton Stakes'. Amongst the landlords who participated in this race were Lord Waterford himself, Lord Clonmell, Lord Howth, George Moore and his brother, Augustus.[86] In the early 1850s, members of the Kilkenny Hunt held steeplechases at Cappenagh.[87] In 1851, the Ward Union Hunt in County Meath transferred their annual steeplechase meeting from Ashbourne to Fairyhouse, a new course that was to become the home of the Irish Grand National.[88] In 1850, the advantages of Punchestown as a race course attracted the attentions of the Kildare Hunt club, which had hitherto been holding race meetings in a variety of places, scattered across the Kildare Hunt country.[89] By the 1870s, it had become the most popular race meeting in Ireland, if not the United Kingdom, and a great landlord society event.

Landlords were involved in all aspects of steeplechasing. As in the case of Lord Waterford, they financed and developed new race tracks. At administrative level, they controlled the organisation of races both as stewards at local meetings and later as members of the governing body, the Irish National Hunt Steeplechase Committee. They also gave prizes at race meetings. In 1872, for example, 'The

Monaghan Steeplechase' was run for the Rossmore Cup and fifty sovereigns presented by Lord Rossmore. 'The Wicklow Steeplechase' was
for the Shillelagh Plate and 100 sovereigns, which Earl Fitzwilliam
presented. 'The Meath Hunt Steeplechase' was for the Slane Cup and
twenty-five sovereigns presented by Marquis Conyngham. 'The
Farmers' Challenge Cup' at Punchestown was presented by Lord
Otto Fitzgerald of Carton and the Earl of Clonmell gave twenty-five
sovereigns as a further prize.[90] As jockeys and owners, they dominated races such as the 'Corinthian Cup' at Punchestown, which was
won three times in a row by Lord Drogheda from 1851 to 1853 and
three times by Lord Howth in 1858, 1861 and 1872. In the 'Kildare
Hunt Challenge Cup' in 1880 Lord Cloncurry owned and rode Kilrue;
Lord Clonmell owned and rode Conjurer; Lord Mayo owned and rode
Dr Tait.[91]

Flat racing was much more lucrative than steeplechasing but
ultimately much more expensive and while it was enjoyed as a spectator sport by all strata of landed society, involvement in the breeding
and training sides became more the preserve of larger landowners.[92]
From the early nineteenth century large landowners began to
develop the Curragh as a training area: Thomas Conolly, Marquis
Conyngham, and Lord Rossmore were amongst those who built
racing lodges there and employed their own trainers and grooms.[93]
The organisation of flat racing in Ireland was given further impetus
in 1868 when Lord Naas, chief secretary of Ireland, successfully cam-
paigned for the passing of the act 'to make better provision for the
management and use of the Curragh of Kildare'. This gave parliamentary legitimacy to the existence of the Turf Club and defined for
it the area it could use for racing purposes.[94]

George Moore of Moore Hall established a reputation in the second
half of the nineteenth century as one of the finest jockeys in the
United Kingdom.[95] He was probably more successful as jockey and
owner at flat racing than at steeplechasing. In 1843, he was elected
steward of the Turf Club which had been established in the late eighteenth century to organise flat racing in the country and which
throughout the nineteenth century remained exclusively the domain
of landlords and those most closely associated with them such as
army officers.[96] But Moore continued to be involved in other racing
areas. In 1846, he landed what was perhaps his greatest betting coup
when one of his most famous horses, Coranna, won the 'Chester Cup'
and Moore and his associates, including Lord Waterford, scooped
£17,000.[97] By the 1860s, Moore Hall had become a veritable racing
establishment. In 1860, Croaghpatrick won the 'Steward's Cup' at
Doncaster for Moore having been quoted at one stage at forty to one

in the ring.[98] Around the same time Master George won six consecutive races 'so that plenty of money flowed into his owner's pockets'.[99] Consequently, Moore Hall was re-roofed, election debts were paid and Moore's eldest son was given a proper education.[100]

In the post-Famine period, horse-racing in Ireland had become more popular than ever. From 1850 to 1878 the number of race meetings held rose by over 60 per cent from 273 in 1850 to 453 in 1878.[101] The prize money on offer rose by around 100 per cent from £15,500 in 1850 to £31,400 in 1878.[102] Similarly, the number of Irish horses in training rose from 520 to 906 over the same period.[103] Landlords' enthusiasm for racing meant that they continued to establish new racecourses. In 1872, Lord Howth financed the building of a new flat course at Baldoyle. His eldest son, who was MP for Galway borough from 1868 to 1874, was instrumental in founding the Galway races. In 1876, a local racing official, W.H. Halliday, wrote to him:

> But for your lordship there never would have been any races in Galway unless mere country runs of the Ennis and Roscommon type, so it is impossible to exclude your lordship's name in the general observations their excellence may give rise to.[104]

Landlords bred horses such as Sir Hercules and Corsair, which helped to establish Irish breeding: their lines produced classic winners such as Coronation, Daniel O'Rourke, Knight of St George, and Faugh-A-Ballagh. For many landlords racing became not only a pastime and hobby but a business as well and it gave an added dimension to their social lives, a dimension, which still flourished well into the last quarter of the nineteenth century. The Earl of Dunraven, himself a successful owner and breeder, wrote in his memoirs: 'As a business or a pastime it is absorbing, and of all phases of society commend me to the racing set as possessing those qualities that make society enjoyable'.[105]

Club Life

In his unpublished memoirs, Sir Shane Leslie wrote: 'A gentleman's standing in his world was signalled by his list of clubs and it was worth paying hundreds of pounds in subs.'[106] The club as a social institution had its roots in the coffee houses of the later Stuart period. This was where gentlemen met on a regular basis and where they made the acquaintance of other habitués who shared their ideas, tastes and culture. Irish clubs took their inspiration from London clubs such as Boodle's, Brooke's and Arthur's which were founded between 1762 and 1765.[107] Around this time, Patrick Daly, a former tavern waiter opened a chocolate house at numbers two and three Dame Street, Dublin, thus founding what was to become 'the most famous of the Dublin clubs prior to the union ... and the chief resort of the nobility and members of parliament'.[108] In 1791, Daly's Club was re-housed in College Green where a much grander clubhouse was built to the design of Francis Johnson. It was furnished in the type of splendour its patrons were accustomed to in their country homes 'with grand lustres, inlaid tables and marble chimney pieces, the chairs and sofas white and gold, covered with the richest aurora silk'.[109] Daly's also acquired the reputation of being 'a fast place where high play and heavy drinking were indulged in and where many a reckless challenge to a duel was thrown down'.[110]

Clubs such as Daly's were political nerve centres where, as R.F. Brooke claimed, much of 'the wire pulling' that was 'part of the procedure of politics went on inside its four walls'.[111] It was, in fact, a political split within the club that led to the foundation of the Kildare Street Club in the 1780s. 'An historical note' on the Kildare Street Club written by George Wood Maunsell in 1880 attributes its foundation 'to an act of hasty tempered blackballing'. In 1782 one of Lord Francis Conyngham's twin sons, Nathaniel, was denied admission to Daly's (Maunsell's note does not specify why) as a result of which 'his friends took fire at the slight and forthwith showed their strength by founding a new club'.[112] Within a short time the Kildare Street Club had taken the lead in the city and in the mid-1850s its members purchased numbers one, two and three Kildare Street where a new club house was built to the design of Sir Thomas Deane.[113]

By the 1880s, the Kildare Street Club was the centre of landlord life in Dublin, all but 10 per cent of its 800 or so members coming from landed families.[114] Membership was exclusively male and was dominated by larger landowners.[115] While the Sackville Street Club was also in existence at this time, its location on the north side of the city, which by the 1880s was becoming increasingly run-down, meant it was less popular.[116] However, there were those who belonged to both clubs such as Lords Clonbrock, Clonmell, Headfort, Longford and Castletown as well as the untitled Henry Bruen and John Madden. (Maunsell wrote in 1880 that 'the two clubs have at all times held friendly relations ... many members being in fact members of both'.[117]) The Kildare Street Club was more centrally located and the splendour of its premises reflected landlord wealth. Mark Bence-Jones writes of it:

There were plenty of comfortable bedrooms, for which the charge was three shillings and sixpence a night, so that the club was a meeting place for gentlemen from all over the country, who before luncheon would congregate in the lofty hall with its staircase of elaborately carved stonework, its big game trophies and its blazing fire.[118]

Moving out from Dublin, there were about thirteen provincial clubs in various large towns and cities such as Galway, Limerick and Cork. These provided local centres for smaller landlords, who did not frequent Dublin on a regular basis, to meet up with peers and large landowners. The Limerick County Club was the first provincial club to be founded in 1813.[119] A town house was bought in Limerick city, which became the clubhouse. The back parlour was converted into a coffee room; the front parlour into a writing room; the front drawing-room into a reading room and the back drawing-room into a card room, while the stable at the rear was reconstructed and converted into a billiard room.[120] The Cork Club was built in 1826 at a cost of £4,000 with, as K.T. Hoppen points out: 'entablature, enormous dining-room, reading, billiard and card rooms so lavish that even the sybaritic sixth Duke of Devonshire was taken aback by its "swagger"'.[121]

Clubs fulfilled certain functions. Shane Leslie wrote: 'London life in Victorian days would have been impossible without the clubs which controlled the etiquette, costume and behaviour of gentlemen and professionals to an extraordinary degree'.[122] In many respects this was true. According to rule xxii of the Kildare Street Club, gentlemanly conduct was expected and demanded: 'Any member ... whose conduct in or out of the club ... shall be derogatory to his station in society shall be subject to expulsion under the award of a general meeting'.[123] Clubs acted as an extension of public school life, enhancing social status and exposing members to influential contacts. In the 1880s, Irish landlords such as Lords Longford, Dunsany, Conyngham, Louth and Henry Herbert of Muckross were members of the Junior United Services Club in London. This club's regulations stated that its members should be drawn from the princes of the blood royal, officers of the navy and army, persons holding appointments in military departments, and lords lieutenant of Great Britain and Ireland.[124] Irish peers who owned large estates, such as Lords Ormonde, Castletown and Talbot de Malahide, all belonged to at least the Sackville, Kildare Street and Carlton Clubs while some such as Lords Doneraile, Headfort and Longford belonged to at least five clubs at this time. There were clubs such as the Garrick in London (founded to facilitate interaction between artists and patrons and to act as a rendezvous centre for all literary men[125]) where Irish

landlords such as the Earl of Mayo, Lord Donoughmore and Lord
Dunraven mixed socially with members of the literati such as
Dickens and Trollope.

Clubs were social centres. While in Dublin, Lord Cloncurry preferred to relax and dine at the Kildare Street than attend formal
functions at the castle.[126] The club had the reputation of keeping the
best table in Dublin. When in season, oysters were sent up from the
club's own oyster bed in Galway and cost members a shilling a
dozen.[127] In the early days of the Limerick Club, dinners were served
between 4 and 6 p.m. A 'chop dinner' consisting of a choice of mutton
chop, veal cutlet, beef steak or salmon 'when not exceeding 8d per
pound' with bread, cheese, vegetables and beer was available at 2s
6d per head. Suppers of hot and cold meats or 'two and a half dozen
oysters with bread and butter and two tumblers of punch from 2s 6d'
were served after 10 p.m.[128] Reading rooms, writing rooms, billiards
rooms, card rooms and smoking rooms in all clubs provided before-
and-after-meals recreation centres.

Clubs were also political nerve centres. Membership of the Kildare
Street Club reflected landlord prejudice towards the maintenance of
the union. Bence-Jones points out that 'although the club was meant
to be non-political, during the years following the land war it was virtually impossible for an active Home Ruler to become a member'.[129]
When Sir Thomas Grattan Esmonde was elected to parliament as a
Home Ruler in 1885, he resigned from the club.[130] Similarly, the lean-
ings of Irish landlords towards the Conservative party was reflected
in the number who were members of the Carlton in London, a club
founded in 1832 to fight the supporters of the Reform Bill and to
serve as a rallying point for the Tories. In the 1870s, over one third of
the 100 sample landlords were members of the Carlton. On the other
hand, its Liberal counterpart, the Reform Club, attracted only one of
the landlords from the sample — Lord Carew.

MARRIAGE PATTERNS

The social exclusivity of the Irish landed class was most discernible
in marriage patterns. To marry a member of a neighbouring landed
family was not unusual. Edith Somerville put this trend down to 'the
impossibility of locomotion ... for to love your neighbour — or, at all
events to marry her — was almost inevitable when matches were a
matter of mileage, and marriages might have been said to have been
made by the map.'[131] As L.P. Curtis Jr. has pointed out, Somerville's
assertion may very well have been based on marital patterns in her
own locality of Castletownshend in County Cork where county families

such as the Somervilles, Beechams, Chavasses and Townsends inter-
married for two or three generations in succession.[132] In the late
nineteenth century there was also a number of marriages between
the Donerailes, Bandons and Frekes in the same county.[133] When
Mary and Henrietta Plunkett, the two sisters of the eleventh Earl of
Fingall, married: 'their marriages took them only a short distance
away, still within the borders of Meath'.[134] Mary married George
Fitzgerald Murphy of The Grange in 1884 while Henrietta married
Robert Gradwell of Dowth Hall in the same year. In 1911 their niece,
also Mary, and the only married daughter of the eleventh Earl of
Fingall, married Captain Cyril Kirk of Tyrrellstown.

However, while this trend was perceptible, it would be too sim-
plistic to put it down to geographical convenience (except, perhaps,
in the case of smaller land-owning families whose social lives were
largely confined to their own counties.) The maintenance of social
status was more pressing. As the nineteenth century progressed and
transportation improved, larger landowners moved out more frequently from their localities for social events in Dublin and London.
The Dublin ball season lasted for about six weeks from the end of
January until St Patrick's Day when it ended with the St Patrick's
Ball. During these months young debutantes were initiated into society.
In 1886, George Moore wrote:

> In Dublin, during six weeks of the year, the arrival of these large offi-
> cial envelopes is watched with an eagerness that words cannot
> describe. These envelopes are the balm of Gilead; and the Land
> League, and the hopelessness of matchmaking are merged and lost
> for a moment in an exquisite thrill of triumph or despair. An invita-
> tion to the castle means much. The grey-headed official who takes you
> down to dinner may bore you, and, at the dance, you may find your-
> self without a partner; but the delight of asking your friends if you
> may expect to meet them on such a night, or telling them afterwards
> of your successes, are the joys of Dublin....[135]

Along with the grand balls held in Dublin Castle, there were balls
every night in houses in Merrion and Fitzwilliam Squares. Members of
the landed class who did not own or lease houses in Dublin stayed in
hotels such as the Shelbourne or Buswell's; the latter, according to
Lady Fingall 'was an old-fashioned, friendly, family hotel, greatly frequented by the country gentry bringing their daughters to Dublin for
the season'. In the 1850s, Georgiana Bond of Farragh, whose father
owned around 8,000 acres in Longford, found her life: 'punctuated by
periodic family visits to Dublin where her parents would take a

house and there would be rounds of social engagements interspersed with shopping and church going'.[136]

During the Victorian period, the London season attracted the wealthiest Irish landlords and their families. It was effectively an extension of the Dublin season lasting from May to the end of July. At the end of April 1874, Lady Alice Howard began packing for the London season. On the boat from Kingstown she met with a number of other Irish families including the Guinnesses, Beresfords and Powerscourts. During her three months in London, her mornings were largely taken up with breakfast at Princes, followed by walks in the park which, more often than not, she found 'very dull'. The monotony of them was broken only by visits to Buckingham Palace to watch polo matches. After lunch came the inevitable round of visits, very much on the same pattern as at home for she dined with Irish families such as the Listowels, Croftons, Conynghams, Clancartys, Annesleys and Dawsons, all of whom kept London houses.[137] Seymour Leslie claimed that to 'exhibit the idleness' of men such as his father at the turn of the century it was sufficient to look at how he spent his days in London. Sir John II spent the morning in Christie's; lunched at the Turf or Beefsteak Clubs; spent the afternoon skating at the Niagara, in Tattersalls or at his fencing club; and the night at Covent Gardens.[138] For children, London was less exciting. Shane Leslie recalled:

> London meant routine, lessons in a foggy schoolroom. Church was a terribly boring Evangelical affair ...
>
> After service with our parents we were taken to Church Parade in Hyde Park ... making up luncheon parties ... or retailing scandal *de luxe* and gossips in gala. The men were always faultlessly dressed as though the unborn Moss brothers had served them personally for Ascot, while the ladies wore the kind of trailing dresses which Mr Cecil Beaton has imagined for scenes in *My Fair Lady*.
>
> On weekdays we played in the corner of Hyde Park ... chiefly in hope of enriching our butterfly collection. Every beauty in society exhibited herself from a pomelled saddle. Here we watched aunts and courtesans, our parents' friends, beautiful bounders and dressy dragoons. Here every midday in the season Mrs [Lily] Langtry rode with the Prince of Wales amid a constant bowing and raising of silken hats from gentlemen, many pretending to know the Prince.
>
> Along the no longer existent rails ... dandies and clubmen, riders and Picadilly loungers watched the ever-passing stream of ladies, not one of whom dared ride astride. Excitements were few save when a horse bolted generally with a lady-rider.

The savour of London was of horse garbage mixed with sooty fog while the distant sound of hoofs on wooden paving was like unceasing tideways — rather a pleasant dreamy seaside kind of rumble. It remains like many smells in the memory when scenes and faces perish.[139]

Perhaps more significantly Sir Shane Leslie regarded Victorian London as 'the Mecca for matchmaking'.[140] While geographical barriers may have been broken down during the Victorian period, social barriers remained. And social barriers often included those between the families of peers and large landowners (often one and the same) on the one hand and small landowners on the other. In a sample of 159 peers (drawn from the 100 sample families) who owned Irish estates and who married between the years 1850 and 1914, 60 per cent married daughters of peers, almost three-quarters of whom were English. Some of the more powerful peers such as the Dukes of Leinster had a tendency to seek their brides from peerage families resident in Britain. In 1818, Augustus Fitzgerald, third Duke of Leinster, married a daughter of the Earl of Harrington; in 1847, Charles Fitzgerald, the fourth Duke, married a daughter of the Duke of Sutherland; in 1884, Gerald Fitzgerald, the fifth Duke, married a daughter of the Duke of Feversham. Of the remainder, just over 30 per cent married into either Irish or English untitled land-owning families, but these families were predominantly large landowners. In 1874, for example, Thomas McClintock Bunbury, fourth Baron Rathdonnell, married a daughter of Henry Bruen of Oak Park. Bruen owned 24,400 acres. There were few peers from 1850 to 1914 with the courage of Geoffrey Taylour, fourth Marquis of Headfort, who, in 1901, married the reputedly beautiful Rose Boote. Rose was a Gaiety Girl belonging to a music hall troupe of dancers. As a consequence of this marriage, Lord Headfort had to resign his commission in the Irish Guards.[141]

The marriage patterns of the younger sons and daughters of peers in a sample of 246 (again drawn from the 100 sample families) who married between 1850 and 1914 showed a similar inclination to stay inside well-defined class boundaries. Almost 75 per cent married into peerage families or families of large landowners. Peers' daughters were aware that marriage to the heir of an estate was a much better prospect than marriage to a younger son because of the law of primogeniture. If they were to marry out of the peerage, marriage to an untitled heir was satisfactory recompense particularly if he was a relatively large landowner. In 1886, Alice Dillon, daughter of Lord Clonbrock, married her cousin, Ambrose Congreve, heir to

Mount Congreve in Waterford. As a result of the occupations chosen by younger sons of landlords, it followed that almost one third of those from the sample married the daughters of clergymen or army and navy officers.

Untitled landowners placed just as much emphasis on social standing as a prerequisite for a suitable partner. In 1833, George Moore of Moore Hall wrote to his mother: 'I am determined to marry none of his majesty's subjects — whether professing the Catholic, Protestant, or Jewish religion — without money ... I am not likely to marry for love'.[142] Some time later, he married Mary Blake, the daughter of a neighbouring landlord in County Mayo. Untitled owners and heirs to large estates frequently married into peerage families: in 1867, Charles Doyne of Wells, for example, married Lady Frances Fitzwilliam, daughter of Earl Fitzwilliam; in 1898, his eldest son, Robert, married Lady Mary Lascelles, daughter of the Earl of Harewood. If they didn't marry into peerage families, they tended to marry daughters of large landowners. From the 1820s to 1914, there were four heirs to Oak Park in County Carlow. In 1822, Col Henry Bruen married a daughter of Thomas Kavanagh of Borris in the same county. In 1854, his eldest son, Henry, married Mary Conolly of Castletown; in 1886, his heir married Agnes MacMurrough Kavanagh, also of Borris; finally, in 1913, his heir married Gladys McClintock of Rathvinden in Carlow.

Daughters of untitled landowners from small to middling sized estate backgrounds do not seem to have been eagerly sought by peers or their sons as only twelve out of a sample of seventy-two on whom information was available married into the peerage. Amongst this group was Elizabeth Burke but her marriage to Lord Fingall was frowned upon in some circles. A great crowd had assembled to greet Lord and Lady Fingall on their return from their honeymoon. But Elizabeth felt that 'it was a great disappointment to them all that Fingall had not married some great and rich lady to bring money to the castle and estate which so badly needed it'.[143] The proportion of younger sons who were upwardly mobile was even smaller, only nine out of seventy-eight who were born to small or middling landowners married daughters of large landowners. Many of these younger sons and daughters married children of army officers or clergymen who were one generation removed from estate ownership.

The fact that members of the landed class rarely married outside that class emphasises the shared common culture that existed between landlords in Ireland and Britain. Marriage was regarded as an important means of regenerating the tightly knit, exclusive

nature of their community. Part of their shared common culture was
what could perhaps be termed their leisured elitism. Landlords had
abundant time to entertain, hunt, race and tour. If there was a
propensity amongst peers to seek brides from other peers' families,
or at least from families of large landowners, it was deemed imperative because the new bride had to be well versed in entertaining on a
grand scale. Anita Leslie claimed that when the seventh Lord
Londonderry 'contemplated wedlock he had met only six or seven
possible girls. Each ... had been purposely placed next to him at dinner because they were by birth and upbringing qualified to entertain
as a great political hostess'.[144] When the untitled Elizabeth Burke of
Danesfield attended her first ball at Killeen, she noted that 'in the
background were some alarming old ladies, Fingall's relatives, exam-
ining and considering me'. The following morning she spent 'a rather
uncomfortable time with a terrifying old aunt of Fingall's, Lady
Henrietta Riddell' who interrogated her about her family, about
where she lived, and about the landed families with whom she was
acquainted.[145]

Dowries were also a prime consideration, especially to the eldest
son who had the responsibility of passing on the family's estate, big
house and heirlooms intact to the next generation. (In the case of the
peerage marriage was regarded as being imperative in the preservation of title.) Estates were kept intact by primogeniture. A strict
settlement was drawn up on the eldest son's marriage or on him
reaching his majority entailing the estate on the eldest grandson,
(usually not yet born), which made the heir merely tenant for life.
Theoretically, this meant heirs' hands were tied regarding the sale of
his property and to whom they could choose to bequeath it. In practice, such settlements were flexible enough to allow the owner
limited rights to sell outlying properties or to mortgage or convey
property to trustees. This was often necessary to meet financial obligations to younger sons and daughters or to pay off debts. The
settlement always contained complex contingency plans should a
grandson never be born, giving priority to males over females, to
direct rather than lateral descent or ascent, and failing that the most
recent branch of the family.

When an heir to an estate got engaged to marry, negotiations
were entered into by both families over the settlement. It was usually settled that a bride received an annual allowance from her
husband's estate, known as pin money, while her husband was alive.
She also brought with her a dowry, which often alleviated some
financial burden of the family she married into, or provided the basis
for her jointure, the annual allowance allowed to widows. When, for

example, Charles Fitzgerald, Marquis of Kildare and heir to the Duke of Leinster, married Lady Caroline Gower in 1847, the settlement stipulated that 'Lady Caroline's fortune should be paid to the Duke whose intentions is to discharge with it encumbrances affecting his estate'. There was also reference to unspecified sums which would 'secure to the Marquis of Kildare during the joint lives of himself and the Duke, £4,000 per annum payable quarterly'. There was provision for the payment of £600 per annum in pin money to Lady Caroline during the joint lives of herself and her husband. She would receive £2,500 during the joint lives of herself and the Duke if the Marquis died in the lifetime of the Duke, and £4,000 per annum by way of a jointure if Lady Caroline survived both the Marquis and the Duke.[146] Such settlements were business based and as such took the form of business arrangements. This is exemplified in the case of the marriage of Ambrose Congreve and Alice Dillon, daughter of Lord Clonbrock, in the mid-1860s. Edward Roper, Lord Clonbrock's solicitor, met with Mr Medlicott, Congreve's solicitor, in the Sackville Street Club on 2 June 1866. A draft agreement was drawn up between the parties. A further series of meetings were, however, necessary at various locations in Dublin between June and the end of July, before final terms were agreed upon.[147]

The role of women in big houses in the nineteenth century was limited. They rarely inherited estates; they had no political influence in the sense that they could not vote or enter parliament; and they were confined to the role of mistress of the household and maid-servants, hostess or occasionally philanthropist. But marriage settlements meant they enjoyed much greater liberty than wives in the classes below them. Marriage settlements guaranteed them separate income, which in the case of Lady Meath of Kilruddery, for example, gave her the wealth to enjoy greater freedom and follow her own interests.[148] However, finding a suitable husband was not always that simple. Olive, in George Moore's *Drama in Muslin*, proclaimed:

> I know that I shall never be married and the perpetual trying to make up matches is sickening. Mama will insist on riches, position and all that sort of thing.... I am sick of going out; I won't go out anymore. We never missed a tennis party last year; we used to go sometimes ten miles to them, so eager was Mama after Captain Gibbon, and it did not come off; and then the whole country laughs.[149]

EDUCATION

The education of a landlord's children began in the big house where a schoolroom was usually set aside for tuition. At Ballynastragh the schoolroom was on the top storey. At Dartrey it was on the bedroom corridor. The latter contained a deal schoolroom table, pine tables and chairs, a blackboard and easel, a walnut marquetry bookcase, Georgian mahogany cabinets and chests of drawers, an oak table with velvety top, a lounge chair, six mahogany framed chairs and a walnut-framed settee. The first agents of education, excluding parents, were nannies and governesses. The latter, particularly in the homes of large landowners, were usually imported from England or the continent: of the twelve governesses returned for the sample houses in 1911, nine were English while the Howards of Shelton employed a French governess; the Croftons of Mote Park employed a Dutch governess and the Gore Booths of Lisadell employed a Scottish governess.

While daughters normally remained at home under the tuition of successive governesses, most sons went on to public school.[150] (However, from the 1890s there seems to have been an increase in the number of daughters who went to English public schools for girls such as Cheltenham Ladies College.) The early life of Lord Castletown was fairly typical of many peers. Born in London in 1849, he went to private school in Ashridge in 1857. On leaving Ashridge, he was sent to Dresden by his parents who employed a private tutor to teach him German. In 1861 he went to Eton to continue his formal education. In 1868, he went to Oxford from where he graduated with a degree in law and modern history. He then went on to join the Life Guards to serve a military apprenticeship before taking over the running of the family estate in Queen's County.[151]

It was to English public schools that the majority of wealthy Irish landlords aspired to send their sons. Of the fifty-five peers who owned sample houses in 1879, forty-five had attended Eton and four had attended Harrow. The same was true of the untitled owners of large estates. Of the twenty on whom information was available, sixteen attended either Eton or Harrow. One of the few exceptions was the fourth Earl of Dunraven who had attended St Columba's in Dublin, a school founded in 1841 by Dunraven's grandfather and Lord Emly as 'a proselytising enterprise' which 'strove to revive the ancient, and in some respects independent, Irish church'.[152] Dunraven later regretted not having benefited from an English public school education. He wrote: 'I lost — and it is a great loss — the education, the discipline and the wholesome training of Eton, or any other great public school, and the intimate friendships that spring from public school life.'[153]

While Sir Shane Leslie might not have agreed with Dunraven, the latter's statement is perhaps a fairer reflection of Irish landlords'

opinions on the benefits of an education at English public schools.
Jessica Gerard contends that harsh discipline and bullying were
dismissed as prerequisites in the necessary inculcation of 'the
public-school ethos of independence, stoicism, courage, honour, loyalty
and manliness'.[154] They were also places where, as Dunraven hinted,
suitable contacts were made that would be beneficial to the pupils in
later life, and where social status was perpetuated. In his memoirs,
Reginald Brabazon, twelfth Earl of Meath, concurred with these
sentiments. Brabazon went to Eton in 1855. Amongst those sharing
his house were the future Marquis of Lansdowne (who was to be the
future leader of the House of Lords, Viceroy of India and Governor-
general of Canada) as well as the future Earls of Camperdown,
Coventry, Kilmorey and Morley. Unlike Leslie, Brabazon 'loved Eton'
believing that there was something 'in its atmosphere which is not to
be found in any other school in the world'. Like Leslie he was aware
of the weaknesses in the educational system practised there and the
lack of material comforts but believed that corporal punishment was
a prerequisite to learning and good discipline for life. He wrote:

> I was sent up to be whipped as soon as my [first] fortnight was over,
> for not knowing accurately the Latin lines I had been given to
> learn.... But was the master wrong in doing so? I don't think so.
>
> Is there no connection between the present [1920s] indiscipline,
> lack of respect for parents or for anything or anybody under the sun
> ... and the change which has almost universally occurred since my
> early days in the attitude of parents towards this question of a sane
> juvenile discipline?[155]

There were also practical drawbacks of having no formal education. Lady Fingall wrote of her husband:

> Never having been to a public school, he had missed that association
> with other boys ... In the ordinary sense he was never educated. But
> he had good Fr MacNamara's teaching. He could not spell either
> English or French — to the end of his days he spelt both *boath* — and
> he wrote such an atrocious hand that I had great difficulty in reading
> the letter in which he proposed to me.[156]

There was no clearly established pattern amongst Irish families
regarding the schools attended by their sons. It did not necessarily
follow that because a landlord had attended Eton or Harrow that his
sons would do likewise. Shane Leslie wrote that 'Irish families did
not suffer from the prejudice which animated the English and often
divided their sons between the rival schools.' His father was the

Etonian son of a Harrovian and sent three sons to Eton. Henry
Leslie, his cousin, and his son, Frank, attended Harrow.[157] Similarly,
Henry Bruen of Oak Park attended Broadfield; his eldest son, Henry,
attended Harrow; in turn his eldest son attended Eton. The eldest
son of Arthur MacMurrough Kavanagh attended Eton; the other of
his four sons on whom information is available attended Harrow.
Those from less affluent Irish landed families attended public
schools such as Charterhouse, Cheltenham and Winchester in
England or St Columba's in Dublin.

As W.E. Vaughan has rightly concluded: 'many landlords did not
go to university', and of those who did few went to Trinity emphasising that they 'were not as "culturally" Irish as they had allegedly
been in the eighteenth century'.[158] (In Shane Leslie's *Doomsland*, one
of the main characters contended that 'the difference between
Trinity and Oxford was the difference between sampling beer and
champagne'.[159]) Of the 100 sample landowners in 1870, forty had
gone to university and of these only seven went to Trinity. Heirs
were more likely to pursue a military career in the intervening
period between completing their formal education and inheriting the
family estate. Such a choice was seen to be the natural extension of a
landlord's perceived duty to lead, something they became aware of at
an early age. In his memoirs, Lord Castletown claimed that he
remembered 'becoming imbued with military ardour at an early age.
Having found an old pistol and loaded it — luckily with powder only
— I constituted myself cavalry'.[160]

Of the 100 landlords in 1879, 76 had military records: two were
lieutenant generals; sixteen were colonels; nineteen were lieutenant
colonels; nine were majors; twelve were captains; eighteen were lieutenants. The most popular regiments with these landlords were the
Life Guards, the Coldstream Guards and the Royal Irish Fusiliers.
The remaining twenty-nine landowners included such as J.R. Garstin
of Braganstown whose lifestyle was more academically orientated.
The Misses Butler of Castlecrine for obvious reasons of gender did
not pursue a military career; and the otherwise remarkable Arthur
MacMurrough Kavanagh who, having been born limbless, was
excluded from the pursuit of a military career.[161] Reginald Brabazon
was the only surviving son of the eleventh Earl of Meath. His elder
brother, Jacques, had died at Naples from diphtheria in 1844 during
the family's grand tour and so his parents were 'naturally loathe to
permit [him] to enter the army'. If he had come to any mishap, his
successor 'would have had to be sought amongst the descendants of
the first Lord Ardee, or some of the very earliest of the Earls of
Meath'. Instead his father directed Reginald into the foreign office

which he joined as a clerk in 1863.[162] Many of those landlords who
served in the army saw active service during the nineteenth and
early twentieth centuries. Lord Farnham served in the Crimea;
George Bellew of Barmeath served in the Afghan war 1878–9 and
South Africa 1900–01; Lord Dunraven, Lord Listowel, Lord Ventry,
Lord Castletown, Sir John Leslie and Lord Fingall all saw active
service in the Boer war.

OCCUPATIONS OF YOUNGER SONS

By the nineteenth century, Irish landlords had become an integral
part of the much broader British landed class, evidence of which has
already been seen in their marriage arrangements and military
careers. They essentially became part of what David Cannadine
terms a 'supra-national' class.[163] As national government was dominated by landlords in the nineteenth century, it became inevitable
that the administration of the state would follow. This opened up
avenues of employment for younger sons (and, indeed, for eldest sons
who wished to pursue a professional career in conjunction with being
a landowner). This choice of career was largely to consolidate social
position for army pay, for example, served only as a supplement to
the allowances received by younger sons from the family estate.
Cannadine points out that the new occupational opportunities of the
nineteenth century were a direct consequence of the expansion of
state bureaucracy from the end of the eighteenth century. From 1784
to 1794, the Home Office was set up and the Board of Trade and
Secretaryship of War revived. From 1815 to 1827, Lord Bathurst
expanded the Colonial Office to administer for seventeen new
colonies. In turn, the expansion of the British army meant that more
army and naval officers were required than ever before to serve
world-wide. From 1792 to 1826, the number of British army officers
rose from 2,000 to 19,000, while the number of naval officers rose
from 1,800 to 8,400.[164]

By the 1870s, the majority of British army and naval officers
were still recruited from the landlord class. Out of a total of 163
younger sons from the sample families on whom information was
available, 75 per cent chose an army or naval career. At least part of
the reason for this landlord dominance was that a private income
was a precondition for a military career. Up to the 1870s, purchase
played an important role in promotion. In July 1854, Wensley Bond
of Farragh in County Longford wrote that he was 'anxiously expect-
ing' a letter from his father regarding the £250 he required to
purchase a lieutenancy. He claimed: 'If ... I do not purchase, Barwell,

the ensign below me, will purchase over me'.[165] There was little financial reward for Bond — the cost of living in the army far outstripped
income — and so in November 1854 he wrote to his father from the
Crimea: 'I have £23 left. Please send me a few pounds as I can buy
plenty to eat and drink in Balaclava'.[166]

Even though entrance to Woolwich and Sandhurst became based
on competitive examination in 1870 and Gladstone abolished the
purchase of commission the same year, the cost of living in the army
continued to limit the officer class to the wealthy.[167] David
Cannadine points out that as late as the 1900s, it cost in the region
of £1,000 to purchase the uniform and horses necessary to join a cavalry regiment and the cost of living could be as high as £700 a year
in excess of salary.[168] While Irish landlords began to fall on hard
times from the late 1870s, they and their sons continued to pursue
the army and navy as a career. Perhaps, as Leopold Amery claimed
in the aftermath of the Boer War, they did this 'simply and solely for
the sake of the social connections they hope to acquire'.[169] The fourth
Marquis of Waterford, who died in 1861, had four sons. In 1859, his
second son, Charles joined the navy eventually becoming an admiral
in 1906. His brother, William, was a colonel in the 9th Lancers, a
recipient of the Victoria Cross and later military secretary to the
Governor of India from 1881 to 1894. The third son, Marcus, was a
lieutenant in the 7th Lancers; the youngest son, Delaval, was a lieutenant in the Leicestershire regiment. A prominent role in the army
was not, however, strictly confined to the very wealthy. While the
Waterfords had a 66,700-acre estate in Ireland in the 1880s, Field-
Marshal Sir Henry Wilson's father had a mere 1,160 acres in County
Longford.

Apart from the army and the navy, Irish landlords and their sons
filled other important positions in the service of the state during the
late nineteenth century. Indeed, long after the home civil service, the
army, the navy, and the law had been taken over by the middle
classes, the Foreign Service remained the stronghold of the landed
class in Britain.[170] When he entered the Foreign Office as a clerk in
1863, Reginald Brabazon was appointed to the 'French department',
which oversaw British interests in France, Switzerland and
Madagascar. From 1868 to 1870 he served as a diplomat attached to
the British embassy in Berlin. In 1871 he was transferred to the
British embassy in Paris and in 1873 was promoted to second secretary at Athens.[171] William Fitzwilliam, son of the sixth Earl
Fitzwilliam, was Governor-general of India from 1880 to 1882.
Herbert Browne, son of the fifth Marquis of Sligo, was a political officer in Lushoi where he was assassinated in 1890. Hamilton Cuffe,

second son of the third Earl of Desart, was solicitor to the treasury
and Queen's/King's proctor from 1894 to 1909; Director of Public
Prosecutions from 1894 to 1908 and British plenipotentiary at the
international naval conference in London, 1908–09. Walter Hely-
Hutchinson, son of the fourth Earl of Donoughmore, was Governor of
Malta from 1884 to 1889, of the Windward Islands from 1889 to
1903, of Natal and Zululand from 1893 to 1901 and of the Cape of
Good Hope from 1901 to 1910. Sir Francis Richard Plunkett, second
son of the ninth Earl of Fingall was Ambassador to Vienna from 1900
to 1905.[172]

These diplomats were drawn from the wealthiest Irish landed
families. It could perhaps be argued that they had the upbringing
necessary to mix at court in other European states: mixing with the
aristocracy of Europe was a natural progression from mixing with
the aristocracy at home. They had the required education and many
had gone on European tours in their youth, which would have given
them experience of other European cultures and languages. As a
child, Reginald Brabazon had gone on the grand tour with his family.
They were 'received with open arms by the members of the Austrian
and Hungarian aristocracies' owing to the marriage of his uncle, the
second Earl of Clanwilliam, to Caroline, Countess Thun, and to the
marriages of two of his first cousins to Count Paul Szechery and
General Count Clem-Martinitz. When his father decided that
Reginald should enter the Foreign Office after leaving Eton, he sent
him to Buckeburg, near Hanover, in order to learn the 'purest
German'.[173] These diplomats drawn from Irish families, therefore,
mixed easily with monarchs and ministers and, at least in the case of
Sir Francis Plunkett were trusted for their discretion for Edward VII
once reputedly said of him that he 'is a great friend of mine and one
of my best ambassadors. He does not talk too much, and always does
the right thing by instinct'.[174]

Following the reorganisation of the Irish Church after 1871, Irish
landlords played a significant role in its government at all levels from
select vestries to the general synod which, according to W.E. Vaughan,
was 'the largest regular gathering of Irish gentry in Dublin since
1800'.[175] Younger sons who wished to perpetuate their social status
saw the church as a further occupational outlet. Of the 163 younger
sons in the sample, 6 per cent entered the church. While the practice
of presentation was more prevalent in England than Ireland, Irish
landlords could and did use their connections there to have their sons
appointed to parishes. James Butler, second son of the fourth Marquis
of Ormonde, was rector of Ulcombe in Maidstone. Rev Edward Talbot De
Malahide was vicar of Evercreech-Cum-Chesterblade. (Interestingly,

his older brother, Monsignor George, was canon of St Peter's in Rome and chamberlain to Pope Pius IX.)[176] In the mid-1880s, the fourth Lord Plunkett was appointed Archbishop of Dublin to succeed Richard Chenevix-Trench who was a member of the Ashtown family. At the same time, the Archbishop of Armagh was a great-nephew of the first Marquis of Waterford.[177]

The proportion of younger sons from the sample who it could be ascertained entered the legal profession — ten out of 163 — probably does not reflect the social prestige that landlords attached to it. David Cannadine quotes an interesting article from *The Times* in 1884 that claimed that 'the main object of the profession is to furnish amusement for gentlemen, an agreeable change from field sports and the pleasures of society. The clients ... occupy very much the same position as the foxes and the pheasants.'[178] There was, however, much more to it than 'amusement'. Law provided younger sons (and, indeed, many eldest sons such as Henry Bowen of Bowen's Court), with a respectable standard of living allowing them to retain their close ties to the landed class which in turn provided them with a great deal of their clientele.

While landlords increasingly turned to professional land agency firms in the nineteenth century, land agency still remained a further career option for landlords' sons.[179] A land agent enjoyed a large amount of autonomy in the day to day running of an estate. He was responsible for the collection of rents, the supervision of the estate's finances and the drawing up of landlord–tenant agreements. He was also entitled to substitute for an absent landlord as resident magistrate or grand juror, which added to his social standing in rural society. Of the agents who gave evidence to the Bessborough Commission in the 1880s, James Hamilton of Ballintra was agent on his father's estate in Donegal and on Thomas Conolly's estate in the same county. The O'Donovan was agent for his father, and for his uncle, William Bence-Jones. F.A.J. Chichester was agent for his brother, Lord Templetown; Foster V. Fitzgerald was agent on the family estates in Clare, Kerry and Limerick.[180]

Although no sons from the sample families were found to be RIC officers, yet Brian Griffin has found that these were also drawn from the landed class, particularly from the families of smaller landowners.[181] In 1861, the *Daily Express* had claimed that 'very many of the officers of the Irish constabulary are connected not only with the first families in the country, but some with nobility'.[182] In 1888, an article in the *Freeman's Journal* generalised that police officers were 'gentlemen of good families, birth and education, but, who, being for the most part without private means, could not support themselves if appointed to the army'.[183] Despite their lowly social backgrounds, RIC officers seem always to have been welcome at big house functions, race meets, hunts and other social occasions because their background meant they shared — along with lawyers, army officers, clergymen and agents — the same culture as landlords.

CONCLUSION

Until the last quarter of the nineteenth century, there seemed to be little indication that the social power enjoyed by generations of Irish landlords was under any type of serious threat. Big house functions continued to proliferate. Landlords indulged their love of fox-hunting, racing and shooting. The London and Dublin seasons were more popular than ever; the shared experience of public school, army or naval careers and club life integrated Irish landlords into the wider British landed class; marriages between Irish and British landed families further consolidated this. However, there were ominous clouds on the horizon. The late 1870s and the 1880s were to be characterised by agricultural depression and land agitation in Ireland. The same decades were also to witness an assault on the political power of landlords. If the politico-economic strength of landlords had enhanced their social status in the past, anything that would threaten this strength could only have grave consequences for their social power in the future.

4

CAUSES AND EFFECTS OF LANDLORD INDEBTEDNESS, 1877–1914

'THE WINDS OF CHANGE'

That terrible Land League would ruin him — that terrible Land League that he could feel about him. It hovered in the air like an evil spirit, and, sooner or later, it would descend and tear and rend him as prey. Yes he was ruined, utterly ruined. But with twenty or thirty thousand pounds he would have been able to fight it and to conquer it....

GEORGE MOORE, *A DRAMA IN MUSLIN* (1886), P. 219

INTRODUCTION

From a purely legislative point of view, landlords were not legally compelled to sell their estates until after 1923. However, it is probably fair to state that at no stage was the transfer of land from landlord to tenant voluntary in the strictest sense of the word. Landlords were pressurised from the early 1880s by government legislation, agrarian movements and mortgagees to transfer their land to appease a growing democracy, to satisfy the land-hungry, and to meet their own financial obligations. To complicate matters further the social revolution, fuelled by Land League rhetoric and agitation, became entwined with the political revolution aimed at independence for Ireland (in one form or another). Inevitably the long-term result was that Free State politicians bowed to the demands of the majority after 1923. The last landed estates were broken up and divided amongst what was essentially a class of people, predominantly Catholic and Nationalist, who felt that their ancestors had originally been dispossessed. For them the ending of the big house was something of a cultural as well as a social victory, if not also a political victory.

For landlords, the seeds of economic decline, somewhat ironically, had been sown during the boom years from the mid-1850s to the late 1870s. This was when many landlords had gone in search of mortgages. They had failed to exploit the commercial values of their estates by raising their rents in accordance with price increases, or continued to live extravagantly spending as if there was going to be no future downturn in the economy. They put very little aside for what were literally to become the rainy days from the late 1870s that were to initiate depression. The plight of George Arthur Hastings, seventh Earl of Granard, was fairly typical in this respect. His relationship with the trustees of St Patrick's College, Maynooth from the early 1870s to around 1903 illustrates the changing fortunes of Irish landlords during that period.

THE GRANARD MORTGAGE, 1871–1903

Under the Disestablishment of the Irish Church Act of 1869, Maynooth College received a capital sum of just over £369,000 (fourteen years' purchase of the previous annual grant of £26,360.) The trustees decided to invest approximately 75 per cent of this capital in mortgages to Irish landowners that would yield 4.25 to 4.75 per cent interest per annum, the best and safest investment option available to them at the time.[1]

In April 1871, the largest single mortgage offered by the college trustees was one of £91,592 to the seventh Earl of Granard at 4.25 per cent.[2] (In June 1876 he was offered a further mortgage of £2,078 by the trustees.[3]) It is not entirely clear why Granard needed so much capital, although correspondence indicates that it was probably secured to pay off a number of inherited debts and charges.[4] The mortgage was secured on Lord Granard's County Longford estate of almost 15,000 acres (including the demesne) and his family home at Castleforbes.[5] In 1871, the rental income on this estate was just under £9,000 per annum. Granard estimated that 'the total amount of outgoings of every nature save only poor rate and county cess payable out of all said lands does not exceed the sum of £680.13s.6d' per annum. There were, he claimed, no estate charges affecting the fee simple of the lands. There was, however, an annuity of £1,000 for the life of Lady Caroline Forbes and a judgement obtained by the Marquis of Lansdowne against the Hon George Forbes in the Court of King's Bench in 1822 for the principal sum of £5,000. Nevertheless, it seems strange, to say the least, that a mortgage, requiring interest repayments of £3,900 per annum, or 43 per cent of gross rental income in a good year, could have been offered so readily by the college trustees. Usually a more thorough investigation of the level of annual expenditure on the estate would be required. The buoyancy of the economy at the time seems to have blinded both parties to what might happen if rents were to fall in a bad year. One can only hypothesise that Lord Granard may have wooed the college trustees with his elitist social credentials. This may have convinced them of his creditworthiness and, of course, the fact that he was a Roman Catholic who had close associations with many of the leading ecclesiastics of the time did not do his cause any harm.

The regular payment of rents on the Granard estate up to the late 1870s meant that interest repayments to the college were met on time and in full. While agricultural depression began in 1877, its effects were not really felt by Lord Granard until 1880. That year, the tenants organised themselves under the Land League and called for a reduction of all rents to Griffith's valuation. This valuation had been carried out between 1852 and 1865 for the purpose of local taxation and was based on 1849–51 prices which meant that by the late-1870s it was very much lower than the real letting value of land. On the estate as a whole rents were 26 per cent above the valuation, although on individual holdings they were as much as 55 per cent above. Although a reduction would have obviously made rents more affordable to hard-pressed tenants, it would simultaneously make it extremely difficult for Granard to meet his financial obligations and so he refused to accede to their full demands. He did, however, grant a reduction of 20 per cent, although it seems that this was not actually a blanket reduction but applied only to some tenants on the estate.[6] However slight the rental decline may have been that year, Granard's agent, F.M. Crozier, claimed that it was 'with considerable difficulty and through the kindness of friends' that Granard was able to raise the money to make his interest payments due to the college.[7]

Local Land League propaganda focused on the fact that any rents above Griffith's valuation were rack-rents.[8] While 26 per cent above may seem quite reasonable, in fairness to Granard's tenants, particularly those around Drumlish, their rents were too high to be sustained by the very poor holdings on which they lived.[9] By 1881, impoverishment was felt most acutely around Drumlish and the Land League spread quickly there as a result, led by the parish priest, Fr Thomas Conefry. At first Conefry was prepared to be diplomatic. In January 1881, he told the Drumlish tenantry:

... allow me to state that while I am under no personal obligation to Lord Granard, yet I will boldly state that I think he is a good-hearted man, who would not oppress you if he could avoid it. In justice to him I say that he was the only landlord of those holding property within this parish who gave me any assistance to relieve your distress during the famine of last year.... He is in distress himself.[10]

That same month, Fr Conefry met with Granard who initially decided to accept a year's rent at Griffith's valuation. However,

Granard 'either through his own pressing necessities or through the advice of misguiding [sic] friends' changed his mind, refused to accept the new terms, and pressed his tenants for their full rents.[11] Granard's intransigence provoked more radical opposition and Drumlish soon became 'noted for its disturbed state'.[12] When tenants struck against the payment of rents, Granard threatened an estimated 100 families with eviction. The Land League saw in the Drumlish case a rallying point. Crowds gathered in their thousands in the village on the third morning of agitation in early January 1881 and, 'horns, Land League drums, and chapel bells were again brought into requisition'. Even the chapel bells at Newtownforbes, 'right in front of Lord Granard's entrance gate, (were) put into motion by two enthusiastic young men'.[13] Granard's process servers 'were driven back' and Granard himself was alerted to the fact that it would 'be impossible to make any practical use of any decrees that may be obtained until things settle down'.[14] In the meantime, his agent hoped that the trustees of the college 'knowing the present state of the country' would 'feel for his lordship' and not compel him to meet his interest repayments.[15]

Shortly after the Drumlish demonstration, scores of the most prominent agitators were arrested and sent to Mullingar jail. Although they were released a short time later, the arrests seem to have taken some of the sting out of the local Land League. Granard took advantage of this and 'ejectment processes ... literally fell like snow flakes over his whole property'.[16] The serving of processes this time: 'was effected ... without serious disturbance, the process server Murphy being protected by a force of 350 constabulary. The Riot Act was read and the police drove back the crowd with their bayonets.'[17] An estimated 100 families on Granard's estate were cleared off their holdings within a three mile radius of Drumlish.[18] Fr Conefry reacted immediately and formed a Parochial Farmers' Defence Association, the aims of which were to restore the evicted tenants to their homes; to prevent any further evictions in the parish and to prevent land-grabbing by every legitimate means. Grants were secured from the Ladies Land League and donations were received from various private charities that allowed the construction of several wooden houses outside the village while out-offices belonging to farmers who had not been evicted were repaired and made habitable for evicted families.[19]

Because of the rent strike, Granard claimed again that he was unable to realise his full rental income and, therefore, was unable to meet his interest repayments. In July 1881, his agent wrote to the college bursar:

I can assure you that I have had the greatest difficulty in trying to get rents from the tenants, as even the tempting offer of 20% [reductions] was not availed of by many, and the consequence is that the arrears have largely increased.[20]

An indication of this rise in arrears is that under the terms of the 1882 Arrears Act Granard had around £11,000 extinguished. Of this amount he recovered only £4,200 from the Irish Land Commission, representing a loss of £6,800 to him.[21]

The 1881 Land Act strengthened the tenants' position while simultaneously weakening that of Lord Granard's. The establishment of the principle of dual ownership undermined his authority as did the imposed restrictions regarding evictions. (After the 1881 clearances, there seems to have been no more evictions on the estate.) Granard was faced with a whole tenantry not willing to pay rents, at least not the asking rents. They began to use the newly established Irish Land Commission courts, set up to deal with the fair rent proviso of the 1881 Land Act, to get wholesale reductions.[22] Not satisfied with the 20 per cent reductions offered by Lord Granard himself, they demanded up to 70 per cent reductions on some holdings.[23] In December 1886, for example, twelve of Granard's tenants entered the courts. The aggregated old rents, which they paid, came to £89.16s.2d. The commissioners lowered these rents to £46.8s.0d, a reduction of almost 50 per cent.[24] In December of the following year, five more tenants went into court. Their aggregated old rents were £48.8s.7d which were lowered to £31.0s.0d, a reduction of around 32 per cent.[25]

Granard now realised that one of the few ways to extricate himself from his financial difficulties was to sell off part of his estate. In 1882, he entered into negotiations for sales but found his tenants unwilling to meet his asking price. The gulf between the twenty-three years' purchase on rentals that he asked and the offer of between thirteen and sixteen years' purchase by tenants was too wide to breach. According to the terms of the 1881 Land Act potential purchasers had to raise a 25 per cent deposit. But this was beyond many of them and as the agrarian agitation of the time closed the door of the land market to all bidders except the occupying tenants, Granard was unable to sell any of his estate. From the beginning of 1880 to the end of 1883, correspondence from him or his representatives with the college authorities indicates amply his financial stress. There were frequent pleas such as: 'It is extremely hard to get rents in this year and we hope you will kindly give us as long a time as possible to pay the balance'.[26] By 1883, the college trustees had not once received a payment of interest from Granard on the appointed gale days since May 1880 with the result that he was almost £3,000 in arrears.[27]

The economy showed signs of recovery in 1883 and 1884. There is not a great deal of correspondence in the Maynooth mortgage papers for these years, perhaps suggesting that mortgagor and mortgagees felt the crisis had abated and the economy would soon stabilise allowing Granard to fulfil his financial obligations to the trustees. However, it was only a temporary aberration from agricultural depression, which was renewed from 1885 onwards. Agitation this time was accompanied by the plan of campaign, which encouraged tenants on estates to stand together. They resolved what abatements they would demand from their landlords and to elect a managing committee to take charge of the half year's rent should the landlord refuse their demand. (This would become known as the estate fund.) They also agreed that as individuals, they would not accept any alternative settlement that was not extended to every tenant on the estate.[28]

In early December 1886, an estimated 500 of Lord Granard's tenants marched to Longford town preceded by the Killoe fife and drum band. They were led by three Catholic priests — the aforementioned Fr Thomas Conefry, parish priest of Drumlish; Fr John Briody, parish priest of Killoe; and Fr Denis Grey, curate of Ballinamuck. At a meeting held outside the Royal Arms Hotel with Granard's agents, Messrs Darley and Roe, they demanded 30 per cent reductions on all judicial rents and 40 per cent reductions on non-judicial rents. Darley and Roe were willing to give only 15 per cent reductions on non-judicial rents and no reductions at all on judicial rents (obviously assuming that tenants had already received a more than fair reduction from the land courts.) The tenants left and resolved at a subsequent meeting 'that they were determined to stand by the plan of campaign'.[29] They had been encouraged to do so by the vinegar-tongued Timothy Healy. He had said that he hoped to see Granard's mortgagees: 'squeezing him out as you would squeeze out a lemon or an orange and when they throw away the skin, I hope to see you give it a kick and send it to its proper place'.[30]

By 1886, the college trustees had become most anxious about their Granard investment. The president's report for that year referred to the accumulated arrears of £3,000 and claimed that:

> this is so serious a question as effecting the working of the college that I must beg of your lordships to mark out what we should do if this financial embarrassment continues, and it is almost certain to continue, and even to increase.[31]

Granard claimed to the college trustees that because of the plan of campaign he received no rents on his estate that November.[32] By February 1887, the college was in crisis and the president, Robert Browne, wrote to Granard:

> I need not explain to your lordship how exceedingly embarrassing to us who are charged with carrying out the work of a large college is this failure on the part of your agents to supply us at the appointed time with so large a portion of our revenue.... In fact I fear we cannot go on long without it. Our contracts are for the most part either for cash or for quarterly payments.... I write to your lordship ... in hope that you may find some way of diminishing our embarrassment — an institution like ours cannot live without its means of support.[33]

As the year of 1887 progressed, it developed into the worst year for agitation on the estate. The tenants' strike against non-payment of rents had gathered momentum and Granard's agent began to anticipate 'some unpleasant work on the estate', hinting at the need to evict the more troublesome tenants.[34] In May, Granard replied to the president's February letter pleading innocence: 'It is, of course', he wrote, 'through no fault of my own that this has occurred and I can most thoroughly sympathise with you as I do not receive a shilling from the estate at present'.[35] Becoming increasingly beleaguered, Granard tried the old landlord expedient of acquiring a loan to pay off a loan. However, he soon realised that mortgage accommodation had all but ceased in Ireland. In 1888, his solicitors wrote to the trustees:

> Acting under instructions received from the Earl of Granard, we have been engaged for some time past in trying to procure a loan to pay the arrears of interest due to the trustees of the college, but owing to the present state of affairs, it is almost impossible to borrow money in any landed security in Ireland, and we should certainly have failed to do so had not relatives of our client come forward to help him in the present emergency.[36]

These were anxious times for the college and, indeed, each year between 1887 and 1891 the bank had to be approached for overdraft facilities.[37]

In May 1887, the college president, Robert Browne, sought 'non official' advice from Judge J.G. McCarthy of the Irish Land Commission. Because of the controversy that had surrounded the Drumlish clearances in 1881, the trustees did not want to draw any more unfavourable attention towards themselves. McCarthy suggested that

at least part of the Granard estate should be sold under the terms of
the Ashbourne Act of 1885 in order to 'save his lordship from evicting'.[38] In September with arrears of interest on the Granard
mortgage standing at £3,500, the trustees resolved that their solicitors be instructed to file a petition for the sale of the Granard estate
in the hope that they could salvage their investment.

Events which subsequently unfolded were rather intriguing.
Having obviously learned of what the college trustees were about to
do, Granard pre-empted their decision by entering his own petition
for sale at the same time, later claiming that the carriage of sale
could be conducted more economically by himself and his agents.[39]
P.A. Chance, the college solicitor, was not convinced: he could see
such an arrangement resulting in heavy losses to the college. He was
even more concerned by the omission of Castleforbes, Granard's
home, and the 1,400-acre demesne from the Granard petition.[40]
(Granard later claimed that he omitted the castle from the petition
in the understanding that the trustees did not want to interfere with
his occupation of Castleforbes.[41])

In the court case which followed, to decide who would get the
sale, held in the second week of April 1888, Judge Monroe gave the
sale to Granard's solicitors, Messrs Crozier & Son, and appointed
Granard's agent, Mr Darley, as receiver. As a further source of disappointment, if not embarrassment to the trustees, it became known
during the court case that Laurence Gillooley, Bishop of Elphin, had
influenced Monroe's decision. At some stage, Gillooley had written to
Granard expressing sympathy for his plight. The letter was read out
in court and according to P.A. Chance: 'had a most injurious effect'.
Chance correctly foretold the trustees: 'I am afraid that as a result of
Dr Gillooley's actions, not only will a receiver be refused to the
trustees, but Lord Granard will receive carriage of the whole proceedings'.[42] Cardinal Logue was somewhat less polite about Gillooley's
interference and what he regarded as Granard's deceitfulness. In
April 1888, he wrote to Robert Browne, president of the college: 'I
feel strongly inclined to send the copy [of Chance's above quoted
letter] to Dr Gillooley. If it did no other good, it might stop any interference on his part in the future.... Lord Granard was too clever
for him'.[43]

There was an even more surprising development during the court
case when it emerged that Lord Granard had been receiving much
more in rents that he had been admitting to. In fact in 1883–84 and
1884–85 (when the economy recovered temporarily) he received
aggregated rents of just over £19,000, or £1,000 above his actual rent
roll. In 1885–86 and 1886–87, his rents did fall because of the plan of

campaign, on average around 16 per cent per annum on his actual rent roll, but they were still substantially greater than the college trustees had been led to believe.[44] The rents collected for 1885–87 suggest that the plan of campaign did have some effect on estate management, although not nearly as much as the organisers would obviously have liked. But more significantly it seems that either tenants were secretly paying their rents through fear of eviction, or that there were those who were willing (and brave enough) to take over the property of evicted tenants.[45]

If Granard was receiving so much in rents, why did he fail to meet his full interest repayments to the trustees? It transpired that there were both new and 'hidden' charges amounting to around £20,000 that Granard had given priority to. When Granard was granted the mortgage in 1871, he had been married for thirteen years but had no children; by 1888 he had married for the second time and had five sons and provision for them took priority.[46] There were also payments made to what the college solicitors termed 'puisne mortgagees' (mortgagees who had granted loans to Granard subsequent to April 1871).[47] But even these charges should have left enough to meet the college's interest. In March 1899, P.A. Chance wrote to Robert Browne, the college president: 'I should like to know what he did with the money'.[48]

In March 1889, the principal owing on the Granard mortgage stood at £93,670 and arrears of interest at £3,723.[49] P.A. Chance feared that the sale of the estate would not produce sufficient funds to discharge Lord Granard's liabilities and feared that he would, therefore, have 'no interest whatsoever in expediting a sale'.[50] (The Irish Land Commission actually deemed most of the land to be 'very bad indeed' which begs the question as to why the trustees regarded it as safe collateral in the first place.[51]) The sale of the estate did, in fact, prove to be very slow. This was partly due to Granard's intransigence (no doubt under the influence of his legal advisers). He continued to exasperate the college trustees by refusing to negotiate sales until a twelve month stay on interest repayments was granted and he be permitted to retain occupation of 2,000 acres of the estate. This annoyed the trustees who felt Granard was attempting to have 'rates, taxes, tithe rent charges and other outgoings paid virtually out of the pockets of Maynooth'.[52] At the same time, Granard continued to plead inability to meet interest repayments. His solicitor wrote to P.A. Chance in March 1889:

> We regret to say that Lord Granard is not in a position to pay the arrears of interest. Through the kindness of friends, he obtained money on a recent occasion for that purpose, but he feels that he cannot

again appeal to them, and in the present state of the money market, and also having regard to the present circumstances of the estate, it is quite out of our power to raise it.[53]

Then in March 1889, Granard successfully instituted a motion to have the sale of the estate stayed for twelve months.[54]

The actual workings of the Ashbourne Act of 1885 hindered progress. By around June 1889, purchase agreements to the amount of £99,980 were reached between Granard and his tenants. But these had to be sanctioned by the Land Commission, which would have to provide the purchase loans to the tenants. When these agreements were submitted to the Land Commission for acceptance, the commissioners accepted, without reductions, agreements amounting to £38,605. They offered a further £34,367 for what tenants had agreed to pay £42,497; refused to buy at any price holdings which tenants had agreed to purchase at £9,814; and held over for further consideration purchases amounting to £8,614.[55] It was always going to be a problem to get the Land Commission to advance money on uneconomic holdings.[56] And those around Drumlish were exactly that. In December 1887, a report was carried out for the trustees. It found that the tenants there 'appeared to be in a great state of destitution and the land ... is so bad that it would be impossible for a person to derive a livelihood from 100 acres without even the payment of any rent'. Most tenants owed three to four years' rent and reports on their individual holdings predominantly described the land as 'very poor', 'bad land only fit for quarrying', 'rocky, all flooded'.[57] From the landlord's and the mortgagees' point of view, the Land Commission was retarding progress which was a source of frustration to both.[58]

The college's solicitor expected that when all negotiations were finalised, and a fair price agreed upon for the residual estates, that the gross proceeds of the sale would amount to about £90,000 (excluding the sale of the demesne and Castleforbes.) Of this he calculated that £22,000 would remain with the Land Commission as the guaranteed deposit (a sum greater than one fifth of the expected gross proceeds!); £14,000 would be absorbed in extinguishing head rents, tithe rents and Board of Works loans. This would leave £64,000 for distribution and fall over £30,000 short of what was owed the college in principal and interest.[59]

In August 1889, Lord Granard died. His heir was still a minor, which caused further legal difficulties with regard to sales. The result was that from the death of Granard to November 1890, 'practically no further sales [were] effected'.[60] There was an 'alarming' increase in arrears of interest. So in late 1890, the college trustees passed a resolution to have a receiver appointed over all the lands included in the Granard mortgage. The intention was that the sale of the residue of the estate (with the exception of the castle and demesne) 'could be completed as rapidly and inexpensively as possible'.[61] But by 1891, when the mortgage should have been redeemed, arrears in interest alone amounted to over £10,000. The townlands of Dyrowley, Greagh and Lettergullion were amongst those proving 'impossible to sell' and the Drumlish tenants refused to buy except at ten to twelve years' purchase.[62] By 1892, only £52,094 of the purchase advances had been sanctioned (of which £10,876 was retained by the Land Commission), leaving £41,188 for allocation. Of this around £30,000 went to the college trustees. Those tenants who had not purchased by now became more reluctant to do so: some were getting rent reductions of up to 70 per cent in the land courts.[63]

In February 1892, the trustees appointed a valuator to appraise the unsold lands. His opinion was that the holdings were 'miserably poor' and that 'the tenants have been worn out by attempts to pay the old rents'.[64] Even the demesne was becoming increasingly run down. In 1891, Fr Thomas Conefry wrote to the president of the college: 'The timber is taken away in cart loads every day; the laurels and young trees were dug up and sold in the neighbouring fairs and markets, and desolation seems to be the order of the day there'.[65]

At the beginning of 1892 it seems that the college trustees contemplated petitioning for the sale of the demesne (574 acres grazing land; 624 acres of wood; and 205 acres of bog) and castle. In February of that year, R.D. Cochrane carried out a valuation of the demesne and castle. In his opinion there were only twenty-five good acres on the demesne and therefore 'ordinary farming profits could not be made out of it'. The castle and out-offices were in good condition but would be suitable only for somebody with an income of £15,000 to £20,000 per annum so that 'no man of moderate means could live in or maintain' them. Finally he concluded that the castle was 'unsaleable in the market and therefore valueless except as building material' as no wealthy man would buy it because of the fact that,

> the County Longford is now almost denuded of gentry, there is no hunting except a scratch pack of harriers got together this winter, there is no general shooting in the county and the place is three and a half hours from Dublin.[66]

In 1894, James Donnellan, the college bursar, wrote to the bishop of Ardagh: 'As far as I know the sale of the residue of the Granard estate is left in the hands of Dr Walsh. The bishops have been very

reticent about the matter, so that I really do not know what conclusions they came to.'[67] The Granard mortgage had become such a huge
embarrassment to the trustees that nobody seemed to want to either
investigate or quantify the final damage caused to the college. As the
volume of correspondence diminishes with the death of the seventh
Earl of Granard in 1889, it is not quite clear what happened either to
the residual estates or the castle. In the case of the former, it seems
that the college trustees agreed to their sale at lower rates because
of the impoverishment of the tenantry. Indeed, it was Fr Thomas
Conefry's insistence that the tenants should not pay any more than
thirteen years' purchase at Griffith's valuation (as opposed to thirteen years' purchase at current rents.[68]) 'An Irish Priest' [possibly
Conefry himself] wrote in 1892:

> ... it is my pleasing duty to narrate that the tenants ... have achieved
> a complete, permanent and final victory. They have now nearly all
> bought out their farms under the Ashbourne Act at a price that leaves
> them their farms at mere nominal rent. The trustees of Maynooth
> College, who have a heavy mortgage on Lord Granard's estate, and
> who are in reality the real owners, true to the Christian spirit of their
> high calling, showed every anxiety, and used every means in their
> power to enable Father Conefry to buy out the farms for the tenants
> on such terms as would enable the latter to support their families in
> comparative comfort. Through the trustees of the college, Father
> Conefry got several years of arrears of rack-rent forgiven.[69]

In the case of the castle, the trustees seem to have accepted the
report of R.D. Cochrane that it would be futile attempting to sell it.
The Granards continued to live at Castleforbes, their fortunes somewhat rescued in 1909 when the eighth Earl of Granard married an
American heiress, Beatrice Ogden Mills.[70] In 1903 the balance due on
the mortgage stood at £31,400 principal plus £3,200 in interest.[71] By
1906, the trustees seemed to have reconciled themselves to the fact
of non-payment. 'The purchase monies resulting from the sale of the
residue of the estate [the demesne and an area known as Kennedy's
Island] would be insufficient to pay the monies still due to the
trustees on foot of their several incumbrances', and so they cut their
losses.[72] The final overall loss, counting non-repaid capital, arrears of
interest, and legal costs was therefore in the region of £35,000.[73]

'THAT TERRIBLE LAND LEAGUE'

After almost three decades of economic prosperity, long-term agricultural depression began in 1877. The post-Famine generation of tenant

farmers (and, indeed, landlord-farmers) suddenly saw the value of their agricultural produce decline by 36 per cent, the value of their crops by 50 per cent and the value of their livestock by around 36 per cent.[74] (Some agricultural prices were not to reach their 1876 levels until 1914.[75]) For the generation of Irish tenant farmers who remembered the hardship of the Famine there was no desire to return to it; for the generation that had grown up with economic prosperity there was no great desire to relinquish it.[76] In the towns there were shopkeepers and publicans who had benefited from tenant prosperity (and many of whom were also farmers themselves) and to whom tenants were financially obligated because of the network of credit facilities that had grown from the 1850s.[77] Such social groupings (strengthened by the influence of a strong Nationalist parliamentary party led by Parnell and by the early support of many Fenians) became more amenable to the rhetoric of leaders of the Irish National Land League, established in 1879. These leaders, often wrongly, vilified landlords as rack-renters in order to combat the threatened reversal of gains. The Land League spread quickly and was soon being exploited by aspiring local leaders throughout the country who saw in the anti-landlord slogans a rallying cry for the populace.[78]

The Land League called for rents to be reduced to Griffith's valuation which, as was pointed out earlier, was very much below the real letting value of land by the late-1870s.[79] However, comparisons of contemporary rents with Griffith's valuation was a tactical ploy exploited by the Land League as rents that had risen in the period could be deemed to be rack-rents when compared to the old valuation. And the fact that such increases, if moderate, had taken place in the 1860s and early 1870s and thus within the living memory of most members of the Land League, added to the philosophy. The successful propaganda campaign of the league, therefore, meant that all landlords were painted with the same rack-renting and capricious evicting brush whether they deserved it or not.[80]

It is plain to see why tenants would clamour for rents to be reduced to Griffith's valuation. It is just as easy to understand why landlords would oppose calls for reductions. For a patriarchal landlord such as Earl Fitzwilliam of Coolattin, whose rents were only 5 per cent above Griffith's valuation in 1881, a reduction would mean a loss of almost £2,000 per annum.[81] For others, as we have seen in the case of Lord Granard, the decline would be much greater. Lord Ormonde, for example, would have suffered a 24 per cent reduction in rents from £21,352 to £16,359. As his annual estate expenditure for the years 1879 to 1890 inclusive averaged £17,400, a reduction of

24 per cent to Griffith's valuation would have made it impossible for him to meet his financial obligations.[82]

Initial reaction amongst landlords to calls for reductions were mixed. Some felt that if they could weather the storm the crisis would abate, as it had done in the early 1860s, and tenants would simply revert to paying their old rents and make up their arrears. One Sligo landlord told the Bessborough Commission in 1881 that he had allowed 25 per cent reductions to ordinary tenants and 15 per cent to leaseholders from the late-1870s. 'From some of them', he claimed, 'I have got no money at all, so we must bear with it until we have a better state of things if possible.'[83] Some took umbrage at being called upon from public platforms to grant reductions but did so out of consideration to the plight of their tenants. Algernon Coote of Ballyfin, for example, perceived demands to be a private matter between landlords and tenants and he resented them being a 'matter for public debate' at Land League meetings that were composed of people other than his own tenants. Nevertheless, in October 1879, he granted 10 per cent abatements on the coming half year's rent to help his tenants in their 'present difficulties' but he told them:

> I regret you have resorted to a public meeting, and resolutions passed there in order to apply to me for a reduction of rent. Such a mode of proceeding is in opposition to the relations of confidence which should prevail between landlord and tenant, and must give the appearance of coercion to a gift of reduction. You have lived long enough on the estate to know that everything affecting your interests would be kindly and fairly considered, and had your applications been made privately, as I think they should have been, through my son, it would have been a gratification to me to respond to them.[84]

And there were other landlords such as John George Adair (more infamous for his Derryveagh evictions during the previous economic depression of the 1860s) who refused to grant any reductions on his Queen's County estates. In October 1879, he told Fr Thomas Murphy of Mountmellick that:

> ... the tenants are aware that my estates are subject to charges, taxes, rents, annuities and encumbrances; these must be paid without reduction. Were I therefore to accede to their request I should be driven to abandon my property. This I am not prepared to do, and consequently cannot grant their request.[85]

A study of local and national newspapers would suggest that most landlords were more accommodating than Adair during the land war of 1879–82. Information on thirty of the sample estates, for example, reported reductions ranging from 10 to 40 per cent. In December 1880, the Duke of Leinster was reported to have granted a 20 per cent reduction on his Kildare estate. In January 1881, tenants were said to have been granted 25 per cent reductions on the King-Harman estate in Longford and Charles Coote accepted rents equivalent to Griffith's valuation on his Queen's County estate.[86] However, one must be careful in assessing the significance of such reported reductions on a landlord's rental income. A report of a 20 per cent reduction did not necessarily apply to all tenants, or to all administrative units of a landlord's estate.[87] When Lady Emily Bury granted reductions in October 1879, they were to apply only to those tenants who had paid their rents in full to 25 March 1879.[88] In the same month, her neighbour, Lord Digby, instructed his agent to allow 10 per cent reductions to those whose half-yearly rent exceeded £40. He allowed 15 per cent to those whose half yearly rent was between £10 and £40, and 20 per cent to those whose half yearly rent was less than £10. However, he stipulated that in the case 'of such tenants as have neglected to properly clean and scour the drains and watercourses and their several holdings, the above allowances will be withheld until such times as the work shall have been satisfactorily performed'.[89]

A study of estate accounts suggests that the granting of reductions probably had less of an effect on a landlord's gross rental income than newspaper reports would suggest. This was certainly the case on well-managed estates such as Lord Clonbrock's. By 1880, his projected rental income was £11,000. In that year and 1881 and 1882 he granted reductions of 2.5 per cent, 5.3 per cent and 4.5 per cent respectively. His average annual rental income for 1880–82 was around £10,300, a decline of only 6 per cent on the 1865–69 average (the last years for which accounts were available prior to the late 1870s).[90] Clonbrock was particularly fortunate with regard to his large tenants, of whom there were twenty-three on the estate in 1880 paying rent in excess of £100 per annum, for between the years 1880 and 1889 these were only £23 in arrears on aggregated rents of almost £50,500.[91]

Much more detrimental to landlords than reductions were the withholding of rents by tenants and the subsequent accumulation of arrears. Landlords who procrastinated or refused to meet tenants' demands for reductions became subject to rent strikes which subsequently denied them a sizeable proportion of their rental income. Lord Clonbrock, because of a firm tradition of good landlord–tenant relations on his estate, did not suffer in this respect to the same extent as many of his fellow landlords elsewhere in the country. On the other hand, when the Earl of Donoughmore refused to accept rents at Griffith's valuation in December 1880, his tenants withdrew *en masse* without paying anything.[92] In December 1881, Lord Dunalley offered a 15 per cent reduction to the tenants on his Cloughjordan estate. But they refused to settle for anything less than Griffith's valuation, while the tenants elsewhere on the estate, who had already secured such a reduction, warned that they would not pay their rents 'until our brother tenant-farmers who are paying over that valuation ... have settled satisfactorily with the landlord'.[93] In 1879, rents collected on the Ormonde estate fell 10 per cent below projected rental. By 1881, they had fallen to 17 per cent below the expected figure and while there was an improvement in 1882 and 1883, they again fell below the projected rental by 14 per cent each year from 1884 to 1886.[94] This is in stark contrast to the period from 1870 to 1878, when rents and arrears paid to Lord Ormonde exceeded his aggregated projected rental by around £20,000. Between 1879 and 1881, arrears on the estate increased from over £7,000 to £12,300. There was a slight decrease in 1882 and 1883 when they fell to below £10,000 each year but after 1884 they began to grow at an unprecedented rate so that by 1890 they were almost 100 per cent higher than the 1881 figure standing at £24,300.[95] The situation was much worse on the Pratt estate in County Cavan where rents received for the years 1880–82 totalled almost £9,000, but arrears totalled over £15,000.[96] In November 1879, arrears on Lord Castletown's estate in Queen's County totalled just over £3,500; by November of the following year they had risen to over £8,300 or almost 50 per cent of the annual rents due to him that year.[97]

'MR GLADSTONE'S BLUNDERING LEGISLATION'

In the midst of this crisis, the introduction of the fair rent provisions of the Land Purchase (Ireland) Act of 1881 was opposed by landlords. The Irish Land Committee might have been unfair to the sub-commissioners responsible for fixing rents when in a pamphlet in 1882 it claimed that:

> ... here we have thirty-six amateurs, with no professional training and, in many cases, with but little practical knowledge of land; they go north, south, east and west; they visit farms at a gallop, and at the most unsuitable season of the year ... and so wonderful is their intrinsic knowledge that next day they assess the value of each farm with the utmost minuteness.[98]

But it captured landlords' antagonism towards what they perceived to be the lack of rationale in the lowering of rents. (Effectively
the fixing of rents came to mean the lowering of them.) From when
the sub-commissioners began their operations in August 1881 to the
end of the first judicial term in December 1902, they dealt with
342,019 cases in which judicial rents were fixed. The former rent of
these holdings aggregated £6.93 million; the judicial rent lowered it
to £5.48 million, representing a decrease of 20.8 per cent.[99]

When in 1882, Evelyn Philip Shirley succeeded his father at
Lough Fea in County Monaghan, he attempted to use his 'right' to
increase rents on succession by 10 per cent, as had been the tradition
on the estate in the past. A tenant named Carragher refused to pay
the increase and questioned the legality of Shirley's attempts to
make him do so. To settle the dispute Shirley agreed to go to the land
court to have a fair rent fixed, but the commissioners actually
reduced Carragher's old rent by 15 per cent. Shirley appealed but the
reductions were confirmed, which encouraged 100 more of his tenants to seek fair rents and all were granted reductions ranging from
15 to 20 per cent.[100] On some estates, or at least parts of them, fair
rent reductions were well above the national average. In December
1887, the commissioners reduced rents on the King-Harman estate
in Longford by 33 per cent and in February 1888 they reduced rents
on the Pratt estate in Cavan by 26 per cent.[101]

It was because fair rent fixing came at a time when arrears on
estates were escalating and landlords were finding themselves in
increasingly difficult financial difficulties that fears of the impact of
the 1881 Land Act grew.[102] While obviously not all tenants entered
the land courts the fact of the matter was that any reduction, no
matter how slight, was decreasing the net income of landlords and
bringing them precariously close to bankruptcy. Under the terms of
the 1887 Land Act, leaseholders were admitted for the first time into
the rent arbitration system and subsequently had their rents
reduced by up to 25 per cent. The terms of fixed rents were now also
reduced from fifteen years to five years, which meant that many
landlords were now faced with a further round of rent decreases. By
1896 twice as many tenants were entering the land courts than had
done in the early 1880s. In the light of further reductions still being
granted, the commander of the northern division of the RIC wrote:
'The feeling on the part of the landlords is decidedly very bitter; they
maintain that their property and their interests are not sufficiently
safeguarded while undue advantages are being secured to tenants'.
What he termed the 'enormous reductions' given by the sub-
commissioners caused 'real consternation' among landlords because

they threatened to 'wipe away the margin of income left them to live on'.[103] Bitter disillusionment amongst landlords became the order of the day. John Madden of Hilton Park told the Cowper Commission that the rents on his estate had not been raised since before his father's time. Referring to £2,300 from 'his own pocket' that he had spent on improvements, he claimed that he had been defrauded of every penny of it because his rents had been fixed below Griffith's valuation.[104] From a landlord's point of view, the perceived hopelessness of their situation was summarised in a letter from the Marquis of Dufferin to Edward Carson in 1897:

> The fact is the whole thing is such a mess, and every principle not only of justice, but of practical good sense, has been so thwarted by Mr Gladstone's blundering legislation, that the situation is irremediable. An enquiry into the proceedings of the Irish land courts might result in showing the blind, capricious and inconsistent way in which they work, and, perhaps, that their general scale of reductions has been excessive; but I should fear that the ultimate upshot of this would not very much improve our position.[105]

Furthermore, the Arrears of Rent (Ireland) Act of 1882 resulted in £1.76 million in arrears being extinguished from landlords' rentals. In real terms the loss to landlords was approximately half this figure as under the terms of the act the Land Commission could make an order for the payment of a sum equal to one half of antecedent arrears to or for the benefit of the landlord. Thus of the £1.76 million extinguished, approximately £767,000 was recovered by landlords.[106] Amongst the landlords who suffered most were Lord De Freyne who had £16,500 extinguished in arrears on his Roscommon rental of which he recovered £5,900. The King-Harmans had £7,500 extinguished of which they recovered £3,600; and Sir John Leslie who had £10,200 extinguished on his Monaghan estate of which he recovered £4,600.[107] However, the greater significance of this act lay in the fact that it was even more demoralising for landlords than the 1881 Land Act for the extinction of arrears was a form of confiscation. In the past landlords had granted abatements when it suited them and at a level that suited them. Now the government dictated the terms and this interference possibly more than any other factor undermined confidence in landed property.

THE PLAN OF CAMPAIGN

From the mid-1880s, in the midst of compulsory reductions and extinguishing of arrears, came a renewal of agricultural depression (after a temporary respite in 1883 and 1884) that was to last until 1888. In 1885, land agitation was re-ignited; this time it was accompanied by the plan of campaign that was ultimately to be adopted on over 200 estates.[108] Again landlords suffered in varying degrees. Where the plan of campaign was adopted by all tenants on a whole estate, rental income declined greatly and arrears grew rapidly. From 1886 to 1890, the rental income of the Crofton estate in Roscommon fell by 14 per cent from the annual average figure of £5,800 for the years 1876–78.[109] From 1885, Lord Cloncurry was faced with severe agitation on his Limerick estate. While for the five-year period 1875–79, he had collected aggregated rents of £17,800 on this estate, the figure fell by almost 46 per cent for a similar five year period from 1880 to 1884, the first stage of the land war.[110] Tenants had demanded a reduction of 20 per cent but from an early stage, Cloncurry argued that such a reduction was beyond him because of his obligations to Maynooth College. He told his tenants in April 1881:

> The annual sum which I pay to the trustees of Maynooth Roman Catholic College as interest upon mortgages of land in Ireland is as large as the whole rental of my property in Limerick, and if you can persuade the trustees of Maynooth college to give me an abatement of 20 per cent in the half year's interest now accruing to them I will have pleasure in giving a similar abatement to my tenants in Limerick.[111]

The situation on his estate was not resolved. From 1885 to 1889, during which time the plan of campaign was implemented there, aggregated rents received remained around 43 per cent below the 1875–79 figure. While only an aggregate of £980 was outstanding in arrears for the years 1875–79, this figure escalated to £8,700 for the 1885–89 period.[112]

Where the plan was not adopted on the whole of an estate, the decline in rental income was less perceptible, if no less worrying. From 1886 to 1887, the plan was adopted on part only of the Clonbrock estate in Galway. Lord Clonbrock seems to have pre-empted its adoption elsewhere on the estate by granting more sizeable abatements than he had done during the previous period of depression. From 1880 to 1882, Clonbrock had granted an average annual abatement of £450. In 1885, the abatement figure rose dramatically to £1,350. There was a further rise in 1886 to £1,700, followed by a decline in 1887 to £1,400. Clonbrock's rental income shows a corresponding decline of around 9 per cent in both 1886 and

1887 on what it had been prior to the beginning of the second period
of depression and the adoption of the plan of campaign.[113]

For landlords who did not sell their estates under the earlier land
acts, arrears continued to remain a constant source of concern
throughout the late nineteenth and early twentieth centuries. Irish
agriculture remained in a state of depression and the rise of the
United Irish League in the early part of the twentieth century simply put more pressure on landlords to sell their estates (and, indeed,
to have large grazing farms broken up and redistributed.) On the
Butler of Castlecrine estate, where the rental was just over £4,300
per annum, expenses were consistently over £3,000 per annum
between 1895 and 1903 and for six of these nine years were not met
by rental income. In 1895, accumulated arrears on the estate totalled
almost £10,000.[114] On the Ormonde estate there was a huge increase
in arrears from £9,100 in 1883 to £24,300 in 1890. Even though they
fell marginally in the following years, the estate auditor was still
perturbed enough to comment in 1896 when they were over £20,600:
'It might be well to, if possible, make the tenants more punctual in
the payment of their rents and prevent accruing of arrears'.[115] It
would seem that Lord Ormonde was unable to do anything about the
situation for the following year arrears increased by a further £1,000
and the auditor repeated his recommendation of the previous year.[116]
Arrears continued to average over £20,000 per annum until 1903.
Meanwhile, Lord Ormonde's personal overdraft at the Provincial
Bank averaged almost £15,000 per annum.[117]

The impression created in the last few pages must be that the
1880s and the 1890s were characterised by one crisis after another
for Irish landlords and the question thus arises as to how so many
actually survived into the twentieth century. The simple answer —
with difficulty! The prolonged agricultural depression marked the
beginning of a long period of economic exigency for Irish landlords
after which it was impossible for many of them, particularly the
small and middle-sized landowners, to revive the position they held
prior to the mid-1870s. The land war was essentially a response to
this depression. But while landlordism had weathered a similar
storm in the early 1860s, this one was different, not only because of
its longevity but because it was accompanied by a particularly hostile anti-landlord mass movement whose leaders were intent on
uprooting landlordism. Rents had been withheld in the past, but
never under such a concerted policy. Reductions had traditionally
been granted but never forced so extensively and successfully as
during the land war and plan of campaign. Furthermore, the continued depression meant not only that the land courts invariably

continued to lower rents after 1881 so that by the 1890s they had fallen to Griffith's valuation (if not below it) but that Irish land was no longer regarded as safe collateral. The fictitious Henry Deluce, a poorly camouflaged Sir John Leslie of Glaslough, epitomised their plight:

> All through the fifties and the sixties he had totted up the great roll of twenty thousand pounds a year, quarter by quarter through the depreciating seventies, and, as one generation died, he lifted the rent off their sons, so that Sir Edward [his son] might continue living the life of the fine old Irish gentleman on a fine estate, until the eighties came and the rents tumbled by a third and a half, and the nineties brought arrears and debt and a strict retrenchment ... Sir Edward must always have enough to keep up ancient state and pay full wage to his pensioners, and keep white ducks and fantails and swans, and pay parsons to pray for his good estate and a full cellar to warm his hospitality, and fifty odd gardeners and bailiffs and keepers and servants and retainers and a coachman and foresters.[118]

'No Capitalist Will Now Lend on Irish Estates....'

As would happen in any period, an economic entity without the power of recourse to borrowing to alleviate cash flow problems, found itself on the brink of bankruptcy. John George Adair, when replying to his tenants' demands for reductions in October 1879, had effectively summed up what was the greatest perceived threat facing landlords at this time: their levels of indebtedness were such that they could not reduce their rents without bringing ruin to themselves. Back in 1874, Lord Dufferin had proclaimed: 'An Irish estate is like a sponge and an Irish landlord is never so rich as when he is rid of his property.'[119] Dufferin was not exaggerating. Besides the expenses referred to by Adair most landlords had to meet a myriad other expenses such as agency fees, legal fees, rates, charitable donations, insurance premiums, entertainment bills, and, not least of all, big house and demesne maintenance. From the mid-1850s to the beginning of the land war, these expenses had been affordable and landlords had continued to live relatively opulent and often extravagant lifestyles. From the late 1870s, the financial strain increased as many landlords were not prepared to compromise some aspects of their expenditure such as ubiquitous family charges and were unable to diminish others such as interest charges. Cumulatively estate expenses soaked up much of the rental income available to a landlord and as rental income declined, net income was greatly diminished. In 1880, Lord Crofton received £5,483 in rents on his Roscommon estate. His estate expenditure was £4,321, leaving him with a net income of just over 21 per cent.[120] However, for the decade 1880–90 as a whole his annual net income averaged just over 5 per cent.[121] The income of the Mahon estate at Castlegar in County Galway fell from around £11,000 in 1881 to £7,300 in 1886, a decline of around 34 per cent. At the same time expenditure remained consistently high in comparison. While it accounted for a massive 93.5 per cent of income in 1881, it was not covered in any of the following years, being on average 7.5 per cent above rental income for the years 1882 to 1886 inclusive.[122]

Landlords, who had borrowed heavily during the 1850s, 1860s and early 1870s, now found a higher proportion of their annual rental income going towards interest repayments.[123] Smaller landowners were hit hardest. In 1891, Lord Inchiquin made a speech in the House of Lords 'on behalf of men who were ruined'. He cited the example of a landlord family who, a decade or so previously, had been in a comfortable position with an annual income of £3,000–£4,000, but who now 'on account of difficulties' was receiving a mere fourteen shillings per week. This was, he said, 'just enough to keep body and soul together from the mortgagees'. A Cork lawyer told the Bessborough Commission:

> The smaller landlords, many of whom may be and no doubt are just as well disposed to act fairly by their tenants are unable to do so in consequence of the charges and mortgages which they have to meet upon their properties.[124]

If one looks to the reports of the Irish Landowners' Convention from its establishment in the mid-1880s to its dissolution in 1919, one is immediately struck by the concentration on landlords with mortgage difficulties and the pleas to the British government to do something to alleviate their indebtedness.[125] Significantly, the Convention was perhaps the most representative of all the landlord bodies in that it was composed of members drawn from all strata of the landlord class. By the 1890s, members of the Convention had become frustrated enough in their quest to do something for the plight of encumbered landlords to ask:

> Why then should we carry on a hopelessly bankrupt business, flaying tenants alive and eternally plunged in scalding waters ourselves, merely for the benefit of some firm of London usurers who are safe out of range of blunderbuss or boycotter.[126]

The state of affairs in Ireland meant that land was no longer regarded as safe collateral. Mortgagees who panicked during the land war began to call in their loans as landlords temporarily defaulted, thus distinguishing this agricultural depression from the one in the 1860s when landlords managed to extricate themselves from financial difficulties through the medium of borrowing. All the available evidence points to the fact that most landlords were unable to meet their interest obligations in the 1880s. In 1886, arrears of interest to the Representative Body of the Church of Ireland (RCB) stood at £35,000; by 1890, they had risen to £81,000; and by 1901 to £135,000. From 1885, in all cases in which a full year's interest had become due upon mortgages, receivers or agents under deed were appointed over estates. The money invested in Irish estates had now become a 'subject of serious anxiety' to the RCB. Its report in 1886 concluded:

> In the present state of uncertainty as to the laws which may be enacted with reference to land tenure, it would be rash to speak positively as to what may, or may not, be the loss on these investments. The Representative Body can only repeat that they hope there will be no ultimate loss of capital, though some loss of interest may be expected.[127]

In December 1880, the agent on the Stewart estate in Donegal wrote to the bursar of Maynooth College informing him of a rent strike on his estate and asking for a deferment of interest payment to the following year.[128] By December 1882 the estate was still in trouble, and Rev Andrew Boylan was forced to write to Sir Alexander Stewart regarding his arrears. He called upon him 'to send ... immediately a cheque for same as very great inconvenience has been caused to the college by the non-payment of this money at the time it fell due'.[129]

Landlords were unable to secure loans to tie them over the difficult times. As early as 1880, Samuel Hussey, whose agency firm annually collected rents amounting to £250,000, wrote to the Duke of Argyll:

> Already the insurance offices, the greatest mortgagees in Ireland, have declined to lend any more money, and all negotiations for loans have been broken off ... I have bought £3,000 per annum worth of land, and no one will lend £5,000 on it.[130]

Some time later, he wrote to *The Times* referring to the further effects of the recent Land Act of 1881. 'No capitalist will now lend on Irish estates as they naturally argue if the government forcibly reduces rents 25 per cent in an exceptionally good year, what in a bad year?'[131] A Cork landowner who informed the Cowper Commission that 'bank accommodation' had 'ceased altogether' was distressed by the fact that 'when men wanted money most they had not the least chance of getting it'.[132] From late 1877 to 1879, the RCB sanctioned no new loans obviously having become aware of the threat which agricultural depression posed to landlords attempting to meet interest repayments on the strength of rental income.[133] By 1886, the amount invested by the RCB in Irish estates was the same as it had been in 1877. Similarly, Maynooth College sanctioned no new loans from the early 1880s. Prior to the onset of depression and the land war the Scottish Widows Company had loaned an estimated £1.2 million to Irish landowners. During the 1880s the company began to call in its loans and by 1894 landlords had been obliged to repay £850,000.[134]

Approaching financiers for abatements on interest repayments proved largely futile and so landlord organisations appealed to politicians and the government to do something to alleviate their distress. In 1883, a deputation wrote to Gladstone pointing out that 'there are few (if any) sources for borrowing money on land in Ireland now open and ... trustees, assurance societies and private lenders are steadily refusing to advance upon mortgages on Irish estates'.[135] In 1886, the executive committee of the Irish Landowners' Convention called on the British government to compensate Irish landlords for losses sustained by them as a result of land legislation from 1881. They asked for advances to be granted, to 'pay off mortgages and family charges' and for 'the incidence of certain public charges, rates and taxes' to be readjusted.[136]

Their pleas fell on deaf ears. The face of British politics was beginning to undergo radical change. Politicians were increasingly becoming aware of the need to woo the expanding electorate leading them to sympathise more with the masses than the besieged minority of landlords. As early as 1881, Lord Dufferin's awareness of this was evident in his comments to the Duke of Argyll:

> The tendency of the extreme section of the Liberal party is to buy the support of the masses by distributing among them the property of their own political opponents, and it is towards a social rather than a political revolution we are tending.[137]

THE LAND ACTS FROM 1881 TO 1896

In Ireland the social revolution and the political revolution became inextricably entwined when the land movement merged with the Home Rule movement. Landlords were perceived to be in direct opposition to both; firstly by being the owners of the land and secondly by setting themselves up as Unionists. The Land Act of 1881 was enacted in an attempt to diffuse the land movement's momentum. However, it did not provide landlords with the necessary incentives to entice them to sell their estates in order to alleviate their debt burdens. Thus the act was more significant for the way in which it infringed on previously sacrosanct landlord rights — by legalising fair rents, fixity of tenure and free sale — than it was for the transfer of land which took place under its terms. The act gave fixity of tenure to a tenant on his holding as long as he paid his rent and observed his covenant. A fair rent proviso provided for the establishment of independent tribunals. This was set up by the newly-established Irish Land Commission, to determine fair rents on holdings. A tenant was allowed free sale of his interest in his holding, thereby compelling a landlord to compensate a tenant for disturbance in his occupancy and for any improvements carried out by the tenant on his holding.[138]

Between 1881 and 1884 only 731 tenants purchased their holdings. Terms of sale suited neither tenants nor landlords. The Land Commission was empowered to make advances to tenants for the purchase of their holdings. However, the amount advanced was restricted to 75 per cent of the purchase price putting the onus on tenant purchasers to raise a 25 per cent deposit. Advances were to be repaid in an annuity of 5 per cent over a period of thirty-five years. There were landlords such as Lord Cloncurry whose relationship with their tenants on outlying estates had become so strained that they would have gladly sold such estates if they could have realised what they considered a fair purchase price. As early as 1881, Cloncurry had written: 'The conduct of the people in the south of Ireland during the last year has been so disgraceful and all feelings of honesty have been so openly repudiated that I shall be glad to sever my connections with the county of Limerick'. But he would not sell for less than twenty-four years' purchase at a time when tenants were not prepared to pay more than fourteen or fifteen years' purchase.[139]

Similarly, in 1884 the Land Commission was asked to negotiate the sale of properties belonging to Col King-Harman in County Longford. The landlord asked for twenty-three years' purchase of the rental of £4,146 which would have brought him £95,358 but the tenants were not willing to meet his demand stating that 'they were unable to pay the necessary one fourth of the price' (the 25 per cent deposit.)[140] Around the same time Lord Lansdowne wanted to sell part of his estate but following negotiations he 'considered the offers

made generally by the tenants insufficient and the matter dropped'.[141]
It may be logical to conclude that in the middle of an agricultural
depression tenants, like those on the King-Harman estate, genuinely
could not raise the capital to provide the one fourth deposit which
was required under the terms of the act. It may also have been
because, as Commissioner Lynch later claimed in 1912, the bitter
agrarian and political agitation of the time closed the door of the
Irish land market to all bidders except the occupying tenants.[142]
Therefore, as Lansdowne realised, this put the tenants in the
strongest bargaining position. It was inevitable that there was going
to be a gulf between what they regarded as a fair price and what
landlords required. As no one else would buy, and as long as rents
remained low, tenants would be in less of a hurry to buy than
indebted landlords would be to sell. Tenants were unwilling to purchase until such time as annuities were less financially exacting
than current rents. There was also, of course, the added consideration that it was land that bestowed economic, social and political
status upon landlords; in the early 1880s it was still very difficult for
them to abandon this. And in many cases landlords' hands were tied
regarding the sale of their estates by complicated legal mechanisms
known as strict settlement that had been devised over preceding
generations limiting landowners' ability to sell their lands against
the interest of their heirs.

It was not until the late 1880s that Irish landlords realised that
agricultural depression and accompanying agitation were not going
to go away. It was becoming clearer that land values and agriculture
in general were in a state of long-term decline. As well as that the
ownership of large estates was no longer a prerequisite to political
power; the Franchise and Redistribution Acts of the mid-1880s had
seen to that. By the end of the decade many landlords, like Lord
Lansdowne, who had lost most of their rents to the plan of campaign,
had resigned themselves to the sale of their estates. In 1887,
Lansdowne saw it as the only hope that landlords had of escaping
financial ruin for he believed that 'the British public is indifferent to
the ruin of the landlords and will not spend a penny to avert it...'[143]
In the same year, Sir Henry Gore-Booth of Lisadell claimed: 'I would
be willing to sell every acre, it would be a great saving to me if I
could get twenty-three years' purchase on the ordnance valuation,
one fourth added.'[144] Lord Cloncurry claimed to have had conversations with 'nearly all the large landed proprietors' and that they
were willing to sell 'all the outlying portion' of their estates. He
himself 'would gladly sell all outlying properties and retain only
that part of [his] estate within a day's drive or journey of [his]

residence'.[145] And John Madden of Hilton Park, Monaghan, told the Cowper Commission:

> If I could get what I consider to be the value of my property and get rid of my house and demesne, on the improvement of which I spend thousands of pounds, if I could get that back I would shake the dust off my feet and leave the country and be glad to do so, because I think prosperity in this country is quite out of the question.[146]

The Land Acts of 1885 and 1891 were more progressive from the point of view of land sales. The incentives, which landlords might have wished for, were still not there for them to dispose of all their lands. But the machinery was in place to allow them to sell outlying portions of their estates to supplement dwindling incomes or to continue to offset debts which were being called in. The Settled Land Act of 1882 had loosened restrictions on the sale of lands and allowed large landowners to sell off outlying estates while still restricting their sale of core estates. (The act forbade the sale of settled mansions thereby effectively inhibiting the sale of core estates.) The 1885 Land Act stimulated tenant interest in purchase as it allowed the tenant to obtain the full purchase price from the Land Commission, lowered the annuity to 4 per cent and extended the repayment period to forty-nine years.[147] The purchase money was advanced to the landlord in cash. However, on the down side, one fifth was retained by the Land Commission as a guarantee deposit. Interest at 3 per cent per annum on this deposit was payable to the landlord but where a mortgagee had first priority, the mortgagee received the interest. Furthermore, as the deposit could be applied to make good any default by tenant purchasers in the payment of their annuity, there was the possibility that the landlord would never realise the full value of the estates he sold.[148]

Under the terms of the 1885 Act, almost £10 million was advanced between 1885 and 1891 allowing 25,317 tenants to become purchasers. Their deteriorating economic position meant some landlords were now prepared to accept less than they had demanded under the 1881 Act. While King-Harman had demanded twenty-three years' purchase on his rentals under the 1881 Act, Lord Waterford sold 14,300 acres in Waterford, Longford and Londonderry for £263,500 or 18.6 years' purchase on his rentals. The Duke of Leinster sold 19,200 in Kildare for £246,400 or 18.9 years' purchase; and Viscount Monck sold 7,800 in Wicklow for £74,700 or 16.1 years' purchase. Furthermore, the average price per acre had fallen from £18 under the 1881 Act to £12.7 reflecting the effects that economic depression and the land war had had on the value of Irish land.[149] On the whole, the majority of sales under the 1885 Act concerned small landowners who had no other means of extricating themselves from their financial difficulties, or large landowners who sold small outlying estates representing only a small percentage of their total acreage. The Earl of Dartrey, for example, the majority of whose estate was located in Monaghan, sold 2,200 acres in Waterford for £13,000; the Earl of Drogheda sold 1,550 acres for £18,400; Sir John Leslie sold 1,350 acres for almost £18,000.

Sales under the 1891 Act followed essentially the same pattern — large landowners lopped off parts of their estates while smaller landowners, who needed to secure a price that would leave them with enough capital for future investment, remained reluctant to enter the market voluntarily.[150] From 1886 to 1902, the average price of 17.3 years' purchase on rentals was not enough to encourage either a significant number of small landowners to sell their estates voluntarily or larger landowners to dispose of all of theirs.[151] Under the 1891 Act, the mechanics of sale were changed. Landlords were no longer paid in cash but in specially created land stock, while the annuity and repayment period remained the same. While payment in land stock was a retrograde step as far as landlords were concerned, it can, nevertheless, be seen that as land stock increased in value more landlords put their estates on the market, emphasising that they were more likely to sell if the proper conditions prevailed. When in 1893, the highest price quoted for land stock was 97.33, applications were made for only 2,391 loans; when in 1898 it reached its highest point of 114.2, applications were made for 6,201 loans (see Table 4.1, p. 283).[152]

Finally, sight should not be lost of the fact that these early land acts did provide a respite to many indebted landlords allowing them to sell parts of their estates in order to remain solvent. (In total almost 2.5 million acres were sold under the land acts from 1881 to 1896 for which landowners received almost £24 million.[153]) The Dukes of Leinster typified this trend. When Charles Fitzgerald, fourth Duke of Leinster, inherited Carton in 1847, he was faced with family charges of over £71,000.[154] The fact that he fathered fourteen children himself led to an enormous increase in the debt burden of the estate, so that when his son, Gerald, inherited encumbrances of over £292,000 in 1887, over half were portions for younger children.[155] The fifth Duke of Leinster was subsequently forced to sell 28 per cent of his estate, around 19,000 acres, under these acts. In 1887, he sold £128,400 worth of land, all of which, except for £940, was used to cancel debts.[156] The following year, he sold £39,000 worth of land,

£33,000 of which went to cancelling debts.[157] On his death in 1893, the *Freeman's Journal* was right to proclaim that: 'his income was not as large as one might be inclined to think from the extent of his estates and the great position he held. Family charges and the lessened value of land cut off much of his ducal resources.'[158]

THE SALE OF BIG HOUSE CONTENTS, 1882–1914

Big houses were ruinously expensive to maintain and the amounts spent on their upkeep could often mean the difference between profit and loss on an estate from the 1880s, but when this became the case cutbacks were all that were contemplated. Even though rental income on the Clonbrock estate had declined by only 9 per cent during the troubled years of 1886–87, the decline was a source of concern. In April 1887, Lord Clonbrock's agent wrote: 'His lordship has reduced his establishment considerably but unless times change he cannot uphold his present one'.[159] In fact, big house expenditure at Clonbrock fell by an average of 30 per cent per annum during the period 1882–89 from what it had been in 1880, while money spent on the gardens also fell by 30 per cent. The consequences of rental decline, therefore, had a disproportionate effect on big house expenditure.

Robert Dillon, Lord Clonbrock, died in 1893. His son, Luke, faced much greater agitation on the estate during the period 1902–07. Unlike his father he does not seem to have been willing to make big house cutbacks but the estate accounts show that the maintenance of the house and surroundings continued to make the difference between profit and loss on the estate. During those years the estate was running at a loss.[160] Table 4.2 (p. 283) compares that loss to the amount expended annually on the house. In any given year expenditure on the house alone accounted for at least 44 per cent of the estate deficit. When expenditure on the gardens, woods and game is taken into account it becomes quite clear that big house and demesne expenditure represented a major drain on declining estate income.

In order to economise some owners closed their houses temporarily or leased them to wealthy Americans. In the late 1880s and again in the 1890s, Killeen in County Meath, home of the Earl of Fingall, was let for at least two winter hunting seasons to wealthy Americans such as the Colliers. Neighbouring Somerville was also let to another American family, the Heskeths (who also took Killeen for a season.)[161] Around the same time, the Earl of Fingall sold his Dublin house in Great Denmark Street to the Jesuits.[162] In 1904, the Taylours closed Headfort and retrenched until 1908 in a rented

house in Hampshire.[163] The Moores of Moore Hall did likewise in the
1910s when 'the Georgian mansion stood exactly as the colonel had
left it, the family furniture covered with dust sheets, and the pictures and the books keeping their ancient places'.[164]

But landlords did not, as a rule, sell their houses in the late
nineteenth century even if they were perceived as proverbial
'white elephants', too large and expensive to maintain. Obviously
as they were not selling their core estates, they were hardly likely
to part with their country seats. Their houses, like their landed
property, symbolised their social standing in a community and
they would have been reluctant to diminish this status. There was
also, of course, the fact that buyers were not readily available.
R.D. Cochrane, as we have seen, pointed out to the trustees of
Maynooth College the difficulties that would have been involved in
selling a house such as Castleforbes in Longford in 1892.[165] New
wealth was not as readily available in Ireland as it was in Britain,
and American plutocrats such as the Astors who bought Cliveden
and Hever Hall in England in the late nineteenth century hardly saw
Ireland as an enticing location. The Jeromes were reluctant even to
visit Glaslough let alone purchase a house in Ireland after having
seen the splendour of Blenheim. The few in Ireland who had accumulated non-landed wealth such as the Guinnesses were more likely
to purchase houses in Britain such as Elveden Hall in Suffolk.
Alternatively, they would build houses in Ireland from scratch such
as Farmleigh and St Anne's in Dublin, equipped with all the modern
conveniences, rather than invest in older and often more dilapidated
houses.

Cutbacks meant that houses often became run down. Lady
Fingall recalled her home at Danesfield in the 1880s:

> My memory of the drawing room at Danesfield is that it was a
> shabby, rather faded room, and very little used.... There were what-
> nots about the room, with bits of old china on them and shells and
> such things, and an Ottoman, on which one might sit as uncomfort-
> ably as in a railway station waiting for a train.[166]

However, the general impression gathered from a study of the 100
big houses would not be one of wholesale decline into dereliction,
enforced neglect of gardens and parkland, wholesale redundancies
and total impoverishment of landed families in the last quarter of
the nineteenth century. Social events and entertaining continued
apace right up to the Great War. The 'Victorian atmosphere' continued
at Glaslough until 1906 when Sir John I and Leonie celebrated their

golden wedding anniversary. It was after they decided to retire to London on an allowance of £4,000 per annum, which greatly impoverished the new owners, that the purge of personnel in the house began with the number of servants being cut from thirteen to seven and then 'the Edwardian age arrived at Glaslough'.[167] It is true that by the early twentieth century money was not as plentiful; Irish families such as the Ormondes had to sell their yachts and the Leslies had to sell their London house and move to a flat instead. But while they may have come down in the world (in London the Leslies had moved from Berkeley Square to Stratford Place to Great Cumberland Place to a flat in St John's Wood), Irish landlords certainly did not disappear from the earth.

Instead of selling their houses, landlords sold off some of their contents. A few paintings here and there or a library of books was not so noticeable as a country house and not as detrimental to social position as the sale of land. At any rate, there was a livelier market for paintings, silver, plate, furniture and rare books, assets that had been unaffected by agricultural depression and which, unlike land, were appreciating. The Settled Land Act of 1882 facilitated sales by allowing trustees to set aside a will in order to sell the contents of a house. At the same time wealthy American families such as the Vanderbilts and the Morgans were intent on building up their art collections. From the 1880s there was 'an American craze' for works by Rubens and after 1906 for works by Van Dyck.[168] Few Irish houses of note did not have works by one or the other or both. At the same time art dealers such as Joseph Duveen, who worked on behalf of American collectors, 'managed to manufacture an extravagant, never-since-equalled market for Gainsborough, Lawrence, Reynolds, Romney and Hoppner'. This was undoubtedly beneficial to Irish landlords whose big houses contained more of these works than they knew what to do with. A Reynolds painting could fetch up to £70,000 while five figure sums were also being paid for works by Romney and Van Dyck, Rembrandt and Rubens.[169]

Some Irish landlords therefore sold heirlooms to meet debts or family charges. In 1889, the president of Maynooth College was concerned about Alexander Stewart's inability to meet the interest repayments on his mortgage. He wrote: 'I am about to reply to the court of chancery for an order under the Settled Land Act giving Mr Stewart liberty to sell certain plate and diamonds which are settled as heirlooms'.[170] During the late nineteenth and early twentieth centuries, the successive Dukes of Leinster had numerous valuations of moveable property at Carton carried out presumably with a view to selling off valuables to meet debts.[171] In 1902, 140 paintings, including works by Gainsborough, Brueghel and Van Der Hayden, and a substantial amount of Irish silver belonging to the Duke of Leinster was sold at Christie's in London.[172] In 1911, Lord Lansdowne sold Rembrandt's 'Mill' for £100,000 to P.A.B. Widener from Philadelphia.[173] There were other landlords who simply sold valuable works of art and furniture to improve the physical structure of their houses. In the late 1880s, the building of west-wing bedrooms at Powerscourt was funded 'by the sale of some valuable pictures'.[174] This may have reflected the changing economic position of Irish landlords at the time, but it was not something that Lord Powerscourt worried about. A few paintings from the massive family collection would not be missed but a new wing would undoubtedly be noticed.

Books were often the first contents to be sold. As early as 1882, J.P. Mahaffy criticised Irish landlords for the apathy they showed towards their libraries: 'They never read a book. The splendid libraries so common before the famine times, are scattered, and it is now an exception to find a good library in any country house'.[175] When landlords came under increasing attack from critics as decline continued into the twentieth century libraries were referred to as symbolic of this decline. W.E.H. Lecky claimed that:

> ... it was noticeable that libraries in country houses in Ireland stop dead at the year 1830, no additions are subsequently made ... that generation and succeeding ones were aware that power and virtue were slipping from them.[176]

Similarly, in 1909, George Birmingham wrote of landlords: 'Beside them on their shelves are their old books, good books which represent the culture of their fathers. They themselves have bought no books since the year in which Gladstone passed the first of his land acts.'[177] (Interestingly, of the 250 lots of books sold from Salterbridge in Waterford in 1916 only lots 1–47 were deemed to be 'in fine condition and handsomely bound' and none were post-1900 publications; nor were any of the vast collection of books sold from Killua in 1920 post 1900 publications.[178])

CONCLUSION

From the 1880s, landlords' worst fears were realised as agricultural depression, the land war, the reduction of rents and the calling in of mortgages all combined to reduce income dramatically. Because of the existence of encumbrances and the everyday expenses incumbent upon running an estate, landlords found that from the 1880s, they had less to spend on the upkeep of their houses as more and more went to the payment of charges. Cutbacks or even the temporary closure of big houses for a period of retrenchment sometimes became necessary. Above all, and with very few exceptions, the remodelling or modification of houses that had taken place at various stages during the previous two centuries had all but come to an end. Libraries were no longer added to. Works of art, curios, silver and valuable furniture were now more likely to be sold than collected. However, there was no major shift towards the sale of big houses themselves before the 1920s. Nor was there a major shift in the transfer of landownership. It was not until the passage of the Wyndham Land Act of 1903 that a revolutionary transfer of landownership began. The next chapter traces the effects, which this transfer of land had upon big houses.

5

CHANGES IN BIG HOUSE LIFE
1914–1960

'THE WORLD WE HAD KNOWN HAD VANISHED'

[Following the sale of the Leslie estate under the Wyndham Land Act] the Leslie investment portfolio soon bulged on his advice [Sir Earnest Cassel] with the most fanciful stocks and shares.... As to my father [Sir John II] his charming désinvolture was leading to difficulties. Any business decision brought on an agonising grimace of distaste and whoever asked for it ... apologised and dropped the matter.

SEYMOUR LESLIE, *THE JEROME CONNEXION* (1964), P. 36

THE LAND ACTS OF 1903 AND 1909

In March 1902, George Wyndham stated in the House of Commons that they had reached 'the end of the landlords who are prepared to sell for a capital sum which can be advanced under the existing law'. In October of that year, the Irish Landowners' Convention adopted a resolution that 'the landowners who have not hitherto sold are, as a body, resolved not to part with their estates on terms under which, in addition to the loss already incurred, their present incomes would be substantially reduced'. Landowners, the Convention claimed, would not part with their estates unless they were guaranteed 'a price, which invested at three per cent [would] yield an income approximately equal to their present net income'.[1] The Convention, which had fought so ardently for the property rights of landlords in the past, was now approaching the stage where it realised the need for a more consensual approach to the whole land purchase issue. And there was a growing body of what could perhaps be termed more pragmatic landlords who were prepared to open negotiations with tenant representatives on the subject including Lord Mayo and Lord Dunraven. Both of these were instrumental in the establishment of the Irish Land Conference of 1902–03 in an attempt to bridge the gulf between what landlords would settle for and what tenants were prepared to offer.[2]

The report of the Land Conference was published in early January 1903. A short time later the executive committee of the

Irish Landowners' Convention adopted a minute welcoming the report 'as a valuable addition to the various suggestions that have been made for removing the grave difficulties of the Irish land question'.[3] As the Landowners' Convention saw many similarities between the report and resolutions, which it had adopted at its October meeting, it claimed the report's recommendations were 'likely to be widely acceptable to the landlords'. Chief amongst these was the conference's recommendation that 'the owners should receive some recognition of the fact that selling may involve sacrifice of sentiment and they have already suffered heavily by the operation of the land acts, and that they should receive some inducement to sell'.[4]

The influence of the report was perceptible in the act framed by Wyndham, which became the first to make purchase a realistic goal for Irish tenants while simultaneously providing the inducements for landlords to sell. Payment of the entire purchase money was now to be advanced to landlords in cash. This alleviated landlord apprehension, which had existed under the 1891 Act, that the nominal price of the estate sold would not be realised by the encashment of land stock later on.[5] The 12 per cent bonus awarded on the sale of estates made them more confident that the capital they would secure would allow them to move from a rental income to an income derived from investments. The bonus had the effect of inflating the price of sales based on the number of years' rental. Under the 1891 Act, land was purchasable for 18.1 times the yearly existing rents in 1901. The bonus inflated this average price to 25.4 years' purchase and to what landlords perceived as being a much more realistic and acceptable figure.[6] More importantly, the tenant for life who received the bonus could do with it as he pleased. It was his and his alone, and was unaffected by any legal settlement that might restrict what he could do with the rest of the money received from the sale of his estate.

Landlords and tenants were still allowed freedom in agreeing upon the purchase price, but now sales were no longer limited to individual tenants or holdings but applied *en bloc* to a whole estate. The purchase price could only be fixed between certain maxima and minima laid down by the act which were termed 'zones'. This guaranteed the tenant that the annuity payable by him represented a 10–30 per cent reduction on his formal rent in the case of second-term judicial rents and 20–40 per cent in the case of first-term rents.[7]

The returns of advances under the Wyndham Act which begin on 1 November 1903 show that many of the estates first onto the market belonged to landlords who were heavily indebted and who had already sold parcels of land under the previous acts.[8] In 1903, for example, the Duke of Leinster sold 41,000 acres for £786,000.

The King-Harmans eventually sold 70,000 acres for £625,000. The heavily indebted Lord Granard had only 340 acres to sell for which he received £3,300. Lord Crofton (whose rental income had declined greatly during the land war and who had sold 5,300 acres for £43,500 under the 1891 Act) sold his remaining 5,000 acres for £67,500. Thus he received £24,000 more for virtually the same acreage under the Wyndham Act than he had done under the 1891 Act.

The prices, which were available, now enticed even the more solvent landowners onto the market. Some, like Earl Fitzwilliam, who spent most of his time on his English estates, were willing to avail of the opportunity to rid themselves of the greater part of their Irish landed investments under what were the most favourable terms likely to be on offer. From 1903 to 1909, Fitzwilliam sold over 53,000 acres for almost £470,000. Similarly, the Earl of Longford sold around 9,000 acres (around half of his tenanted estate) for £145,000 during the same period having sold only thirty-four acres under the 1885 Act.

By the end of 1907, landlords had realised that the terms on offer under the 1903 Act were the best they could hope for and that the Liberal government that had replaced the Conservatives in 1906 would be more in alignment with the Irish parliamentary party and the farmer interest.[9] Alvin Jackson claims that when Birrell introduced his bill, which slightly modified would become the Land Act of 1909: 'Irish landlords reacted by rushing to lodge their purchase agreements before the bill became law'.[10] Sales for the 100 sample estates reflected this to some extent. In 1907, the 100 landlords sold 38,400 acres for just over £404,000; in 1908, they sold 52,900 acre for almost £602,000.[11] Amongst those to sell in 1908 was Somerset Saunderson of Castlesaunderson who formally initiated the sale of his Cavan estate before 24 November 1908 in order to benefit from the terms of the 1903 Act. Within three years he had received £98,000 for 9,400 acres.[12] Lord Dunalley left it too late. In January 1909, his agent, C.H. Maude, wrote to the estates commissioners claiming that Dunalley was 'most anxious the tenants should get the benefit' of the 1903 Act.[13] Dunalley's motives seem, however, to have been more self-centred. In July the estates commissioners claimed that Dunalley was unwilling to go ahead with the negotiations for sale because he feared the sale would not be carried out in time to come under the terms of the 1903 Act and so he would not be guaranteed the 12 per cent bonus.[14]

From 1909, land sales through the estates commissioners slowed down considerably compared to what they had been in the previous six years. From November 1903 to the end of 1909 around £7.2 million was advanced to the 100 sample landowners compared to £4.3 million for the years 1910 to 1925 inclusive. Only 435,798 acres were sold by these landlords in the latter sixteen year period, an average of just over 27,200 per annum, compared to 480,652 acres, effectively from 1904 to 1909, an average of over 81,100 per annum.

Declines in sales post-1909 may be put down to a number of factors. Firstly, applications for sales under the Wyndham Act had been greater than the government's ability to deal with them. As early as 1904, the Landowners' Convention was expressing concern about the great disparity between the amount of advances applied for and the financial arrangements made for meeting them. In December a landlord delegation met with George Wyndham and proposed to him 'that the arrangement with the treasury should be revised and sufficient funds provided to prevent delay in closing cases'.[15] Wyndham explained to the delegation that there was little prospect of more than £5 million per annum being provided in the first three years.[16] The landlord/vendor had to accept a relatively low rate of interest on the purchase money in lieu of his rents from the date of purchase agreements. Therefore the allocation of only £5 million per annum certainly did not favour landlords who continued to remain liable for the full annual charges payable in respect of mortgages and other encumbrances until the distribution of the purchase money. By 1905, there was the realisation amongst landlords that they would have to wait up to five years from the lodging of purchase agreements with the Land Commission to the payment of the purchase money and bonus.[17] By 1910, the Landowners' Convention contended that:

> ... sale entails on the vendor an immediate and serious loss of income and a delay of several years before he will be paid his purchase money and the bonus, and as long as these two conditions exist it is not reasonable to complain if some owners cannot see their way to sell.[18]

It was not exaggerating. When William Mahon tried to sell part of his Castlegar estate in 1910, his agent wrote back to him:

> In the list of pending cases prepared by the estates commissioners early this year, there was £18,287,000 in front of your estate ... as the treasury are at present allowing only 2 millions a year for all cash cases, it will, of course, be some years before your estate is reached.[19]

As late as 1923, there were still 432 estates, totalling 474,000 acres, awaiting advances of £3.86 million under the 1903 and 1909 Acts and it was not until 1928 that most of these cases were disposed of.[20]

Secondly, the Landowners' Convention considered the terms of the 1909 Act to be retrograde: 'framed not to promote and encourage but to wreck and kill voluntary land purchase'.[21] The reversion to payment by land stock was a major grievance. Because of fluctuations in government stock and a decreased bonus the Landowners' Convention calculated that a landlord would lose four or five years' purchase under the 1909 Act as compared to what had been obtainable under the 1903 Act.[22]

In 1918 the Irish Convention set up a sub-committee to deal with land purchase. A confidential report from this sub-committee pointed out the gravity of the situation for those landlords who had agreed to sell prior to the outbreak of the First World War but whose negotiations had subsequently been suspended. Total purchase money in all such cases amounted to £4.5 million. At the time the value of stock stood at over eighty, but in consequence of the war and the issue of government stocks bearing higher rates of interest, land stock fell to under sixty.[23] Any landlord who had not received payment would suffer a heavy loss if he had to sell at post-war value to pay off charges. Take, for example, a landlord who agreed to sell his estate for £10,000 to be paid in 3 per cent stock and who had charges of £3,000 on his estate. If at the time he agreed to sell, stock stood at eighty, he would have to sell £3,750 worth to redeem his charges. If, however, the value of stock had fallen to sixty by the time the purchase money was paid over, he would have to sell £5,000 to redeem the same charges. It did, in fact, happen that some estates, which were solvent when sold became insolvent by the time the purchase money was paid over because of the depreciation in the market value of stock in the interval. Sir Roger Palmer's estate in County Mayo was a notable example of this. When Palmer accepted £292,000 for his estate in 1911, stock stood at eighty-five. When he got paid in 1916, the market price had fallen to 59.25 representing a depreciation in cash value of £75,190.[24]

There was one other reason why land sales fell off: some landlords had sold as much land as they wanted to or had to. Landlords, such as Lord Clonbrock, claimed they were too sentimentally attached to their Irish estates to sell them off. In an article in the *Morning Post* in 1903, Clonbrock put forward his 'hereditary ties' theory:

> At the end of the scale we may suppose a landowner, who is wearied out by the uncertainty and trouble to which he is exposed, who has no particular sentiment for his property, perhaps from having purchased it not so long ago, while freedom of contract still existed in Ireland, or

perhaps from never having resided on it. At the other end we may take a man who has had but little trouble from the land courts, who has constantly resided on his property, and whose life is therefore identified with it; who is attached to his tenants, as such by strong personal and hereditary ties, and who has always entertained the most friendly relations with them. It is obvious that such a man would require a far higher inducement to sell than the former, who would be glad to escape the precarious position of an Irish landowner on almost any terms.[25]

As his was a well-managed estate Clonbrock saw hardly any benefit in shifting from a rental income to an income derived from investment and felt that there was 'no moral obligation on landowners to sell'.[26] However, once his tenantry (and those in the area who had no land) became willing to purchase under the enticing terms of the 1903 Land Act they organised themselves for the first time under the United Irish League. Clonbrock's reluctance to sell drew upon him the wrath of the Nationalist press and he was now seen as 'a fossilised bigot', in opposition to the public will.[27] From 1903 to 1907, the estate was subjected to extreme agitation. Demands for reductions were accompanied by frequent cattle drives as small holders and landless labourers demanded the break up and redistribution of the large grazing farms on the estate.[28] By 1907, his rental income had fallen by around 15 per cent (as a result of fair rent fixing and rent strikes) while arrears had risen at an unprecedented rate from £4,362 in 1902 (twice the level of what they had been even in 1882) to £6,370 in 1907. All this time, estate expenditure remained consistent and for the years 1902 to 1907 inclusively, aggregated £67,781 compared to £59,000 in income. This was the first time during the period under study that the estate was running at a loss. Clonbrock was faced with no option but to sell. By 1915, he had sold his entire estate except for six townlands on which there were forty-four tenants paying a total of only £240 in rents (see Table 5.1, p. 284).

From the late nineteenth century much of what had formerly been tenanted land had been consolidated into larger farms following evictions during the land war and let to graziers on the eleven-month system. Under this system, which became particularly predominant in the west and midlands, the highest bidder secured the use of the land for an eleven month period after which it went up for auction once again. The most obvious advantages to the landlord were that the occupiers could not claim formal tenancy and thereby could not avail of the rent fixing terms of the 1881 Land Act and they could be evicted without notice to quit. Furthermore, landlords seem to have been able to collect their rents much more easily and punctually from large graziers than they had been from a mass of small tenants.[29] Retaining large tracts of untenanted land was therefore economically beneficial to many.

There were also landlords like Lord Cloncurry or Lord Ashtown who themselves had become substantial graziers and farmers and who wanted to continue as such by retaining as much untenanted land as that required. In 1907, Ashtown claimed that since the passing of the various land acts: 'a landlord now has only two inducements to remain in Ireland, 1) farming his own land and 2) sport'.[30] In that year, Ashtown also made £1,330 from letting land on the eleven-month system. He emphasised that the importance of untenanted land to a landlord lay: 'not only in the income or annual profit he may be deriving from it, but also his proprietorial rights, which are often of great value'.[31]

Section 3 (2) of the 1903 Land Act allowed landlords to sell their demesnes and other untenanted lands to the Land Commission and then to repurchase these lands under the same purchasing terms as tenants. The Land Commission could advance a maximum of £20,000 to each landlord wishing to repurchase. From 1903 to 1921 a total of 355 demesnes consisting of 122,100 acres were repurchased for £1.9 million. (Of this amount £1.68 million, or 88 per cent, was advanced by the estates commissioners, the balance being paid in cash by the purchasing landlords.)[32] These transactions were significant for two reasons. Firstly, the landlord, selling his demesne to repurchase it under the terms of the 1903 Land Act, was effectively receiving a substantial loan at very low interest rates. Secondly, he still retained his property which meant that repurchasing landlords such as Lord Wicklow (who sold and repurchased 1,960 acres) and the hard-pressed W.H. Mahon of Castlegar (who repurchased 1,650 acres) could continue to farm on a large scale.[33]

FROM RENTAL INCOME TO INCOME FROM INVESTMENTS

In 1905 Lord Dunraven, referring to the Wyndham Land Act, claimed: 'As a class there can be no question that the financial circumstances of the landed gentry will be improved by sale'.[34] What Dunraven essentially hoped was that the 1903 Land Act would extricate landlords from the indebtedness that threatened to ruin them as a class. By providing them with a large capital sum, it would leave landlords with enough to remain solvent in the future, and resident, even after all charges had been met. His ideal was that landlords would continue 'farming their own land, retaining the amenities of their position and finding ... a larger scope for usefulness than they have hitherto enjoyed'.[35] While they were unable to retain the amenities of their position or influence the politics of the Free State, they did, in many cases, manage to retain substantial tracts of untenanted land down to the 1930s. Significantly, many (former) landlords had described themselves in the 1911 household schedule returns as farmers. Thomas O'Donnell of Newport considered himself 'a farmer'. John Lenigan of Castleffogarty stated that he was 'a retired lieutenant-colonel in the British army and a farmer'. Charles Mervyn Doyne of Wells also stated that he was 'a farmer', while John Ribton Garstin of Braganstown stated that he was 'deriving income chiefly from land rents, dividends, in fact what the French call "rentier" and retired farmer'. By 1923, only around half a million acres of untenanted and demesne land had been sold out of an estimated total of 2.6 million acres.[36] Sir John Leslie still had a very large untenanted estate of over 12,000 acres in Donegal. Lord Dunalley farmed around 1,300 acres in Tipperary. Lord De Freyne farmed almost 1,100 acres in Roscommon. Lord Fingall had 1,500 acres in Meath. Lord Cloncurry farmed 2,700 acres in Kildare, and Lord Ashtown almost 4,000 acres in Galway.

The fact that many landlords retained large untenanted estates meant that they could continue farming on a viable basis. Smaller landowners who sold the bulk of their estates slipped into the large farming class and continued to exist comfortably, maintaining their modest big houses. More significantly the larger magnates who sold huge tracts of land received very substantial capital sums. Even after they met their charges they were still left with a considerable amount to invest. After the heavily encumbered Leinster estate was sold, the family still had £600,000 to invest at 3.5 per cent. An unencumbered landowner such as Lord Clonbrock had almost all of the £250,000 that he received from land sales to invest. Similarly the Shirleys of Lough Fea had around £300,000 to invest while Lord Ormonde had around £250,000. Effectively, this meant that there might not have been any major dislocation of the economics of big house life had not other factors impinged upon landlords' investments.

During the First World War, agricultural prices exploded for the first time since the beginning of the agricultural downturn in the late 1870s. Landlord farmers reaped the same rewards as their former tenants. Those who retained tenanted estates, such as the Farnhams in Cavan, found their rents better paid than they had been for years. Those who retained untenanted land and instead of farming it themselves leased it out on the eleven-month system found a much more vibrant and competitive market for it. Those who had invested wisely the capital they had received from the sale of their estates accrued substantial income from investments. However, the post-war economy changed everything. Agricultural depression struck once again, decimating farming profits. A new phase of land agitation targeted landlords who had retained tenanted and untenanted land; the payment of rents ceased once again and agitation for the break-up and redistribution of untenanted land (including landlords' demesnes and farms) escalated. Worse still, the world wide economic depression of the late 1920s was to infringe severely upon those who had invested the cash from sales under the 1903 Act in stocks and shares and those who had been paid in government stock under the 1909 Act.

The capital that landlords received from their land sales was, it seems, invariably invested outside Ireland. This was the type of move anticipated by Lord Ashtown in 1908 when he claimed that if his fellow landlords sold their Irish property 'the money they invest will leave the country. It will not be invested here [Ireland]'.[37] This is one area for which primary sources are extremely scarce, but it is the impression that was gained from what is available. Alvin Jackson has found that the capital received by Somerset Saunderson from the sale of his 10,000 acres in Cavan was 'converted into an extensive colonial share portfolio' and that 'only in Ireland did Somerset resist investment'.[38] Similarly, Lord Clonbrock's share portfolio shows large-scale investment in Canadian stock, Argentinean and USA railway companies, Indian stock, Australian and New Zealand stock. Only £2,000 was invested in Great Northern Railway preference stock.[39] Lord Ormonde's share portfolio was also an extensive colonial one while the Duke of Leinster invested his entire capital in English property and mortgages.[40]

Families such as the Clonbrocks did not cut back on big house or demesne expenditure after their estates were sold. In fact, as in the case at Clonbrock, both big house and estate expenditure rose considerably after 1914. This can be partially explained by the rise in farming profits as a result of the Great War, remembering that Lord Clonbrock continued to farm extensively after he had sold his tenanted estate.[41] But more importantly, the estate was obviously receiving considerable income from the investment of sales' capital in stocks and shares. Clonbrock was one of the few relatively unencumbered landlords in Ireland at the time of sale with the result that the bulk of the capital he received from land sales could be invested. From about 1919 the family had at least £250,000 invested in stocks and shares paying between three and four per cent interest per annum.[42] No longer having expenses such as quit rents, head rents, improvements, bailiffs' salaries and so on to meet, he was at least as well off as when he had been dependent upon rental income.[43]

However, during the great depression of the late 1920s and early 1930s, everything changed dramatically presumably because the crash in stocks and shares (allied to the agricultural depression at home in the 1920s) wiped out a large part of the family fortune. In 1930, the year after the Wall Street Crash, house expenditure dropped from £698 the previous year to £274, estate expenditure from £6,029 to £4,894, and while £323 was paid in big house salaries in 1929, nothing was paid in 1930 (see Table 5.2, p. 284).[44] From that year onwards the estate and house went into irreversible decline. By then, Ethel Dillon, sister of the last Lord Clonbrock, was living alone in the house except for an old butler.[45] It was a situation that became all too familiar in big house communities from the 1920s.

Perhaps the point needs also to be considered that the generation that received huge capital sums under the Wyndham Land Act were, if not naive, then certainly inexperienced in the world of business. Some of the older generation, like Sir John Leslie, regarded 'making money in the City as rather dishonest and certainly fit for no gentleman'.[46] Having been accustomed to estate management and the relatively unsophisticated (if at times difficult) procedure of collecting rents, wheeling and dealing in shares was anathema to them and dealing with stockbrokers was much more intricate than dealing with land agents. There was perhaps a certain amount of naiveté on Edward Fitzgerald's part (even given his fondness for gambling) when he entered into agreement with the much more City-wise Sir Henry Mallaby-Deeley in January 1918. The agreement was to have his gambling debts of £67,500 paid off in return for a £1,000 allowance per annum and the 'sale' of his rights to the ducal income from Carton should he ever inherit. There was a reversionary clause which made provision for Edward to buy back his rights to Carton for £400,000 if he wished to do so (and could afford to do so) in the future.[47] At the time it seemed a good gamble as his two older brothers were still alive. However, before the end of the war, Desmond was to be killed in action and his other brother, Maurice, died prematurely in 1922. Carefree and reckless behaviour characterised Edward's life. He was declared bankrupt three times during his lifetime and so was never in a position to buy back the reversionary rights to Carton. Three days before he died in March 1976, Edward was interviewed by Roger Williams, an *Evening Herald* journalist, who found him living in a tiny London bed-sit meagrely furnished with twin beds, a wardrobe, chest of drawers, a broken easy chair, a coffee table, a small ring stove and a refrigerator. Williams appropriately headlined his article: 'From £2m[illion] mansion to squalid bedsitter'.[48]

The Socio-economic Effects of The Great War, 1914–18

From a personal point of view the war had at least a psychological effect on landlord families. As the landlord class was an isolated, self-contained society it was inevitable that a great sense of loss would permeate it. The death of a member of a landlord's family was taken personally by members of the whole class whether they knew the person their whole life or merely knew of them. As early as November 1914, Shane Leslie noted, 'At this rate everybody in a year will be mourning'.[49] In 1915, Douglas Hyde wrote to a friend:

> Nearly everyone I know in the army has been killed. Poor Lord De Freyne and his brother were shot the same day and buried in one grave.... MacDermott of Coolavin, my nearest neighbour, has lost his eldest son shot dead in the Dardanelles. All the gentry have suffered. *Noblesse oblige.* They have behaved magnificently.[50]

Lady Elizabeth Fingall's neighbour, and kinsman of her husband, the eldest son of the seventeenth Baron Dunsany was killed in action. After the war, she wrote in her memoirs:

> I used to think and say, during the war, that if ever that list of dead and wounded would cease, I would never mind anything or grumble at anything again. But when the armistice came at last, we seemed drained of all feeling. And one felt nothing. We took up our lives again, or tried to take them up. The world we had known had vanished. We hunted again but ghosts rode with us. We sat at table, and there were absent faces.[51]

Of the 100 sample landlord families, seventy-nine were represented in the army or navy by a father, son, grandson or son-in-law during the First World War. In total, there were 146 serving members of the armed forces, an average of almost 1.5 members per family, a figure that would almost certainly be much greater if nephews, cousins and uncles were included. This is consistent with the impression created by Irish writers whose works were set against the backdrop of the big house and which claim that the landed class accepted enthusiastically 'the call of the empire'. Molly Keane's Major Chevington in *Mad Puppetstown* (1931) and Desmond French-McGrath in *The Rising Tide* (1937) join up without hesitation and with the support of their families. In Elizabeth Bowen's *The Last September*:

> Mrs Fogarty's drawing room was thronged with photographs; all the dear boys who for years had been garrisoned at Clonmore, many of whom, alas! had been killed in that dreadful war. You could not stoop to put down a cup on one of the little tables without a twinge of regret and embarrassment, meeting the candid eyes of some dead young man.[52]

The enthusiasm to become involved in the war is just as evident in surviving correspondence. In 1916, Arthur Maxwell, eldest son of Lord Farnham, who at the time was stationed at Woolwich barracks waiting to be sent to the front, wrote to Aileen Coote:

> They don't seem to be in a bit of a hurry to send me out bad luck to them.... I had a letter from [?] the other day and he told me he was off [to the front]. 'Lucky divel' [*sic*] ... I am getting to hate the sound of the name Woolwich now, I am quite certain I shall commit suicide if I stay here much longer.[53]

Maxwell's letter suggests that his reasons for wanting to go to the front were, in the main, because of the general enthusiasm for war amongst the landed class. It has been argued by Patrick Buckland that this enthusiasm was the natural response of a class of people who had traditionally led the armed forces of the British empire.[54] However, it must be remembered that a very high percentage of landlords and their sons were officers in the army or navy and thus were serving members who were put in a situation rather than volunteering for it.

There is, however, some evidence to suggest that some Irish landlords and their sons who went to the front were motivated by non-political and non-traditional considerations.[55] The case of Charles Monck, heir to Charleville, offers the rather poignant reason that he saw the Great War as a means of escape from the realities of land-lord decline in the early twentieth century — a trend that had left him constrained in his financial dealings, his social life and in what he could offer as a local or national figure. An extract from a letter written by him to his solicitor is worth quoting at length:

> I fear after reading this letter, that any regard you may have had for me before, will disappear and you will only think of me as a coward and a hypocrite ... I am about to acquaint you with the grave state of my finances, but I want you to understand that it is not the present life that I am living that has prompted me to do so but, since I have

been away, certain of my debts, though a small part only of them, have become known to my wife who has heretofore been ignorant of them.... When I started out here I fully realised that the odds were very long against my ever returning, and if I die today my difficulties and those of my family would to a great extent disappear with me. But although I have seen two thirds of our original number of officers struck off the roll and there is still more work to be done, I realise that the 100 to 1 chance may yet come off.... At present I cannot myself see anything but disaster [at home], which is far worse to face than what is at present going on here.[56]

Captain Charles Monck was killed in action a short time later. He was one of a total of 215 peers or their sons killed at the front, twenty-eight of whom were from Irish landowning families.[57] Because the contribution of Irish landlords or their families was predominantly to the officer class, it was inevitable that they would suffer heavy casualties in the type of warfare that characterised the First World War. The mode of Norman Leslie's death was typical of the early days of the war before the battering of trench warfare begun. His niece later wrote: 'An attack had been ordered and, being an officer, Norman walked ahead waving his men on with his cane. A sniper got him and he died instantly'.[58] Having led his men 'over the top' Thomas Pakenham, fifth Earl of Longford, 'was never found and the whole of the brigade staff disappeared with him' at Gallipoli in 1915.[59] The losses suffered by individual families were great. Of the six sons of the fourth Baron De Freyne of Frenchpark who fought in the war, three were killed in action and one died a prisoner of war. Of the five sons of Duc De Stacpoole, two were killed and one returned so severely wounded that his father later claimed: 'I fear he will never be his former self again'.[60]

How significant was this casualty rate to the decline of the big house in Ireland or even to the decline of family dynasties? In his introduction to the 1958 edition of *Burke's Landed Gentry of Ireland*, Mark Bence-Jones described the 4 August 1914 as 'the last day of Ireland's ancient regime' and claimed that 'this was not just the beginning of a war but the end of a nation'.[61] Some time later he wrote: 'In all too many houses in 1919 the young master was no more than a memory and a photograph in uniform on a side table. [There was] no heir but a grandson under age or a daughter....'[62] Lennox Robinson had previously written in his biography of Bryan Cooper:

It [the Great War] was to be the last chapter in the history of many families. Behind the high stone walls at the end of the long avenue, in that Georgian house or sham Gothic castle, there remained now only an old father and mother and a couple of ageing daughters.[63]

However, the decline of too many big houses has been hyperbolically linked to the death of an heir during the war overshadowing the role of the more powerful, but less heroic, economic factor. The fact was that almost three-quarters of those from the 100 families who served, returned from the war. Therefore this raises the question as to what extent the implications of landlord losses were more psychological than tangible. Did the war provide the Irish landed class with a plausible and more glorious explanation for their own decline than they could previously lay claim to? The idea of the 'lost generation' seems to have grown in mythical proportions, becoming for some the primary catalyst in the decline of the big house. These psychological effects, while important in their own right, need to be contextualised, and not allowed to overshadow the other factors which were already undermining the position of the big house in Ireland before 1914.

Casualties had few implications from the point of view of succession.[64] Although Norman Leslie was killed at Armentières in October 1914, his father lived another thirty years before being succeeded by his grandson, Jack, himself a formidable character in his own right. Hercules Langrishe, fifth Baronet of Knocktopher, fought in and survived the war. His eldest son, also Hercules, was less fortunate, being killed in 1917. However, the Baronet lived until 1943 when he was succeeded by his only surviving son, Terence. Edward Stafford-King-Harman was killed at Klein Zellebecke in November 1914. He was survived by his father, Sir Thomas, who lived until 1935. Frederick Mason Trench, third Baron Ashtown, lost his eldest son in 1916, but the Baron did not die until 1946 when he was succeeded by another son, Robert.[65] Down through the years as many landowners or their heirs, if not more, had died unmarried or childless and caused as great a dislocation of continuity. Houses had passed to brothers, uncles, nephews, cousins and so on.[66] Yet, there had not been the same claims that the effects of such social factors had left big houses futureless as were made in the aftermath of the Great War. An economic entity can survive the loss of its management structure; but management cannot survive bankruptcy.

Take the case of Captain Charles Monck's family. Between 1887 and 1889, the bulk of the family estate in County Wicklow was sold to the Irish Land Commission. By the end of the war the remainder had been sold under the terms of the 1903 Land Act.[67] Presumably, the sale of his estate was for the same reason as the majority of his peers — unsustainable indebtedness. (Between 1878 and 1918, the estate was subject to indentures totalling £20,950 and this excludes a deed poll of £10,000 imposed in 1897 and a reversionary charge of £10,000 in 1904.[68]) In 1894, Henry Monck inherited what was left of the estate. His financial situation continued to deteriorate, a decline which, if anything was accentuated by the reckless behaviour of his two sons. His younger son, George, died intestate in July 1912, leaving a list of sixty creditors seeking payment from the estate. Charles Monck was informed:

> One thing we must not shut our eyes to distressing tho' it must be. Your brother was a veritable wild Irishman when on a racket and no doubt did many harum scarum feats which cost him dearly. A lot of turf plunges were done when he was not fit to bet ... I have seen him myself in the course of sprees (I must be blunt) make the most astonishingly freakish wagers.... It simply meant taking advantage of a fellow under the influence of drink.[69]

While Charles seems to have done everything in his power to meet George's debts, he seems to have learned little from the experience himself. In the aforequoted letter from him to his solicitor, J.E. MacDermott, he wrote:

> It is only a little over two years since you last helped me over a financial crisis [unrelated to his brother's] and yet through sheer carelessness I soon found myself drifting into another one, and I was curiously enough too shortsighted to see what it must eventually lead to. I had, anyhow, not the courage to go to my father or to you, or anyone else for advice but simply got advances whenever I could trusting to luck in the matter all coming right.[70]

Charles asked his solicitor to find 'a way out without letting the burden fall too heavily on those dependent on me and on my father'. MacDermott's reply emphasised the difficulties facing landlords who sought in vain for loans to alleviate their financial burdens from the late nineteenth century onwards. He felt there was little he could do to secure a mortgage to offset debts because 'of the ever-increasing disinclination among lenders to advance on estates which are subject to heavy paramount charges'.[71] This letter of MacDermott's, dated 19 October 1914, would not have reached Charles Monck who was killed in action at Ypres on 21 October. Despite Charles's fears, the burden of his debts fell on his father who was in no position to honour them: MacDermott's letter had pointed out that 'I know your father can do little in this direction'. By the 1920s, encumbrances on the estate amounted to almost £30,000.[72] In 1925, Viscount Monck, then 'in delicate health' appointed MacDermott to oversee the estate management which included control of domestic expenditure at Charleville.[73] However, MacDermott had only a shoestring budget on which to operate. In 1926, the net income on the estate was only £4,500 while ordinary expenditure on estate and house maintenance, taxes and other expenses amounted to £3,600, leaving less than £1,000 to meet other encumbrances. When Viscountess Monck died in 1930, funeral expenses and death duties of £2,400 had to be met by the sale of securities and the use of dividends.[74] In 1933, Viscount Monck was forced to sell off Dublin property in order to pay a charge of £10,000 that had been created under a settlement of 1874.[75] The previous year the contents of Charleville itself had been sold by private auction realising in the region of £11,000.[76] In 1939, the house and demesne were also sold. The death of Charles Monck at the front had not made the decline of his family estate inevitable. That had already been effected by the wider economic crisis that faced most landlord families.

A NEW LAND WAR, 1917–23

While the Land Acts of 1903 and 1909 had made a major contribution to the transfer of land from landlords to tenants they did not end landlordism in Ireland. Prior to the enactment of the 1923 Land Act, there were approximately 114,000 holdings on three million acres that had not been sold.[77] In Kerry, the Marquis of Lansdowne retained almost 49,000 acres; in Donegal, the Earl of Leitrim retained over 39,000 acres; in Cavan, Lord Farnham retained almost 20,000 acres; in Monaghan, Lady Edith Windham retained almost 11,000 acres; in Carlow, the Kavanaghs still retained around 7,000 acres. During the First World War, advances had been suspended for the purchase of holdings and the Congested Districts Board had also stopped purchases.[78] (The Congested Districts Board had been established under the 1891 Land Act to relieve the problem of congestion especially along the western seaboard.[79] A total of 398 electoral divisions in counties Galway, Leitrim, Mayo, Roscommon, Sligo, Donegal, Kerry and Cork were deemed congested areas. The 1896 Land Act empowered the board to secure advances from the Land Commission for the purchase of estates from landlords instead of having to buy them out of board funds. The 1903 and 1909 Land Acts further extended the powers of the board making more money available and conferring authority upon it to compulsorily acquire land for the relief of congestion. By the time the board was dissolved in 1923 it had purchased 874 estates totalling 1.77 million acres for £8.9 million.[80]) The allocation of land previously acquired proceeded at a very slow rate. The agricultural boom of the war years had proved an incentive to landlords to retain their lands and farms as they saw little sense in selling them for land stock that had been greatly reduced by wartime uncertainties.[81] At the same time, David Fitzpatrick concludes: 'the frustration of land-hungry men began to assume more organised form, potentially far more dangerous to the landowners'.[82]

After months of isolated agrarian disturbances in the west, Eamon de Valera encouraged every Sinn Féin club in County Clare in February 1918 to form a company of the Irish Volunteers 'to help divide the land evenly'.[83] In the western and midland counties of Sligo, Roscommon, Leitrim, Galway, Clare, Mayo, Limerick, King's County (Offaly), Queen's County (Laois) and Westmeath, large bodies of men with ploughs, bands and Sinn Féin flags marched to grazing farms and forcibly took possession of as much land as they required.[84] The inspector general of the RIC concluded:

> Subsequent agrarian activities give reason to assume that henceforward that in districts where Mr. [Laurence] Ginnell and other leaders who share his views possess influence, Sinn Féin clubs and Volunteer companies will be employed in agrarian agitation.[85]

He feared a general outbreak of agrarianism because of 'a great deal of irritation in consequence of the suspension of land purchase'. He also felt that the recent attempts to commandeer land under the pretence of the necessity for increasing tillage were a mere pretext to renew agitation for the sale and division of grass lands.[86] He associated the recrudescence of lawlessness and crime in the west and midlands with the growth of the Volunteers, the speeches of Sinn Féin leaders 'inciting their followers to ignore British authority' and 'the land hunger of the people' and thus effectively linked land agitation to revolutionary activity.[87]

His fears were realised when the desire of the landless, whose numbers had been swelled by the restrictions on emigration during the First World War, to secure lands for themselves led to an upsurge in agrarian crimes directed against landowners. As the War of Independence intensified, agitation grew throughout the country, particularly in the west and midlands. In May 1920, an unoccupied house belonging to Lord Ashtown in King's County was destroyed 'as the land attached to it was wanted for division'.[88] A few months later, the employees on the estate were attacked in a further bid 'to drive

Above: This sketch of the Earl of Glengall's Carnavilla House, Cahir, County Tipperary, was typical of the type that appeared in estate valuations and maps of the mid-nineteenth century.
Courtesy National Archives

Below: This map is typical of the type that appeared in estate valuations in the mid-nineteenth century. Clonkyne Estate, County Cavan, c. 1845.
Courtesy National Archives

Below: Accounts and Rental of the estate of Lady Howard Bury, Charleville, King's County, 1909.
Courtesy Offaly Historical and Archaeological Society

Above: *Mrs Dunne of Brittas Castle, County Wicklow, 18 July 1887.*
Fetherston Haugh Collection, courtesy Offaly Historical and Archaeological Society

Above: *Meet of Lord Huntingdon's hounds, Sharavogue, King's County, c. 1870.*
Fetherston Haugh Collection, courtesy Offaly Historical and Archaeological Society

Above: Sketch of Dartrey Castle, 1880 by Eilíse O'Hart.
Original courtesy Monaghan County Museum

Below: Conolly's Folly, Castletown,
County Kildare.
Courtesy Jim Campion

Below: Clonbrock, County Galway.
Courtesy National Archives

these men from Lord Ashtown's employment and thereby secure division of farms for local people'.[89]

In June 1920, the town workers of Westport in County Mayo were said 'to have been clamouring for some time for land for tillage'.[90] When they appealed for land from the Marquis of Sligo he refused and so two hundred to three hundred people turned out 'armed with sticks and proceeded to fields which were recently added to his lordship's demesne', broke locks on his gates, drove off his cattle, took possession of about fifty-six acres and began to graze their own milch cows.[91] The following month, at Abbeylara in County Longford, several hundred people were reported to have been involved in a cattle drive on the lands of William Bond. Placards were placed around the estate saying that the cattle had been 'evicted' because the land was needed by the people.[92] In Galway, notices were posted warning people against having anything to do with local landlords whose lands were wanted for division.[93] The diaries of W.H. Mahon of Castlegar are littered with entries in the early 1920s referring to 'large groups of men' or 'unwelcome visitors' and 'landgrabbers' who 'demanded great extent of land'.[94] In March 1920, Frank Shaw Taylor was murdered in Galway. A week previously he had been visited by a deputation of locals who called on him to sell his estate, only to be told by Taylor: 'You'll never see a perch of my land'.[95] In Clare employees on H.V. McNamara's estate at Ennistymon were warned to cease working for him because his land was wanted for division.[96] There were reports of similar outrages to secure division of lands on the Walpole estate in County Roscommon, the Agar estate in Queen's County, the Longfield estate in Cork and the Westropp estate in Limerick all between the months of May and November 1920.[97]

Art O'Connor informed the Dáil in 1921 that during the spring of that year: 'the land war broke out with a virulence and presage of danger which made the worst of previous years seem positively tame' and that 'large numbers of terrified landowners [from Connaught] came up to the city for the purpose of seeking interviews with responsible Republican officials and beseeching the Dáil for our protection.'[98] In his memoirs, written the following year, the Duc de Stacpoole, a Galway landowner, supported O'Connor's claims stating that conditions were much worse in County Galway that at any time during the land war of 1879–82. He wrote:

> Even demesnes and land immediately round the owner's house, and already farmed by him may be considered suitable for division. In many cases the landlord has been compelled to give up farming

altogether, owing to threats from those who consider that he is in possession of too much land, while others have not sufficient.[99]

Following the establishment of the Free State, landowners continued to seek protection. In January 1922, the solicitors of
J.M. Wilson wrote to the Minister for Home Affairs stating that two
families had taken over the yard and demesne of Currygrane in
County Longford. It was not until the following November that the
minister made any attempt to enquire into the situation on Wilson's
estate (having been harangued by Wilson's solicitors in the meantime). But the commissioner of the guards pointed out to him that
there were many more similar cases throughout the country and too
few guards who were limited in what they could do, as they were
dependent upon the goodwill of the people.[100] In May of the same
year, Lord Castletown wrote to W.T. Cosgrave complaining that his
tenants were refusing to pay their rents and that cattle drives were a
regular occurrence on his estate.[101] In June, Lord Powerscourt wrote
to the Minister for Home Affairs drawing his attention to the robbing,
looting and intimidation on his estate in Enniskerry.[102]

The attitude of the Provisional government towards such landlords was not always sympathetic. Nor was action immediate, if it
followed at all. The new state was having too many teething problems
for ministers to immerse themselves in the needs of landlords, even
if they wanted to. Throughout 1922, H.P. Maxwell, Lord Lansdowne's
agent, wrote on numerous occasions to the Minister for Home Affairs
regarding the state of lawlessness around Kenmare. In May 1922, a
letter from him claimed that Dereen had been looted a number of
times, the adjoining garage had been commandeered and used as a
dance hall, and the woods and lands were full of trespassing cattle.[103]
No efforts were made by the minister to investigate Maxwell's
claims. However, when Maxwell wrote to the minister again in June
reporting that salmon in local rivers around Kenmare were being
endangered by dynamiting and poisoning, the minister's secretary
wrote the same day to the adjutant general, marking the letter
'URGENT'. He requested him to 'please have immediate inquiries
made into the matter with a view to the prevention of further outrages and to the saving of the fishing industry in that district'.[104]
Even after Dereen was burned, all the Minister for Home Affairs
could do was express his regret at 'the outrages which have taken
place on his lordship's estate and at the condition of the county of
Kerry generally'. He added that 'owing to the disturbed conditions
existing in that county and the adjoining counties, it has been as yet
impossible to post thereto members of the new police force'.[105]

Reports of outrages on their estates by individual landlords were only the tip of the iceberg. In April 1923, Patrick Hogan, Minister for Agriculture, informed President W.T. Cosgrave that the civic guard reports showed that in every county there were numerous cases of land seizures that had never been reported by landowners.[106] It was largely inevitable that landowners, who retained either tenanted or untenanted land, would be targets of intimidation to force them to divide their estates considering the land hunger that prevailed. While in the past, a price had to be paid for land, there were now those who saw the social chaos as being an opportunity to acquire land for little or nothing. By 1923, land grabbing had become endemic. Civic guard reports informed Hogan that 'owners apparently acquiesce in the seizures apparently considering it the lesser of two evils'. Hogan claimed it was 'landless men who would not be entitled to land under any scheme' who were seizing it.[107]

The social chaos was also used by tenants on unpurchased estates as a pretext for not paying their rents. In December 1922, Patrick Hogan claimed that:

> for the last couple of years, there has been practically a general strike by tenants against the payment of rent to landlords. Generally speaking the cause alleged was inability to pay due to the depression in agriculture. Possibly the desire to force land purchase has given its chief strength to this no rent movement.[108]

In April 1923, landlord representatives pointed out that only on about 10–15 fifteen per cent of tenanted estates were rents paid up to date; on others they were anything from one and a half years upwards in arrears. In April 1923, Patrick Hogan concluded that 'while tenants are not paying rents, and while they consider that they need not pay rent in the future, they don't want a land bill, except on terms which would amount to confiscation'.[109]

THE FREE STATE LAND ACTS, 1923–33

It was largely with confiscation in mind that the terms of the Land Act of 1923 were formulated.[110] Under its terms: 'all tenanted land wherever situated and all untenanted land situated in any congested districts county and such untenanted land situated elsewhere as the Land Commission shall before the appointed day, declare to be required for the purpose of relieving congestion or of facilitating the resale of tenanted land, shall by virtue of this act vest in the Land Commission on the appointed day.'[111] There were limited exceptions such as land purchased under previous land acts, home farms and

demesnes.[112] But all exceptions, other than public authority or corporation lands, could be disregarded by the Land Commission if it
declared any holding to be important in the relief of congestion.

Under the financial terms of the act, an automatic method of fixing the price payable to the landlord for tenanted land was provided
which was commonly referred to as the 'standard price'. Landlords
were entitled to the equivalent of fifteen years' purchase. A purchase
annuity set at 65 per cent of rent and capitalised at 4.75 per cent left
the landlord with 13.68 years' purchase and an annual income of
£61.12s per £100 rent. From a tenant's point of view, the new standard purchase annuity amounted to a reduction of 25 per cent on a
first term judicial rent or a reduction of 30 per cent on a second term.
The government provided a contribution of 10 per cent of the price
bringing the landlord's total income to 15.05 years' purchase or
£67.15s per £100 of rent. The advances to vendors were paid in
4.5 per cent land bonds to be accepted by the vendor as the equivalent of the corresponding amount of purchase money.

In the case of every tenanted holding to which the act applied,
rent and arrears of rent due up to and including the gale day preceding the date of the passing of the act ceased to be payable. No
proceedings against the tenant for recovery of arrears could be begun
or continued after the passing of the act. All arrears of rent up to the
final gale day in 1920 were cancelled and those accruing from that
gale day to the one preceding the passing of the act were compounded at 75 per cent of the total.

From January 1924 to December 1930, the Land Commission compulsorily acquired substantial estates belonging to landlords who had
not sold under previous acts. In total, around 200,000 acres belonging
to seventy-eight of the 100 sample owners were acquired during this
period. In April and June 1925, the commission acquired over 10,000
acres from Lord Cloncurry. Much of this was untenanted land including his Galway estate of 3,400 that he and his predecessors had used
for grazing purposes. It also included 2,700 acres on the Kildare–
Meath border which the Land Commission 'declared to be required for
the purpose of relieving congestion'.[113] In February 1926, the commission
acquired almost 9,000 acres from Lord Ashtown in Galway. In June
it acquired 20,300 acres from Lord Leitrim in Donegal. In October it
acquired 10,000 acres from Viscount De Vesci in Queen's County and
6,800 from Lord Powerscourt in Wicklow and in November 1926, the
commission acquired 11,300 acres of tenanted land from Lord
Farnham in County Cavan.[114]

The price landlords received for their tenanted land was around
ten years' rental purchase below the highest price available under

the Wyndham Act and, worse, they were paid in land bonds yielding 4.5 per cent per annum rather than cash. The estimated income on these land bonds, represented a decline of around 30 per cent on gross rental income. For example, Lord Farnham's tenanted estate of 11,000 acres was the largest compulsorily acquired by the Land Commission in the early 1930s. His annual gross rental up to that time was £9,346. He received almost £141,000 for the land, but had he sold under the 1903 Act he would probably have realised around £240,000 (taking the years' purchase at 25.4). Income on land bonds realised only £6,334 per annum, a decline of 32 per cent. Viscount Powerscourt had to sell a tenanted estate worth £4,700 per annum for £72,000. He would have received almost £120,000 under the 1903 Act. Land bonds now provided him with an income of £3,200, a decrease of 31 per cent.

The transfer of tenanted holdings under the 1923 Land Act was slow and unsatisfactory from the government's point of view and was hampered by legal constraints. The Land Act of 1931 was intended to speed up the process.[115] This act enabled the vesting of holdings in the Land Commission to be accomplished by means of the gazetting of lists of vested holdings in the *Iris Oifigiúil* subject to the correction of errors and omissions that might be found necessary. Every tenant of a holding included in the published list was deemed to have entered into a purchase agreement for the purchase of his holding on the appointed day at the standard price. However, loopholes continued to be exploited. Speaking in the Dáil in July 1933, Frank Aiken pointed out: 'very few realise the legal and other difficulties, which the Land Commission have to surmount before they can divide even a single estate'.[116] There were, he claimed, lengthy procedures which led to administrative difficulties. There had to be a declaration that the land was required for the relief of congestion; this then had to be published in the *Iris Oifigiúil*. Next came the hearing by the Land Commission of the landowner's objections; a decision was reached after a further inspection of the property if necessary; but this could be followed by an appeal by the landowner which again could be followed by further hearings, inspections and so on. Furthermore, Aiken claimed that 'it has been found that the safeguards given to home farms and demesne lands have operated to impede the work of the Land Commission in the relief of congestion'.[117] Aiken's comments were primarily aimed at landowners, who had exploited loopholes in the 1923 Land Act in order to retain untenanted land. His final sentiment that 'the day of the large and lazy rancher is over' sounded the death knell for many big houses dependent on agricultural acres to sustain them.

The 1933 Land Act empowered the Land Commission to redistribute any property it found suitable with the exception of ordinary owner-occupied farms.[118] This prevented landowners from laying claim to outlying farms as they had done in the past. The commission could now acquire holdings of individuals who did not reside in their immediate vicinity or who did not use their property: 'in the same manner as an ordinary farmer in accordance with proper methods of husbandry'. Under the previous acts, residential property had been exempted from their scope, which meant landlords could claim untenanted land was residential even if only a derelict ruin stood on it. By the late 1930s, the old landed estates had eventually been broken up in Ireland. The Free State Land Acts had vested 113,800 holdings on just over 3 million acres in the Land Commission for £20.8 million.[119]

The reduction of retained land below a viable level began a downward economic spiral that was impossible for big house owners to reverse. It was tantamount to ruin especially with the rise in taxation.[120] One 'western landowner' wrote to the editor of *The Irish Times* in July 1922, saying that he had received no rents on his tenanted land for the previous three years and that he inevitably found himself in a precarious position:

> Now I have received an income tax note. The taxes have to be paid and the mortgagees threaten to call in the mortgage. The small amount I make on the lands in my own hands [150 acres] is barely able to pay for the necessaries of my family.[121]

Of course, much more than 150 acres was required to maintain a great mansion. Unfortunately for those landowners who wanted to remain in Ireland, and who were not driven out by events of the revolutionary period from 1919 to 1923, the Free State government had little sympathy for anyone holding on to thousands of acres when there were so many smallholders and landless men clamouring for land. Thus, between 1923 and the late 1930s, the Land Commission acquired almost 4,000 acres in demesne and untenanted land from people like Lord Ashtown in Galway. 2,400 acres were acquired from Lord Cloncurry in Kildare; 1,500 acres from Lord Fingall in Meath; 1,300 acres from Lord Dunalley in Tipperary; 1,100 acres from Lord De Freyne in Roscommon; and 700 acres from Willoughby Bond in Longford. Within thirty years all of their big houses had been sold.

For those who continued to struggle as farmers, the agricultural depression of the 1920s brought further ruin. From 1920 to 1923, agricultural output fell by 38 per cent and the price of store cattle by

40 per cent which was 10 per cent more than the fall in the cost of living, thereby exasperating landowners' hopes of remaining resident in Ireland.[122] When the economic war with Britain broke out it was to prove even more damaging to agricultural development in the Free State, particularly to the cattle rearing farmers with whom the old landlord class were now associated. The war resulted from the new Fianna Fáil government's refusal to transfer to Britain the annuities paid by Irish farmers to the Land Commission to redeem the money advanced under the pre-1923 land acts. In reprisal the British government imposed penal duties on Irish agricultural produce: cattle were subject to duties first of 20 per cent and then of 40 per cent. By 1934, the value per animal, depending on age, had fallen by 68 to 88 per cent and from 1931 to 1935, the average price of cattle exported declined from £16.5 per animal to £8, while during the same period, the value of cattle exported fell from £12.7 million to £4.3 million.[123]

By the mid-1930s Lord Wicklow's farming ventures no longer supported Shelton Abbey. His auditor expressed concern about the fact that payments over the three years 1934–36 exceeded receipts by an average of £5,455 per annum.[124] The house and gardens of Shelton Abbey accounted for the bulk of Lord Wicklow's expenditure: in 1937, almost £5,000 was spent on the maintenance and running of the house; £2,000 on the gardens; and £460 on wages. Rates and taxes consumed another £2,000.[125] The deficit had been supplied in cash each year by Lord Wicklow presumably from income from investments or money held in deposit accounts but it was a drain that he could not afford. As farming had become so unprofitable, Lord Wicklow decided to open Shelton Abbey as a hotel in 1947 in a bid to make it a viable commercial enterprise. However, it failed to be successful and his level of debts forced him to sell it in 1951.

The case of the Butlers of Castlecrine in County Clare is also rather typical. Most of the estate was sold under the 1903 Land Act, but the family managed to retain enough land to continue farming and thereby maintain the big house. From 1896 to 1915, the Butlers bought a total of 1,755 cattle valued at over £13,200. During the same period they sold 1,910 cattle for £20,788. The most profitable five year period was from 1916 to 1920 coinciding with the economic boom of the war years when 193 cattle were bought for over £2,600 and 304 were sold for £7,800. However, from 1925 to 1930, only ninety-three cattle were bought (roughly 17 per cent of the 1896–1900 figure) and only 159 were sold (roughly 30 per cent of the 1896–1900 figure.)[126] Castlecrine was eventually sold in 1950 and later demolished.

THE RISE IN TAXATION AND DEATH DUTIES

In the late nineteenth century the attack on the privileges of the landed class became a feature of British politics with a rising group of more radical non-landed politicians pressing for the abolition of privilege. In the past the landed class had benefited from certain exemptions in the assessment of death duties. The probate duty on personal wealth was levied at 3 per cent and succession duty on land at only 1.5 per cent in 1888. Personalty under settlement was not liable to any duty because successors were deemed unable to benefit from the sale of heirlooms. Land, whether under settlement or not, was valued for succession duty not on its capital value but on its nominal value over the lifetime of the possessor and as most land was under settlement, exemptions amounted to what were impressive privileges to the landed class.

During Lord Rosebery's ministry in 1894, Radical pressure on financial policy became irresistible. The Liberal Chancellor of the Exchequer, Sir William Harcourt, came under increasing pressure to meet huge demands on government expenditure (and to appease Radical demands for even greater reform.) In the budget that year he introduced a consolidated death duty, called estate duty. This was to fall on realty as well as personalty settled as well as free, and to increase progressively with the size of the estate. It would increase from 3 per cent on estates valued at over £1,000 up to a maximum of 8 per cent on fortunes over £1 million, thereby allowing the state to take substantial toll of the capital wealth left by deceased persons.[127] In the so-termed 'People's budget' of 1910, there was an unprecedented rise in the level of death duties when Lloyd George was forced to raise money to fund old-age pensions and to provide finance for eight new dreadnoughts. There was a 2 per cent increase on estates valued at over £20,000 and below £50,000, while on much larger estates valued at over £1 million, there was an increase from the 1894 rate of 8 per cent to 15 per cent.[128] In 1919, death duties increased even further, ranging from 7 per cent on estates valued at over £20,000, to 28 per cent on estates valued at over £1 million. All of this hit landowners disproportionately and further emphasised the post-war government's desire to capitalise on the wealth of the landed class.[129] The Free State inherited its rates of death duty from Britain but by 1950 the rates had increased dramatically rising progressively from 6 per cent to 41.6 per cent in the intervening years.[130] While from 1925 to 1930, a total of £5 million was paid in death duties in Ireland, this amount rose to a total of £13.4 million for the period from 1945 to 1950.[131]

Lloyd George's 'People's budget' also saw the introduction of 'super tax' levied at 6d in the pound on incomes over £5,000 and because it was levied on gross rather than net income, it became a grave source of concern to landlords who had substantial outlay on debts and charges. It was especially burdensome when one considers that interest rates rose from 3.5 per cent to 6 per cent during the war years, 1914–18. Then in 1914, super tax was raised to 10d in the pound for the first £500 in excess of £2,500 rising to 3s 6d in every pound over £10,000. In 1923, the rate of super tax in Ireland rose progressively from 1s 6d in the pound for incomes over £2,000 to 6s in the pound for incomes over £30,000. By 1950 it had been decreased at the lower end of the scale to 9d in the pound for incomes over £2,000 but increased significantly at the upper end to 8s 6d in the pound for incomes over £30,000. Similarly between 1914 and 1921, ordinary income tax rose from 1s 3d in the pound to 6s. This rate was inherited by the Free State government who lowered it to 3s in the pound in 1928. However, in the face of economic depression and the economic war with Britain, it rose from 3s 6d in the pound in 1932 to a high of 7s 6d in the pound in 1942.[132] As Table 5.3 (p. 285) shows, over half of earned or invested incomes of over £10,000 per annum was lost to taxes by 1950.

The consistently high level of rates was another contributory factor to decline. A dismantled house was rates free, but rates on one that was habitable could be as high as £500–£600 per annum. In a sample of twenty-five of the 100 houses, it was found that the highest rateable valuation in 1950 was that of Powerscourt at £450.[133] The total valuation of the houses was £4,475, an average of approximately £179 per house, at a time when rates collected in the twenty-six counties averaged £1 5s 4d per £1 valuation.[134] This was a significant increase from ten years earlier when rates collected averaged 17s 11d per £1 valuation.[135] (In 1935, this average had been at a high of £2 18s 4d per £1 valuation.[136]) Shane Leslie claimed in 1939 that, 'Irish big houses are still treasure houses of the arts but they and their contents will entirely disappear under rates and death duties by the year 2,000 AD'[137] Within a decade, his prophecy had come true for one of his neighbours. In 1950, Lady Edith Windham claimed that she had no option but to have Dartrey demolished as its rates were too high and a buyer could not be found.[138] The demolition was carried out by Hammond Lane Foundry from Dublin and realised a profit of £3,000, less than 10 per cent of what it had cost to build Dartrey over a century before.[139]

Not surprisingly, landlords felt snowed under by increased taxation from the late nineteenth century. In 1897, the combined rates and tax bill on the Headfort estate was £712; by 1916, it had trebled to £2,300; and by 1920 had again increased dramatically to £5,900.[140] For the period from 1903 to 1910, the Ormondes paid an average of £990 per annum in income and super tax, but for the period from 1931 to 1940 they paid an average of £3,200 per annum.[141] In the early 1920s, Irish landlords and their representatives expressed their concerns regarding increased taxation and pointed to the imminent dangers for their big houses. In August 1921, the editor of *The Irish Times*, fearing the worst in Ireland, wrote of the situation in England:

> The burden of taxation is crushing the life out of rural England. During the last two years many great landowners have been forced to sell their historic mansions and estates.... The Duke of Portland has just told a gathering of his tenants that he fears 'there can be little doubt that those who come after him will not be able to live at Walbeck.' The charges on land, the demands of the income tax collector, and the prospect of heavy death duties, he added, made a closing down of the larger country houses almost inevitable.

The abandonment of Kilkenny Castle and the sale of its contents in 1935 exemplifies the effects that the rise in taxes, death duties and worldwide depression could have on an Irish big house. By 1915 the Ormondes had sold the bulk of their tenanted estates in Tipperary and Kilkenny, almost 21,000 acres, for approximately £240,000.[142] Like the Clonbrocks, they invested their capital globally.[143] Until 1919, life within the castle continued much the same as it had been from the beginning of the century, an average of around £4,500 per annum being spent on its upkeep. That year, James Butler, the third Marquis of Ormonde died and the estate was faced with death duties and legal expenses of almost £166,000.[144] In order to meet these payments the family was forced to sell off much of its English property realising £48,500 in 1920 and £132,000 in 1921.[145] They were also forced to withdraw £16,600 from deposit accounts and to encash Victory bonds to the value of £61,000 to meet other estate charges, super tax and charges payable to Ladies Beatrice and Constance Butler, daughters of the third Marquis.[146] The estate became heavily burdened as a result. While the Ormondes had been receiving almost £22,000 in rental income in 1880, they were receiving only £9,000 from investments in 1930. The great depression seems to have wiped out virtually all of the family's investment portfolio. By 1950 investments yielded only £830.[147] In the meantime, the castle suffered from cutbacks. Throughout the 1920s, an average of only

£2,166 per annum was spent on its upkeep, less than half of what it had been the previous decade. By 1930, this figure was halved again. The whole demesne became neglected, with demesne expenditure declining from £10,500 in the early 1900s to £3,400 by 1922. In 1935 the Ormondes took the decision to vacate the castle in favour of their London home and that year the entire contents of the castle were sold for a mere £6,000. For the next thirty years the castle was to stand empty and deteriorating.

THE SALE OF BIG HOUSES AND THEIR CONTENTS

The depression that set in after 1921 not only depreciated investment income, it also diminished the hopes that many landlords had of becoming successful farmers. The convergence of the two forced big house owners to abandon the visible symbols of their exclusivity. In September 1921, the Earl of Meath held a gathering of his workforce and tenantry at Kilruddery to inform them that he was compelled to close his conservatory, hothouses, kitchen and pleasure gardens and to place several men on the pension list. He claimed: 'My father was always a poor man. His income was never more than from £1,500 to £2,000 a year' and 'he never knew anything about the present heavy taxation of 6s in the pound income tax and super tax'. The Earl made no secret of the fact that he himself had married 'a wife with money' but when she died in 1918, her income ceased to go to him under the terms of her father's will. 'For some considerable time', the Earl claimed, 'I have been living on money I had to withdraw from capital ... this could only lead to bankruptcy'. In 1921, tax payments alone of £4,436 accounted for 43 per cent of the estate charges. The Earl contended that he could no longer afford to live in Kilruddery as it would cost him £2,000 to £4,000 per annum to run and he was no longer prepared to draw on his invested income to supplement its upkeep.[148] A few months later, the Marquis of Waterford gave a luncheon for his employees on the Curraghmore estate. There he told them that 'in consequence of the rise in wages and the abnormal taxation it was found very hard to keep up an estate like Curraghmore' and that he had no option but 'to do things on a greatly reduced scale'.[149]

The sale of big house contents grew at an unprecedented rate from around 1918 (possibly coinciding with the loss of investments to Irish landowners in places such as Russia). Heirlooms and works of art were no longer sold to refurbish houses or to provide extra finances to maintain a leisured lifestyle; they were sold in order to help their owners to survive. The available catalogues of Bennett and Son show that by 1920 landlords such as William Stanley Monck, Lord Massy, and Charles Hamilton had sold huge quantities of silver plate; paintings by Gainsborough, Rembrandt, Van Dyck, Brueghel, Verner, Kneller (all of whom continued to remain in fashion) as well as large collections of Dutch and early Renaissance masters; Sheraton and Chippendale furniture and rare books. In 1917, Lord Courtown had to sell paintings from his home to meet legacy payments of £1,800.[150] In 1918, the contents of J.R. Garstin's library at Braganstown were sold to meet debts.[151] In 1919, furniture was sold from Shelton Abbey for £3,500 to meet estate duties.[152]

From the early 1920s, the combination of economic decline, the dramatic change in the socio-political climate during the revolutionary period, and, indeed, the desire to cling on to an extravagant way of living forced or influenced many big house owners to dispose of their Irish assets on an even larger scale. The columns of *The Irish Times* were filled with notices advertising the sale of 'very superior early Victorian and modern furniture'; 'oil paintings and engravings'; 'rare Irish books' and 'Irish silver plate and antiquities' from big houses. In June 1920, as the War of Independence heightened in the area, the contents of Killua Castle in Westmeath were sold including a fine collection of paintings: Holbein's *Portrait of Gustavus Vasa*; Kneller's, *William III*; Rembrandt's *Samson threatens his father-in-law*; Caravaggio's *The death of Seneca* and *Alexander and Diogenes* and Cuyp's *Portrait of the Artist's Wife*.[153] In 1923, the spendthrift Edward Fitzgerald, seventh Duke of Leinster, was forced to sell a great deal of the furniture from Carton to meet income and super tax debts.[154] Then in 1925, with the consent of the trustees, a collection of Old English and French furniture, tapestries, painted leather and lacquer screens, Oriental and European porcelain, curios, Irish coins, oil paintings by the Old Masters, eighteenth century French and English pastels and mezzotints were also sold from Carton. Most of these were bought by William Randolph Hearst and exported to his castle in California.[155] In her memoirs written in the 1930s, Lady Fingall recalled a portrait of Hermione, wife of the fifth Duke of Leinster, and lamented that:

> it is the only thing hung in the room now. Everything else was taken out to be sold that tragic day when fourteen pantechnicons took away most of the treasures of Carton that were not entailed.... The house is stripped of its great treasures. Even many of the precious books had to go.[156]

There was no respite in the 1930s. In 1932, the Moncks, unable to keep their estate solvent, sold the remaining contents of Charleville

over a five-day period for £11,000.[157] By the 1930s, Lady Edith
Windham found Dartrey too expensive to maintain. She moved into
the steward's house and sold the contents of the castle over a four-
day period in April 1937 including paintings by El Greco, Hamilton,
Zoffany and Coates and 5,000 books from the library. Special buses,
with reduced fares, were laid on for potential buyers taking them
direct from Dublin to the castle and back again. It was brought to
the attention of potential buyers from Northern Ireland and Great
Britain that furniture over 100 years old could be imported duty free
into the United Kingdom, a fact that was largely responsible for the
loss of so many Irish big house treasures to this country.[158]

Those families who retained their houses found it increasingly
more difficult to maintain them in anything like their former splendour. Elizabeth Bowen wrote of her ancestral home in the 1930s:
'The drawing room is now quite empty, but for a grand piano: it is
hung with a white, grey and gold scrolled wallpaper, put up when my
grandmother was a bride'. In the library, there were 'smells of dry
calf bindings, polish, plaster, worn carpet and wood smoke'.[159] When
David Thomson first visited Woodbrook in the 1930s, he felt that it
was 'dark and unlived in'. His impressions were conditioned by 'a
faded Indian carpet, Persian rugs torn in places and the brass rail
of a fender by the empty fireplace'.[160] In the 1930s, the owners of
Woodbrook, the Kirkwood family, ran into financial difficulties with
their banks and the family was forced to sell off land they had
retained for farming purposes to meet their debts. This, Thomson
tells us, upset them knowing 'that hope of solvency lay in expansion
not contraction'.[161]

Contraction was, however, as important for some big house owners
in the twentieth century as expansion had been in the eighteenth
and early twentieth centuries. As income declined owners such as
Bryan Cooper found that the most sensible way to approach the
problem was to demolish or close part of their houses. In 1927 he
closed off the basement and the 'too large and rather gloomy dining
room' of Markree.[162] Similarly Captain F.B. Barton demolished four
bays of the main block of Straffan in 1937, while much later, in the
1960s, the Maxwells of Farnham demolished the additions made to
the house in 1839 and remodelled it on a much smaller scale.[163]

From the 1920s, big houses themselves began to pour onto the market. Before 1935, Battersby and Sons alone had sold at least sixty big
houses in Ireland including Bishopscourt; Killashee; Kylemore Abbey
and Ravensdale. As entire landed estates were sold under the compulsory terms of the Free State Land Acts, big houses were sold with
them. When the bottom collapsed out of the shares market during the

depression of the 1920s and farming was thrown into economic disarray it was simply impossible to retain houses and when contents were
sold, shells were no use. By the 1960s, only 37 per cent of the houses
in the sample of 100 were in existence (but mainly decaying) and in
the original families' ownership. (Since then at least six more have
been sold — Bellamont, Malahide, Abbeyleix, Gurteen de la Poer,
Knocklofty and Adare.) Even more illuminating is Mark Bence-Jones's
recent claim that only about 200 of the 2,000 or so big houses in his
Guide to Irish Country Houses are presently in the ownership of the
original families.[164] It would be difficult to argue that there was a typical reason for their sales, but each sale was in some way connected to
the socio-political and economic changes from the late nineteenth century that infringed upon all big house communities.

After the Land Commission succeeded in dividing untenanted
lands and demesnes in the 1930s, houses such as Knockdrin, Woodlawn,
Granston Manor and Harristown were sold in the 1940s. Some of
these houses continued in private ownership: Woodlawn was bought
by Derek Le Poer Trench and Granston Manor was purchased by
Kenneth Harper. Others, particularly the great houses, assumed a
totally new role as educational centres, hospitals, hotels or industrial centres. In the 1920s, the Patrician Brothers bought Ballyfin
and established a college there; in the 1940s, Moore Abbey was sold
to the Sisters of Charity who ran it as a hospital. In the early 1960s,
Oak Park became an agricultural research centre; in 1962, Lyons
was sold to University College Dublin; around the same time Cabra
Castle became a hotel and continues to remain so; Mount Juliet and
Straffan have more recently become country clubs. It would be interesting to gain an insight to the old landed class's attitude towards houses
being used for such purposes. In 1880, on hearing rumours that
Leixlip Castle was to be turned into a convent, Sophia Trench wrote
to Mrs Henry Bruen: 'I cannot feel but great regret at the thought of
this fine old place being given for such an object'.[165]

Other big houses were demolished after sale. Burton Hall was
sold to the Land Commission in 1927 and demolished in 1930. Coole
Park was sold to the Department of Lands in 1927. Its owner, Lady
Gregory was allowed to live there until her death in 1932, but the
house was demolished in 1941. Desart Court and Kilboy, both of
which had been rebuilt after having been burned during the revolutionary period, were sold and also subsequently demolished. Many
other houses, such as Dunsandle, Courtown, Mote Park, Frenchpark
and Castlecrine, were demolished in the 1950s, a time when it became
profitable to dismantle big houses because of the shortage of materials
in post-war Ireland.[166]

Most of those who purchased estates that had been divided by the Land Commission had little interest in the big houses which stood on them. Even if they could afford their upkeep, few may have wanted the stigma of being associated with the old landed class. They had come to symbolise colonial rule and their houses were symbols of an old order that the majority of people would at least have feigned delight at being rid of. In 1946, Hazlewood in County Sligo was put up for sale by the Land Commission with a stipulation that the buyer had to demolish the house, remove all materials and level the site. To encourage potential buyers, the advertisement of sale pointed out that the roof had a high quantity of lead.[167] The editor of the *Sligo Champion*, one of the few to oppose the move, condemned what he perceived to be the Land Commission's policy of acquiring houses simply to demolish them whereas in England the National Trust was attempting to preserve them. The editor sarcastically proclaimed: 'In Ireland the value of such a house is measured by the contents of lead in the roof'.[168] But there were very few who agreed with him that big houses were part of a shared heritage.[169] Forty years later, Desmond Guinness was just as critical of Land Commission policy at that time:

When it [the Land Commission] came into possession of what is loosely termed nowadays an 'historic property' the consequences were dire. The buildings were emptied and left shuttered up for years while the dreamers decided how to carve up the place. A favourite ploy was to run the statutory concentration camp fence ten feet or so from the front steps. The trees were cut, the garden went wild and no longer gave any employment. In terms of national investment it was a waste. The house would be advertised for sale, through the means of a five line advertisement on the back page of a local paper, to ensure that no one except the demolition men could possibly be mis-guided enough to buy it.[170]

Other big houses were simply abandoned by their owners who either could not afford their upkeep or who did not want to continue to live in a changing Ireland. Dalyston, Derrycarne and Hollymount were allowed to fall into decay having been left derelict for years. The Rossmores tried to live at Rossmore Park for a time after it developed dry rot but when mushrooms began to grow on the drawing-room ceiling and guests were forced to wipe their feet on a disinfected mat when leaving so as not to spread the disease, they decided it was time to abandon it in favour of Camla Vale.[171] Having sold his estate under the 1903 Land Act, a rather innocuous IRA raid

for arms in September 1920 provided Somerset Saunderson with the
pretext to leave Castlesaunderson and to spend the rest of his life in
Newbury or on the Côte d'Azur. Alvin Jackson captures his feelings:

> In Ireland he had lost everything beyond a derelict mansion. The pop-
> ular political authority of the family had died with his father in 1906;
> the high political influence of the family ended with his brother,
> Edward Aremberg's, resignation from Dublin Castle in July 1920.
> Land purchase had obliterated the estate; land purchase had finally
> broken the social ascendancy of the family.[172]

CONCLUSION

The period from 1903 to 1933 was perhaps the most catalytic in
terms of the decline of the Irish big house. Even during the extended
economic depression and land war of the 1880s and 1890s most Irish
landlords had managed to retain their big houses, even if some contents, most notably valuable works of art, had had to be sacrificed.
Cutbacks had undoubtedly been made, there were signs of dilapidation in some homes and others had even been closed temporarily as
families retrenched. However, the capital secured under the terms of
the Wyndham Land Act and the chance which it afforded to landowners
to retain enough land for farming purposes offered a respite to the
big house. In total Irish landowners had received almost £86 million
under the Land Acts of 1903 and 1909 between November 1903 and
March 1921.[173] (They had already received almost £25 million under
the terms of the land acts from 1870 to 1896.[174]) The Taylors managed
to return to Headfort, for example, in 1908 and lived there quite
comfortably until the great depression of the 1920s and 1930s. While
they spent an average of around £2,000 per annum on the upkeep of
the house throughout the 1920s, the depreciation of investments
meant this expenditure was cut to just over £270 by the 1940s.
Unable to maintain the house as formerly, Lord Headfort leased out
three-quarters of it to a boys' preparatory school after the Second
World War.[175]

Big house social life certainly retained much of its former grandeur
up to the war years. Servants were still plentiful, the 100 houses
in the sample returned almost 800 servants in 1911 (and one must
consider that in many houses there was only a skeleton staff on the
night.) While big houses may have become something of an anachro-
nism without their vast landed estates, they were still affordable as
long as investments paid regular dividends and farming remained
viable. And, of course, they did not look totally out of place as long as

they continued to be surrounded by hundreds of acres of demesne and parkland as of yet undisturbed by land acts.

The economic crash and prolonged agricultural depression, which followed the First World War, sounded the death knell for Irish big houses. When these were added to political revolution, a campaign of big house burnings, a social revolution in the form of a new land war, a land act aimed at compulsory acquisition of all tenanted and un-tenanted land and a rise in rates and taxation, the decline of the big house became all but inevitable.[176]

6

SERVANT LIFE IN THE BIG HOUSE
1860–1960

'WILLING AND RESPECTFUL, ILL ACCOMMODATED
AND POORLY PAID'

James Vogan [head gamekeeper] proved more potent than governesses
or tutors. James Vogan had that honesty, devotion, fidelity and absolute
content with his lot which alone made the feudal system a part of
Christian civilisation.... A world has grown up where such servitors
and retainers are unknown. So much the worse for the world!

SHANE LESLIE, *THE FILM OF MEMORY* (1937), P. 27

INTRODUCTION

Servants are largely the anonymous members of Irish big
house communities. Their names appear in estate account
books with usually only the bare information regarding
what position they held in the house and the wages they
received. Servants appear in short stories and novels, most notably
in those of Somerville and Ross, but invariably they are mere stereo-
types. They sometimes appear in the memoirs of big house owners,
most notably those of the Leslies referred to throughout this work,
but they were the favoured few, presented as loyal retainers who
never questioned their status or role in big house life. Unfortunately
they themselves did not write their memoirs or leave any type of
diaries behind that might provide an authentic insight into their
daily lives, how they perceived their role in the big house or the relationship they had with their employees.

However, in order to continue the trend of this work it has been
decided to use an essay by Elizabeth Bowen, which deals with a servant, Sarah Cartey, who worked in Bowen's Court right throughout
the period under study. Extracts from an interview carried out by
this author some years ago with Annie MacManus, who worked in
Clohamon in the early 1920s, will also be used.[1] Dependence on oral
history may have its drawbacks, and Bowen's account may be somewhat elegiac but both sources provide at least an insight to servant
life in the big house.

SARAH CARTEY AND ANNIE MACMANUS

Sarah Cartey was born in the early 1860s. At the age of fourteen, she
left her home in Tipperary, where her father was probably a tenant
on the Bowen's Tipperary estate, to become a kitchen-maid at Bowen's
Court. It was a journey of fifty miles and Elizabeth Bowen wrote that
at the time Sarah 'did not know when, if ever, she would see home
again':

> Ireland looks so small from the outside, it is hard to realise how big
> the distances feel: for the simple people, each county might be a
> different continent — and way back in the last century this was even
> more so. Young Sarah, face set towards County Cork, might have
> been driving off into Peru.[2]

She travelled that day with her new employer, her 'master',
Robert Cole Bowen, whom she would have known only by sight as a
man who travelled weekly between his Tipperary and Cork estates.
On leaving home: 'her mother and all her neighbours had told her
she was a lucky girl, to get such a start — legends of Bowen's Court
grandeur were current in Tipperary'.[3] The house was, indeed, at the
height of its Victorian prime, lavishly kept up and maintained by
eight indoor servants who catered for the needs of the Bowens, their
nine children and frequent guests.

At first Sarah saw very little of the upstairs rooms in Bowen's
Court for 'the basement claimed her'. It was here that the kitchens
were located and where Sarah spent the best part of her day in a routine
that literally meant she went from bed to work and work to bed.
Work was carried out 'at exacting pressure' for if a meal was not on
the table on time 'the master would "roar aloud", at which the whole
household quaked'.[4] As in all big houses, the servants at Bowen's
Court formed a hierarchy from the butler down and it was with the
upper servants that the family had most contact. There was very little
contact between the lower servants such as Sarah and members of
the Bowen family, although Sarah was later to form a close working
relationship with Sarah Bowen, the eldest of the Bowen daughters.
'As a rule' Robert Cole Bowen 'ignored the servants, who for their
part gave him a wide berth'.[5] Within a few years of Sarah's arriving
at Bowen's Court, much changed in the house. First Mrs Bowen died
of smallpox; then Robert Cole married a second time but the children
from his first marriage resented the woman who had taken their
mother's place. Robert Cole suffered a mental breakdown and the
estate, lacking his tight financial control, began to run at a loss.
When he died his heir found that a period of retrenchment was

necessary. Most of the farm labourers and the indoor servants were dismissed. Sarah was one of the few to be kept on.[6]

Sarah's workload increased — fewer servants meant that she had to turn her hands to a myriad of other tasks besides working in the kitchen. Elizabeth Bowen wrote: 'Meanwhile, she was doing the work of six, turning her hand to everything — cooking, laundering, scrubbing. I don't know how many times a day she plied up and down between the basement and attics.'[7] Sarah did not marry until she was thirty: 'Her comeliness and her fame as a cheerful worker could not fail to bring many suitors around — but she had literally no time to listen to them'.[8] Then she married Patrick Barry, who worked on the Bowen estate, and Sarah moved out of the big house for the first time to a little cottage on the outskirts of the demesne. However, she continued to work in Bowen's Court every day even after the birth of her only child, Paddy. Elizabeth Bowen was the third generation of the family that she served. This is how she recorded her childhood memories of Sarah:

> To escape downstairs to the laundry where Sarah worked became my dominating idea. Happiness stays, for me, about the warm smell of soapsuds. I remember her short strong arms red from the heat of water, and the hilarious energy with which she turned the wringer.... Under her hand the iron sped effortlessly over the steaming linen.... One of the pleasures of growing older was that of growing more fully into her confidence.[9]

Some years after her husband died, and Elizabeth Bowen inherited the house, Sarah and Paddy moved into quarters at the back of Bowen's Court acting as caretakers during Elizabeth's absences in London. As the years went by Elizabeth became more attached to Sarah but her and her husband's work in London meant that she became more detached from Bowen's Court. From the late 1930s, rooms in the house were necessarily closed off as they were no longer used and Sarah packed away the pictures and other furniture. She had witnessed great changes at Bowen's Court during her sixty years there. Her girlhood had been in the days of the Land League. She saw the 'bad times' and further economic depression that followed the First World War. 'She saw horizons scarlet with burning mansions and farms' during the War of Independence and Civil War. She witnessed the sale of the Bowen estate and the financial decline of the family that was eventually to force Elizabeth Bowen to sell Bowen's Court sixteen years after Sarah's death in 1943. She saw the number of servants reduced from eight to one, herself. During her time at Bowen's Court the significance of her perceived role in the life of the house is evident in the following passage written by Elizabeth Bowen shortly after Sarah's death:

> At the start, I pictured Bowen's Court standing empty. But that is not the picture Sarah would want you to see — and more it is not a true one. Her presence is still to be found there, and from no place where Sarah reigns can life turn away for too long. I believe in her power to magnetise people home again; in the rooms will be heard again the laughter she liked to hear. You may say she gave her genius to a forlorn hope — to a house at the back of beyond, to a dying out family.[10]

Annie MacManus's story is somewhat different from Sarah Cartey's. While Sarah worked in a big house almost throughout the period under study, Annie worked in one for only three years, 1922–24, which were very much the twilight years of the big house in Ireland. Annie was born in 1906 into a labouring family in Enniscorthy, County Wexford. At the age of fourteen she left school — 'you didn't get a chance of secondary education in those days' — and went to work for two years in a local shop. However, she was never happy there and aspired to work in a big house instead. She was, she claimed: 'like many young girls who used to love to go to these houses because they were THE jobs'. As far as Annie was concerned the advantages of working in a big house were that one's parents did not have to pay for an apprenticeship and accommodation and uniform were provided free. At the age of sixteen, having got a recommendation from her employer, Annie went to work for the Hudson-Kinahan family at Clohamon near Bunclody village, a two-storey eighteenth-century house.

Annie began her service as a between-maid, her workload effectively divided between the eight upstairs bedrooms and the four main reception rooms on the ground floor. Her first wages were £15 per annum for a six and a half day week which she considered to be 'very good' at the time. Annie got up at 5.30 a.m. and effectively worked from then until bedtime. There were only two maids in the house, herself and Molly Wilson, a Protestant girl also from Wexford. They had a very heavy workload that makes one wonder how Annie had the time to savour the 'great fun' of the big house that she referred to. First, she swept and dusted the drawing-room, dining-room, front-hall and sitting-rooms. Then she lit the fires while her companion, Molly, prepared the kitchen for the cook. At 7 a.m., she brought Colonel Hudson-Kinahan and his wife a cup of tea in bed. At 7.30 a.m. during the winter months, she lit the twenty-five lamps that were located throughout the house. At 8 a.m. she waited at the breakfast table. After breakfast, Annie and Molly made the beds, re-arranged the rooms and cleaned the front staircase and hall. During the day, the fires had to be attended. At 4 p.m. she went up to Mrs Kinahan's bedroom and set out her clothes for the evening. In the evening she did a further round of the bedrooms, drawing curtains, turning down bedcovers and heating the beds with hot-water bottles. She usually got to bed around 10 p.m.

In the early 1920s, the Hudson-Kinahans still hosted large dinner parties for up to thirty guests. These parties took place mainly dur-ing the hunting season as Colonel Hudson-Kinahan was MFH of the Island Pack in Wexford. Setting the dinner table for such an event took Annie and Molly 'the whole evening', the family silver had to be polished, the glassware had to be 'sparkling', and the linen 'spotless'. Annie recalled one dinner party given at the end of the hunting sea-son when she spent the whole of the evening building an imitation mountain of cotton wool in the middle of the huge dining-room table. It was then decorated with figurines of huntsmen and women that Mrs Kinahan had gone especially to Paris to purchase. While setting the table, and for their morning and afternoon work in general, Annie and Molly wore plain black cotton dresses and white aprons, but when serving dinner they had to change into a uniform of brown lustre and white lace aprons. Dinner compromised seven or eight courses but it was always a great source of disappointment to Annie that 'the guests ate so little, just a pick of everything'.

There was neither housekeeper nor butler at Clohamon. The day-to-day running of the household was the responsibility of the cook: 'every complaint went to her' and every Monday she was informed of the week's itinerary by Mrs Kinahan. Also on Mondays, a local butcher delivered a whole lamb and a side of beef to Clohamon, which the cook carved into the different joints required. The servants ate in the servants' hall on the ground floor, enjoying the same food that was served to the family and their guests.

Annie was loath to describe her life at Clohamon as one of 'drudgery'. She enjoyed every day of it, the 'great jollity' and the endless 'bits of fun' amongst the staff. (She was aware, from her conversations with servants employed elsewhere, that this did not exist in all such houses). She also remarked upon the kindness of her employers, who, for example, on Christmas Eve would leave presents for the servants in their bedrooms. She loved the 'beautiful bedrooms' with 'carpet and lovely suites of furniture', which each of the maids had on the top floor. (The cook and her husband, the yard manager, slept in a room off the kitchen). The central heating that allowed her to wash her stockings at night, hang them on the pipes and have them dry in the morning, was a luxury 'that no one had around home'. The responsibility of caring for Mrs Kinahan's valuable collection of jewellery; the social events organised by Mrs Kinahan for her servants; and 'the food ... which was the very best' all contributed to Annie's appreciation of her job there. All in all, Annie thought that working in Clohamon was: 'a great life, a great life'. In 1924, Annie left Clohamon having met her husband who was contracted there for a time as a carpenter. She told me:

> It's very hard when you're working there to knuckle down to the ordinary way of living when you come out. It's all so nice. When I left I missed all the company and the different living. I was heartbroken.

SERVANT LIFE IN THE BIG HOUSE

Right up to the end of the First World War, and in some cases beyond that period, servants were an integral part of big house life in Ireland. They ensured a luxurious and leisured lifestyle for landlords by undertaking everything from caring for the richly-furnished interiors of houses to cultivating extensive and elaborate gardens; from driving carriages to raising and preserving game. A great house such as Carton could not be maintained without an army of servants and even the houses of smaller landowners required several. Thus, in 1880, *The Servant's Practical Guide* claimed that 'without the co-operation of well-trained servants, domestic machinery is thrown completely out of gear, and the best bred of hostesses placed at a disadvantage'.[11] However, while at the height of landlord grandeur the number and diversity of big house servants symbolised the social status and economic strength of a landlord, enhancing his reputation amongst his peers, it must also be considered that the running of a big house was extremely labour-intensive. The very size of these houses with their numerous rooms and extensive furnishings required that an adequate number of servants be on hand to keep them presentable. Landlords' propensity for entertaining, for dining formally, for acting as hosts during the hunting and shooting seasons or during race meetings such as Punchestown necessitated more than the two or three maid servants that sufficed in a middle-class urban home. The larger the house, the larger the number of servants required to cope with the multitude of tasks involved. In 1911, Marquis Conyngham, for example, employed a private nurse, a governess, two lady's maids, a butler, cook, housekeeper, valet, two footmen, a hallboy, as well as scullery, kitchen, parlour, dairy and house maids at

Slane. As socio-economic strength declined, so too did the dependence upon servants who became less affordable. In this way the decline of the role of servants in big houses reflected the much wider decline of the big houses themselves.

House servants formed a hierarchical structure from butler and housekeeper down to hall-boys and scullery-maids. The butler and housekeeper were both responsible for the day-to-day organisation of the household schedule and supervision of the other male and female servants. The butler was also responsible for the safekeeping of the household plate and in charge of the wine cellar. If there was no valet employed in a house (and these tended to be exclusive to the homes of the very large landowners) the butler was also responsible for his master's wardrobe. He waited at breakfast, luncheon, tea and dinner along with the footmen. In houses where footmen were not employed, he answered the door. Few were likely to have been as busy as the butler at Woodbrook who: 'seldom turned up in time to wait at table ... because something usually happened to delay him in the stables and when he did come the smell of horse dung from his boots was mingled with the food'.[12]

Moving down the manservant line, the valet was next. He was his employer's personal servant, being in charge, for example, of his wardrobe, but, as noted earlier, valets were employed principally in the houses of the very large landowners. Footmen were directly subordinate to the butler and they attended the carriages, cleaned boots, carried coal to the fires, and waited at table. Again, footmen were employed principally in the houses of the larger landowners; in smaller houses maids doubled as footmen when required. In addition the bigger houses such as Castletown, Slane, Carton and Powerscourt employed a variety of other male servants such as scullery-boys, hall-boys, pantry-boys, clock-winders, chamber-pot boys and messenger boys.

The housekeeper was the female counterpart of the butler, directing the female staff, consulting with the mistress of the house about the week's time-table, supervising the household linen and china, and ordering supplies. Elizabeth, Countess Fingall, said that she 'often marvelled at the way in which a housekeeper or butler could carry the whole weight of some big house on their shoulders — not the house only but the people who live in it as well.' Her housekeeper, Mrs Jones, 'was the real butler' at Killeen, keeping even the Countess 'in her place severely'.[13]

In the houses that did not employ a housekeeper, the roles of housekeeper and cook were amalgamated. In larger houses, cooks were assisted by scullery and kitchen-maids, who were at the bottom of the female servant hierarchy. Annie MacManus said that her experience of cooks was that they 'tended to guard their positions in the household' and that 'an old cook mightn't let you see her recipe for a cake for five years'. In 1880 *The Servant's Practical Guide* suggested that a cook's position was worth guarding:

> Some ladies stand very much in awe of their cooks, knowing that those who consider themselves to be thoroughly experienced will not brook fault-finding or interference with their manner of cooking, and give notice to leave on the smallest pretext. Thus when ladies obtain a really good cook, they deal with her delicately, and are inclined to let her have her own way with regard to serving the dinner.

Whereas in small houses such as Clohamon the workload of maids was relatively diverse, in larger houses it was more specialised with kitchen-maids, parlour-maids, chamber-maids and so on each with responsibility for maintaining certain areas of the house. 'Head housemaids' or 'first housemaids' basically supervised the work of their subordinates in houses where several maids were employed.

Positions in a big house usually offered security, good living conditions, ample food and a possible pension at the end of service. (On occasion, as wills show, a possible legacy was made upon the death of their employer). In addition, for most, working in a big house offered the opportunity to be part of a glamorous lifestyle that was far removed from the one into which they were reared. There was the opportunity for trips to race meetings or to the theatre and for travel to London or further afield if they were fortunate to be chosen to accompany their employers on continental tours. One former servant who worked in Louth Hall took great satisfaction in telling how she 'used to long for her ladyship to go back to England' so that she 'could dress up in her gowns and necklaces and bracelets and waltz up and down the avenue'.[14]

Servant life was not, however, an easy one. This was particularly true in smaller houses where servants were less numerous and less specialised than in the houses of larger landowners and, therefore, had to turn their hands to most types of housework. There were contemporary commentators who regarded it as a life of drudgery. In 1857, Mary MacMahon wrote:

> The servant should be regarded as one of the family — allowed time to read — and time for open air relaxation and refreshment. The servant on a miserable pittance is expected to have the virtues of a seraph and the capacity for drudgery of a slave. She must not think of dress, of news, of acquaintance, or of pleasure of any kind....

It is impossible for them to make provision for old age or sickness, and yet in many families there is no kindly consideration shown for them. Many a lady that drives in her carriage and sports needless finery on her person, is overbearing, and penurious to her servants.[15]

Having bedrooms in the attic (or basement) of a house was the landlord's way of segregating the servants from the family. In her autobiography, Anita Leslie recalled servants' quarters at Glaslough:

The servants lived in a separate wing with its own stone staircase, at the bottom of which was a row of bells beneath which were written 'Sir John', 'study', blue drawing-room', 'red room' etc. Miss Meade, the housekeeper, who had her own room somewhere on the stone stairs so that she could know who passed up or down, issued forth and ordered us [Anita and her brother] back to what she called our proper quarters. Later on we would discover that young housemaids slept in rooms which could only be reached through that of the head housemaid, who was always over forty. Men servants inhabited a suite of their own with a separate staircase.[16]

At Rockingham, extreme measures were taken to keep servants out of view. Fuel was brought across the lake in boats, unloaded below the view from the windows, and wheeled under the house through a tunnel; goods coming in by land came through another tunnel; while servants came and went through yet another tunnel.[17]

However, servants' living quarters were in the main quite comfortable. At Straffan, each of the maids' bedrooms had a white enamel or brass bed, an oak sofa, oak table, oak sideboard, a small toilet mirror, a white enamelled chair and a bathroom seat. There was Axminster carpet on the floor, which possibly had once been used elsewhere in the house. Here, as in most of the larger houses, the servants also had a sitting room with an oak circular top table, an oak sideboard and reclining chairs.[18] While such furnishings may not have been up to the standard of what was available to the family, they were, nevertheless, of a higher standard than servants would have been used to at home.

Servants had little time for socialising. Live-in servants were literally at the family's disposal all day long. They were expected to be deferential and could expect to have their lives controlled by their employers. They had no set hours, working as long as their employers required them and usually for six and a half days per week. Even the individual task of lighting and heating a house such as Killeen was an arduous one in the late nineteenth and early twentieth centuries. Lady Fingall wrote:

The house [Killeen] was difficult of course to light and heat in those days when we had only oil lamps and candles. There were two boys to do the lamps and keep the fires of wood and turf going, and carry enormous cans of hot water for baths. I believe it took nearly a hundred lamps to light the house, and even then there were many dim corners.[19]

A lady's maid was expected to wait up for her mistress to return from a ball; this could be 5 a.m. where Lady Alice Howard was concerned. And even when a lady's maid travelled with her mistress, she was inevitably kept busy: Lady Fingall recalled changing her dress as often as five times a day during her visits to Carton for riding, tennis or croquet, tea and dinner. 'Our frocks were voluminous', she wrote, and 'our luggage, of course, absurd'.[20]

Farm work, the cultivation of extensive and often elaborate gardens and the preservation of game provided a good deal of employment on demesnes as at Powerscourt, where up to fifty men were employed at high season. Demesne employees, the functions of whom are largely self-explanatory, included gardeners, grooms, coachmen, agricultural labourers, herds, shepherds, gamekeepers, yardmen, blacksmiths, foresters or woodrangers, carpenters, masons and plasterers. It was the job of the steward to supervise the overall activities of demesne employees but within each group such as gardeners, yardmen, grooms and farm labourers there were also supervisors or 'headmen'. Many of these men (and their families) lived in cottages provided by the landlord on the demesne or, as in the case of grooms and yardmen at Dartrey, in rooms above the stables.

Demesne employees, as we have already seen in the case of Glaslough, were often members of the same family and worked as retainers for generations. Such families seem to have accepted their role in life as being one of servitude to the local landlord and servants like James Vogan devoted their whole lives to the landlord and his family and to caring for his property. On the other hand, it is also important to recognise that the employment of a father and/or son(s) or daughter(s) provided steady work and much needed income in a society where labouring conditions on a farm were much less comfortable or rewarding. In 1911, at Gowran in County Kilkenny, two members of the Millea family were agricultural labourers, two were gardeners and one was a servant in the castle. At Farnham in Cavan, George Harper was a coachman, his wife, Margaret, was a laundress, and their son, James, was a garden-boy. Some families specialised in certain areas of demesne work: at Borris in Carlow, four members of the Kelly family were masons; at Howth in Dublin, three members of the Hartford family were gardeners; at Hazlewood in Sligo, a

father and his three sons were gamekeepers. As with household
servants, demesne staff, particularly stewards and gamekeepers,
often moved from estate to estate. Take, for example, D.[?] MacLeish,
the gamekeeper at Slane in 1911. He was born in Kildare, his eldest
son was born in Fermanagh, his next two sons were born in
Monaghan, while his youngest son was born in Meath.

There are surviving sources detailing contractual agreements
between landlords and estate employees which do not seem to exist
for household staff. In 1861, for example, the steward on the
Ballyglunin estate in Galway entered into the following agreement
with his new employer, Walter Blake:

> I, Thomas Burke, in acknowledging that I have no claim of any kind
> against the late Mr Martin J. Blake and that I have been paid in full
> for all services I may have rendered to that gentleman herewith offer
> the whole of my time and service to the best of my ability to you,
> Mr Walter Blake, for an annual stipend of fifty pounds and in getting
> in addition to this sum two shillings and sixpence per day, for every
> four and twenty hours you may require my attendance from home to
> defray my board and lodging expenses while away[21]

A lodge-keeper on the same estate was allowed: 'grass of a cow,
eight pounds a year, the use of both the garden attached to and the
gate house' which he promised 'to keep in good repair and order and
... evacuate at any time' his employer so desired.[22] At Kilkenny Castle,
the lodge-keeper had to open the gate at 6 a.m. to admit the demesne
workers. He had to sleep in the lodge and have breakfast and tea
there. He could vacate it at 1.15 p.m. for dinner (where is not stated)
and return by 2 p.m. providing an 'oddman' or stable hand took his
place; he was not allowed to let any servant pass out through the
gate after 9 p.m. unless they had special permission.[23]

As most of their waking time was taken up with work, it is small
wonder that only 2 per cent of the females and 4.6 per cent of the
males amongst the 772 household servants who appeared on the
1911 census returns for the 100 sample houses were married.[24] While
employers preferred singles, the high rate of spinsterhood and bache-
lorhood amongst these servants was undoubtedly also due to the
minimal amount of time they were allowed for interaction and the
lack of potential partners to whom they were exposed. Lady Fingall
has written that housemaids in at least one big house 'seem to have
been kept somewhat like novices in a convent'.[25] On most estates,
demesne workers were not allowed inside the big house, nor was
friendship encouraged between them and the maids 'who were ever

under the watchful eye of the misthress (*sic*)'.[26] (It should be pointed out, however, that there were cases such as at Clohamon where the cook was married to the yard manager and where Annie MacManus met her husband who was employed there as a carpenter.) Sarah Cartey, as we have seen, was too busy to marry until she was over thirty. David Thomson offered another interesting reason for Winnie, the elderly cook at Woodbrook, not marrying: 'So many years in the big house had given her expensive tastes such as cake and meat, and no doubt she hated the prospect of life on a small farm'.[27]

REMUNERATION

Some sources such as memoirs suggest that servants in various households got paid very little, if anything at all. Lady Fingall was not sure if all the servants at Killeen received regular wages; she thought they were probably 'content with their meals in the big kitchen'.[28] When Shane Leslie recalled life at Glaslough at the turn of the century, he remembered the servants as being: 'poorly paid'.[29] David Thomson claimed that servants at Woodbrook were not paid every week. When the young Mrs Kirkwood became aware of this and inquired of her mother-in-law as to the reason for it, she was told:

> They wouldn't know what to do with it. They never had money at home.... Can you imagine Winnie bicycling into Carrick for that [a new dress]? The shop people would cheat her and she'd come home looking a fright.[30]

It is possible that servants in many big houses did not receive regular wages as the economic position of Irish landlords deteriorated from the late nineteenth century. Some may quite willingly have stayed on with little or no pay, having nowhere to go and knowing no other way of life. However, even in the big house's heyday, as Leslie pointed out, they were poorly paid for the amount of work they did. Furthermore, there were often wide variations in the rates of pay from one household to the next and, indeed, between one servant and another. In 1884, at Carton, the housekeeper, cook and lady's maid all received £60 per annum; the house-maids between £12 and £16 per annum and the kitchen and scullery-maids £12 per annum.[31] Comparatively speaking, these wages were high. Even at Kilkenny Castle, during the early 1880s, the average wage of the housekeeper was only £32.5 per annum while house-maids received around £15 per annum and kitchen and scullery-maids between £8 and £11 per annum.[32] A glance at the advertisement columns of *The Irish Times* for April 1911 shows that house-maids in large houses could by then earn around £22 per annum, although wages as low as £12 per annum were quoted for maids in smaller houses. No figure higher than £40 per annum was quoted for housekeepers.

The same variations were evident for male servants. In 1884, the butler at Carton earned £100 per annum whereas his counterpart at Kilkenny Castle was paid £47 per annum.[33] (Even the wages of the housekeeper and cook at Carton far outstripped those of the butler at Kilkenny.) On the demesne, the highest paid employee was the steward who usually received a number of perks along with wages, which again varied from estate to estate. In 1898, the steward on the Farnham estate received £75 per year plus 'a free house, three ton of coal, cut timber as required, potatoes, vegetables, and the grass of a cow'.[34] In 1888, the steward on the much smaller Ballyglunin estate in Galway received similar perks but only £8 per annum.[35] In 1902, the steward on the Clonbrock estate received £120 per annum.[36] In 1879, the head gardener at Powerscourt received £52 per annum, while around the same time the head gardener at Kilkenny Castle received £40 per annum.[37]

Indoor servants also received certain perks. Money wages did not take into consideration the board and lodgings of servants. In 1906, the female servants at Powerscourt were paid nine shillings per week and the male servants eleven shillings per week in board wages.[38] A servant formerly employed at Louth Hall claimed that her wages in the 1920s varied according to whether or not 'her ladyship was at home or away'. When her employers were away she received one shilling per week extra to feed herself.[39] This practice seems to have been widespread in the late nineteenth and early twentieth centuries although it was criticised in 1899 in a Board of Trade report on the money wages of servants in Great Britain and Ireland:

> Another disturbing feature in many Irish households is the practice of paying 'breakfast' wages in some cases and 'full board' wages in others. Although in such cases the servant is supposed to provide her food out of this allowance, there can be little doubt — at any rate where breakfast allowances are made — that the allowance goes to increase wages, and that the servant manages to serve herself from her employer's provisions.[40]

This report also concluded that vails or 'tips' to servants, particularly in big houses where a considerable number of guests were entertained, greatly supplemented their real earnings. However, it was also pointed out that this was an issue 'on which little trustworthy information would be available'. Of the estate papers scrutinised by this author, only the Clonbrock accounts for 1904 and 1905 make reference to tips (ranging from one to five shillings) paid by members of the Dillon family to servants in other big houses.[41]

There were other less material perks. At the beginning of the twentieth-century, bathrooms in rural Ireland were exclusive to big houses. Lady Fingall has pointed out that 'the mistress could offer a bath to the cook as a privilege, a share in the luxuries she enjoyed herself'.[42] Some maids, when they married, partially furnished their new homes with chattels that had been discarded by their former employees (or which they had perhaps taken from the big house.) On leaving Woodbrook to get married, one maid took with her a load of chattels. When the Kirkwoods visited her new home they were surprised to find themselves eating off their own plates![43]

Perhaps more importantly, the big house offered at least some security that servants may not have been willing to give up. Even though wages were not very high, servants did at least eat as well as their employers and relatively decent accommodation was provided. The Ormonde and Powerscourt estate papers also show that long-serving employees were traditionally given small pensions and sometimes a demesne cottage on retirement. To be made redundant late in life could be disastrous. In 1893, Joseph Chamberlain told the royal commission on aged poor that in Britain no one would employ a servant 'past fifty years of age and accordingly, almost by the necessity of the case, they will have to go to the workhouse'.[44] There seems, however, to have been a greater sense of security amongst servants in Ireland. In 1899, the aforementioned Board of Trade report on servants concluded:

> The process of elimination of the unfit and infirm does not seem to go on in Ireland with the same completeness as in England, and the elderly and the incompetent appear to be retained with more tolerance in Ireland. Perhaps also in Ireland capable servants are more inclined to stay on with mistresses to whom they are accustomed, without much thought whether they could earn higher wages elsewhere.[45]

A comment by Shane Leslie in his unpublished memoirs concurs with this conclusion:

> In those days joining service with the Leslies was like joining a clan or taking a sacrament. They joined for life and Glaslough held a number of retainers who had already done forty years' service. There was an old nurse who had nursed my father.[46]

The same could be said to have been true of Lady Fingall's long-serving housekeeper, Mrs Jones. Another example is probably the servant about whom J.R. Garstin of Braganstown found it necessary to note on his 1911 household schedule return: 'I asked her [her age] five times and could get no reply but "What you like". I think she must be at least sixty-five'.[47]

EMPLOYMENT OPPORTUNITY IN THE BIG HOUSE

With the exception of five servants — three born on the continent, one in Bermuda and one in the USA — the remaining 767 returned in the 1911 census returns for the 100 sample houses were born in Britain or in Ireland. Of these, only 14 per cent were locally born (within the county where the house was located); 47 per cent were born in Ireland outside the county of employment; while 39 per cent were born in Britain. All those returned for Curraghmore (twenty) and Convamore (twelve) were born in Britain as were ten out of four-teen in Glenart; seventeen out of twenty in Castletown and fourteen out of seventeen in Slane. These were all homes of large landowners and as they commuted more regularly to Britain, they undoubtedly preferred to employ servants who could adapt more readily to condi-tions in London. Anita Leslie, recalling Glaslough at the turn of the century, claimed that 'men servants were invariably English. Irish butlers or valets did not seem to exist'. She recounted a story of two Irish footmen who were brought to London for the ball season during Queen Victoria's golden jubilee year and who 'celebrated' by 'getting drunk and running down Oxford Street shouting, "To Hell with your bloody old queen" — a terrible humiliation for the Leslies', which seems to have been taken as a warning to avoid the employment of Irish footmen in the future.[48]

Of 470 Irish servants, only 14 per cent were locally born empha-sising the fact that landlords preferred to 'import' their servants. Because of this, big houses were not of great economic benefit to locals seeking employment on a permanent basis.

This trend is more pronounced when we focus on the upper ser-vants, those such as butlers, cooks and housekeepers who were at the top of the staff hierarchy. Information was available on fifty butlers. Of these twenty-eight were born in Britain; eight were born in the six counties that now constitute Northern Ireland; and eight more outside the county of employment. Only six were locally born. Similarly, of seventy-eight housekeepers, fifty-five were born in Britain; thirteen outside the county of employment; and only ten were locally born. Of seventy-two cooks, thirty-one were born in Britain;

thirty-four outside the county of employment; and only seven were locally born. In total, only 11.5 per cent of upper servants were locally born. Furthermore, of eleven governesses, seven valets, thirty-seven lady's maids and ninety coachmen/footmen, chauffeurs, only three were locally born. Again this serves to emphasise the fact that land-lords were extremely reluctant to give prestigious posts to locals, or positions in which there was a good deal of contact with the family.

There are a variety of reasons why landlords filled vacancies in their houses, particularly posts of responsibility, with employees from outside the locality. Fifty-five of the sample houses belonged to large landowners who moved frequently between Britain and Ireland. Many of them were married to English wives who may have brought some of their personal servants with them from their own homes when they moved to Ireland. This was undoubtedly true in the case of lady's maids. Most of these Irish landowners retained English houses and socialised with English landlords. They, therefore, had considerable English connections from whom they would have found out about capable servants looking for places. The professionalisa-tion of servants in England had developed during the mid-nineteenth century with the establishment of servant training schools from which many more servants working in Irish houses were recruited.

Ninety-two of the sample houses were Protestant-owned. Between them they returned 717 servants, of whom 71 per cent were also Protestant. Some houses such as Carton and Glenart returned no Catholics at all. These statistics would seem to point to what today might be termed unequal employment opportunity. But one must analyse them in the context of the time to which they applied and the nature of servants' tasks in order to understand them. It would probably be unfair to state that there was a deliberate policy amongst all Protestant landlords to discriminate against Catholic employees (or, indeed, amongst Catholic landlords to discriminate against Protestant employees.) Landlords in the nineteenth and early twentieth centuries took, for example, the education and moral and spiritual development of their children very seriously. Education began in the home. It was, therefore, desirable that nurses, governesses, nannies and whatever other servants children were in regular contact with should share the family's religious beliefs. Perhaps this explains why so many Catholics employed in Protestant big houses tended to have the more menial tasks as scullery or kitchen-maids or laun-dresses. Such jobs kept them out of contact with the family. Of the fourteen servants returned for Shelton in 1911, only the scullery-maid was Catholic (and Welsh). Of the thirteen servants returned for Dartrey, only the laundry-maid and a third house-maid were Catholic (neither was locally born); of fourteen servants returned for Ballyfin, only a house-maid and laundry-maid were Catholic (again neither was locally born). The situation was no different in Catholic-owned big houses. While there was an overall propensity by Protestant land-lords to employ Protestants, there would seem to have been a similar propensity amongst Catholic landlords to employ Catholic servants. Of the fifty-five servants returned for the Catholic houses in the sample, 95 per cent were Catholics. Moore Hall, Dalyston, Dunsandle, Castleffogarty, and Gurteen returned no Protestant servants at all.

The demand for trained Protestant servants is perceptible in estate records and newspaper advertisements. In 1871, Lord Inchiquin was informed that 'it is also a difficult thing to get a man without children — who is also a Protestant'.[49] The Farnhams in Cavan were devout Evangelicals; Lady Farnham frequently used the Protestant Servants' Registration Office in Dublin when wishing to fill a position. From her correspondence it seems that potential employees knew the importance of religion as a prerequisite to employment at Farnham. In the early 1890s one young servant wrote to her: 'My age is 21. Wages 18£ [sic]. I am a Prodestant [sic].'[50] Around the same time, the director of the office wrote to Lady Farnham explaining that the delay in finding a house-maid for her was because 'there is such a demand for Protestant servants'.[51] In the 1911 census, all ten servants returned for Castlegar were Protestants. In January of that year, Lady Mahon had advertised for a house-maid specifying that she be a Protestant. All twelve servants returned for Courtown were Protestant. Again, in January 1911, its owners advertised for a house-maid who had to be: 'Protestant, young, of good height and appearance, early riser....'[52]

Servants were often in closer contact with a landlord's children than were parents themselves. The moral conduct of servants and their religious practices may, therefore, have been deemed important to landlords who wanted their children to be disposed only to what they considered proper influences. The tenth Earl of Fingall 'did not pay a great deal of attention' to his children after his wife died, but he made sure his Catholic son was 'educated first by his sisters' governesses, a stern martinet, and later by an old priest, Fr MacNamara, whom he loved'.[53] In 1871, a fellow landlord inquired of Lord Inchiquin about James Hawkins who had been employed as a butler at Dromoland 'whether he [was] sober, honest and equal to his duties'.[54]

Similarly, there may have been problems with Catholic servants such as cooks and kitchen-maids who would have difficulties with the preparation of meat dishes on a Friday. In rural Ireland, where the local community tended to be staunchly Catholic, and the local big house was more often than not Protestant, Catholic parents may have been just as reluctant to have their children exposed to the very strong influence of the landlord's personality, beliefs and actions.

Religion was only one consideration. The vast majority of Irish landlords were Protestant but from a social point of view the sons and daughters of local Catholic tenants had also distinct disadvantages in landlords' eyes as potential employees, possibly being perceived by landlords to be lacking, for example, the relevant domestic skills.[55] Better training facilities for servants were in place in England, while those training facilities in place in Ireland were geared towards the domestic education of Protestants.[56] The demand for trained Protestant servants in Ireland led to the establishment of institutions such as the Providence Home in Charlemont Street, the Protestant Registration Office in Duke Street, and the Protestant Servants' Registration Office in Anne's Street in Dublin alone in the early to mid-nineteenth-century period. By 1904, the Providence Home had sent 7,000 Protestant girls of 'good moral character' out 'into the world to earn their bread in honourable independence'.[57] Its annual report that year claimed that 'the demand at the home for servants is always much greater than the supply'.[58]

EMPLOYMENT OPPORTUNITY ON THE DEMESNE

There was an almost equal distribution of Protestants and Catholics amongst the 1,054 demesne workers found for the 100 demesnes using the 1911 household schedule returns (48 per cent were Protestants and 52 per cent were Catholics.) On the eight Catholic-owned demesnes, it was found that 86 per cent of workers were Catholics. However, of the four stewards found for these estates, three were Protestants born in Britain. Out of a total of sixty-two stewards, 84 per cent were Protestant; 47 per cent were born in Britain; 31 per cent were born outside the county of employment; and only 22 per cent were locally born. As in the big houses, posts of responsibility on demesnes were largely held by stewards born out-side the county of employment and even stewards employed on Catholic-owned demesnes were usually Protestant. Back in 1871, Lord Inchiquin was having some difficulty in finding a suitable steward. One man, he was informed, 'who would suit you in every way' was 'unfortunately a Roman Catholic'.[59]

The employment situation on demesnes, at least from the 1880s, is partially explainable by the widespread intimidation and boycotting many landlords and their employees were subjected to as the land war gained momentum. There are no statistics that specifically categorise attacks on estate employees but a study of sources such as police reports for the period from 1880 to 1911 suggests that the life of a demesne worker was anything but secure during the period. In September 1882, Lord Kenmare's rent-warner, Daniel Leahy, was murdered by 'Moonlighters' in Kerry.[60] In the same month, one of Lord Ardilaun's bailiffs and his son were found drowned in Lough Mask, their deaths attributed to agitation in the area.[61] In the late 1880s, Purdon Coote, a Cork landowner, said that several local Catholics were anxious to take up vacancies on his estate but were prevented from doing so by the National League. Coote claimed that when he did employ a man from outside the locality:

> A large party of men came with blackened faces and guns, and broke into the house, and asked him if he would leave my employment. He refused to do so, and he was then most severely beaten kicked, struck with a gun over the head ... and left lying for dead.

His wife was also badly beaten and his dog shot dead.[62]

In February 1898, the inspector general reported that 'herds on grazing farms have been hunted and assaulted and other individuals have been violently attacked'.[63] In June 1902, tradesmen on the Clifford estate in Kilkenny were boycotted. In February 1909, a herd on an estate in Clare was murdered because he worked on an estate 'his neighbours wanted divided'. In March 1909, a carpenter on the Blake estate in Galway who ran a poacher off the demesne was later found murdered. In the same year, the gamekeeper and the bailiff on the Pratt estate in Galway had to be afforded 'constant protection' and by February 1913, Richard Kingston and his employees at Mitchelstown Castle had been boycotted for almost a decade.[64]

The simultaneous growth of the land and political movements had left many landlords almost paranoid about their future in Ireland and even about the employment of local Catholics on their estates. In 1893, Lord Ardilaun, in an anti-Home Rule speech, made specific reference to his fear of employing members of his Catholic tenantry in the future. He had heard 'that these people believe that my house is to be turned into three or four factories' in the event of Home Rule becoming a reality.[65] Such fear and mistrust led landlords and their agents to diminish their dependence on local Catholic employees and sometimes to dismiss them and replace them with 'imported' Protestants whom they regarded as more dependable.

Take, for example, T.R. Blackley who became agent to Lord Farnham in Cavan in 1896.[66] Blackley's early correspondence with

Lord Farnham reveals his dissatisfaction with some of the employees on the estate. He first recommended to Lord Farnham that the vacant posts of under-steward and gardener should be filled by English Protestants.[67] Then in February 1897, Blackley and two under-keepers from the locality came upon a poacher on the demesne, but Blackley found he had to apprehend him on his own as neither keeper would come to his assistance 'despite being only 100 yards away'. Thus, he suggested to Lord Farnham that 'a young Scottish or English keeper be got and these two dismissed. A complete stranger would be worth a good deal to the game'.[68] Blackley's recommendation epitomises the dangers, real or imaginary, of employing local Catholics too emotionally involved with their community to be of benefit to the landowner.

In turn, diminishing the number of local Catholics employed on an estate focused resentment upon a landlord. In November 1901, Lord Ashtown dismissed a number of herds at Woodlawn. The county inspector of the RIC reported: 'An ugly feature of this case is the [writing becomes illegible at this point] of the religious element by the enemies of Lord Ashtown. They allege that he is bent on driving all Catholics from his employment'.[69] Extra police protection had to be established on the estate as resentment spread and six months later the police again reported that 'the dismissal by Lord Ashtown of another herd and his alleged intention to replace him by a Scotchman is certain to intensify the bad feeling already existing'.[70] Similarly, T.R. Blackley's policy on the Farnham estate focused much resentment upon him. Almost thirty years later, in April 1922, during the Civil War, this manifested itself in a murder attempt upon him by 'a large number of armed and unknown men purporting to be members of the Irish Republican Army'. Blackley and his son thwarted the attack and in the process are believed to have killed three of the raiders. However, in a later raid his house was burned and he and his family had to leave Ireland and 'seek refuge in England under an assumed name'.[71]

CHANGES POST-FIRST WORLD WAR

The First World War became an important turning point regarding the employment of servants in big houses, as it did in so many other respects. Unfortunately, no household schedule returns are at present available for later than 1911 that would undoubtedly throw much light on the servant situation in Ireland from that year until the end of the period under study. However, some information can be gleaned from the general reports of censuses to show a national decline in the number of people involved in domestic service. (Domestic service does, of course, include city houses, lodging houses and so on.) Between 1881 and 1911, the numbers employed in domestic service declined by 57,000 from 211,000 to 154,000. By 1951, the number employed in domestic service had fallen to 53,000.[72] Therefore, just over one quarter the number employed in 1881 was employed in the domestic service sector in 1951.

What caused this rather dramatic decrease? Although these figures include city houses, lodging houses and so on, one would have to point to the simultaneous decline of the big house and landlord fortunes as a major contributory factor. A popular area in cutbacks would seem to have been a reduction of personnel in big houses and demesnes during times of financial crisis. We have already seen how in 1887, when the plan of campaign was established on his estate, Lord Clonbrock was forced to reduce considerably the number of servants employed in the house.[73] In the late 1890s, Lord Farnham found it necessary to cut back on his demesne staff.[74] Cutbacks such as these led to the closure of domestic servants training institutes such as the one in Charlemont Street before the First World War: its report for 1911 stated that it was impossible to maintain the institute 'owing to the lack of adequate support from the public'.[75] It was, however, in the aftermath of the war that the most drastic cutbacks were made. In 1921, the Earl of Meath was forced to close his conservatory, hothouses, kitchen gardens, and pleasure gardens and thereby 'place several men on the pension list' because the expenditure on Kilruddery was beyond him.[76] Around the same time, the Marquis of Waterford reduced his staff numbers because of the 'rise in wages and abnormal taxation'.[77] When Viscount Monck was forced to alter the management of his estate in 1925, he appointed his solicitor to:

> ... check all domestic accounts so as to obviate any extravagance in domestic expenditure or waste in consumption and to dismiss any servant if there is a cause of complaint of neglect of duty or if in his opinion the service of such servants are not required or that the retention of such servants will be inadvisable for any reasons.[78]

From the 1920s, many big house owners were forced to, or chose to, close their houses thereby ending them as significant rural employment centres. Pre-First World War, the Ormondes were spending in the region of £4,200 per annum on the upkeep of Kilkenny Castle, much of which went to the payment of wages.[79] In the 1920s, this figure fell to an annual average of £1,800 and by the

1930s to £800. In 1935, the Ormondes vacated the castle and from
that year onwards there were no servants employed there on a full-
time basis. By the 1930s, there were no servants employed in
Woodbrook and what would have seemed an unbelievable scenario a
few decades before was now a reality dictated by necessity — members of the family were forced to take turns in keeping the house. As
the Kirkwood's financial situation worsened, Charlie Kirkwood was
called in by the bank and advised to cut down on his number of
employees but at that stage: 'there was no gardener, not even a
proper stable boy. James Currid worked almost single-handed in the
stable yard'.[80] When Sarah Cartey took up her duties as a maid in
Bowen's Court, it was, 'Lavishly kept up, it was at the height of its
Victorian prime. Mr and Mrs Bowen, their nine children, eight
indoor servants and frequent visitors more than filled it'.[81] However,
shortly afterwards, the estate began to run at a loss, severe retrenchment had to be made and 'labourers were turned away from the farm
and most of the indoor servants were sent away'. Sarah was the last
and only servant in the house up to a few years before it was sold
and subsequently demolished in the late 1950s.[82]

There are several other factors to be considered for the decline in
the number of people employed in domestic service. The growth of
the Labour movement in Ireland after the First World War led to a
call for the increase in wages and an improvement in working conditions.[83] A Women's Advisory Committee, set up in Britain 'to consider
the present problems which exist in connection with the question of
domestic service' after the war, recommended wage increases of
around 30–35 per cent on pre-war levels.[84] Although, these increases
were only recommendations, they were indicative of the wage levels
that were now deemed necessary to entice people into service after
the war. It is difficult to assess the wages on offer in Irish big houses
in the 1920s because of the variation from one house to another. But
a study of advertisement columns in *The Irish Times* in 1923 suggest
that cooks and housekeepers were commanding £40–50 per annum,
an increase of around 25 per cent on pre-war levels, while house-
maids were commanding £14–26 per annum, an increase of over
60 per cent on pre-war levels.

People became more reluctant to go into service after the war as
new opportunities opened up in other sectors. In December 1918, the
Women's Advisory Committee pointed out that 'the majority of girls
prefer other occupations, and also that parents are reluctant to let
their daughters take up domestic service as an occupation' because of
'the lack of social status which is at present attached to the occupation'. The loss of social status, the long hours of work and the lack of

companionship were regarded as the three most important reasons for the decline in interest in domestic service in Britain.[85] In January 1920, the *Weekly Irish Times* claimed that 'the servant difficulty in Ireland as elsewhere has assumed serious proportions in recent times, and at the moment many employers have the greatest difficulty in securing domestic servants'.[86] It is probable that many Irish servants took the same course as 400,000 female servants in Britain who, during the war, left service for work in factories.[87] In 1922, a letter to *The Irish Times* claimed: 'The short lived experience of munitions factories etc. and high wages, with free evenings has thoroughly demoralised many and has left to all a new conception of the "rights and liberties"'.[88] In the past, the length of a servant's working day was accepted without question. But in the changing climate of post-war Europe and with the growth of trade unionism long and unsociable working hours became less acceptable.[89] Those wishing to go into service preferred to do so in the growing hotel, restaurant and catering sectors where the length of the working day and week was more structured than in private houses. Between 1926 and 1951, the numbers in private domestic service declined by 32,000, while the numbers employed in hotels, restaurants and catering rose from 7,200 to 14,100.

One should perhaps also take into consideration the coincidence in the scarcity of servants in post-war Ireland with the rise in terrorism that characterised big house life in the early 1920s.[90] The diaries of William Mahon of Castlegar make frequent references to his home being raided during the Civil War. By the end of 1923, his diaries suggest that he had great difficulty in retaining servants: two left his employment in November, followed by three more in December.[91] Elsewhere, other servants suffered at least as much as their employers. In April 1921, two servant girls in Donegal received threatening letters because of their association with some soldiers.[92] In November of the same year, 'terror stricken servants' had to flee from Summerhill to the plantation for shelter during the raid, which resulted in its burning.[93] During one of the many raids on Dunalley, the 'terrified servants' were locked in a room while the rest of the house was ransacked.[94]

Demesne workers found themselves in a similar position. Gamekeepers' houses were frequently raided for arms; some, like John Lyne, gamekeeper to Lord Kenmare, were shot and wounded whether they resisted the raiders or not.[95] As the struggle for the division of demesnes and estates intensified from 1919, employees were forced to give up their jobs in order to make life more difficult for targeted landlords. In November 1919, four armed men entered the home of Martin Lally, herd to Major Hall at Knockbrook, and ordered that he and his four sons stop working for the major as his land was wanted for division.[96] On 11 July 1921, the day the Anglo–Irish truce was called, the home of E.J. Beaumont-Nesbitt's steward in King's County was burned and he was forced to flee Tubberdaly.[97]

Finally, another consideration would have to be the technological developments which began pre-1914 and which were hastened by the war. By the time this study ends in 1950, housekeeping had been revolutionised chiefly by the advent of electricity and the development of labour-saving devices such as vacuums, washing machines and more efficient cooking methods.[98] Staffing levels were reduced as indoor toilets saw the demise of pot-boys; the increase in the number of cars meant footmen were replaced by a single chauffeur; farm machinery reduced the need for so many farm labourers; and businesses began to produce goods formerly made in homes. But the role of labour-saving devices could only be considered significant if big houses had continued to exist in the same way into the twentieth century as they had done beforehand. They did not. The economic decline of landlords had grave consequences for big houses and, subsequently for the servant class. And this was mutually detrimental to both. A big house, which could not afford the employment of a retinue of servants, was one that would suffer decay despite the advent of labour-saving devices.

Conclusion

Servants, perhaps more than anything else, were the outward symbols of the luxurious and leisured lifestyles led by Irish landlords and their families during the Victorian period. They were an integral part of the values and style of living that characterised big house life. In the same way that landlords were acutely conscious of standards in the way that they built up art collections and libraries during the nineteenth century, they were conscious of the standards of servants. The guests they invited to their homes were used to moving in high society milieus, where the quality and number of servants indicated the status level of a home. For that reason professionally trained servants and particularly English ones were widely employed.

During the last quarter of the nineteenth century and the early part of the twentieth century big house cutbacks were gradual and uneven. But the number of servants employed in Irish big houses prior to 1914 is a solid reflection of the fact that Irish landowners clung on to certain aspects of their old way of life. Pride and the necessity of maintaining outward displays of grandeur amongst the larger landowners may have been a factor. Elizabeth Bowen once wrote that 'big house people admit only one class distinction: they instinctively "place" a person who makes a poor mouth'.[99] Similarly, Lennox Robinson, in his youth, was told that it was very vulgar to 'bemoan your poverty' and that 'you must never hint that you had not the food, the clothes, all the pleasant things of life you could desire.' In this context an anecdote related by Mark Bence-Jones in his *Twilight of the Ascendancy* is appropriate. In 1904, a young girl recently married into a Kilkenny landed family paid her first visit to Kilkenny Castle. She was amazed by the display of liveried footmen, the Ormonde gold plate and the selection of priceless tapestries on display. However, she was even more astounded when Lady Ormonde confided in her: 'We are very poor'.[100] And yet, this was the same year that the Ormondes had doubled household expenditure in order to entertain royalty!

Much changed in the post-war period. There was to be no rejuvenation of the domestic service industry. With the spread of education and new ideas and alternative forms of employment domestic service went into irreversible decline. Young women were no longer prepared to be perceived or treated as skivvies in an age when social equality was gaining more and more credence and any work deemed to be demeaning was considered unacceptable.[101] As the twentieth century progressed, those who retained big houses in Ireland found themselves increasingly unable to replace servants as their old ones died. In the early 1960s, Major Carew of Ballimona in Waterford summed up this predicament:

> A couple of years ago the housemaid died suddenly — she had been here twenty-six years. Last year three old retainers died and last April my housekeeper died. She had been here nearly all her life. So now I have no help in the house.[102]

7

THE BURNING OF IRISH BIG HOUSES 1920–23

'A BONFIRE FOR A GENERATION'

If there is a war of extermination waged on us, that war will also exterminate British interest in Ireland; because if they wage a war of extermination on us, I may not see it finished, but by God, no Loyalist in north Cork will see its finish and it's about time someone told Lloyd George that.

SEAN MOYLAN DURING TREATY DEBATE, 21 DECEMBER 1921
*DÁIL ÉIREANN OFFICIAL REPORT: DEBATE ON THE TREATY
BETWEEN GREAT BRITAIN AND IRELAND* (N.D.), P. 146

INTRODUCTION

In many ways, the revolutionary period from 1919 to 1923 realised the fears of Irish landlords which had been growing since the land war began some forty years previously. During these years, landlords, largely because of their socio-political, economic and religious backgrounds, were to suffer outrage and intimidation on a scale the like of which their class had not experienced in living memory, not even at the height of the land war in the 1880s. This is one of the more deplorable features of the period that historians have largely failed to address.[1] A major feature of this intimidation was the burning of big houses.[2]

'THE ORANGE BRIGHT SKY CREPT AND SMOULDERED'

February, 1920. The War of Independence was very much in its embryonic stages. IRA activity was largely concerned with the acquisition of arms and the neutralisation of the RIC as a law enforcement body. The burning of big houses had not yet begun in earnest. (From the beginning of that month to the end of May, only four houses were to be burned.) Instead the IRA were intent on destroying evacuated RIC barracks throughout the country. Rumours began to circulate that abandoned big houses, whose owners had gone to live on a more permanent basis in England since the Troubles began, were to be used as substitutes for destroyed barracks. With few exceptions, the county inspectors of the RIC were reporting a rise in crime rates in their areas and a decreasing ability on their behalf to identify perpetrators. In February, the Meath county inspector of the RIC reported:

> ... this county has not been in a peaceable state during the month of February. A large number of outrages [twenty-one] have been committed and there is a marked unrest in all sections of the community. Rich and poor alike are in constant fear of raids. Information of any kind is becoming more and more difficult to obtain as the people are afraid that their neighbours may think that they are in league with the police and fear subsequent intimidation or worse.[3]

He felt that while the people of Meath were generally: 'law abiding ... outside influence and example and proximity to Dublin seems to be changing the character and disposition of the people for the worse'.[4]

At the beginning of that month, Summerhill, formerly the home of Lord Langford, and now the home of his successor Colonel Rowley, became one of the first big houses in the country to be burned. On the night of 4 February the only occupants in Summerhill were the butler and a number of servants, as Colonel Rowley had been living in England since December 1919.[5] At 10 p.m., the butler heard a knock at the back door. Having consulted with the servants, he decided not to open it, obviously fearing at least a raid for arms. The raiders, between thirty and forty of them, then broke down the back door (or depending on which report is more accurate broke into the house 'in a number of different places'), seized about thirty gallons of petrol, poured it over the floors and set the house on fire. The terrified servants escaped out through a passage and hid in the plantation until the raiders left.

When it was safe for the servants to come out they raised the alarm by sending a telegram to Trim police station. By the time the police arrived: 'the fire had gained such a hold that there were no hopes of saving the building'.[6] The police fired rifle bullets into a large tank of water on the top of the house but the water made no impact on the flames. The absence of proper fire extinguishing appliances meant that the police and some civilian helpers could do nothing to prevent the house being 'reduced to a mass of blackened ruins' with the complete loss of its contents. The estimated cost of the damage was £200,000.[7]

What was the motivation behind the burning of Summerhill? On 5 February an official report, issued from Dublin Castle, claimed that the vacated Summerhill had been burned by the IRA in order to prevent military occupation by British forces.[8] The rumour regarding its proposed occupation seems to have been quite widespread. Lady Fingall, for example, had heard that Col Rowley had been corresponding with the military authorities and that one of these letters was intercepted by the local IRA.[9] This was largely corroborated many years later by Sean Boylan, the local IRA leader:

> In the spring of 1921 I received a letter from GHQ to the effect that the Auxiliaries were about to occupy Summerhill Castle ... it appears that the information was received by Mick Collins from one of his men in Dublin Castle who had seen a decoded message to that effect. I called on Battalion Adjutant, Bernard Dunne, and instructed him to have Summerhill Castle burned down immediately. He conveyed the message to Michael Graham, Captain of the Summerhill Company, who carried out the order within twenty-four hours.

Boylan claimed that the burning of Summerhill was imperative because of the castle's strategic position, located as it was 'on high ground which commanded one of the routes to the west. The Auxiliaries with field glasses could have swept the country.'[10]

June–July, 1921. On 20 June Col-Cmdt Lambert, commanding officer of the 13th Brigade, Athlone, and Colonel Challoner and their two wives were driving through Glasson in County Westmeath when six IRA men attempted to stop their car. Col-Cmdt Lambert accelerated but the IRA men opened fire, killing Lambert and wounding Mrs Challoner.[11] The police believed that the original intention of the IRA men had been to kidnap Lambert and hold him hostage, bargaining his release for that of Seán MacEoin, the leader of the Longford IRA, who had recently been captured.[12] A week later, General H.S. Jeudwine, commanding officer of the 5th Division at the Curragh, issued the following statement:

> His [Lambert's] brigade will best avenge his death, as he himself would have wished, by the strict adherence to duty which he did his best to inculcate, and by a determination to maintain, by regular methods, at all risks and through all difficulties, the sovereignty and authority in Ireland of the King and his government, whose servants we are.[13]

Jeudwine's statement went unheeded. A week later, a number of Black and Tans burned five farm houses in Coosan. The 'terror' began at 2 a.m. on 1 July when a 'number of masked men [estimated at twelve] who carried revolvers and wore trench coats and tweed caps' called at the home of Thomas Duffy. Duffy, his wife, four children and ninety-year-old aunt were told to 'clear out'. Petrol was poured on the beds and furniture in their house and set alight. The Black and Tans then burned four neighbouring houses belonging to the Wansboro, Farrell, Coghlan and Moore families. Some of the families attempted to save their possessions but were prevented from doing so and were 'roughly handled'.[14] Next, the Black and Tans moved on to nearby Mount Temple where they burned the home of Anne Hanevy, one of whose sons was interned at Ballykinlar.[15]

At 3.30 a.m. on the morning of 3 July an estimated sixty armed men arrived at Moydrum Castle, the home of Lord Castlemaine who was in Scotland at the time. Lady Castlemaine was in the house with her only daughter and eight servants. The raiders, a party of 'young men dressed in civilian attire', knocked at the front door and when they were refused entrance they smashed the lower windows and entered. Some of them made their way upstairs where they met Lady Castlemaine on the landing. She was told by one of them: 'We will give you five minutes to clear out. We are burning your house as a reprisal of [sic] the recent burnings at Coosan and Mount Temple'.[16] The raiders spent the next thirty minutes going into each of the thirty or so rooms in the house, collecting all the furniture and placing it in piles in the centre of each room. They then saturated these piles with petrol they had commandeered from Lady Castlemaine's chauffeur. In the meantime the family and servants managed to evacuate some of their personal belongings and the family silver plate collection. By the time the police and military arrived: 'the castle and its contents were beyond salvage'. The damage was estimated at £150,000.[17]

The following day Mr Justice Dodd, addressing the grand jury assembled at Mullingar, said that he:

> ... did not know why these beautiful residences throughout the country should have been burned. There seemed to be an idea that they were to be used for military occupation. But from inquiries he had made this was a delusion, as not one of these residences had been taken over by the military and not one was intended to be taken over.[18]

But such rumours were prevalent throughout the country — well-founded in a number of cases — and provided the motive, or, perhaps, the pretext, for the burning of such big houses as Summerhill. However, in the case of Moydrum (and Creggan burned the same night) revenge for the burnings carried out by the Black and Tans in the area seems to have been the main motive.

January, 1923. County Kildare, as a whole, had largely escaped the ravages of the War of Independence. Until then there had been no real animosity shown towards the landed class, only two big houses had been raided for arms and no big houses had been burned.[19] However, the Civil War was to infringe much more upon Kildare life and the burning of Palmerstown on 29 January 1923 became the first such attack on private house property in the county.[20] Shortly after 9 p.m., as Lord and Lady Mayo were finishing dinner, a party of armed men arrived at the house. They first knocked on the front door but the butler refused them entry.[21] Five minutes later they knocked on the servants' entrance door at the back of the house. When Patrick Behan, the hall-boy, opened the door, three armed men forced their way past him, one of them claiming to be 'an orderly officer of the Irish Republican Army'.[22] When they met the Earl of Mayo they told him that they were going to burn his house in reprisal for the execution of six Anti-Treatyites at the Curragh.[23] However, another of the raiders later asked Lady Mayo if her husband was a senator.[24] The same party of raiders may, therefore, have had different motives for burning Palmerstown: some of them may have wished to burn it in response to the government's policy of executions introduced as part of the Public Safety Act the previous November, while others may have wished to burn it in response to Liam Lynch's order issued around the same time that all senators' houses should be burned.[25]

The Earl of Mayo asked for time to remove his paintings. The raiders who 'behaved courteously while in the house' granted him his request but limited his time to fifteen minutes. Only three of the more valuable paintings, the family plate, some of the contents of the housekeeper's room and the study, and clothes belonging to the family were removed. The raiders then saturated the carpets in the main reception rooms on the ground floor with petrol and set them alight. Lord Mayo and a groom named Hurt made futile attempts to extinguish the fire in the dining-room. The Curragh military fire brigade arrived around midnight but: 'could do nothing, the whole house being then in the grip of the fire, and the hose lines insufficiently long to secure any considerable quantity of water'.[26] The fire raged all through the night, floor after floor collapsed with 'deafening noise', cut-stone window facings and turrets split with the heat and 'flew in splinters and crashed to the ground'. By morning the wine cellar was the only part of the main building that was undamaged. However, the outoffices and servants' quarters built at the northern end of the house were practically unscathed.[27]

April, 1923. At 2 a.m. on the morning of 15 April, armed men arrived at Tubberdaly the home of E.J. Beaumont-Nesbitt, located outside Rhode in King' County.[28] Beaumont-Nesbitt was not in residence at the time, having lived there only occasionally since the recent deaths of his son who had been killed in action during the

Great War in 1917 and his wife who had died in 1918. The raiders broke into the house, ordered the servants out and as in the other burnings described above, they sprinkled the floors and furniture with petrol before setting them alight. These raiders were even better prepared and seemingly less patient than most for when they realised that the petrol was 'not doing its work quick enough', they used home-made bombs.[29]

The motivation for the burning of Tubberdaly can be traced back to the day the Anglo–Irish truce was called. On that day, 11 July 1921, agrarian agitation began on the Beaumont-Nesbitt estate, or more particularly the 1,225-acre demesne that the landlord had retained for ranching and the breeding of pure-bred Aberdeen Angus cattle.[30] This initial agitation was linked to the earlier dismissal by E.J. Beaumont-Nesbitt of three demesne labourers, one of whom, Christopher Jones, later became the alleged ringleader of local people who wanted Nesbitt's demesne land divided.[31] The first person to suffer as a reprisal for the dismissal of the labourers was Lewis Frazer, the Beaumont-Nesbitt's land steward whose home was burned on 11 July and he and his family forced to flee the area. Jones reputedly sent threatening letters to Lewis Frazer's successor, Mr McMullan, warning him not to interfere or 'he would get what Frazer got'.[32] However, McMullan was intent on carrying out his duties and so he ignored what he considered to be idle threats.

McMullan had no more trouble until September 1922 when he received more threatening letters. At this stage Jones started to graze his own cattle, without authority, on the Tubberdaly estate. McMullan called the estate employees together and informed them that 'if Jones was allowed to graze the lands, it would lead to others doing the same, and eventually Mr Nesbitt might be forced to give up the lands with the result that they would lose their employment'.[33] Some of the employees helped McMullan to drive Jones's cattle off the estate (seven refused to do so.) The night of the drive a party of nine or ten men arrived at McMullan's house, dragged him out, put him on his knees and threatened to shoot him. Again McMullan refused to be intimidated and continued to carry on his duties.

The culmination of the intimidation was the burning of Tubberdaly House in April 1923. In June McMullan was revisited by a party of raiders:

> The windows were broken, door forced, and McMullan pulled out of the bed into the yard, put on his knees and threatened to be shot. He was then conveyed to the road by five or six of the raiders, made get on his bicycle and ordered never to put a foot inside Tubberdaly again.[34]

This time McMullan had had enough and he and his family moved to England. In July Beaumont-Nesbitt himself received a letter from Jones which Beaumont-Nesbitt forwarded to the Minister for Home Affairs as part of his plea for help. Jones's letter read:

> This is the fourth letter I wrote you. Got no reply about the farm. I have my case entered this two years. I expect you have a letter from IRA headquarters.... I am willing to buy the farm honestly as no one else will be allowed to do.[35]

The minister acted on Beaumont-Nesbitt's behalf and Jones was subsequently arrested and tried for 'illegal possession of a farm of land'. But there were difficulties in securing a conviction because, a guard reported, Jones's family was: 'connected with the Irregulars [and] he would get a certain amount of assistance from that section of the people in the locality'. The only person who was likely to give evidence against Jones was the steward, McMullan, but he was by then in England, 'out of harm's way'.[36] Jones remained in custody at least until early 1924, but his family remained in possession of land and a house at Tubberdaly belonging to Beaumont-Nesbitt.[37]

There is little doubt but that the burning of Tubberdaly was primarily motivated by agrarian issues. The involvement of Christopher Jones also suggests that there was something of a personal vendetta against E.J. Beaumont-Nesbitt because of his dismissal from the latter's employment. But Jones and his allies saw in the social chaos of the time an opportunity to secure land for themselves and their families. This was just as obvious to the authorities of the time. A local guard reported that the whole campaign of agitation had been originated: 'with a view to terrorising Mr Nesbitt and his employees and ultimately to succeed by such methods to have the ranch divided up and distributed'.[38] In 1925, the Land Commission compulsorily acquired 1,225 acres of untenanted land at Tubberdaly, paying E.J. Beaumont-Nesbitt £10,200 in 4.5 per cent land bonds. The families of some of those who had been involved in the burning of the house and the raids on Frazer and McMullan were amongst those who received parcels of land ranging from four acres to sixty acres. From these people's point of view the burning of Tubberdaly had been a worthwhile exercise.

The motives behind the burning of Summerhill, Palmerstown, Moydrum and Tubberdaly essentially summarise the reasons for the arson attacks on big houses throughout the country. Some were burned for what could loosely be termed political or military reasons — in revenge or as reprisal for atrocities carried out against civilians during the War of Independence (who may or may not have been active supporters of the IRA and Sinn Féin). Some were burned to prevent occupation by the British forces or later by either of the Civil War IRA factions; some houses were burned because they were the homes of Free State senators; while many more were burned because local people wanted land held in landlords' hands divided. The motives behind the burnings of these individual houses may seem fairly clear-cut, but as we shall see below nothing is clear-cut when trying to determine what drove the various factions to burn big houses. W.J.H. Tyrell of Ballindoolin illustrated this when he tried to figure out why an unsuccessful attempt had been made to burn his house in December 1922. He wrote that it could have been because he allowed the British military to stay in a vacant house belonging to him at Monasteroris outside Edenderry. It could have been because he had been a justice of the peace for forty-eight years. Perhaps he was chosen because he was a deputy-lieutenant 'always ready to help the government'; because he had a son in the British army; or because he had 'tried to get rid of a herd and caretakers' for allowing local people to graze their cattle on his lands.[39]

LANDLORD INTIMIDATION DURING THE WAR OF INDEPENDENCE

Big house burnings were, however, just one aspect of a much wider form of intimidation directed against landowners (who were not all necessarily landlords) from around 1917 to 1923. Social revolution thrived amidst political revolution. The IRA action directed against the forces of law and order created the chaotic conditions that allowed agrarian agitators (many of whom were IRA members themselves) free rein to give physical outlet to the emotional frustration that had been gathering and festering since the late 1870s.

In the past, even at the height of the land war, the houses and property of landlords were rarely harmed inside their demesne walls. One of the main reasons for this was the protection afforded by the RIC.[40] The judicial system may not have been all that effective in convicting perpetrators from the late 1870s, but this did not prevent the RIC from fulfilling their primary duties as law enforcers. When the War of Independence began in late 1919, the RIC became the IRA's primary targets, their ability to maintain social order in the countryside was destroyed and landlords subsequently became more vulnerable to attack than they had been for generations. During the first three months of 1920, approximately 500 police barracks and huts were evacuated by the RIC in outlying areas. By the end of June, the IRA had destroyed 424 of these to prevent their future re-occupation. A further sixteen occupied barracks were also destroyed and another twenty-nine damaged.[41] Consequently, in Tipperary, the police reported that 'well disposed persons were terrorised and could not be given adequate protection'. In Donegal, 'Loyalists' were reportedly 'dismayed at the further concentration of the police, which delivered them into the hands of the lawless element'. Meanwhile, in Monaghan, the county inspector wrote: 'It is unfortunate that this course of action could not be avoided as it has caused apprehension among law abiding citizens in the localities affected who feel they are left without adequate protection'.[42]

The consequences of the withdrawal of protection from outlying districts are exemplified in a letter from a Clare landowner to the Irish Unionist Alliance (IUA). In April 1920:

> The conditions of affairs in my neighbourhood in Co. Clare are beyond description; there is no protection whatever for life or property. Recently an attempt was made by some forty masked men, armed with rifles, revolvers and axes, to raid my house. They got in by rushing the back premises of the house. They reduced the servants to a state of terror by threatening to shoot them, seized the steward's gun and tried to gag him with a rifle butt. I immediately armed myself with a repeating rifle, and fired at the raiders from the lobby, forcing them to retire, one of their number being wounded. I have since been warned repeatedly that my life is in danger. The houses of most of the respectable people in my neighbourhood have been raided, but such is the terrorism that exists that many who have suffered in this way are afraid to report what has occurred lest worse should befall them. I reported the raid on my house to the authorities, who sent down a small detachment of infantry, but recalled them after about three weeks. The police were then withdrawn from Scariff, and the barracks closed, leaving no police at all for a distance of over fifteen miles.[43]

He found himself with no option but to shut up his house and take his family away, presumably to England, fearing that when he was gone his house would be 'broken into and destroyed'.

The growth of a new land war and the type of agrarian crimes directed against landowners at this time have been discussed elsewhere in this work. There were many other equally if not more deplorable crimes directed against the landlord class and their associates which do not seem to have been motivated by agrarianism but rather by sectarianism or loosely defined political reasons. In August 1920, seventy-year-old Major Johnstone was bludgeoned to death with sticks and iron bars near his home at Ardara in Donegal. An inquest

was called but: 'no juror daring to attend fell through'.[44] The following month, during a raid for arms at Hilton Park, the sister of Major
John Madden was shot and seriously wounded.[45] In May 1921, John
Bagot and his wife of Ballyturin in Galway, Margaret Gregory (widow
of Robert Gregory of Coole), Captain Blake (the district inspector of
the RIC), Captain Cornwallis and Mr McCreevy were ambushed outside the gates of Ballyturin by a number of armed men. Mrs Gregory
was the only survivor. She later wrote:

> For myself, I felt that death might come at any moment and hoped
> that the bullet might come through my head and terminate that long
> drawn out agony. Mrs Blake was still kneeling and I heard the sound
> like running water from a tap, as the blood poured from a lacerated
> wound in her neck and chest. A volley was then fired at Mrs Blake:
> she fell sideways pierced by eleven bullets, her head just resting on
> her husband's feet.[46]

As such crimes and continuous raids for arms on big houses grew,
landlords and their representatives called for government protection.
In July 1920, at the Orange celebrations in Monaghan, the British
government was called on to deal resolutely with: 'the cruel and
treacherous warfare which is being carried out in the country involving the sacrifice of the lives of loyal men and the senseless
destruction of life and property'.[47] The following year, at a meeting in
Cavan, Rev Little interpreted the deeds of the IRA as, 'an alarming
attempt to rout Protestants out of the country' and added that he
thought it a shame that the British government 'should allow good
citizens to be hustled about'.[48] In April 1921, the inspector general
was gravely concerned about the 'intimidation of Loyalists' that
ranged from 'murder downwards'. He emphasised to the chief secretary that: 'THE OPINION OF CIVILIANS IS THAT THE GOVERNMENT CANNOT
AND WILL NOT TAKE ADEQUATE STEPS TO ENFORCE LAW AND ORDER'.[49] In
June, the county inspector of Cork West Riding wrote that Loyalists
there felt they had been 'deserted by the government and that
politics are engaging the government's attention rather than their
protection'.[50]

Police patrols were not seen as the answer to the problem by
landowners. In March 1920, R.E. Longfield, a Cork landowner,
thought that 'the chance of their being in the right place at the right
time' was 'very remote' and that the small police barracks should
have been 'strengthened and not vacated'.[51] The introduction of
the Auxiliaries and Black and Tans was not seen to be any more
beneficial.[52] On the other hand, army officers, despite their close

association with the landed class, failed to understand the latter's lack of support or, indeed, to understand their growing fears to co-operate. The reaction of Captain Despard in Lennox Robinson's *The Big House* is indicative of this. In a drunken outburst, Despard tells Kate Alcock:

> Not guts enough. 'Scuse my language. But true. Whiners, that's what you are. 'Why doesn't the government.... Must establish law and order.... But Black and Tans are rather naughty.' Compromise, conference, save your bacon. Wow, Wow.[53]

Even one of the landed class's arch supporters, *The Irish Times*, claimed in April 1920 that they had 'only themselves to blame' for their lack of initiative. The editor argued that after 'the whole machinery of law [had] been thrown on the scrap heap' and the police had withdrawn from outlying areas, landlords should have persuaded the British government to intervene.[54]

However, one must consider that landowners' fears were more real than imagined. Nora Robinson, sister of Lennox, wrote about her anxieties during 1921:

> English people in their law abiding country had no conception of the horror and dread and all pervading misery of a war fought round one's own home, in one's own countryside: a war which meant daily and hourly suspicion and discomfort as well as fear of maiming and death.[55]

In 1922, Nora's mother wrote to her: 'We are all right and nothing has happened to us beyond the constant nervous strain, especially at night, when the firing around has sometimes been very tiring, I thought I was very brave but I have felt it very much'.[56] The inspector general was aware of the prevailing fear. In March 1921 he wrote: 'Behind the blocked roads, the houses of Loyalists have been raided and money and property stolen. The injured persons do not complain to the police as they fear their lives would be forfeit'.[57]

THE BURNING OF BIG HOUSES DURING THE WAR OF INDEPENDENCE

During the third Home Rule crisis, George O'Callaghan-Westropp, a Clare landowner, sketched out 'Notes on the defence of Irish country houses' in which he wrote that landowners should be prepared to defend their houses from raids by groups of land-hungry Nationalists in the event of Home Rule becoming a reality.[58] O'Callaghan-Westropp obviously feared attacks on his house for agrarian reasons. While seventy-six big houses were burned in the twenty-six counties from the outbreak of the war of independence to the calling of the Anglo–Irish truce on 11 July 1921, it is extremely difficult to estimate with certainty the number which were actually burned solely for agrarian reasons (see Table 7.1, p. 286). The simultaneous growth in military activity and the fact that agrarian agitators and IRA members were often perceived as being, and probably were, one and the same, confused perception of the motives.

In February 1920, when the first big house was burned, agrarian agitation was endemic throughout large areas of the country. IRA attacks on RIC barracks became a precondition for the burning of big houses which, in turn, became a new and more frightening form of intimidation aimed at pressurising many landlords to part with their retained lands. The burning of Derrycastle in Tipperary, for example, was linked to local agrarian agitation and the struggle to have its demesne divided.[59] There was a hint of agrarianism in the burning of Portumna, situated as it was in the traditionally disturbed county of Galway, and which had been leased by Captain Shawe-Taylor, one of the few landlords to have been murdered during the War of Independence. Shawe-Taylor's murder was linked to local agitation and his refusal to sell part of his estate. Sir Arthur Vicars was murdered on 4 April 1921 and his house, Kilmorna, was burned. A note was pinned to his chest warning spies to beware. However, IRA headquarters later disclaimed all responsibility.[60] There is the possibility that Vicar's murder may have been perpetrated by a local agrarian society. They may have used the more potentially effective name of the IRA in the same way that local societies had used names such as 'Captain Moonlight' or 'O'Donnell the Boo' during the land war of the 1880s in an attempt to intimidate.

Military reasons, if rather dubious at times, were in the main cited as the reasons for the burning of big houses. From April 1920 to July 1921 marked the second phase of the war, which saw the introduction of the Black and Tans and Auxiliaries to Ireland and the growth of reprisal and counter-reprisal. Prior to the end of April, only four big houses had been burned but the growth in terror forced many owners to abandon their homes which then became regarded by the military as convenient substitutes for the empty or destroyed RIC barracks in rural areas. At least one third of the seventy-two big houses burned during the second phase of the war were destroyed by the IRA either because the military were reputedly about to take them over as billets or because the military had already occupied them and left. From November 1919 to May 1920, Moorock in King's County had been uninhabited. At the beginning of May the IRA burned nearby Ballycumber barracks and a rumour subsequently circulated that Moorock was to be used as a substitute. Lest this should happen, the IRA burned Moorock later that month.[61] When, in June 1920, three big houses were burned in Galway, the county inspector wrote to the inspector general: 'The military were warned not to send men out to stay at these kind of houses. The CO disregarded the warning with the above result'.[62] However, an official military order not to use 'Loyalist homes' as billets was largely responsible for the fact that no big houses were burned from September to the end of December 1920.

When the Black and Tan war intensified from the beginning of 1921, arson attacks on big houses once again became a major feature of IRA policy, official or otherwise. From the beginning of January 1921 to the end of April nine big houses were burned. Again, military occupation continued to be a prime motivating factor. From 22 to 26 March, for example, Ballyheigue in County Kerry was occupied by the RIC, Black and Tans and the Auxiliaries. A day or two after they left the house was burned.[63]

An IRA ambush at Kilmichael in County Cork on 28 November 1920, in which eighteen Auxiliaries were killed, led to the introduction of a system of martial law and official reprisals in the south-western counties, allowing for the burning of houses of those implicated in an IRA ambush. In June 1921, IRA headquarters issued their own retaliatory general order officially authorising the burning of houses 'belonging to the most active enemies of Ireland' as legitimate targets. A warning was added that 'no one shall be regarded as an enemy of Ireland, whether they may be described locally as Unionist, Orangeman etc. except [when] they are actively anti-Irish in their actions'.[64]

It was from the beginning of June to the calling of the Anglo–Irish truce that the heaviest concentration of big house burnings took place. During those six weeks, thirty-three big houses (or 43 per cent of the total) were destroyed. Big house owners were regarded as being 'anti-Irish'. This was not necessarily as a result of their actions but rather because of their cultural and political alienation from the majority of the population in the twenty-six counties. Local IRA leaders perceived big houses to be suitable targets for reprisals, and, of course, they were also soft targets. The county inspector of Tipperary reported in June: 'It is thought that the campaign of burning country gentlemen's houses is only just starting and that we may expect to see a lot more of it done in the near future'.[65] At the end of that month a headline in *The Irish Times* referred to the 'House burning mania' that was sweeping the country.[66]

The worst affected county was Cork which alone accounted for over one-third of all big houses burned during the War of Independence. By May 1921, the IRA there had developed its own system of reprisals. At the beginning of that month three big houses were burned by the Cork IRA in reprisal for the burning of six houses allegedly owned by 'active supporters of armed rebels' by order of Col Cameron, commanding officer of the 16th Infantry Brigade at the end of April. When the raiders arrived at one of them, Convamore, Lord Listowel's niece was handed the following note, which was addressed to her uncle:

> On Wednesday the 13th inst., the enemy bombed and destroyed six houses of Republicans as reprisals for IRA activities on the 10th inst. You being an aggressively anti-Irish person, and your residence being in the battalion area of enemy reprisals, I [cmdt. Cork no. 2 brigade] have hereby ordered that same be destroyed as part of our counter reprisal.[67]

The county inspector of Cork reported in May: 'Counter reprisals in the form of burning Loyalist houses is a more or less new feature'. The following month he was shocked by the fact that 'Loyalists are being persecuted, their mansions and houses are being burned, and a huge number of them have cleared out of the county'.[68] Tom Barry, leader of the West Cork IRA who had carried out the Kilmichael ambush, later wrote in his memoirs that when the authorities decided on a policy of burning the houses of IRA supporters they: 'forgot to take into consideration [that] Ireland was studded with the castles, mansions and residences of the British ascendancy who had made their homes here'.[69] Barry claimed that: 'a note was sent to the British military commander in West Cork, informing him that for every Republican home destroyed from that date, the homes of two British Loyalists would be burned to the ground'.[70] The tone of Barry's writing suggests that the local IRA had little sympathy for big house owners and that their policy was not only dictated by the British reprisals but also their own sense of ancestral grievance:

> Castles, mansions and residences were sent up in flames by the IRA immediately after the British fire gangs had razed the homes of Irish Republicans. Our people were suffering in this competition of terror, but the British Loyalists were paying dearly, the demesne walls were tumbling and the British ascendancy was being destroyed. Our only fear was that, as time went on, there would be no more Loyalists' homes to destroy, for we intended to go on to the bitter end. If the Republicans of West Cork were to be homeless and without shelter,

then so too, would be the British supporters. West Cork might become a barren land of desolation and misery, but at least the Britishers would have more than their full share of the sufferings.[71]

Analysis by Erhard Rumpf and A.C. Hepburn shows that British reprisals were primarily located in the Munster counties of Tipperary, Cork, Kerry, Limerick and Clare.[72] Peter Hart's more recent analysis of the geography of revolution in Ireland from 1917 to 1923 shows that these were also the counties where IRA violence was most intense during the War of Independence.[73] It is hardly surprising then that forty-two of the seventy-six big houses (55 per cent) burned during the War of Independence were located in these counties (see Table 7.2, p. 286). Cork, where twenty-six big houses were burned, had the highest number of towns and villages affected by British reprisals and by far the highest incidence of IRA violence. On the other hand, Connaught involved itself very little in the war. Here only four big houses were burned, three in Galway and one in Sligo. In the three Ulster counties, eleven big houses were burned. Donegal, where two houses were burned, had the highest incidence of British reprisals but the lowest level of IRA violence. Four houses were burned in Monaghan which had one of the highest levels of IRA violence outside of Munster and where the War of Independence was fought very much along sectarian lines with the local IRA being faced with Protestant paramilitaries as well as the British forces. Disregarding Dublin because it was the headquarters of both the British and IRA organisation, large tracts of Leinster saw little significant military activity during the war particularly the prosperous farming counties of Kildare, Meath, Wicklow, Carlow and Queen's County. No big houses were burned in Kildare or Carlow and only one was burned in each of seven of the other Leinster counties. Westmeath had the highest number of burnings, six. Significantly, it also had the highest number of towns and villages affected by British reprisals, six as well and after Longford had the highest level of IRA violence in the province outside of Dublin. Here, as we have seen, Moydrum was burned in July 1921 as the result of a spiral of reprisals. On the other hand, only one big house was burned in Longford despite the fact that during 1920 in particular it had the second highest rate of IRA violence in the country, surpassed only by Cork.[74]

It is difficult to generalise that all big houses were burned for agrarian or military reasons when the War of Independence engendered such bitterness on both sides. There was a feeling in Loyalist circles that some houses were burned because their owners 'showed themselves on too friendly terms with the forces of the crown'.[75] After one big house was burned in Tipperary in April 1921, an official report from Dublin Castle claimed that it was because there had been a rumour that the owner 'had suggested that the Black and Tans should come to the district'.[76] Around the same time, Timoleague, home of Robert Travers, was burned because he was reputed to be on friendly terms with the British army officers stationed locally.[77] Furthermore, houses other than Doolin in Clare, the home of Francis MacNamara, may have been burned by the Black and Tans because their owners were reputedly Sinn Féin supporters.[78]

Almost a year earlier, Oakgrove, home of Captain John Bowen-Colthurst was burned in Cork. On the night of 25 April 1916, Bowen-Colthurst had taken the pacifist, Francis Sheehy Skeffington, as hostage with him when doing a tour of duty in Rathmines. Sheehy Skeffington witnessed Bowen-Colthurst's murder of a young man named Coade that night. The following morning Sheehy Skeffington and two other prisoners were shot in Portobello barracks. A court-martial followed but the plea was accepted that Bowen-Colthurst had been of unsound mind at the time of the murder in Rathmines.[79] During the latter part of 1919, the Bowen-Colthurst family was subjected to intimidation, which the inspector general put down to the fact that 'some persons were shot at Portobello barracks in 1916'.[80] It seems as if the culmination of this intimidation was the burning of Oakgrove.

Possibly many more big houses would have been burned during the War of Independence had not potential arsonists been deterred by the large military presence in the country. Also, the Republican police and the Dáil courts filled rather successfully the vacuum left by the RIC and the collapse of the judicial system.[81] Landlords may have had more protection than they believed, for when law and order disintegrated completely during the Civil War, they were exposed to even more atrocities than during the War of Independence and the growth in big house burnings escalated dramatically.

THE COMMANDEERING OF BIG HOUSES DURING THE TRUCE

The Anglo–Irish truce, which began on 11 July 1921, brought little respite for the big house. From July to the end of December, the IRA continued to drill and prepare in the event of another outbreak of hostilities. During this period at least thirty big houses were commandeered by the IRA and used as training camps in much the same way they had been used by the UVF in the northern counties (with the consent of their owners) less than a decade previously. These camps were seen by some county inspectors as part of a settled plan 'to train and equip and organise the IRA' and 'to overcome the non-combatant and neutral sections of the population'.[82] A rather tongue-in-cheek county inspector in Kildare reported in September: 'Training camps [are] run on comfortable grounds here. Only the largest houses are fit to be commandeered'.[83] Amongst these was Harristown, home of the late Percy La Touche, which had been lying empty for some time, and where 200 IRA men were billeted for a week. In turn, they then used Kildangan and Dowdenstown in the same county.[84]

Similar camps were established throughout the country. In October 1921, the police received information that Duckett's Grove in Carlow was being used as a prison 'for loyal subjects' although no further information was found to substantiate this.[85] Around the same time, an estimated 150 IRA men spent two weeks training at Ashfield in Queen's County. Fifteen men trained at Highpark in Wicklow. IRA men moved between Annadale and Clooncarrig in Leitrim; fifty men trained at Lough Bawn in Monaghan; Carrigmore and Clongee were among the houses used in Mayo; Stonehouse was used in Louth; Cornelane in Cavan; Runnamote and Mantua in Roscommon; Ballymacoll in Meath and Kilfine in Westmeath. Some secondary residences or hunting lodges were also commandeered such as Sir Josslyn Gore Booth's hunting lodge, Cabra, and the Marquis of Sligo's Delphi Lodge in Mayo.[86]

There seems to have been little actual damage done to these houses. After Kildangan and Dowdenstown were evacuated by the IRA, the county inspector of Kildare wrote: 'The rebels have in each case left the house perfectly tidy and undamaged except for a badly needed wash'.[87] However, their occupation had set a dangerous precedent for the Civil War.[88] When the split occurred in the IRA, big houses were often regarded as safe havens by both sides and where neither side felt they could allow particular big houses to be occupied by the opposing forces, they were burned. However, as during the War of Independence this was merely one reason amongst many for the renewed, more intense and more damaging, campaign of burnings.

THE BURNING OF BIG HOUSES DURING THE CIVIL WAR

On 6 December 1921, articles of agreement were signed by the British and Irish negotiators in London bringing the War of Independence to an end. According to Michael Hopkinson, the signing of the Anglo–Irish treaty was, 'the decisive event, which led to the Civil War. No document could have more effectively brought out into the open the

divisions in the philosophy and leadership of the Sinn Féin movement'.[89] Following a heated and bitter debate between December
1921 and early January 1922, the Dáil ratified the treaty by sixty-
four votes to fifty-seven. Unable to accept the ratification, Éamon de
Valera and his followers withdrew from the Dáil. Although the treaty
had the overwhelming support of statutory public bodies, Church
leaders and the majority of the public, a split began to appear in the
IRA within days of the Dáil vote. For the next few months attempts
were made to heal the rift but to no avail. On 14 April 1922, Anti-
Treaty forces occupied the Four Courts in Dublin, signalling the
beginning of Civil War.

The disorder which followed made it increasingly difficult for an
embryonic government to establish its authority or any form of law
and order. There was no recognised law enforcement body as the RIC
had been disbanded and in January 1922 the Republican police force
was also disbanded. In large tracts of the country, IRA military fac
tions and local agrarian organisations were virtually free to do as
they pleased. It was a scenario that had been dreaded by Loyalists.
In April 1923, Lord Midleton, who had been the most prominent southern Irish Unionist leader, wrote to King George V:

> The hasty withdrawal of British troops, against which your majesty's
> government were repeatedly warned, has left the South of Ireland
> without any force to preserve order and even if individuals were made
> amenable, there are no courts sitting effectively to deal with them....
> The mutiny of the IRA is probably the least serious element in crime.[90]

In the various localities, the landed class, and Loyalists in
general, became subjected to an increasingly vicious type of intimidation. Big houses were subjected to incessant raids; many land-owners
such as Major Blennerhassett in Clare were viciously assaulted and
threatened with being shot; demesne walls were pulled down and
trees cut and carted away; livestock was stolen; big house employees
were intimidated and even murdered. In June 1922, in County
Galway, the intimidation of Protestants was so intense and widespread that one commentator feared that if it continued 'in similar
intensity for a few weeks more, there will not be a Protestant left in
the place'.[91] In the same month in the Templederry, Silvermines and
Ballinclough districts of Tipperary there was: 'scarcely a Protestant
family ... which had escaped molestation.... Houses have been burned,
Protestant families have been forced to leave the neighbourhood,
altogether a state of terrorism exists'.[92] Around the same time
Protestants on Lord Lansdowne's Luggacurrane estate in Queen's

County were told by local agitators that it was 'time they and their sort were out of the country' and so twenty Protestant tenants were forcibly ejected by 150 armed men to make way for 'local landless Catholics'.[93] The rate of emigration (or migration to Northern Ireland) of Protestants from the worst affected areas such as Cork and the border counties increased dramatically causing something of a refugee crisis in Britain.[94]

The most visible form of intimidation directed against the landed class was again the burning of their big houses. From January 1922 to the end of April 1923, an estimated 199 big houses were burned in the twenty-six counties, almost three times more than during the War of Independence which, in itself, is an indication of the extent of lawlessness that prevailed during the Civil War. However, the simultaneous existence of political strife, agrarian agitation and sectarianism once again makes it difficult to categorise the reasons for the burning of individual houses.

Geographically, there were more big houses burned in every province during the Civil War (see Table 7.3, p. 287). In Munster, the number rose from forty-two to sixty-nine; in Leinster from eighteen to seventy-four; in Connaught from four to thirty-nine; and in the three Ulster counties from eleven to seventeen. There were reported burnings in twenty-five out of the twenty-six counties in comparison to twenty-one out of twenty-six during the War of Independence. The only county for which no burning was reported during the Civil War was Queen's County, which ironically had a noticeably higher incidence of IRA violence than during the War of Independence.[95] The marked increase in burnings in Connaught is probably a reflection of the fact that almost all the IRA in Mayo, Sligo and West Galway went anti-Treaty.[96] The number of houses burned in Leinster almost quadrupled because of the increase in IRA activity (though not necessarily violence directed against persons) in previously dormant counties such as Kildare, King's County and Wexford. The number of burnings in Wexford rose from one to eleven, while in King's County the number rose from one to twelve. In Munster, Tipperary and Cork once again had the highest incidence of IRA violence in the country, and the highest rate of burnings, between them accounting for forty-eight big houses. Seven houses were burned in Waterford, a county that had seen hardly any military activity and where no big houses had been burned during the War of Independence.

Chronologically, only about 10 per cent of the 199 houses were burned in the first seven months of 1922 (see Table 7.4, p. 287). These months witnessed sundry attempts to heal the rifts caused by the

Anglo–Irish treaty. It was not until June of that year that the Civil
War began in earnest and from then until the end of December seventy-
four houses were burned. From January to the end of March 1923 was
the most intense period of burnings resulting in the destruction of
53 per cent of the 199 houses. Ironically, this was at a time when the
Anti-Treatyites were very much on the run and the government was in
a much stronger position than it had been since the outbreak of hostilities. Anti-Treatyite resistance had diminished in even its strongest
areas of support and many of the most prominent leaders had been
either executed or arrested.[97] However, with their backs to the wall, the
Anti-Treatyites began a campaign of wanton destruction. A Free State
military report of 21 January 1923 claimed that,

> ... with depleted numbers, lack of resources and unified control, and
> almost complete ineffectiveness from a military standpoint their
> [Anti-Treatyite] policy of military action is slowly changing to one of
> sheer destruction and obstruction of the Civil Government.[98]

The growth in burnings was linked in some respect to the Anti-
Treatyites' response to the government's policy of executions, which
had been introduced as part of the Public Safety Act in November
1922. Under its powers, Anti-Treatyite leaders such as Liam Mellows,
Rory O'Connor, Joe McKelvey and Dick Barrett had been executed in
December as well as a number of lesser leaders in the various localities. As we have seen, some of the raiders who burned Palmerstown in
January 1923 said they did so as a reprisal for the execution of six
men at the Curragh.[99] The same month Ballygassan in Louth was
burned. Its owner thought at first that it was for sectarian reasons but
when he put this to the leader of the raiders, he was told that it was: 'a
protest against executions.... We care nothing for religion'.[100] When
Greenhills was burned in King's County the following month: 'the
leader announced they were Republicans who had come to burn
the house as a reprisal for the execution of Patrick Geraghty'.
Geraghty had been tried on 5 January and charged with having
possession, 'without proper authority', of one automatic pistol at
Croghan in November 1922. He was executed at Portlaoise prison on
27 January.[101]

Following Liam Lynch's order to burn the houses of senators, a
total of thirty-seven were burned, sixteen of which could be described
as big houses.[102] These included Cappoquin, home of Sir John Keane;
Desart Court, home of Lord Desart (even though it was his sister-in-
law who was a senator); Moore Hall, home of Maurice Moore and
Mullaghboden, home of Sir Bryan Mahon.

Reprisals for the execution of Anti-Treatyite leaders, or because they belonged to senators, accounts for probably no more than 15 per cent of those big houses burned during the Civil War. Many more were burned for agrarian or what again can be loosely termed military reasons. Anti-Treatyites and Free Staters burned houses in order to prevent them being used as billets or barracks by the opposing faction. From June to August 1922, Anti-Treatyites occupied Mitchelstown Castle but on hearing of the approach of the Free State forces they evacuated and burned the castle.[103] In August 1922, Geashill, home of Lord Digby in King's County was burned for a similar reason.[104] In January 1923, Castlehackett was burned. *The Irish Times* reported that: 'the reason given was that they [the Anti-Treatyites] expected the national army to occupy it. The raiders also said they had no ill feeling towards Col Bernard ... as he was a good man to the people of the locality'.[105] The night after Free State soldiers evacuated Dunaree (sometimes Kingscourt) in January 1923, it was burned by Anti-Treatyites.[106] Woodstock in Kilkenny was burned in May 1922 by Anti-Treatyites not only because it had been occupied by Free Staters but because it had also been commandeered in August 1920 by the Auxiliaries and used as an interrogation centre where IRA prisoners had allegedly been tortured.[107]

Of at least equal significance in the rise of burnings was the continued growth in agrarian agitation. By 1923, land grabbing was endemic.[108] Patrick Hogan informed President W.T. Cosgrave that 'the shooting of Land Commission officials [had] become widespread' and 'house burning [had] become a matter of course'.[109] Hogan claimed that he had: 'noted the cases through the country where houses have been burned and in more than 50 per cent of these cases the circumstances make it plain enough that the destruction was not for political but for agrarian motives'.[110] On 15 March 1923, the editor of the *Manchester Guardian* argued that 'Irregularism and land grabbing go together, so much so that many of the shootings and burnings are due more to economic than to political motives'. This as we have seen was exemplified in the burning of Tubberdaly. Similarly, in January 1922, agitation for the division of J.M. Wilson's Currygrane demesne in County Longford began when two families, with the support of the local branch of the Labour movement, took forcible possession of outoffices and houses on the demesne. Wilson was forced to flee to England. From there he wrote a number of times to the Minister for Home Affairs to see if anything could be done to stop the agitation and allow him to return home. When the minister made inquiries on Wilson's behalf, he was informed by the commissioner of the guards that:

... there are many cases of this kind now engaging the attention of the guard [*sic*] and that places where our men are in outposts, few and far between, we cannot move in such matters as energetically as might be wished, and must perforce hasten slowly. This I consider is much more desirable than adopting rushing tactics at the outset, which we might not at the moment be able to support by the necessary executive action.... The civic guard as an unarmed force relies more on moral than on physical force at this time.[111]

Currygrane was burned in August 1923.[112]

With regard to some burnings there is a difficulty in separating political and agrarian motives as is illustrated in the case of Lord Lansdowne's house, Derreen, in Kerry. The Kerry IRA went predominantly anti-Treaty. The new government found it difficult to establish any semblance of authority there, particularly around Kenmare. As the war intensified so too did agrarianism on Lansdowne's estate to force him to sell what land he retained. Conditions were described as 'anarchic' as boathouses were burned, poaching became the order of the day and robberies from the house and demesne (including trees and even stones from the demesne wall) became 'frequent'. Derreen was burned in late 1922. The extent to which agrarianism and politics were intertwined is suggested in a letter to the Minister for Home Affairs in 1923: 'The offenders were Republicans and Free Staters in about equal proportions and acting on no mandate but their own'.[113]

Finally, perhaps there was no motive for some burnings. In January 1923, Milestown, one of the finest houses in County Louth, was burned by ten unmasked raiders. An eye witness claimed that 'most of them were hardly seventeen years of age' and hinted that they had simply nothing better to do.[114] Lady Fingall's comment on the burnings may also deserve mention. She wrote that the revolutionary period:

> ... became a bonfire for a generation that was having its full fling and escape from the dullness of Irish rural life! Some made the most of this wild hour before they went back to the hard work on the farm and the parental tyranny that existed to a peculiar degree in Irish country life.[115]

REACTIONS TO BURNINGS

Whatever the reasons for the burning of big houses, their destruction was widely condemned, not only by Loyalist supporters but also by many sectors of the wider population. An editorial in *The Irish Times* in August 1922 claimed: 'Everyone is puzzled to find out what purpose the mutineers [Anti-Treatyites] can serve, even from their own crazy point of view by destroying these stately mansions'.[116]   Nowhere is the sense of bewilderment and loss more obvious than in the correspondence of Sir Thomas Esmonde whose house, Ballynastragh, was burned in March 1923.[117] (Esmonde had been a Nationalist MP for North Wexford from 1900 to 1918 and was the first chairman of Wexford county council in 1899.) Initially Sir Thomas himself was somewhat philosophical about the burning: 'The only reason for such an act is that I am a senator of the Free State, and, of course, I am in no worse a position than anybody else'.[118] As time went by he became more bitter and despondent as the realisation of what he had lost sank in. He was particularly affected by the loss of the library at Ballynastragh, which contained a wealth of archival material: 'After my burning I lost heart and gave up books altogether, so much so that I refused to accept books from several literary friends who wanted to give me their publications as I had no place to keep them.'[119] He also began to feel aggrieved that his house should be burned in light of the contribution he had made to Irish political life as a Nationalist.[120] In 1925, Esmonde wrote to President W.T. Cosgrave:

I need not delay on the irreparable loss the destruction of such a home has been to me and mine; but I may state that we have never been voluntary absentees from our country; and that we have done what we could in changeful conditions of Irish life, for local development and improvement from generation to generation.

He claimed that 'as an agriculturalist — a tillage farmer' he had given all the local employment he could; he had built over fifty houses in the locality and planted over a million trees'.[121] But as Esmonde and many of his fellow landowners were to find out, past improvements meant very little in the hostile climate of the early 1920s that was characterised by a new land war. It was felt by some of those who sympathised with him that the odium in which landlords had been held since the 1880s had finally caught up with them and was manifesting itself in a physical assault upon them and their property. Paula Hornstein, for example, wrote to Esmonde: 'Can it possibly be that a whole life of devotion to your country, so many sacrifices, are rewarded with the blackest ingratitude.... We live in a very sad time, hatred, revenge ruling everywhere'.[122]

Hornstein was just one of scores of friends, relatives, acquaintances, representatives of public bodies and members of Church bodies who wrote to Esmonde after the burning of Ballynastragh. 'Wanton' was by far the most popular adjective used by them to describe the destruction. All Esmonde's sympathisers failed to see the rationale behind the burning of big houses such as his. P.J. McGrath was 'shocked' at the news and wrote to Esmonde:

> I sincerely hope for the sake of the future prosperity of the country, as well as its reputation, that Ireland has seen the last of the crazy acts of a minority the best excuse for whom, I suppose, would be to plead that they do no know what they are doing.[123]

Fr J.J. Rossiter of New Ross, County Wexford, claimed that there was 'universal sorrow and indignation at what had been done. Some form of mania seems to have seized on a section of the people and at the present moment they are capable of anything'.[124] William Stafford of Baldwinstown Castle wrote that 'it makes one almost despair of the future to think that the series of similar outrages which have covered the country with disgrace could have been inflicted by a section of our own countrymen'.[125] Lord Courtown, a fellow landowner in Wexford, feared that his house might be next:

> I do not know how soon I may be in a similar position to you as the whole country seems to have gone mad and a certain class are burning all the houses. What the reason is I fail to see as this destruction of property cannot help their cause and besides that it is bringing financial ruin.[126]

Reaction to the news of burnings was much the same elsewhere. The Nationalist editor of the *Leinster Leader*, for example, condemned the burning of Lismullen in County Meath in April 1923: 'The burning of this beautiful building seems inexplicable as the owner has not been identified with any political organisation, merely confining himself to his principal occupation as a large farmer and breeder of pedigree stock.'[127] When Tubberdaly was burned a week or so later, the same editor wrote:

> Widespread sympathy is felt for Mr Beaumont-Nesbitt in the great loss he has sustained.... He worked very hard to ameliorate the conditions of the people around him, took the deepest interest in their works and doings and aided the district council very materially in their administration by his energy, initiative and help.... Why was his residence destroyed and what possible good can be achieved thereby? ... The resultant loss will not touch him to any great extent, except possibly from a sentimental point of view. It is the ratepayers who will be affected and who will have to foot the bill.[128]

Many years after the burning of Woodstock, Hubert Butler wrote: 'The Tighes were friendly charming people who did not deserve the misfortune that happened to them'.[129]

DESTRUCTION

Those who burned big houses were usually thorough in what they did. Houses were invariably reduced to ruins and most of their contents destroyed. Raiders left little time for family or servants to save furniture or treasures. The notice served on Lord Listowel's niece by the IRA gave the family half an hour to remove valuables and foodstuffs from Convamore, but stated that they were not allowed to remove furniture.[130] There was much truth in how Lady Fingall saw it:

> Often it was valueless things that were stacked on the lawn, to be examined when the cold day broke on the blackened walls and ashes, while the Romneys and the Chippendale furniture and Waterford glass, or old Irish silver had perished.[131]

Large quantities of petrol were usually sprinkled throughout the bottom floor rooms and windows were opened to ensure a plentiful supply of air so that the fire would spread rapidly, thereby ensuring maximum damage. In some cases, as at Tubberdaly and Kilteragh, bombs or dynamite were used. When Castlebernard was burned in June 1921, all that remained of the building was the kitchen. After Mary Gaussen, Lord Bandon's niece, visited the ruins some time later she wrote: 'The ruin is absolute and all one can do is to wander across the mass of debris in those precious rooms'.[132] After Castleboro was burned in February 1923, a newspaper report claimed that 'it was impossible to save any portion of it. It appeared to have been fired in several places.... All the furniture in the west wing as well as in the caretaker's apartment was destroyed'.[133] In February 1923, the steward wrote to Col Maurice Moore regarding Moore Hall: 'There is absolutely nothing left but the walls, not a vestige of glass, timber or even plaster from the ground floor up, such wholesale destruction in a few hours is difficult to understand'.[134]

After houses were burned (or, indeed, simply abandoned) moveable contents or valuable fittings that survived were looted. One night shortly after Derreen was burned, the housekeeper and maid, who had continued to live in the surviving servants' quarters, were locked in their rooms by a group of raiders who carried off: 'all the beds, bedding and linen ... and also some of the smaller furniture and smashed more'. Three days later the estate agent visited Derreen and this is his description of what greeted him:

On arrival at Derreen the scene that greeted our eyes beggars description, crowds of every description around the house, men, women and
children, pulling, hauling, fighting for what they could take. The
house is absolutely destroyed, doors all smashed, every particle of
furniture taken.... A. [?] tried to save a few things, but as fast as he
and his men got them out they were seized and carried off. On
Sunday and Sunday night A. says it was perfect hell, they got at the
cellars and the men were all half drunk, fighting and revolver shots
going off.... Everything is gone, all the windows, doors, floorings etc.
have been taken, motor garage gone. A.'s house burned to the ground,
all outbuildings either removed or burnt, green houses smashed up,
laundry pulled down and removed. Joss's house looted and walls only
remain. In fact there is nothing left of Derreen or its surroundings.[135]

The absence of an effective police force in rural areas was seen as
a precondition for such looting.[100] In March 1923, Mr Justice Devitt
described the looting at Glenfarne, County Leitrim, thus:

From far and near — from Fermanagh, Cavan and Leitrim — the people
came with carts and carried away from Glenfarne everything that
was portable — the timber, the rails, the whole interior of the house
so that only the four walls and the roof were left, and the roof went
eventually.

Devitt found no evidence of this looting being: 'the concerted action
of people banded together in an unlawful or seditious association' and
concluded that it 'was done by people of the neighbouring counties
with the object of enriching themselves'.[137] The silver at Mitchelstown
Castle was not destroyed in the fire but looted afterwards, as was
what furniture had survived.[138] When Castlesaunderson was abandoned
by its owners, it became: 'a sort of Tom Tiddler's ground for the countryside. Baths, fireplaces, water pipes, doors, windows, and fittings of
all descriptions vanished like magic; even the lead from the roof was
stripped off and stolen'.[139] Even servants got in on the act. Shortly
after Moydrum Castle was burned in July 1921, Michael Grady, the
butler, and Patrick Delaney, a footman, were both charged with the
larceny of a fur coat, dress suits, a bicycle and other goods to the
value of £360 from Lord Castlemaine. Both men pleaded guilty to the
charges and were sentenced to between four and six months' hard
labour.[140]

Before Kilboy was burned on 4 August 1922, it had already been
raided a number of times and silver plate, jewellery and farm imple-
ments stolen. The night after it was burned the conservatory, garden
out-offices and farmyard were all looted and the farm machinery and

twenty-eight sheep were stolen. Dunalley's steward wrote to him in England: 'Such wanton destruction was never witnessed'.[141] Later Dunalley 'heard on excellent authority' that the furniture saved by the servants: 'was stolen and is now in many of the houses round about'.[142] In October 1924, the garda sergeant in Silvermines told Dunalley that his furniture was in farmers' houses in Upperchurch but Dunalley's solicitor advised his lordship not to undertake the task of identifying it personally: 'It would be putting you in a most invidious position and would, I think, cause great ill feeling, which has now happily died down'.[143] Similarly, at the beginning of the Civil War, the Free State army occupied Markree and caused £10,000 worth of damage which its owner, Bryan Cooper, described as 'wanton, mischievous and filthy'. Cooper goes on to claim that when the Free Staters evacuated Markree: 'nearly all the furniture left behind was to disappear, some to a neighbouring military camp, some to cottages in Co. Sligo'.[144]

PRE-TRUCE COMPENSATION CLAIMS

To replace big houses, their contents, or both required large-scale funding. In the vast majority of cases, big house owners were unable to claim on their insurance as their policies did not cover riot and civil commotion. In 1924, Lord Dunalley's solicitor informed him: 'The Northern Assurance Company refused to pay at the time of the occurrence [the burning of Kilboy] on the ground that the loss was due to civil disturbance'.[145]

Initial claims for compensation by big house owners for the period before the calling of the truce on 11 July 1921 came under the terms of the 1898 Local Government (Ireland) Act[146] and the Criminal Injuries (Ireland) Acts of 1919 and 1920.[147] Under the 1898 Act, application for compensation could be made against the council of the county in which the damage occurred. The 1919 Act modified this: compensation could now be levied against either the council of the county in which the house was located or against that council and the council of any neighbouring county or counties. The power of the county court judge or judge of assize to fix the area off which the compensation was to be levied included the power to apportion the award on specific townlands or parishes. Increased claims during 1920 and an increased burden on ratepayers led to a further change in terms under the 1920 Act. This act stated that if the county council made representation to the lord lieutenant that the amount of compensation could not be raised by means of a rate in one year 'without imposing an excessive burden on the ratepayers', the lord lieutenant could direct that the amount be paid in instalments over a maximum of a five-year period.

By its very nature, it was inevitable that the whole area of compensation would become a very thorny and complicated one and in the long term big house owners were not to be adequately compensated for the loss of their property. (Nor indeed were smaller householders, businessmen etc.) Awards initially made by county court judges in respect of big houses were uncontested because Nationalist dominated county councils refused to appear as defendants. The county councils then refused *en bloc* to pay the sums decreed as members were in no position to be seen to be imposing exacting rates on relatively impoverished ratepayers in order to rebuild landlords' houses.[148] (At the same time it was very difficult to collect rates as ratepayers were angered that they should be responsible for compensating landlords and were generally taking advantage of the political chaos to avoid paying them.[149]) The British government responded to the crisis by deducting the amount payable in awards from the grants that the county councils were entitled to receive.[150] By July 1921, most of the personal injury claims for the deaths of officers and men of the British forces received had been met but this was not the case regarding those who had suffered material loss.

From the spring of 1920 to the signing of the Anglo-Irish Treaty in December 1921, big house owners made claims for compensation through the county courts and awards were made. However, in most cases the awards bore little relation to the claims. In September 1921, a claim for £100,000 was made at Trim quarter sessions for Summerhill and £30,000 for its contents. However, Judge Fleming awarded only £65,000 for the house and £11,000 for contents.[151] The following month a claim of £100,000 was made for Castlebernard, but the judge awarded only £62,000. Lady Bandon had also claimed £70,000 for contents but was awarded only £14,000.[152] George Moore put in a more modest claim of £25,000 for Moore Hall but was awarded only one third of that sum.[153] In November 1921, the MacNamaras claimed £29,000 for damages to Doolin but were awarded only £4,500.[154] It was one thing to have an award made in a landowner's favour; it was quite another to have the compensation actually paid to them. These big house owners became just some of the many property owners who were awarded compensation in the British administered courts but who were not actually paid due to the state of the country. At the beginning of December 1921, the chief secretary, Hamar Greenwood, admitted in the Commons: 'Those who have lost their property only are not likely to receive much consideration'. Even if

years after the first claim for compensation had been made. The delay was too much for some. By 1923, Captain Cooke Collis of Castlecooke in Cork had received nothing of the compensation awarded to him over two years before and so he wrote: 'I have to leave the country forthwith. Until I get some of the £26,716 awarded to me I have nothing to live on ... merely because I am and ever have been loyal is the only cause of my appalling state'.[168] In 1920, R.C. Williams had been awarded £16,000 for the burning of Coolcower, also in Cork, but over two years later had received nothing. He was by then 'in urgent need of cash' and feared that if he did not get at least an advance he would lose his herd of Angus cattle (of which he claimed he was the largest breeder in the Free State) and therefore his livelihood.[169]

DAMAGE TO PROPERTY (COMPENSATION) ACT, 1923

The Shaw Commission did not deal with post-truce cases. In its early stages, as it was working its way through the claims for damage during the War of Independence, Civil War was raging throughout the twenty-six counties. By the time the Civil War had ended, a new and larger crop of claims by big house owners had to be dealt with. These came under the terms of the Damage to Property (Compensation) Act 1923 passed by the Irish Free State government.[170] All proceedings under previous acts, which were pending at the passing of this act, and in which no decree had been made, were declared to be void and discharged. Injuries committed after the 11 July 1921 on which a decree had been made prior to the passing of the act were to be re-opened and re-heard on the application of the applicant or the Minister for Finance. In May 1923, J.J. McElligott, secretary of the Department of Finance, pointed out that the machinery of administration should be put in position quickly as the 'aim must be to be in a position to oppose every claim when it comes up for hearing'.[171] He was making it quite clear that the levels of compensation to be awarded were not to be a burden on his department.

The funding of the act fell once more upon the county councils; the sum required to be paid by the county at large was to be assessed and raised in much the same manner as under the earlier Criminal Injuries Acts. Again this was ominous for big house owners as Nationalist county councils were just as unlikely to look favourably upon huge claims as they had been under the 1919 and 1920 Acts.

This act met with much opposition from big house owners. The right to compensation was limited to damage done to the house during its burning and did not extend to consequential damage, the loss

of the use of the property, or the loss of 'articles of personal orna-
ment' such as jewellery. In the case of chattels such as furniture,
which came under the terms of the Act, it would have to be proved
that those who stole them had been 'engaged in or purporting to act
or who might reasonably be presumed to have been acting in the
name or on behalf of any combination or conspiracy' for the overthrow of the Provisional government or the Free State government or
who belonged to any 'unlawful or seditious association'. Because of
the amount of looting that took place by locals who, as in the case of
Glenfarne, more often than not belonged to no such association, big
house owners were to be hard pressed to prove the legitimacy of their
claims. When Lord Dunalley's claim for compensation for the loss of
contents was dismissed by the county court judge in May 1924, his
solicitors wrote to him:

> We were unable to prove that the things were taken by the Irregulars
> and as a matter of fact I believe they were not taken by these people
> for the whole place was plundered principally by the 'mountainy'
> people [locals around the Silvermines area] after the burning.[172]

Furthermore, when assessing the amount of compensation, judges
took into consideration 'the steps taken or which might reasonably
have been taken by the owner of the property, his servants or agents'
to protect the property from any anticipated injury, or to resist, prevent or defeat the committal of the injury. This was an interesting
clause considering the fact that so many big houses were actually
vacant when burned. And rarely in cases of raids was any type of
resistance forthcoming from a family if resident, or a skeleton staff if
not. In April 1923, an article in the *Morning Post* illustrated the
apprehensions amongst the Loyalist community: 'Take the case of the
Loyalist owner having to leave the country to save his life. He may be
deprived altogether of compensation by the judge for failing to take
steps to protect the property from an injury he could anticipate'.[173]
  Even more contentious was clause 10 which stipulated that compensation would be payable only upon fulfilment of conditions which
the court might impose requiring the building to be wholly or partially reinstated. Full reinstatement entailed the erection of a new
building on the old site or the restoration of the old house. Partial
reinstatement meant the erection of another building on a nearby
site. Early in 1923 the Duke of Devonshire wrote to Timothy Healy,
Governor-general of the Free State: 'There are owners of property
who feel that they cannot with safety return to Ireland or in view of
the destruction of homes to which they were attached, do not wish to

return'.[174] President W.T. Cosgrave was aware that 'there are some who feel that it would not be safe to return to the insecurity in which the loss has been occasioned'. But he was also at pains to point out that the big houses burned were, 'property of a description which is to a large extent out of date, and not easily marketable, if at all'.[175] A draft of an earlier statement of Cosgrave's, intended for delivery to the Dáil at the final stages of the debate on the bill, stated that the government was not going to grant huge sums of compensation to facilitate the rebuilding of big houses. The reason given was that, 'the size and cost of the maintenance of these premises is out of all relation to either the comfort or the means of the owners'.[176] Unofficial government policy, suggested in another statement added to this draft, shows the reluctance to accommodate (former) landlords:

> Practically every claim for financial accommodation to economic interest is accompanied by a statement [from Loyalists] that the government can find millions to compensate a class which never benefited the nation and drew its revenues from rents and lands etc. etc.[177]

The compensation case of Sir Thomas Esmonde of Ballynastragh is indicative of what happened. Ballynastragh had been burned on 9 March 1923. It was Sir Thomas' intention to rebuild it from the start. In June 1923, he wrote to Lord Eversley:

> I have only the one country after all and there is a place in it where the happiest and the best and holiest of my memories are centred. If I can rebuild I certainly will, but these things take time. It will be months — if not years — before whatever compensation I am to get is awarded me.[178]

His words were to prove prophetic.

Esmonde made a claim for £77,500 under the 1923 Act. However, his case was not heard until February 1925 by which time Esmonde was becoming increasingly disillusioned and embittered. (By May his award had not been paid and so he wrote to President W.T. Cosgrave that he had not found 'a suitable house' and that the 'increasing discomfort ... of the nomad existence I am forced to lead' had prompted his action.[179]) During the hearing, the solicitor representing Gorey District Council claimed that while the burning of Ballynastragh was 'wanton and outrageous' the claim was 'somewhat excessive'.[180] Mr Costello SC, representing the Minister for Finance, argued that the old walls could be used for rebuilding and that £21,000 would be sufficient compensation.[181] Judge Doyle was satisfied, however, that 'it would be a far too dangerous risk' to require Esmonde to rebuild on the old walls and awarded £55,100. A reinstatement clause was attached to the award which was not as much as Esmonde had hoped for but as Myles Higgins pointed out to him: 'I think in the present times the amount sufficient to replace not all, but middling things, is sometimes best.'[182]

In March, the government used its right to appeal the county court judge's award. The appeal was held in the High Court in Dublin in July and the award was reduced by Justice Sullivan to £44,800, or by around 25 per cent. Esmonde therefore was awarded less than 60 per cent of what he had originally claimed and was disappointed not only by the way his award had been diminished but also by the way he felt he had been 'treated as a criminal during his trial'. He claimed that the award was totally inadequate and that he would have to spend 'many thousands' of his own in order to rebuild Ballynastragh. His disillusionment with the new government is clear from the ending of his letter:

> You must excuse me if after the treatment I have received from the officers of your government I do not continue to support it with enthusiasm. I shall reconsider my purpose of rebuilding as well as remaining in a country where such things are possible.[183]

Here then was a (former) landlord who had suffered for being a member of the Senate and who felt very much aggrieved by the fact that he received no apparent sympathy from the system. Esmonde then sought legal advice regarding the reinstatement clause, presumably hoping that he could use the award to build elsewhere. However, he was informed that the Minister for Finance: 'would probably not consent to any alteration in the order unless under special conditions if at all'. He could, he was told, approach the Minister and 'accept a smaller sum of compensation for deletion of the reinstatement clause'.[184] This proved to be a deterrent and Esmonde went ahead with the rebuilding of Ballynastragh. From mid-1925 to around the end of 1926, Esmonde received his award in 'instalments' according to the completion of various stages of the rebuilding project.[185] The rebuilding of Ballynastragh was not completed until 1937. The new house, a two-storey Georgian-style structure, was much smaller than the original.

Even though Esmonde was eventually awarded only 60 per cent of his original claim, he does seem to have done better than most. A register of claims under the 1923 Act survives which records the claims of individual big house owners throughout the country and the final awards granted along with any conditions attached.[186] From this register a random sample of fifty big houses was chosen. In total the owners of these houses made claims for £1,908,605. They were awarded only £493,428 or around 26 per cent of what the claimants felt would have been necessary to rebuild their houses. Twenty-six (52 per cent) of these big houses were rebuilt including Ballynastragh. Cecilia Burrows, owner of Milestown in Louth had claimed £17,400 of which she was awarded £11,750 (£8,500 subject to reinstatement). Milestown was rebuilt in 1925 using the old walls. Lord Lansdowne had claimed £30,000 for Derreen. He was awarded £13,000 for the house and £3,370 for the contents. Derreen was rebuilt in 1924. Sir John Keane had claimed £24,600 for Cappoquin and was awarded £10,800. He rebuilt the house as before.

In the case of Lord Dunalley, he made a claim for over £70,000 for Kilboy but was awarded only £17,400 which Dunalley's solicitors claimed was 'quite inadequate to rebuild the old structure'.[187] A reinstatement clause was added and Dunalley's solicitor claimed that 'the reason why this condition was attached was to render it impossible for an owner to obtain a substantial decree and then to expend only a portion of the money on rebuilding, retaining the balance for his own use'.[188] With the diminished award, it became necessary to plan for rebuilding on a reduced scale. Dunalley was advised that 'if the cellars were sealed up altogether and the top storey taken off', it would allow him: 'sufficient space for a smaller staff of servants but with sufficient accommodation for a fair sized ordinary house fitted up with modern requirements such as central heating, electric light etc.'[189] Kilboy was rebuilt without the top storey and Dunalley, it would seem, kept the rebuilding within the budget provided to him by the award.[190] His son was not, however, impressed by the new design later complaining that his 'parents had not included some very necessary conveniences. There was no strong room, no box room, no larder, no dairy'.[191] Around 1955, the house was demolished and a single-storey house built in its place.[192]

Other owners did not rebuild either because their awards were inadequate to allow them to do so or because they were reluctant to come back to live in Ireland. Lord Desart was awarded £19,000 for the burning of Desart Court, of which £12,000 was conditional on it being rebuilt. His daughter later wrote:

As it was impossible for my father to undertake the rebuilding of Desart, he handed the property to his niece, Lady Kathleen Pilkington.... She restored the house and for some while spent part of each year there, until the anti-English feeling in the neighbourhood made that impossible.[193]

Desart was sold some years later and subsequently demolished. It is interesting that the Earl of Desart's niece should feel it necessary to leave Desart Court because of 'the anti-English feeling in the neighbourhood'. E.J. Beaumont-Nesbitt did not rebuild Tubberdaly. Again there may have been a mixture of reasons. Firstly he had claimed £35,000 but was awarded only £8,100. Secondly, the socio-political climate in Ireland as a whole and the agitation, which had taken place on his estate in particular, had made him disillusioned about ever returning to Ireland. In 1925, he wrote to his cousin:

> But in the face of all the opposition it isn't worthwhile to try to build any other houses, and I have nobody there to look after my interests in the least, and if I started to rebuild or build anything new, I should just be robbed.[194]

Neither did the equally disillusioned J.M. Wilson, who claimed £59,000 but was awarded only £12,000, rebuild Currygrane. In 1925, Col Charles Warden made his feelings known about rebuilding Derryquin which was burned in 1922, he and his mother being forced to flee to England:

> I bought Derryquin [and 25,000 acres in 1879] to live in, and to end my days in, and I expended thirty years of labour on it, but after my experiences there in 1922, it would be impossible for me to have any further pleasure in living there, and therefore, I do not care to rebuild Derryquin Castle.

Jonathan Darby had claimed £28,000 for Leap Castle but was awarded only £4,100, which was totally inadequate and so the castle was allowed to fall into a 'sinister ruin'.[195] As we have seen in the case of Summerhill the compensation awarded had been greatly diminished and bore little relation to the original claim. Its new owner, Col Rowley sought advice from his relatives about the prospect of rebuilding. But Douglas Rowley wrote to him from the Riviera: 'Much as I should like to see the old house rebuilt, one must remember that even if this was done you could not put back the old things that formed part of it'.[196]

No level of compensation could have enticed people like Beaumont-Nesbitt, Warden or Wilson to return. They, like many more of their class, took whatever compensation they could negotiate (without the reinstatement conditions) and moved permanently to England. Others built smaller houses elsewhere in Ireland, particularly in south County Dublin or north Wicklow, away from their original estates where they felt they would be safer. In 1991, almost seventy years after Tubberdaly had been burned, Brian Beaumont-Nesbitt, grandson of E.J. Beaumont-Nesbitt, became the first member of his family to return to see the ruins of the ancestral home. After returning home to Shropshire he wrote to Bobbie Tyrell who lived at Ballindoolin (about eight miles outside Edenderry and whose family had been friends of the Beaumont-Nesbitts) that he was filled with,

> ... a mixture of anger against the blackguards who burned it, nostalgia for something I never knew — and regret that the site had been invaded by so many buildings, including the power station [at Rhode] and all those electricity pylons.

Tyrell, who had been born in 1905, remembered the night the IRA tried to burn his own home during the War of Independence. He replied that he no longer enjoyed 'going to Rhode and passing the places that were destroyed, when I think of old times and the good people who lived in those places and the way that they were treated.'[197]

8

THE POLITICAL PLIGHT OF IRISH LANDLORDS, 1880–1960

'THROWN TO THE WOLVES'

They [landlords] just watch with peevish irritation the slipping of slate after slate from the roof of their castle of power, the sagging of eave shoots choked long ago, the loosening of rusty hold fasts from their walls. Over their lives there has gathered a nerveless melancholy: a grey mist charged with insidious damp is settling down on them.... It is the sense of a hopelessly lost cause which blights them so utterly, that they have not displayed, not once in the last half century, a single flash even of the desperate courage of despair.

CANON S.O. HANNAY (*NOM DE PLUME* GEORGE BERMINGHAM),
WESTMINSTER GAZETTE, 16 JANUARY 1909

INTRODUCTION

The above quote from S.O. Hannay encapsulates the criticism directed against landlords by concerned contemporaries who viewed with dismay landlords' lethargic reaction to the invasion of what were perceived to be their political rights during the last quarter of the nineteenth century. It is an appropriate quotation from the point of view of this work as the extended metaphor that Hannay uses compares landlords' apathy towards their political decline to their apathy towards the deterioration of their houses. In the early twentieth century, Hannay and others associated with the landed class such as Horace Plunkett and Shane Leslie took a step back to judge Irish landlords. They felt that with the growth of democracy from the mid 1880s landlords could have either shown 'a single flash of the desperate courage of despair' to at least fight their own corner, or they could have been more adventurous and put themselves in the forefront of the new democratic movement, supporting Home Rule rather than opposing it, and in that way ultimately accomplishing more for themselves and their supporters both locally in rural communities and nationally in a re-established Dublin parliament. In *Noblesse Oblige*, published in 1908, Plunkett argued:

The abolition of landlordism, so far from destroying the usefulness of
the Irish gentry, really gives them their first opportunity, within the
memory of living men, to fulfil the true functions of an aristocracy.
They have ceased to be the masters; they are no longer dealing with
dependants. My appeal to them is that they should recognise this
fact, and take their new position as men who, working among others
in a rural community, have by their wealth and education special
advantages which they desire to use for the common good; and I
assure them that for men who are willing and qualified to take that
position it will open.[1]

In a similar vein, Leslie wrote:

I grew up amongst the remains of a class who had had everything and
were rapidly reducing themselves to nothing. In vain Charles Stewart
Parnell gave them a lead which would have restored their position as
leaders of the people.[2]

However, it was not quite that simple. Even in Britain in the late
nineteenth century the idea that the landed class had some traditional right to parliamentary representation and political leadership
at local and national level was fast becoming anachronistic as the
rapidly expanding electorate and a rising urban middle class clam-
oured for a share of power. In Ireland, landlords had the further
distinct disadvantages of being separated from the vast majority of
the people not only by reasons of religion and culture but also
socially by reason of a 'land question'. Furthermore, they were politically estranged by reason of a wider 'Irish question' both of which
were to become inextricably entwined when the land and Home Rule
movements merged in the early 1880s. To a rising generation of
Nationalist politicians, the abolition of landlordism as a system was
seen to be the answer to both questions.[3]

THE ASSAULT ON LANDLORD POLITICS IN LATE-VICTORIAN IRELAND

In 1880, Benjamin Disraeli, former Conservative prime minister,
wrote that the politics of Great Britain would 'probably for the next
few years mainly consist of an assault upon the constitutional position of the landed class'.[4] His words proved prophetic although he
hardly envisaged how complete this assault would be over a relatively short period of time. Politically, as well as economically, Irish
landlords were in a very vulnerable position by the 1880s. While
their level of indebtedness had grown since the Famine, the farming
class had become more prosperous. Farmers, as well as shopkeepers,

publicans and traders were clamouring for political representation
that would reflect their new-found prosperity. When economic
depression hit in the late 1870s, landlords found themselves in direct
opposition to a new rural alliance; it was a powerful anti-landlord
alliance that was soon exploited by Davitt, Parnell and the Land
League.

Of the 105 MPs returned in 1859, eighty-seven had been landowners and sixty-five of these owned more than 2,000 acres while
twenty-nine owned more than 10,000 acres.[5] Although the 1850
Reform Act had quadrupled the county electorate, R.F. Foster claims
it continued to be dominated by middling and strong farmers over
whom landlords exerted their 'fair and legitimate influence'.[6] Property
qualification, the personal expense involved in contesting elections
— between 1832 and 1878 a successful campaign could cost a candidate between £2,000 and £15,000 — and the ability of landlords to
curry favour with farmers and priests as needs demanded ensured
landlord dominance.[7] Irish landed MPs were very much at home in a
British parliament, which was dominated by what David Cannadine
terms an 'integrated and supra-national class'. They were bound
together by common ties of landownership, growing social bonds
formed in public schools and clubs, careers in the army, navy, civil
and diplomatic services, and through marriage alliances between
succeeding generations of Irish and British landed families.

A significant shift occurred between 1868 and 1874. In the 1868
general election, fought on the question of the disestablishment of
the Irish Church, sixty-six Liberal MPs were returned for Ireland,
providing W.E. Gladstone with half of the majority in the House of
Commons that led to his appointment as prime minister in December
of that year. However, the 1874 election proved a turning point; only
ten Liberals were returned while the Home Rule party won sixty
seats. These years, therefore, witnessed the demise of the Liberal
party in Ireland (and by extension the election of Liberal landlord
MPs) and the growth of the Home Rule party (which attracted very
few landlord adherents), so that only the Conservatives were representative of the landed class. In 1868 seventeen MPs of commercial
backgrounds were returned which, as K.T. Hoppen puts it, reflected
the fact that: 'the landed grip upon the Irish representation was
being modestly relaxed'.[8]

From 1872 the slowly expanding electorate was better placed than
ever before as the Secret Ballot Act of that year diluted landlords'
powers of intimidation at election time. Similarly, the land acts from
1870 to 1885 curtailed landlord powers over their tenants as legislation
regarding evictions, for example, strengthened the tenants' position

while simultaneously weakening that of landlords. The growth of the Land League signalled the beginning of the end of political deference towards landlords once and for all. At no stage previously had existing or aspiring Nationalist politicians directed such concerted hostility towards landlords from platforms all over Ireland. Their rhetoric was a potent weapon threatening violence on landlords or anybody who might be tempted to support them. In 1881, Timothy Healy proclaimed: 'We believe that landlordism is the prop of English rule and we are working to take that prop away. To drive out British rule from Ireland we must strike at the foundation, and that foundation is landlordism.'[9] In 1887, William O'Brien asserted:

> The grand army of Irish freemen will march unconquered and unconquerable until they have trampled down in its last ditch alien landlordism and ascendancy, and hauled down from its highest pinnacle the last shred of English misrule.[10]

Such speeches were highly inflammatory. The fact that they were met by 'loud applause', 'sustained applause' and 'shouts of hear, hear' suggests that they often had the desired effect of inciting the masses to exact revenge for what was portrayed as years of suffering and hardship at the hands of usurping colonists. In their quest to prove this, Nationalist leaders had only to concentrate on the actions of a minority of rack-renting landlords to taint all others with the same brush. The rise in evictions during the land war simply added fuel to their fire. Propaganda, or even gossip, was a powerful weapon in rural Ireland, the truth of which is evident in the picture that tradition has painted of Irish landlords. As the Marquis of Sligo later pointed out: 'Before 1916, and long after, the old time landlords were convenient bogeymen, gifts to a rising politician'.[11]

The anti-landlord resentment aroused by the Land League and the continued growth in the Home Rule movement saw landlords (and the Conservative party) routed in the 1880 election. The results of the 1885 election (fought in the aftermath of the passing of the Franchise and Redistribution Acts of 1884–85) when Parnell and his party captured eighty-five of the 103 seats, confirmed that landlords had virtually lost all of their electoral power. It was clear that the newly expanded electorate were more amenable to Nationalism. The new political aspirants were increasingly professional men. Of the 103 MPs returned, only five were landlords with more than £1,000 valuation, no less than seventy-five were Catholics, and of the total only forty-two still served on grand juries.[12] Landlords who contested this election did so as Unionists. With the exception of Parnell and a handful of others such as Sir Thomas Esmonde and the Redmonds, landlords politically isolated themselves from the majority of the electorate outside the six north-eastern counties, effectively destroying whatever hopes they may have retained for political participation in the future. Their own acceptance of the new order was evident in the 1886 election when Unionist candidates contested only nine out of the sixty-six constituencies in the twenty-six counties and five of these were in the Ulster counties of Donegal and Monaghan.

While these developments were taking place at national level, landlord political power was also being corroded at local level. In their localities landlords had dominated local government.[13] It was as justices of the peace that their influence was perhaps most pronounced as they presided at the petty and quarter sessions as administrators of justice. JPs were appointed by the lieutenant of the county, invariably a large and influential landowner, who was entitled to hold this position for life. Theoretically, the lieutenant had responsibility for the order of the county and had control over the local militia. Below him were a number of deputy lieutenants (again invariably drawn from the landed class) whom he had the authority to nominate and who were responsible for order in their respective localities. The position of high sheriff was one which an individual was entitled to hold for one year, having been appointed by the lord lieutenant from a list of three names submitted to him by the judge of assize on the summer circuit. Landlords who were appointed as high sheriffs represented the sovereign within the county in the execution of the law and were entrusted with the conduct of parliamentary elections, the execution of writs and the appointment of the grand jury.[14] Similarly the grand juries were dominated by landlords and their representatives, such as agents. The principal matters administered by the juries were related to public works such as the construction and repair of roads and bridges, the erection and repairing of gaols, court houses and so on. To local landowners, membership of the grand jury was essential to the maintenance of their influence over local affairs and local expenditure. Finally, landlords and their representatives dominated boards of poor law guardians, which had been established back in 1838 to implement the Irish poor law of that year. W.L. Feingold tells us that during and immediately after the Famine: 'the boards developed into an important administrative network, to which parliament assigned numerous new functions in areas related to poor relief, public health, the care of orphans, voter registration and emigration'.[15] Guardians were chosen in annual elections by the ratepayers of a union. Both landlords and occupiers contributed to the poor rates (with the exception of occupiers whose holdings were valued at below £4 who were excluded from the tax) and so both could vote. In practice, however, local landlords used their influence to ensure that elected representatives were favourable to the continuance of their power. As voting papers were brought to the homes of electors who indicated the choice of candidates, signed the paper and returned it to the clerk of the union, the voting system facilitated this.[16] Until the late 1870s, as Feingold has found, the three principal offices on each board — those of chairman, vice-chairman and deputy vice-chairman — were dominated by landlords or their agents.

During the land war, the poor law boards, because they were the only administrative body in rural Ireland with directly elected members, became specifically targeted by the Land League as potential local power bases. On 1 March 1881, Parnell, in an open letter to the *Freeman's Journal*, encouraged local league branches to:

> ... see that all exertions are made to secure the return of Land League candidates as poor law guardians and to drive from office the agents, bailiffs and landlord nominees who have hitherto been allowed to fill these important positions.[17]

By the mid-1880s, the tenants controlled a majority of the chairmanships, vice-chairmanships and deputy chairmanships of poor law boards throughout the country. By 1900, the situation had changed even more dramatically: the Government of Ireland Act of 1898 had abolished ex-officio poor law guardians, thereby further diminishing landlords' powers of representation and influence on these boards. And newly composed boards were quick to assert their Nationalism. In 1901, it was proposed by a Unionist member of Monaghan poor law guardians to send an address of welcome to Horace Plunkett on his visit to the town to open the local agricultural show. The majority of the members rejected the proposal, Patrick Whelan claiming that:

> ... it was very inconsistent for a Nationalist board appointed on political principles to present an address to a member of a government that had done so much to ruin their country.... Horace Plunkett had done a good deal to develop the industrial resources of the country and to help the people in many ways, but they would not forget he was a bitter Unionist.[18]

The assault on the offices of the poor law guardians provided much experience to aspiring Nationalist politicians at local level.[19] This was invaluable when the functions of the grand juries (as well as other important administrative duties) were placed in county councils under the Government of Ireland Act of 1898. The initial threat of local government for Ireland brought a wave of protest from the landed class, their fears perhaps best summarised by Sir Stephen De Vere in 1891, who envisaged county councils being controlled by the same element that had controlled the Land and National Leagues:

> Those who inflame and pervert the minds of men will find a ready-made arena at their own doors, costing them nothing, in which each orator can air his eloquence, and his malevolence against the landlord, the law and the State, safely and profitably, not as a volunteer adventurer, as at present, but as a 'chartered libertine', the representative of a large constituency elected under the law. He will enjoy the double privilege of being dangerous to others and safe himself.[20]

A sense of anxiety pervaded the landed class that under elective representation, landlords and their representatives would form only 'a contemptible minority' with the inevitability that rather than bow to their fellow councillors they would opt out of local government and so 'release themselves from a position of humiliation'.[21]

By 1907, only eighteen out of 694 councillors in the twenty-six counties could be considered Unionists, and just over a third of these could be described as landlords.[22] This came as no great surprise to supporters of the landed class. After the first elections, the editor of the *Morning Post* wrote: 'It would have been absurd to expect that in the first flush of their new powers, the democratic electorate of the Irish counties should have returned the landed gentry, who they have been taught to regard as hereditary enemies and oppressors'.[23] County councils effectively reversed the policy of their predecessors on the grand juries, questioning the right of non-democratically elected officials to interfere in any aspect of local administration. In the past the high sheriff had, for example, the power to appoint the court house keeper. When the high sheriff of Mayo, Robert Orme, appointed a Protestant to this position in 1901 he drew upon himself the wrath of the totally Nationalist and Catholic county council who believed that this type of appointment should be their preserve. Having threatened High Court proceedings to test the case, the council won out when Orme back-tracked and appointed a Catholic instead.[24]

In December 1901, a similar controversy erupted in Tipperary when the county council objected to the appointment of a Protestant as returning officer for the forthcoming elections. K.E. O'Brien told the council that 'they were a popularly elected body and it was their duty to make popular appointments'. The appointment should have been a Nationalist, and by inference a Catholic, as 'it was absurd to talk of not letting politics enter these matters when they had such a brilliant example in the action of their predecessors who never allowed a Nationalist to have a look-in in such appointments'.[25] The council assumed responsibility for electing a returning officer at its next meeting. In July 1902, a meeting of Louth county council decided that as it paid the salary of the sub-sheriff, they would in future have sole control over the appointment.[26] In December 1904, the chairman of the Longford county council inquired if they, as a body, had the power to strike the name of J.M. Wilson of Currygrane off the agricultural committee because his father had travelled to England to speak at Unionist meetings.[27] This, the *Daily Express* claimed, was 'deplorable' and contended that that type of spirit was 'not confined to any one county or group of counties' but was 'rampant' throughout the country since 1898.[28]

LANDLORDS AND UNIONISM, 1885–1914

The socio-political developments that took place in Ireland from the early 1880s left landlords and their associates, as well as the Protestant business and professional communities, apprehensive about their prospects under a Home Rule government. Following the Franchise and Redistribution Acts of 1884–85 and the results of the 1885 election, old party divisions were forgotten as Protestants of all classes and denominations, former Liberals and Conservatives, united as Unionists 'in an attempt to maintain minority ascendancy interests and influence'.[29]

Growing apprehensions coincided with the growth in agitation and the rise in crime during the land war and the plan of campaign.[30] While landlords, their bailiffs and agents escaped the more serious type of outrage relatively unscathed — of fifty-seven agrarian-related murders from 1880–82, only four were of landlords — they still attracted 35 per cent of lesser agrarian outrages even though they made up only 5 per cent of the population.[31] It was the judicial system's enforced inability to do anything about the rise in crime that caused most concern to landlords and their representatives. Samuel Hussey, a leading land agent in the south, went so far as to claim that one fifth of crimes were not being reported because of fear.[32] James Hamilton, a Cork judge, claimed that 'if there is evidence of a conspiracy, no doubt the magistrates would send the case for trial, but no jury in the country parts of Ireland would convict'.[33]

Landlords perceived the political struggle to be intrinsically linked to the agrarian struggle.[34] As Laurence Geary tells us, they watched with apprehension as Nationalist leaders exploited the patriotism of the tenantry by linking the land struggle with the whole question of Home Rule. Arthur Smith-Barry, the leading landlord opponent of the plan, argued it had 'really nothing to do with landlords and tenants' but was 'a great political movement started by the leaders of the Irish rebellion to prevent the possibility of government being carried out in Ireland by the English government'.[35] It was one thing to be subjected to intimidation while there still existed protection from the British administration; it was quite another to be left stranded in a self-governing Ireland dominated by an Irish parliament that, according to the newly formed Irish Loyal and Patriotic Union in 1886, would be:

> ... composed of the same elements as are to be found among the Irish members now gathered under the banner unfurled by Mr Parnell; only its members will be more numerous, more hostile to the friends of England, more unscrupulous — if that be possible — more rapacious, less restrained by decency or prudence than they are now. And then there is the further consideration that then they will have full power to give effect to their hostility.[36]

Many landlords were demoralised by how indiscriminate the land war was in that it affected improving landlords in the same way as it affected negligent ones. In 1881, Finlay Dun reported that the Fitzwilliam estate was run by a 'liberal and generous landlord' but was 'still subjected to league agitation'.[37] When the Earl of Meath returned to London from his Wicklow estate in 1884, his wife noted in her diary:

> Pleased to get him back safe and sound from Ireland, where he had a dreadful time of it, what with the Bray town commissioners to whom he went to hand over the market house and the Land Leaguers. They even threatened his life on Christmas Day. So much for the gratitude amongst the poor, easily led Irish.[38]

Sir William Gregory of Coole, who felt that he had always shown 'the strongest sense of duty to his tenants', was even more disillusioned in 1881 when he returned to Coole from Ceylon where he had been Governor-general, to find that despite having reduced his rents by 10 per cent in 1879 a no-rent combination was 'creeping on like lava, filling every cranny' on his estate. Equally as disconcerting to him was the fact that his tenants no longer doffed their caps to him! He wrote to a friend:

I must tell you with deep regret that I feel so deeply the way I have been treated that it is my intention no longer to reside at Coole.... I will certainly not expose my wife and child to the risk of vengeance and outrage ... I meant to dismantle the house and to remove every-thing of value to a safe place, and if they blow up the residence, I shall be very much obliged to them — I only regret that I have laid out very foolishly so much money on it of late years which I did from the happiness of living among tenants who had, I thought, the affec-tion for me that I had for them.[39]

By the mid-1890s, and despite the defeat of the first two Home Rule bills, landlord apprehensions regarding the prospect of being governed by Home Rulers had changed very little. In 1894, the Irish Landowners' Convention passed a resolution condemning Nationalist leaders who had delivered: 'hundreds of speeches in Ireland, inciting the Irish tenants to withhold payment of their rents, and promising that if Home Rule were granted the Irish legislature would reduce or abolish rents, or compel the landlords to sell on terms to be fixed by the tenants'.[40] The retention of large tracts of land by landlords even after the passing of the 1903 Land Act exposed them to further agita-tion from the UIL. In 1900, threatening letters sent to landlords in Cavan 'failed in their effect, but they unpleasantly recall[ed] the practice of Land League days'.[41] In December 1901, attempts to boy-cott Lord Ashtown were 'feeble' but the inspector general of the police contended they were indicative of the return of the type of agi-tation that had characterised the 1880s.[42] The establishment of UIL courts in many areas of the country led the Irish Unionist Alliance (a reformed ILPU established in 1891) to condemn their 'cruel and unscrupulous' method 'of enforcing its decrees against those who transgress its despotic rule'. 'What would be the state of things in Ireland if the loyal minority found themselves in close conflict with the powers that would represent a glorified UIL?' they wondered.[43]

The close association of the Catholic Church with both the social and political revolution led to another fear that Home Rule would equal Rome Rule. In 1886, the ILPU had claimed that it was the influ-ence of the Catholic clergy over the tenantry that was responsible for the political overthrow of landlords.[44] At a national level, landlords had witnessed and decried the involvement of prelates like Bishop O'Donnell of Raphoe and Bishop Kelly of Ross in the land movement and the almost universal support of ecclesiastics for the plan of campaign. They resented the role of the parochial clergy in promul-gating the evils of landlordism. Fr Gaughran of Carrickmacross, County Monaghan, for example, vowed to 'trample upon landlordism with the help of God'. Fr Lane in Cork promised to continue his role in the land movement until landlordism was 'utterly crushed'.[45]

Finally landlords feared that Home Rule would sever their much-cherished link to the British crown. They did not have the same degree of attachment to successive British administrations, which they blamed for the precarious position in which they found them-selves by the late 1880s. Indicative of this is the fact the political resolutions of the ILPU, the IUA, and the Orange Order tended not to refer to Ireland under the British government but rather Ireland under the British crown. In 1910, Michael Knight, county grand master of the Orange Order in Monaghan, claimed: 'Loyalty to the throne has ever been a strong point in the practice of the Orange institution'.[46] The following year, the programme for a demonstration of southern Unionists organised by the IUA in Dublin concluded: 'We protest against any change that will deprive us of our birthright, by which we stand on equal ground with our fellow countrymen of Great Britain as subjects of our king and as citizens of the British empire.' Inevitably, it ended with the sentiment: 'GOD SAVE THE KING'.[47]

Essentially, the Irish Unionist movement became characterised by two different outlooks. There were the Unionists of the nine-county province of Ulster who adhered to the more rigidly defined concept of the union, to be enforced by an armed struggle if necessary. Then there were the Unionists of the three southern provinces who, because of their different circumstances and their greater sense of isolation were less aggressive. The latter's anti-Home Rule campaign was mainly propagandist; they channelled their energies towards informing the British electorate of their perceived position in a self-governing Ireland.

On 16 October 1885, the ILPU issued its initial manifesto. They emphasised that it was an organisation 'affording to those Irishmen of all creeds and political opinions ... an organised opposition to the efforts being made by the party led by Mr Parnell to sever the legis-lative connection between Ireland and Great Britain'.[48] The new organisation was to be 'entirely unsectarian in its character'. However, it became almost exclusively Protestant and dependent on the support of the landed class.[49] Of its nine founding members, seven were landlords: William Pakenham, Henry Bruen, Arthur MacMurrough Kavanagh, Bernard Fitzpatrick, John Vesey, Richard Bagwell and Thomas Butler.[50] In the 1885 election, the ILPU were dependent predominantly on landlords and their sons to act as candi-dates. But none of their fifty-two was successful, emphasising to its members that outside of the University or Dublin South constituen-cies, they had little hope of winning any seats in the three southern provinces. In the general election of the following year, only eleven landlord Unionists contested seats in the twenty-six counties and none of these were returned; in 1892 they contested thirty-four seats, but won only two; in the election of December 1910 they contested only four seats but won none.

From the mid-1880s, too many southern Irish landlords were pre-occupied with their economic survival to have the heart to fight for their political survival. Even if they had the finances and the heart to do so, they saw little prospect of being able to turn the tide of Nationalism. Sir William Gregory, for example, refused the invitation of Arthur MacMurrough Kavanagh to become involved in the ILPU. Considering Gregory's political record, this must have been quite a blow to the ILPU, but as Gregory's biographer puts it: 'Gregory was sceptical of its prospects in electoral contests with the Nationalists, fearing that its candidates might make laughing stocks of themselves, yet stimulate American subscriptions to the National League'.[51]

Just as the founding members of the ILPU were substantial land-owners, it was the same class who composed the executive of the IUA in the 1890s and acted as presidents of Unionist clubs throughout the country.[52] Smaller landowners were less active. It is possible that this was because they spent more time in their localities and felt more susceptible to outrage if they were openly to oppose the will of the majority of the people. After all, Unionism in the south did not have the numerical support that it had in Ulster. Lionel Pleignier, an officer of the IUA, did a tour of the country in 1891. He found in County Louth, for example, that: 'Unionist strength underneath the surface, which is afraid to put itself forward unless backed by an organisation of some sort, is undoubtedly greater than is generally supposed'.[53] He found a 'lack of energy' amongst landlords, which he claimed was at least partly 'due to the series of blows they have received'.[54] Similarly regarding the 1885 election, an ILPU pamphlet regretted that many of those 'whose position ought to make them independent in their actions never voted at all partly through fear of the unwritten law of the land'.[55] In 1886, the same fear was present when the ILPU made a plea for funds to its supporters but did not publish the names of subscribers as a safeguard against possible recrimination.[56] When, some years later, in 1907, the Marquis of Waterford made a contribution to the IUA, both Dungarvan and Carrick-on-Suir rural district councils passed resolutions 'condemn-ing and stigmatising' his conduct.[57] In the same year, a meeting of Longford UIL passed a resolution condemning Lord Longford for his donation of £500 to the same fund; he 'had no right to devote any

portion of his income to such a purpose'.[58] When in 1912, the IUA
organised a series of anti-Home Rule demonstrations in the south,
they were met with opposition from hostile crowds of Nationalists.
Opposition was overt in areas such as Limerick, or more subtle as at
Kilkenny Castle where a local firm that had lent some barrels for the
construction of the platform withdrew them when they found out
what the platform was to be used for.[59]

The ILPU and the IUA therefore failed to gain a foothold at
grassroots level in the twenty-six counties because they were too
dependent on the initiative and energy of a limited number of individuals.[60] Even at its height in 1913, the IUA boasted no more than
around 700 members. Yet while neither movement made any significant impact on politics in southern Ireland from 1885 to 1914, their
propagandist campaigns in Britain should be given some credit for
thwarting the Home Rule movement during the first and second
Home Rule crises. This was facilitated by their links with British
Unionists many of whom would have objected themselves to Home
Rule on constitutional grounds. It should also perhaps be considered
that some Irish landowners, who would have failed to win seats in
Ireland continued during these crises to represent British constituencies. The fifth Earl of Dunraven was MP for South Glamorgan from
1895 to 1906. Charles Beresford who had been MP for Waterford
from 1874 to 1880 continued to sit successively for four separate
English constituencies from 1885 to 1916. And William Fitzwilliam
who had been MP for Wicklow from 1868 to 1874 sat for Yorkshire
from 1880 to 1885 and for Doncaster from 1885 to 1892.

The situation in the three counties of Ulster (where the Protestant
population ranged from 19 per cent in Cavan to 25 per cent in Monaghan)
was somewhat different. Landlords in these counties very much put
themselves out on a limb to support the Unionist movement. The
1880 election in Monaghan which saw the return of two Liberals —
John Givan and William Findlater — and the continued growth in
Land Leagueism in 1881, encouraged landlords in that county to look
increasingly towards the Orange Order as a bulwark against the
spread of agitation and a means of maintaining at least some of their
political rights. According to Sir Shane Leslie, his father and grandfather, 'joined the Order in a desperate effort to save the family
seat'.[61] In neighbouring County Cavan (where two Home Rule MPs had
been returned as early as 1874), Colonel Edward Saunderson had
already come to regard the Orange Order as the only 'organisation
capable of dealing with the condition of anarchy and rebellion'.[62]
Families such as the Leslies, Murray-Kers, Dartreys, Maddens and
Rossmores took a more prominent and leading role in the Orange

Order's activities. Through the Orange Order, they re-established themselves as the leaders of a Protestant tenantry who, despite their shared agrarian grievances, were gradually becoming more alienated from their Catholic neighbours because of the growing association of the Land League with the Catholic clergy and the Home Rule movement.[63] The speeches of Orange leaders at the 12 July celebrations in the three counties from the early 1880s closely associated Land Leagueism with sectarianism, land agitation and plunder. As a child of the 1880s, Shane Leslie grew up with such associations:

I had not long grown out of nursery or schoolrooms before I realised that nothing really mattered in Ireland except Home Rule, a rumour of ill omen against which all the Orangemen and good men on the estate were pledged to fight. The mountainy men would descend on the village and gardens and divide up the beautiful grounds in which we played. Mr Gladstone, who was more wicked than any bad man in the bible, had promised to give all our woods, house and demesne to the Catholics who already had them divided up and were playing dice for them in the public house.[64]

In June 1883, a by-election was called in Monaghan because of the resignation of John Givan who had been appointed crown solicitor for Kildare and Meath. This provided Parnell with the opportunity to begin his so-called 'invasion of Ulster'. Timothy Healy contested the seat for the Home Rule party and defeated the Conservative John Munroe QC by 2,376 votes to 2,011.[65] (The third candidate, Henry Pringle, secured only 274 votes emphasising the collapse of the Liberal party.) Healy's election had been achieved largely with the help of the Catholic clergy. Munroe later wrote:

The priests of the county were his sponsors, his canvassers, his personation agents, his clerks. I do not speak merely of the younger clergy, who might still be powerfully possessed by a strong fellow-feeling for the people with whom they are so intimately associated. I include the older clergy, the parish priests, the canons, and the higher dignitaries.... To no one is Mr Healy so much indebted for his success as to the Very Rev Canon Hoey, parish priest of Castleblaney. At Carrickmacross he never for a moment relaxed his exertions, aiding to the booths the weak and helpless. Indeed so complete were his arrangements that one agent, seeing the death-like pallor on the faces of these independent electors, asked the reverend gentleman if, having exhausted the poorhouses and hospitals, he had now taken to the graveyards.[66]

The election campaign that Healy fought emphasised the division in the county between Catholic Nationalists (who no longer feared landlord retribution) and Protestant Unionists (even though that term does not effectively become applicable until 1885). Shane Leslie later claimed that Parnell's 'audacity to send a whipper-snapper of a secretary' and the failure of the Monaghan landed class to 'guide the mane of slow galloping opportunity [meant] it had fallen to the priests and been consequently nailed to the counters of Belfast as Rome rule disguised'.[67] After Healy's election, Nationalists organised meetings throughout south Ulster, but wherever they did so, an Orange counter-demonstration was called. The most famous stand-off occurred at Roslea on the Fermanagh–Monaghan border in October 1883. The fifth Baron Rossmore, county grand master of the Monaghan Orangemen, issued a provocatively-worded invitation to Orangemen to assemble in their thousands to counteract the effect of the 'rebellious party' who had organised a Nationalist meeting there.[68] Only a minor skirmish ensued. But the Roslea meeting was to mark an important stage in the emergence of the Orange Order to political leadership in the province as a whole.[69]

Within a short time, the Ulster Unionist movement became more and more independent of its southern counterpart. The Nationalist invasion of Ulster led to the formation of the Ulster Loyalist Anti-Repeal Union in 1886 which was shortly to team up with the Orange Order voicing opposition to Home Rule. The formation of Unionist clubs in Ulster during the second Home Rule crisis of the 1890s, a phenomena which did not effectively stretch beyond the province (although there were a few clubs in counties such as Sligo, Leitrim, Wicklow and Cork), emphasised the divide between Ulster and southern Unionists.

After the defeat of the second Home Rule Bill in 1893, the land question once again threatened to weaken what was still a relatively unstable alliance of landlords and Protestant farmers. The latter were now being organised under the Ulster Tenant Defence Association led by T.W. Russell who by 1901 was addressing meetings through-out the province, largely attended by Presbyterian farmers.[70] However, the advancement once again of the Home Rule movement, especially after the devolution crisis of 1904–05 (allied to the gener-ous terms of the 1903 Land Act) alleviated the crisis. In response to the devolution crisis when Balfour's government was suspected of fostering a policy of Home Rule by instalments, a meeting of Ulster Unionists in Belfast in 1904, formed a central Unionist association. In March 1905, it assumed the name of the Ulster Unionist Council and comprised Unionist MPs, all local Unionist associations, Unionist clubs and Orange lodges in Ulster. The UUC was to become the virtual directing power of Ulster Unionism during and after the third Home Rule crisis of the 1910s.

The opposition to Home Rule, which had largely fallen into abeyance until then, was reawakened in the three Ulster counties. In September 1912, the signing of the Solemn League and Covenant outlined the stance that the UUC was prepared to take in the event of Home Rule being passed.[71] Landowners throughout the three counties took the initiative in organising the signing of the Covenant: in Monaghan over 5,000 men signed it; 4,600 signed it in Cavan; and 'a considerable number of people' signed it in Donegal, later estimated at around 3,000'.[72] Around the same time, members of the Unionist clubs throughout Ulster began drilling. Again, in Cavan, Monaghan and Donegal it was landlords who provided the leadership. By September 1913, there were seventeen Unionist clubs in Cavan and fourteen in Monaghan. The previous May, the Cavan county inspector reported that 'its country gentry, many of whom are retired military officers, appear to be head of the movement'. They included Lord Farnham, Colonel Somerset Saunderson, Captain Pratt, Major Hamilton and Colonel Nugent.[73] By October 1913, there were nineteen clubs in Donegal where drill was 'regularly practised ... under the instruction in most areas by men who have served in the army or who are still connected with it', the most prominent leader being the Earl of Leitrim.[74]

At the UUC's annual meeting in January 1913, it was decided to co-ordinate those who had taken up drilling into a body to be known as the Ulster Volunteer Force. By November 1913, there were 3,400 UVF members in Cavan and its leaders were reported to be Lord Farnham, Henry Maxwell of Mount Nugent, Somerset Saunderson, Major Hamilton of Castlehamilton, Captain Pratt of Cabra and two Church of Ireland ministers.[75] Of these, Lord Farnham (Arthur Kenlis Maxwell, eleventh Baron Farnham) was the most active. In January 1914 he told the Unionists of Cavan that they had: 'to do their utmost to put their whole moral and spiritual courage and feeling in the Ulster Volunteer Force, and to do their utmost to make it a success and a real disciplined military force'.[76] By November 1913, there were 2,746 UVF members in Donegal who by May 1914 were said to be: 'well drilled and a well-organised body under capable leaders'. The following month the county inspector reported that 'all through the county the local gentry with few exceptions are Unionists.... Where units of the UVF exist in their respective localities, they lend their support to that organisation'. The Earl of Leitrim, who was the county commander, was busily 'involved in transportation of arms, a

sub target gun belonging to him being transported from Orange hall
to Orange hall for instructional purpose'.[77] By August 1913 there
were 1,152 members of the Ulster Volunteer Force in Monaghan
divided into two battalions.[78] Of the members of the county committee of the UVF in September 1912, four were landlords — the Earl of
Dartrey, Sir John Leslie, John Madden and Major E.J. Richardson;
the fifth was Michael Knight, a Clones solicitor and county grand
master of the Orange Order. The divisional representatives were
made up of three other landlords, three large Protestant farmers,
one land agent and one doctor.[79]

Landlords in the three Ulster counties opened their demesnes
to facilitate the training of the UVF and they allowed arms to be
hidden in their houses and out-offices. In March 1912, one of the
first demesnes in Ulster on which drilling was reported was
Castlesaunderson in Cavan.[80] In April 1913, there was a review of
the first battalion of the Monaghan UVF in Sir John Leslie's demesne
at Glaslough. In March 1914, a camp was set up on Farnham estate
in Cavan for one week, attended by 230 UVF members, 'for the
purpose of receiving instruction in drill'.[81] In June of the same year:
'about five tons of provisions [were] stored' at Drumbarnett in
Donegal 'in preparation for an hospital or a camp of instruction'.[82]
After the Larne gun running, there were 1,374 rifles in Cavan of
which 300 were stored at Farnham (as well as two maxim guns); 114
in Major Hamilton's house; and 120 in other big houses in the
county. There were 1,784 rifles in Donegal of which seventy were
stored at Mulroy, sixty at Boyd's of Letterkenny and over 300 in
smaller quantities in other big houses.[83] Of the estimated 1,678 rifles
in Monaghan, 300 were stored at Dartrey Castle; 150 at Glaslough
and 125 at Hilton Park.[84]

Why were landlords in these three counties more prepared to go
out on a limb by assuming leadership of a militant organisation that
could only draw upon themselves the wrath of the Nationalist
majorities in their respective counties? Numerically they were better
placed, being part of a wider Ulster Unionist society that offered a
more hierarchical framework of support from industrialists and
businessmen as well as tenant farmers that was not available
further south. Although this level of support from the business
community was not as forthcoming in the three counties, there was
still more of an attachment to industrialised Belfast than to Dublin.[85]
During the third Home Rule crisis, some landlords were at pains to
emphasise their pride in being part of the flourishing northern
economy. Sir John Leslie asked in 1913 if Nationalists had 'ever
shown any ability to farm on scientific methods or when had they

proved that they would be capable of industrialising and developing the agricultural south as Protestants had done in the north'?[86]

Despite the 'invasion of Ulster' landlords in the three counties had escaped relatively unscathed the ravishes of Land Leagueism. They had not witnessed first hand the type of intimidation and terror that prevailed on the estates of their fellow landowners in the south, and where they did they were largely successful in combating it. Allied to this was the effective organisational Unionist structure that characterised Protestant politics in Ulster. The UVF meant they had a well-organised and well-armed force at their backs so that rather than succumbing to decline they found themselves with an alternative not fashionable amongst the more isolated and more out-numbered Unionists in the south: they could stand and make a fight of it. As such, this could perhaps be seen as the natural response to a crisis expected of men with a long political and military tradition of leadership. Such traditions were still carried on in the army by land-lords such as Col John Leslie; Lt-Col John Madden; his brother, Major Gerald; Captain Somerset Saunderson and Captain Mervyn Pratt to name but a few. Some like Leslie who fondly recalled memo-ries of his father, a man 'whose word was law to lay folk and clergy and to Catholics and Protestants', may have lived in hope that that day would return.[87]

They at least wanted the maintenance of the union which they, no different in this respect from their peers further south, considered vital for the maintenance of their civil and religious liberties. The growth of the UVF in the three counties coincided with the rumoured proposals to exclude the four north-eastern counties from the scope of the third Home Rule Bill. This caused great anxiety amongst Unionists in the three counties for if such rumours were well founded, landlords needed to mobilise as much support for the UVF as possible in order to win the gratitude of the UUC. They would need to convince that body that Cavan, Monaghan and Donegal were worthy of a place in a separate state should partition become a reality.[88]

LANDLORDS AND THE WAR EFFORT, 1914–18

Although the contribution of the First World War to the socio-economic decline of the big house raises some questions, there is little denying the detrimental effect it had on landlord politics.[89] In the south, the IUA virtually ceased political activities and did not seri-ously oppose the third passage of the 1912 Home Rule Bill in 1914.[90] At a local level, Unionist organisation broke down completely. By

January 1916, there had been no Unionist meetings in County Clare since the outbreak of war. In Sligo, it was 'absolutely dormant since the war started'; in Tipperary, there was 'nothing doing' and Unionists were said to be 'lying low.... Everybody is quiet and everyone who used to support the cause has gone to the front'. In Waterford, Unionism was 'a negligible quantity. The committee hardly exists. Every Unionist has gone to war'.[91] The permanent or temporary loss of Unionist landlords such as the fifth Earl of Longford, Richard Levinge, Edward Stafford-King-Harman, and Bryan Cooper weakened the organisational structure of Unionism at both national and local levels.

Similarly, the war led to a weakening of Unionist sentiment which although not quantifiable was at least perceptible. Southern Unionists deemed the wartime needs of the empire to be far more pressing than the 'domestic controversy' at home. John Redmond's emotional speech in the House of Commons on 3 August 1914 pledging Irish support for the war effort and urging the government to leave the defence of Irish shores to the volunteers, north and south, led to a new conciliatory stance by the IUA. (His speech on 20 September at Woodenbridge pledging the National Volunteers to go 'wherever the firing extends, in defence of right, freedom and religion, in this war' was to lead directly to a split between moderate and radical Nationalists.)[92] Immediately afterwards, the Earl of Fingall joined the National Volunteers in the hope that that body would provide manpower for the armed forces at the front. The Earl of Bandon, who had been president of the Cork Unionist Association, became patron of the Cork Volunteers along with the Nationalist mayor of the city. Lord Headfort 'proposed forthwith to join a corps'. Sir Algernon Coote and the Duke of Leinster allowed the National Volunteers to drill in their demesnes. Lord Mayo said he would 'gladly help in the equipment and maintenance of the Volunteer movement in the south of Ireland'. Lord Courtown, on behalf of the Unionists of Wexford, said they all appreciated Redmond's stance.[93]

In dozens of letters by landlords to national newspapers in August 1914, there was a sense of optimism that the war crisis might somehow lead to conciliation amongst the divided parties in Ireland at a later stage. Sir John Keane appealed to all classes and denominations 'to pull together without prejudice to their political opinions' so that when the war was over they might find that 'political differences are not so acute as they appeared in the past'.[94] At the front in 1915, Lord Powerscourt told a reporter of the *Freeman's Journal*: 'If we could only come together in Ireland what a country we would make of it'.[95] In 1918, Bryan Cooper claimed that his war experience

had a profound effect on the way that he perceived Irishmen who did
not share his political ideology:

> The bond of common service proved so strong and enduring that
> Catholic and Protestant, Unionist and Nationalist, lived and fought
> and died side by side like brothers. Little was spoken concerning the
> points on which we differed and once we had tacitly agreed to let the
> past be buried we found thousands of points on which we agreed.[96]

As his biographer, Lennox Robinson, later pointed out, Cooper
was a much-changed man when he returned to Ireland. He was prepared to look for a settlement based on Home Rule and even to
consider adopting the ideals of Sinn Féinism. He was no longer the
hard-liner throwing 'on the counter every used coin of Unionism'.[97]

The conciliatory attitude of Southern Unionists was brought with
them to the Irish Convention of 1917. By then the political scene in
Ireland was in a state of chaos. The 1916 rebellion, the failure of
Redmond's party to settle the Home Rule question, and controversies
such as the threatened extension of conscription to Ireland had led to
a swing away from constitutional Home Rule towards the more militant Sinn Féin.[98] The Ulster Unionists were not so conciliatory. For
them partition was becoming a viable option and it did not necessarily include the counties of Monaghan, Cavan and Donegal. The idea
of partition had been floating around since June 1912 but it was not
until the Buckingham Palace Conference of July 1914 that the
Unionists of the three counties became fearful of their position when
the idea of a six-county split was mooted. The outbreak of war
shelved the partition problem for the time being but it was brought
out of cold storage again after the 1916 rebellion when David Lloyd
George, Minister for Munitions, was determined to exact a settlement in order to consolidate relations between Britain and the USA.
Without reference to the cabinet, Lloyd George proceeded to effect a
settlement based on the implementation of the 1914 Home Rule Act
with a proposal for the exclusion of the six north-eastern counties.
He misled Sir Edward Carson into believing that the cabinet supported
these terms and so Carson laid them before the UUC on 6 June 1916
and urged their acceptance.[99]

For the next week, the delegates of Monaghan, Cavan and Donegal
debated the terms and at a meeting of the UUC on 12 June, they
informed its members that if the future of the empire was dependent
on the terms proposed they would abide by any decision reached.[100]
The UUC gratefully acknowledged their decision and proposed that
Carson should continue negotiations on the basis of a six-county split

'in the interests of the empire'.[101] Carson claimed that 'this sacrifice' was 'the greatest piece of lasting evidence of their devoted, unselfish loyalty to the king, constitution and empire' that he had seen in his political career.[102]

However, there seems to have been some dissension amongst the delegates of the three counties as one of the Cavan delegates, Major Somerset Saunderson, left the meeting 'with a feeling of dismay and a sense of betrayal'.[103] A short time later, Saunderson was in London where he found out that Lloyd George's proposals had, in fact, never been before the cabinet. He wrote to Carson to discontinue negotiations but although Saunderson's revelations were borne out by Lord Selborne and Lord Lansdowne, Carson refused to accept their validity.[104] Saunderson then wrote to William Martin, secretary of the North Monaghan Unionist Association, calling on that body to pass a resolution informing Carson that the 12 June decision, based on 'misconception', could not stand.[105] The NMUA refused to do so and at a meeting on 13 July 1916 they stood by the decision to allow Carson to negotiate a six-county split.[106] Carson wrote to William Martin welcoming the NMUA's continued support, describing Saunderson's claim as 'a tissue of misapprehension from beginning to end', and claiming that 'no one has suffered more than I have from the knowledge that it was impossible to include the three counties'.[107] As Carson and the UUC were now in the process of negotiating terms that would safeguard their position within the United Kingdom, it is hardly likely that they would admit to the truth of Saunderson's allegations.

When Lloyd George failed to implement his proposals, Unionist leaders in Monaghan assumed that their position reverted to what it had been prior to the 12 June meeting.[108] But the die had been cast, the principle of a six-county exclusion had been accepted by the UUC and their adherence to this principle at the 1917 Convention reflected this. Inevitably, the Ulster leaders welcomed the government's intention to tackle the Irish question on the basis of partition in the aftermath of the war. At the same time the Unionist organisation in Monaghan, Donegal and Cavan had been thrown into chaos during the war. Protestant farmers and their sons who had joined the UVF so readily had failed to respond to recruitment.[109] Fifty-two members of the Monaghan UVF joined the army in September 1914, but the reluctance of their comrades to do so became a characteristic of the war years in the county.[110] As early as December, the county inspector noted that there was 'scarcely anyone' coming forward. The response remained essentially the same during 1915 and 1916 and by February 1917 the county inspector reported that recruitment for the army in Monaghan was at a standstill. From that month on, police reports (for Donegal and Cavan as well as Monaghan) were littered with statements such as: 'recruiting has practically ceased in this county'; 'recruiting is practically nil'; 'recruiting for the army is practically at a standstill'.[111]

From a political point of view, the war years affected not only Unionist organisation and activity, but also the very cohesiveness of the movement. The poor response of Protestant farmers to recruitment led to a schism between them and landlords. In December 1915, Col Lucas Scudamore of Castleshane claimed that 'no set of people in the world ... had more done for them by the government than the farmers of Ireland and no set of people had done less for their country'.[112] Sir John Leslie also denounced them. But he was aware of a reason other than personal gain from war-time agricultural profits that may have underpinned the reluctance of Protestant farmers to recruit: the fear that if they were sent from Ireland, their holdings would be in danger from people 'whose political opinions were not quite the same as theirs'.[113] This fear stemmed from the equally poor contribution of Nationalists to recruitment, the halting of emigration, the growth of agrarian agitation particularly in Monaghan and Cavan due to the rejuvenation of the United Irish League from 1915 and the growth of Sinn Féin during the war years.[114]

From 1914 to 1918 big houses were emptied of many of the Unionist movement's leaders; some, like Gerald Madden and Norman Leslie, were to die at the front while others such as Col Lucas Scudamore, W.F. de Visme Kane and John Moorehead died at home from illness or natural causes, thereby depriving the movement of many of its established or potential leaders. Those who had remained at home concentrated on the war effort to the exclusion of Unionist activities. Col John Leslie, the Earl of Dartrey and Major Richardson devoted their energies to recruitment. Michael Knight considered recruiting meetings 'more important' than attending meetings of Monaghan county council and so communicated more with the council through letters than in person from 1914 to 1918.[115]

As early as September 1914, it was reported that drilling 'was not as active as previously' in Unionist clubs in Monaghan.[116] A year later both the Unionist clubs and the UVF there were said to be totally inactive.[117] By 1920, there was only one Unionist club in the county with a mere thirty members.[118] Similarly, the Orange Order lost much of its traditional vigour and for the three years, 1916–18 inclusive, it held no Orange demonstrations: 'in view of the serious war in which our country is engaged in'.[119] By January 1917, the UVF in Donegal was 'inactive and nominal'.[120] Likewise in Cavan: in November 1914 there were only 187 active UVF members.[121] Even if the Unionists of the three counties had been better prepared, the UUC as a body had decided that the best way forward was a six-county split. When Lord Farnham, who as well as being a member of the UUC was a leading member of the IUA, wrote to Charles Craig, brother of James, in 1919 proposing a joint committee of Irish Unionists north and south, he received the following reply:

> With regard to the question of a joint committee we felt that while desiring to work with you to the utmost of our ability in the common cause it would not be possible to have any formal and permanent committee for this purpose. We feel we must have a free hand, and although we realise that our aims are the same as those of the Irish Unionist Alliance, we feel that there are occasions on which the attainment of these aims will be sought along different lines.... This applies to questions of policy, but the same difficulties arise even in the question of propaganda, as we have found in the past, and I might mention as an instance of this, the difficulty with regard to pamphlets sent out from the Ulster point of view, which sometimes offend the susceptibilities of people coming from the South.[122]

The Government of Ireland Bill, introduced into the House of Commons in February 1920, proposed to set up two parliaments: one for the twenty-six counties that presently constitute the Irish Republic and one for the six counties of Ulster to be styled Northern Ireland. To Charles Craig the new bill gave Unionists in the proposed exclusion area 'practically everything that they had fought for, everything that they had armed for, and everything that they had raised the volunteers for in 1913 and 1914'.[123]

In a desperate bid to have the whole of the province excluded, the Monaghan, Cavan and Donegal delegates made a plea to the UUC in the form of a pamphlet entitled *Ulster and Home Rule: No Partition of Ulster*. The pamphleteers argued that anything less than the exclusion of the whole of the province would be a breach of the Solemn League and Covenant, and they set out the political, geographical and economic reasons why the whole of the province should be excluded.[124] On 10 March 1920, Lord Farnham of Cavan moved and M.E. Knight of Monaghan seconded the following resolution:

> That this council abiding by its covenant refuses to accept any form of government which does not include the whole geographical province of Ulster and calls upon its parliamentary leaders to take such steps

as may be necessary to see that the term Northern Ireland in the permanent bill is altered to include the whole province of Ulster.[125]

The resolution was rejected. The majority of the UUC agreed that the new bill recognised the rights of the six counties to separate treatment, which was a preferable alternative to the 1914 Home Rule Act.[126] The Unionists of the three counties became disillusioned and bitter with the UUC's decision. In April 1920, the Monaghan, Cavan and Donegal delegates resigned from the UUC.

At the end of March, a meeting of the Cavan Unionist Association passed a resolution 'protesting against the breach of the Ulster covenant by the UUC in deserting their fellow covenanters'.[127] A descendant of Somerset Saunderson later wrote:

> Being himself the most punctilious of men, Somerset's feelings may be imagined when he saw his ancestral home and family estates handed over to his bitterest enemies by the country which he and his forebears had served so loyally and so long. 'Now', said he. 'I have no country'.[128]

Saunderson emigrated to England where he died in 1922. His fellow Cavan delegate, Lord Farnham, wrote in April 1920:

> Our people look upon themselves as betrayed and deserted.... How can we remain members of a body that have plainly told us they don't want us and that we are an encumbrance to them and have ... broken a solemn covenant in order to get rid of us.[129]

By April 1920, the Monaghan delegates had resigned from the UUC, deploring their treatment as part of 'a selfish policy'.[130] The Ulster Unionist leaders were denounced by John Madden who claimed at the 12 July celebrations that year that Sir Edward Carson had given to Monaghan Unionists 'the most perfect example of legal quibbling' he had ever seen.[131] Madden went on to encourage his fellow Orangemen to owe allegiance to a southern parliament and to help in every way to carry out the business of the country and of Monaghan.[132] Michael Knight, a former member of the UUC standing committee, was equally as vehement that the betrayal of Monaghan Unionists 'by those who professed to be their friends' had been 'in order to make for themselves places of trust and emoluments'.[133]

Nowhere was the sense of desertion, betrayal, resentment and subsequent acquiescence to the new order more perceptible than in the activities of the Orange Order. In 1922, the Orangemen of Monaghan sent a resolution to the Grand Orange Lodge of Ireland in Belfast stating that as they considered the union no longer existed for them, they could not pledge loyalty to it. The resolution ended: 'If Orange-ism is to exist at all it must have its own organisation which will not clash with the laws of the Irish Free State'.[134] An attempt to form a separate Free State lodge was unsuccessful due to lack of support given to a meeting in Clones in April 1923.[135] On 12 July that year, the only Orange celebration in the Free State was held at Analore, near Clones. Michael Knight told those present that 'they owed noth-ing to British statesmen (cheers). To them was due the present position in which they in that part of the country found themselves'.[136] The following year, the editor of the *Northern Standard* noted the trans-formation which had taken place in the speeches of the Orange leaders in just over a decade: there was no longer an appeal to pas-sions, a note of challenge in every sentence or the emphasising of sectarian differences.[137] Instead the message was that 'the sphere of usefulness' open to Orangemen of the Free State was in working for 'the realisation and universal application of the root principles of the Orange movement, the principle of liberty and equality for all creeds and classes'.[138] It should, of course, be remembered that these Orangemen were in a very different position than a decade previously when they had the UVF at their back and the support of Unionist Ulster. Having been discarded, they were now very much in the minority. And having witnessed the terrorism of the revolutionary period 1919–23 in the county and the monopolisation of parliamentary representation and local government by Sinn Féin their acquiescence had undoubtedly been hastened.[139]

LANDLORD POLITICS IN THE FREE STATE

The main contributory factors to post-war decline were largely out-side the control of Unionists in the twenty-six counties. There was nothing they could do to stem the flow of support towards Sinn Féin which swept the boards at the 1918 election and then took control of the local government bodies in 1920. The conciliatory attitude adopted by Southern Unionists at the 1917 Convention led to a split in the IUA. Some of the most influential landlord Unionists, such as Lords Desart, Donoughmore, Bandon, Courtown, Headfort, Mayo, Sligo and Wicklow, opted to become members of the new Anti-Partition League, while hard-liners such as Lord Farnham, Lord Dunalley, E.J. Beaumont-Nesbitt and J.M. Wilson remained with the IUA.[140]

The turmoil of the country during the revolutionary period from 1919 to 1923 prevented either body from effectively rejuvenating

Unionist politics in the south. The terrorism to which landlords were exposed made many question the wisdom of remaining in the country let alone the idea of involving themselves openly in a political movement that would expose them to even greater threat from those seeking complete independence from Britain. In August 1921, J.W. Garvey of Tulley near Westport wrote:

> I would have preferred to see the union cemented rather than dis-membered but the union is now a thing of the past. We have our all in the west and our only chance of saving anything we have is by silence in the midst of this great revolutionary change.... Any aggressive word or act would be fatal to us now and our chances of security and safety are not very hopeful.[141]

The disillusionment which landowners felt with the degree of protection offered to them by the British government diluted their Unionism. In June 1921, Lord Dunraven claimed in the Lords:

> Outrages and murder are committed, not for any political motives, but purely for personal motives of malice and revenge, hate and spite. There is in Ireland today absolutely no protection whatever for life or property. Honest, decent citizens have no protection, and can get no protection from the police and are not allowed to protect themselves.[142]

Even the less politically active felt the same. In December 1921, Lady Alice Howard wrote in her diary: 'Such a dreadful year of rebel-lion and murder — and now England has cast us off and given us to the murderers'.[143]

Other Unionist landlords decided to leave the country altogether, with no great desire to return. In March 1922, Lord Bandon went to England to recover from a kidnapping ordeal. He wrote:

> In areas where these outrages were most frequent and most cruel no protection was afforded to human life, and many of the exiles would not dare run the risk of placing themselves again in the power of criminals who desire to injure them.[144]

Lord Desart was living in England a long time before his house was burned in February 1923. After its burning he felt that 'the end of his life in Ireland had arrived'.[145] Shortly after J.M. Wilson's house, Currygrane, was burned in 1922, Edward Carson informed the Lords that Wilson was 'now living in humble lodgings in an English village, shattered in health and broken in spirit'.[146] Having

heard of Carson's speech, Wilson wrote to him: 'A thousand thanks
for your *great* speech, from a poor Irish refugee, who is nearly heart-
broken at the duplicity, mendacity & cowardice of our former friends.
God help those of us belonging to the south or west'.[147]

Those landlords who remained saw the inevitability of their position and in their capacity as deputy lieutenants or officers of local
Unionist clubs sought to make peace with the new administration.
During 1920, *The Irish Times* was teeming with resolutions passed
by landlord-dominated bodies which reflected that they no longer
regarded Unionism as an acceptable or practicable political ideology.
In August 1920, for example, a meeting of the deputy lieutenants
and magistrates of Queen's County called for dominion Home Rule.
Col Cosby of Stradbally Hall revealed his change of heart: 'I am an
old Unionist — as you know a life long Unionist — and now I have to
pocket my feelings and to do what I can for the good and benefit of
my beloved country'.[148] In October, a meeting of Mayo JPs expressed
their lack of confidence in the British government, deplored the state
of anarchy and resolved that law and order could only be restored 'by
an Irish parliament having complete authority'.[149] Even though landlord bodies still preferred a form of dominion Home Rule to a total
dismemberment of the union, their resolutions showed that an Irish
parliament was now more acceptable to them than at any other time
in the past.

At local level, landlords effectively lost all political power. In the
1920 local elections, Sinn Féin captured all the county councils in the
twenty-six counties. There was little room for landlords on them and
even where the very few were elected in counties such as Monaghan,
their influence was negligible.[150] The titles which landlords continued
to hold up to the 1920s such as lieutenant of the county, deputy of
the county and high sheriff had merely become honorific. Gradually
their duties were whittled away and all power passed to elected local
bodies. In September, 1920 Algernon Coote resigned his position as
lieutenant for Queen's County claiming that his experience was that
'his majesty's lieutenants are not now consulted in any way in reference to the maintenance of law and order in the country'.[151] Sinn Féin
dominated local councils and were at pains to emphasise that the old
regime had passed and that there was neither place for obsolete
offices nor for landlords who had traditionally filled them. Before the
meeting of the new Dublin county council in 1920, it was said to be 'a
matter of controversy' as to whether or not it would recognise the
office of the shrievalty. The lord mayor, Alderman O'Neill, said: 'he
would not touch the position with a forty foot pole'.[152] In the same
month the Sinn Féin members of Cork corporation nominated Fred

Murray for the post of high sheriff for the city. Murray was in jail at the time on charges of having shot and wounded an RIC officer the previous May and one member of the corporation pointed out wryly that if he was elected, Murray would have the power to summon 'a special jury' to try himself![153] In Limerick, 'no action' was taken to appoint a high sheriff in 1920 as the county council refused to discuss the matter.[154] As the War of Independence and later the Civil War gained momentum nationwide, the shrievalty in the twenty-six counties fell into 'a state of dissolution'.[155] An article in *The Irish Times* in January 1923, pointed out that nobody was even aware of who held the positions in each county that year.[156] Finally, and perhaps most significantly, the District Justices (Temporary Provisions) Act of 1923 took away the judicial functions of JPs. Section 4 of this act made provision for the appointment of new peace commissioners.[157] Very few peace commissioners in the Free State could be said to be representative of the old landed class (with the exception of the likes of George O'Callaghan Westropp in Clare, Sir Walter Nugent in Westmeath and Edward Bellingham in Louth). As W.E. Vaughan points out: 'the abolition of the lay magistracy in the Free State took away not only the gentry's status, but their main occupation as well'.[158]

Dominion Home Rule as favoured by landlords was not the Sinn Féin priority. With the establishment of the Free State those who may have wanted to add their political experience to the new parliament found that the electorate did not see it as being a place for former landlords or Unionists. The dwindling support for the old Unionist ideology in the twenty-six counties resulted in the winding up of the IUA and APL in 1922 and 1923 respectively: their *raison d'être* was gone and a Unionist party was not to re-emerge in the twenty-six counties.

THE SENATE

The only political outlet for (former) landlords in the Free State was the Senate. It had its origins in the schemes of 1914 and 1920, as proposed by the British government in an attempt to dilute the full force of national democracy, and also in talks which were held between southern Unionists and leading Free State politicians, the aims of which were to resolve how the interests of the minority could be safeguarded. Article 82 of the act establishing the Senate lay down that thirty members, or one half of the house, were to be nominated by the president of the executive council.[159] He was to take into consideration the provision of representation for groups, who were not adequately represented in the Dáil (effectively ex-Unionists.) Of these thirty, fifteen, to be selected by lot, were to hold office for the full term of twelve years, the other fifteen for six years. The remaining thirty senators were to be elected by the Dáil voting on the principle of proportional representation. Vacancies caused by death, resignation and so on were to be filled by a vote of the senate itself. In subsequent elections to the Senate, the whole country was to form a single electorate area. Voting was to be by PR with the electorate composed of all those over thirty-five years old. Candidates were to be drawn from a panel made up of three times as many qualified persons as there were members to be elected. Two thirds of these were to be nominated by the Dáil and the other third by the Senate.

Of the sixty members of the first Senate, eight were peers, four were baronets, one was a knight and eleven others had served as officers in the British army.[160] Sixteen out of the thirty nominated by President W.T. Cosgrave could be described as ex-Unionists.[161] Former landlord families were represented by such as Lord Dunraven who had been lieutenant of Limerick since 1894. He had also been an officer in the British army, ADC to the lord lieutenant of Ireland as far back as 1868, under-secretary to the colonies, chairman of the Irish Land Conference 1902–03 and a member of the Irish Convention in 1917. The Earl of Mayo had also been a member of the Irish Land Conference of 1902–03 and a representative peer for Ireland since 1890. The Earl of Granard, a veteran of the First World War, had been lord-in-waiting to King Edward VII, and ADC to Lord Cadogan when he was lord lieutenant. Sir John Keane an extensive landowner, a director and future governor of the Bank of Ireland was another senator. Still others were the Countess of Desart who had re-established the Kilkenny Woollen Mills and Sir Nugent Everard then chairman of the Great Southern Railway Company. These ex-Unionists did have political experience. They had contributed to Irish life in various ways, some like Keane were added assets because of their experience in the financial world, but they were also representative of the less hard-line element of the southern Unionist movement, more amenable to government support than opposition.

On the opening of the Senate and the election of a chairman, members were at pains to emphasise the goodwill that existed between former parties. Sir William Hutcheson-Poe asked his fellow senators, 'to bear in mind that whatever the colour of the political coats these candidates wore nine or ten years ago, that has nothing to do with the question today'. All were now: 'united in a determination to loyally support the Free State government and to carry out the constitution'.[162] John McLaughlin rebuked the scepticism of

Ulster Unionists regarding the usefulness of the Senate, and supported the candidature of the eventually successful Lord Glenavy for the chair. He said that: 'by electing Lord Glenavy we will give them a guarantee of fair play and let them see we are prepared to treat every Irishman, irrespective of what his politics were in the past or his religion is in the present'.[163]

It was, however, clear from the outset that the Senate was not to become a very powerful representative platform from the old landed class's point of view. In the same debate Col Maurice Moore acknowledged the fact that 'the Senate has not very much actual power'.[164] In fact, the powers of the Senate were greatly restricted in comparison to second chambers elsewhere. The Dáil was effectively given exclusive legislative authority over money bills. The Senate was given a power of suspension of 270 days on other bills received from the Dáil. But if it decided to amend or reject in total any bill, the Dáil could wait for a period of nine months and then have it deemed to be passed by both houses in its original form.

Former landlords accomplished very little in the first Senate. This was partially their own fault. Some showed an obvious apathy towards attending debates. Dónal O'Sullivan, a former clerk in the Senate, tells us that from 1922 to 1928: 'The bad attendance of certain senators was a grave scandal which was the subject of frequent discussion in the Senate'.[165] Poor attendance amongst former landlords may be explained by the fact that the Earl of Dunraven, for example, was eighty-two years old when elected and probably lacked the vitality for the political arena that he had shown previously. When Sir Thomas Esmonde proposed Dunraven as chairman, Sir Nugent Everard informed him that Dunraven was unwell.[166] On the other hand, Everard also informed the Senate that the Earl of Granard would be an unsuitable candidate as he had to go to America.[167] Others such as Sir William Hutcheson-Poe lived for the most part in England and although he regularly attended Senate meetings in the early period of its existence, he resigned his seat in 1924.

There were other factors outside their control, which undoubtedly proved to be disincentives to attendance, most notably the campaign of terror directed against senators by the Anti-Treatyites in early 1923. This campaign originated on 30 November 1922 when Liam Lynch, De Valera's chief of staff, sent orders to all battalions of the Anti-Treatyite forces to commence operations against the 'enemy' who included members of the Senate. On 9 January 1923, Marlfield, home of John Bagwell, was burned. Three weeks later Bagwell was kidnapped and held captive for three days before he managed to escape.[168] On 29 January, Palmerstown, home of the Earl of Mayo, and Kilteragh, home of Sir Horace Plunkett were burned. In February, Moore Hall, home of Maurice Moore; Mullaboden, home of Sir Bryan Mahon; Cappoquin, home of Sir John Keane; and Desart Court, home of the Earl of Desart (whose sister-in-law was the senator in the family) were all burned.[169] On 26 February, two land mines were placed in Castleforbes, home of the Earl of Granard and although only one of them exploded it did cause extensive damage. On 9 March, Ballynastragh, the home of Sir Thomas Esmonde, was also burned.[170]

Even when in attendance, the landed class showed very little initiative. The attitude of the chairman, Lord Glenavy, before the summer recess of 1924, did not augur well for the future. He told the Senate:

> There are nineteen bills for our consideration when we meet tomorrow. Twelve months ago it would have occurred to me that that would mean two days protracted sitting of the Senate. But seeing that we have dispatched fifteen bills today in the space of an hour I see no limit to the speed and powers of this house. Therefore, I think we will be able to dispose of these nineteen bills tomorrow.[171]

They made no attempt to act as an organised party. Even competent senators like the Earl of Mayo got carried away with issues that were hardly going to further the cause of the former landlord class except to provide them with more comfortable travel arrangements between Ireland and Britain: in 1924 he proposed that the Senate 'request the government to improve the accommodation on Dún Laoghaire pier for passengers crossing from Dún Laoghaire to Holyhead and vice versa'.[172] Nor was there any enthusiasm from former landlords in the three Ulster counties to become involved in the Senate: only Lord Farnham sought election in 1925 and he was unsuccessful.

Within a decade, the representation of former landlords had all but ended. The Earl of Dunraven died in 1926. Lord Mayo died the following year. In 1928, Lord Headfort did not seek re-election; by 1932, Everard, Nugent, Hutcheson-Poe, Esmonde and Plunkett had all gone; in 1934 Granard did not seek re-election and Sir John Keane failed to be re-elected. Keane had been the most active of all the former landlords and an enthusiastic senator from the beginning. His personality, while gaining respect, did not, however, endear him to his fellow senators. Dónal O'Sullivan has written of him:

> Ever since the beginning he had proved himself to be, on the widest variety of subjects, a convincing and well-informed parliamentarian.

He had originated debates on probably more occasions than any other
member of the House, and he was as good a debater as he was a
public speaker.... His great defect lay in his unwillingness to co-operate with any group or party, and his aloofness was the cause of his
defeat.[173]

By now the usefulness of the Senate had been under close
scrutiny by Fianna Fáil who wished to see it dismantled. Writing in
1958, J.L. McCracken argued that a certain stigma was attached to
the Senate because of the fact that provision had been made for the
establishment of a semi-nominated second house by the Home Rule
Act of 1914 and the Government of Ireland Act 1920. Both of these
'were obnoxious in all their parts to the men who had successfully
carried through the revolution'.[174] Secondly, he claimed that the Dáil
members were not in favour of the fact that the establishment of the
Senate was a result of an agreement with 'a group, which, rightly or
wrongly, was regarded as inimical to the national cause'.[175] In 1932,
Fianna Fáil came to power and although landlords exerted little
influence in the Senate, De Valera still viewed it as a nuisance to the
constitutional changes he had in mind. He saw it as: 'a remnant, a
part of the defensive armoury of the ascendancy class ... in favour of
vested interests and privileges'.[176] Sean Lemass saw it as 'a bulwark
of imperialism' that 'was always hostile to the interests of Irish
Nationalism' and that 'gave political power to a certain class that
could not get that power if they had to go before the people'.[177] In
1934, a memo from the Department of the Taoiseach claimed
that the Senate had 'set itself in opposition to democratic ideals'. By
holding up the Oath Bill from 19 May 1932 to May 1933, the
Local Government Extension of Franchise Bill from 28 June to
27 December 1934, and the Local Government (Dublin) Bill from
7 June 1933 to 6 December 1934, the Senate, the memo alleged, had
proved this.

It was on these grounds that De Valera introduced a bill to abolish the Senate in 1934, a move that was fiercely attacked by the
chairman of the Senate, T.W. Westropp Bennett, who, in a speech
published as *Pro Domo Sua*, wrote: 'Mr De Valera is out for uncon-
trollable power, and this is why he regards the abolition of the
Senate as a necessity.... No one can doubt that Mr de Valera's real
aim is to establish a dictatorship'.[179] Whatever De Valera's real aim,
the Senate was abolished in 1936 and so ended the only political
safeguard, albeit largely a notional one, that former landlords had
from those who had framed the new Free State constitution. Amongst
the old landed class, the generation that followed, with few exceptions,

showed little or no enthusiasm for Irish political life. The seventh Marquis of Sligo, as his successor noted, typified their mood:

> He took little interest in the arts or in politics and perhaps he did not miss much. The 1930s in Ireland were curiously stagnant years as though, exhausted by rebellion and civil war, and by the unparalleled literary achievement of the previous half century, the country was content to play safe, safe in politics, safe with a censured literature, safe in industry behind tariff walls.[180]

CONCLUSION

Irish landlords had traditionally remained aloof from the majority. They cherished their social exclusivity. And as long as the majority was disenfranchised political ascendancy went along with social and economic ascendancy. From 1879 they found themselves under attack from the Land League which they perceived to be both a social and political movement, 'a powerful and unscrupulous organisation', intent on usurping their land as well as their social, political and even religious liberties. In 1869, their Established Church had been attacked because W.E.H. Lecky believed: 'it was regarded as an English garrison sustaining an anti-national system'.[181] This may not be true but it does say much for landed perceptions at the time that an Irish parliament would only 'build up a wall of separation between Protestants and Catholics'.[182] The Home Rule movement politically alienated landlords completely. As a class they were not prepared to throw in their lot with the few such as Parnell or Redmond. 'Now and again', S.O. Hannay wrote in 1909, 'out of this class comes one or another with a message of hope [but] the gentlemen of Ireland who will not lead will not follow either'.[183] When landlords were 'assailed by lying Irish rebels and by some misguided English radicals'; when they were subjected to 'every kind of misrepresentation'; when 'every sort of odium [was] stirred up against them', what, John Pentland Mahaffy asked in 1882, did they do to protect themselves?

> They remained silent, separate, perplexed. With ample funds at their disposal, they made no attempt at a strong and central counterorganisation; the partial efforts of two associations started by a small number of men received no general support.... [Taken] as a class the landlords have spent neither time nor money in defending themselves. They say they expected government to do it; as a matter of fact they were waiting and hoping for somebody, anybody, anything,

to intervene, which would save them any exercise of public spirit and public self-denial and leave them to hunt foxes.[184]

When they continued to hold on to their attachment to the Union, they destroyed any prospects they might have had of sharing some degree of political power in an independent Ireland. The political tidal wave that swept through Ireland from the 1880s was, in the twenty-six counties, undoubtedly Catholic and Nationalist. Not being English in England, the landed class was certainly not perceived by the new ruling class as being Irish in Ireland. As Stephen Gwynn wrote in 1926: 'I was brought up to think myself Irish, without question or qualification; but the new Nationalism prefers to describe me and the likes of me as Anglo-Irish.... So all of my life, I have been spiritually hyphenated, without knowing it'.[185]

9

THE STRUGGLE FOR SURVIVAL
1914–60

'STILL STRANGERS'

... the war found William Kirkwood little better off than his Catholic neighbours, poorer than some Catholics already on the rise. He had a drawing-room and library and lawn and orchard and spreading fields within stone walls: but the lawn was like a meadow; many of the books on the high shelves of the library had been damaged by the damp; the orchard was wild, his father's beehives rotting away unseen in the high grass at its foot; the many acres had been understocked and half farmed for too long, and there were broken gaps in the stone walls. Nearly all the other Protestant landowners ... seeing the erosion of their old ascendancy, had emigrated.... William Kirkwood stayed, blessedly unaware that he had become a mild figure of fun.

JOHN McGAHERN, 'THE CONVERSION OF WILLIAM KIRKWOOD' IN
HIGH GROUND (1985), P. 123

INTRODUCTION

In this final chapter it is intended to examine the social changes that affected Irish landed families, particularly those who remained in Ireland, from around 1914 onwards. As we have already seen the war was not responsible for any great financial disaster as far as Irish landlords were concerned; in fact, if anything, it improved the lot of many landlords who were substantial farmers or who were dependent upon rental income from tenant farmers. The casualty rate amongst big house families, most notably heirs, was not so catastrophic (although proportionately higher than other classes) as to significantly affect succession lines, no more so than the Boer War had been at the beginning of the century, or social factors such as unmarried heirs or childless families had been in the past.[1] In other respects the war did prove to be a watershed in big house life. It had at least a psychological effect. The sense of loss that pervaded landed circles meant that it was emotionally painful for most to enjoy the same type of social life in its aftermath to which they had formerly been accustomed. (Seymour Leslie wrote: 'The London season resumed but many faces were missing, many were dead or ruined, or still mourning'.[2])

Perhaps more significantly, the war radically changed society as a whole in the western world. In Britain, the elitist socio-political position, which landowners had held, was greatly undermined by the torrents of democracy and by politicians. Lloyd George, most notably, had for years 'taunted them, threatened them, taxed them, tormented them', taken away their hereditary powers and threatened to take away their hereditary acres so that by the end of the war landowners 'hated him as much as he hated them'.[3] In Ireland their political power had already been taken and the bulk of their estates had been sold, but socially and economically they still remained a powerful group. The years following the war were to throw them into total confusion and disarray. Economically they were to flounder on the rocks of economic depression and government legislation aimed at the compulsory acquisition of their remaining acres. Socially their whole world was turned upside down as they became exposed to a more virulent form of intimidation from a community they had long kept outside their demesne walls. While in Britain their position was merely resented, in Ireland it was detested particularly because the culture they represented was the one that the new order in Ireland was attempting to suppress. While their isolation in the past had been voluntary, it now became enforced.

'No Money Dears to Entertain in the Old Way'

As chapter two opened with a case study of the social life of Glaslough up to 1914, it is appropriate that this penultimate chapter should trace the changes that took place there in the years after. The bulk of the Leslie estate in County Monaghan was sold under the terms of the 1903 Land Act, for which the family received around £200,000. Being a relatively unencumbered family, the bulk of the capital was available for investment and 'the Leslie investment portfolio soon bulged' on the advice of Sir Ernest Cassel 'with the most fanciful stocks and shares'.[4] If invested at the going rate of 3.5 per cent, the Leslies were receiving around £7,000 per annum. And with the demesne farm in still quite a healthy position by 1913 and further rental income accruing from their estates in Donegal, the Leslies were no worse off than they had been before sales. If the family wealth did diminish as a result of the loss of rental income, there were no outward signs of it before 1914. At any rate there was a great reluctance to expose penury to the outer world; 'never talk of

money, illness, children or servants' was Leonie Leslie's Edwardian
motto.[5] And so social life continued at Glaslough for a number of
years in much the same way as it had done for generations.

The most notable social function held at Glaslough prior to the
outbreak of war was a celebration ('a large house and garden party')
to mark the golden wedding anniversary of Sir John I and Lady
Constance in 1906. Shortly afterwards, they handed the house over
to Sir John II and Leonie and retired to live in England at 22 Manchester
Square, London, and Brighton in the summer.[6] At Glaslough entertaining continued, if anything becoming more fashionable, as the Leslies
now frequently entertained the late Queen Victoria's son, the Duke
of Connaught.

The level of deference shown towards landlords like the Leslies is
hardly quantifiable, but the Leslies were aware that as time passed
attitudes towards them changed. As a child Sir Shane recalled arriving late at Glaslough station for the Belfast train to find it pulling
off. The coachman reined the horses, drew the sociable in line with
the engine and waved his whip at the train driver who saluted and
reversed the train to the station: 'After all it was our own station
and why not this piece of snobbery', Leslie contended.[7] With his
brother Norman they 'went the rounds' of tenant houses with Sam
Cunningham, a retainer, 'and were received with feudal delight'.
However, by the late 1880s every one of the Catholic tenants on the
estate reputedly put their hat on inside the rent-office instead of outside, a sign to Leslie that deference was becoming a thing of the
past.[8] Within fifty years everything had changed around Glaslough
'save the rooks'.[9]

By 1914 Sir John and Leonie's sons had grown up. The youngest,
Seymour, who had been a sickly child, was making his way in the
world as an electrical engineer, having qualified in 1914 and gone to
America to join General Electric. For him: 'it was certainly good
shock treatment to escape from the Edwardian hot-house into the
purposeful middle-class atmosphere of London university'.[10] Their
second son, Norman, had followed a more traditional path for a landlord's son and had joined the army. As a young officer he enjoyed the
adventure of high life before 1914, his brother Shane claiming that
he was the last of his class to fight a duel to defend the honour of a
lady friend on the continent in 1910. But their eldest son, christened
John Randolph (and whose godfather was Sir Randolph Churchill),
was very atypical of an heir to an Irish landed estate. In the 1890s
he had become influenced by the Gaelic revival ('How angry [J.P.]
Mahaffy was when I met him at a railway station wearing an Irish
kilt'[12]); changed his name to Shane ('in an outburst of Celtic fervour'

after Shane O'Neill whom he referred to as 'the romantic rebel whose kingdom had been bordered like the Leslie estate by the River Blackwater'[12]); converted to Catholicism ('he let his heart become fast entangled in the ways of the Roman religion because it was the religion of Ireland'[13]) and became a Nationalist who fought the 1910 Derry by-election as a Home Ruler losing narrowly to Lord Hamilton, the future Duke of Abercorn.

Shane had few qualms either about his political or religious conversions. Nonetheless, from a political point of view he did 'grieve bitterly' that he had hurt his grandfather 'who had stood for the old order for so long and had been slowly wrenched out of the family seat by no less than Tim Healy, then the henchman of Parnell'.[14] He was aware that what he had done would not go down very well either at home or amongst members of his class in general: 'If I was comforted by the thought that Patrick Sarsfield and Robert Emmet were on my side I realised that behind each corner waited Oliver Cromwell and William of Orange'.[15] The agent of the Leslie estate exaggeratedly 'predicted a mass emigration of the Protestant villagers, the Presbyterian farm bailiff would resign, it would all cause scandal'.[16] While none of his prophecies came true, Sir John, a staunch Unionist and Orangeman, reacted rather predictably by disinheriting Shane in favour of his younger brother, Norman, at great expense to the family as hundreds of tenants had to be reconveyanced to break the entail.[17]

The war exacted a heavy toll upon the Leslies. Immediately after its outbreak, the family vacated Glaslough and moved temporarily to London, Sir John coming home occasionally to assist in recruitment drives.[18] As a serving officer in the British army, Norman was sent to the front at an early stage. Before he left, he wrote to a friend, Zoë Farquharson:

> Try not to worry too much about the war anyhow. Units, individuals cannot count. Remember we are writing a new page of history. Future generations cannot be allowed to read the decline of the British Empire and attribute it to us. We live our little lives and die. To some are given chances of proving themselves men, and to others no chance comes. Whatever our individual faults, virtues or qualities may be, it matters not, for when we are up against big things, let us forget individuals and let us act as one great British unit, mixed and fearless. Some will live and many will die, but count the loss not. It is better by far to go out with honour than survive with shame.[19]

His letter not only seems to encapsulate ideas of chivalry that were an implicit part of landlord culture but it could also be regarded as an expression of the contemporary cult of patriotism that was very much in vogue at the time. It was even parallel to the type of patriotism espoused from a different viewpoint by P.H. Pearse. The harsh realities of the First World War were to sweep away any romantic notions attached to warfare and the type of cavalier lifestyle heretofore enjoyed by people like Norman Leslie. He was killed at Armentières on 18 October 1914.

Understandably, the death of Norman came as a great blow to the family. Neither Sir John nor his wife, Leonie, ever got over the death of their favourite son.[20] Sir John 'did not really break down until the treasury sent in a cold-blooded £2,000 bill for death duties for one who had never inherited', a bitter reminder of Norman's 'lost expectations'.[21] When Anita Leslie and her brother arrived at Glaslough for the first time in 1919, she found that 'one room frightened us. It had been that of our Uncle Norman, who had been killed five years previously and it was kept just as he had left it ... a bunch of withered flowers lay on the pillow'. During her first tour of the house Anita also found signs that Glaslough had suffered from being vacated during the war years and most likely from declining fortunes: 'We found bedrooms that had not been used for years, and a cobwebby box-room lined with enormous hanging cupboards designed to hold dresses of the last century'.[22]

The revolutionary period did not affect Glaslough; a largely Protestant village outside the demesne walls full of former UVF men may partially explain why the local IRA was reluctant to raid it. Initially there was a sense of bitterness amongst family members at having been excluded from Northern Ireland and left 'to make their peace with their supposed enemies. They were welcomed to share in the privileges and taxes of the new state'.[23] Afterwards, the Leslies prided themselves on the fact that while 'mansions with memories and heirlooms were burned and families which counted as Anglo-Irish removed their capital and future out of the country' they stayed.[24]

Sir Shane contended that between the wars, those who had grown up in the Victorian or Edwardian eras would 'have been content to restore the old roundabout between club and countryside, between the old seasonal sports and the remaining mansions of Mayfair'.[25] But big house social life had been severely disrupted by the Great War: houses throughout the county had been closed up; entertaining was not deemed appropriate at a time when so many families were suffering bereavements and sporting activities were halted.[26] Big house social life was not to return to its former splendour in the aftermath. Families were still in mourning for lost relatives and friends when the country was plunged into revolution that was to last from 1919 to 1923. By then landed families were psychologically more isolated than ever from mainstream Irish life; their economic base was much weakened by depression; and the new Free State government was threatening to diminish the acres they had held on to. In Monaghan, the parties in neighbouring big houses all but ended as there were few houses or families left to visit. By the mid 1920s, the Dartreys and the Blaneys had died out; the Ancketells had long since gone having sold their estate in the 1890s; Castlesaunderson, Gola and Ballybay had been burned during the revolutionary period and the Shirleys were too far away in the southernmost corner of the county. The 'only friends' of their own age that Shane's children had were John and Charlie Madden and they lived twenty miles away at Hilton Park.[27]

After the war, the London season effectively ended for most Irish families (but not the Leslies.) No longer able to afford them, they sold their London houses. Sir Shane regretted the passing of London society. The sale of 'great palaces' such as Lansdowne House that was to become the Waldorf Astoria and then Selfridges marked the end of an era. Dorchester House with its 'carriage drive always laid down with ground red-brick, the immense stairway and the glass cases full of Shakespearean folios' was sold and became the American embassy.[28] Sir Shane himself was forced to move into a London flat in the 1920s despite the fact that he found such a move distasteful: 'the universal flat could never become a home'.[29] In 1938 he wrote, 'I have to presume that my family have been going down in the London world'. His great grandmother had lived in Berkeley Square, his grand-parents in Stratford place (which they sold in the 1890s), his parents in great Cumberland Place (sold before the war — it was 'much too large for [them] as their Irish income fell'). Now he found himself in a flat in St John's Wood.[30] After the economic (and, indeed social) crashes post 1918 the type of lifestyle that had characterised Berkeley Square came to an end. When Selfridges took over Lansdowne House their first party, attended by Sir Shane: 'was a complete and comic contrast with the previous party [he] had attended when [he] witnessed Lord Lansdowne receiving the Chinese ambassador in full costume'.[31]

In the long term the longevity of Sir John and Lady Constance (they died in 1916 and 1925 respectively) had a detrimental financial effect on the family fortune. The £4,000 jointure, which they retired to London on in 1906, proved too great a financial drain. Sir Shane's brother, Seymour, claimed that 'as long as my grandparents lived [my parents] had to count every golden sovereign'. The payment of what was a very substantial jointure to his widowed mother left Sir John II 'with little to run' Glaslough 'even when the long overdue purge of the personnel took place' and the number of indoor servants was cut from thirteen to seven.[32] After her husband's death, Lady Constance was asked to sell the house in Manchester Square so that the family could economise but she refused and lived out the remainder of her days there.[33]

From the early 1920s, the family's financial fortunes were on the wane. The 'most fanciful stocks and shares' were most likely depreciated by depression, the farm was no longer profitable and family charges had still to be met. The Leslie diamonds were in temporary pawn and 'the real goldmine' of Sir John I's — his collection of Old Masters — was being sold off.[34] By the 1930s, the agent at Glaslough 'had given up all hopes of financing the mending of the fences, cleaning the ditches, replacing the heifers and castrating the lambs'.[35] However, the crisis cannot have been all that bad for all this time 'the London seasons were faithfully attended' and the Leslies continued to cling on to the old lifestyle. At home shooting parties and dinner parties continued at Glaslough right throughout the 1930s, with guests including Prince Pierre (father of Prince Rainier of Monaco) and Anthony Eden, while John Betjeman stayed there during the war years.[36]

Unlike his father and grandfather Sir Shane had no time for clubs, much preferring the reading-room of the British museum. The only club that he did aspire to joining was the Athenaeum but he never applied for membership as he felt that he would be blackballed because of his novel *Oppidan* which was a scathing criticism of Eton and Etonian values.[37] Like his father he had married an American, Marjorie Ide, daughter of Henry Clay Ide, one time Governorgeneral of the Philippines and Samoa and ambassador to Spain. Her lifestyle was symbolic of the changes facing the Irish landed class — she belonged 'to the new American world of jazz and cocktails, which had emerged after the First World War'.[38]

As in the past, the Leslies continued to look to England as their mother-country so to speak after the establishment of the Free State. In the early 1920s, Sir John II and Leonie Leslie spent much of their time in London and further abroad 'accompanying the Connaughts on such royal missions as the opening of the Aswan dam.'[39] Sir Shane may have refused to send his sons to Eton because of his own experiences there, but he still sent them to English public schools, Jack to Downside and Desmond to Ampleforth. His daughter, Anita, was presented to King George V and Queen Mary at Buckingham Palace during her 'coming out year'. When the Second World War broke out

Shane left his wife and parents 'safe in Ireland' and went to London where he joined the Home Guard in Sloane Square. His eldest son, Jack, was captured and spent five years a prisoner of war; Anita served as an ambulance driver with the First Armoured Division of the French army, while Desmond joined the RAF.[40] The rest of the family remained at Glaslough where they entertained British and American troops stationed across the border, who had to change into civilian clothes before crossing into Monaghan. Wells, 'their very English butler' painted the top-floor windows at Glaslough dark-blue to show solidarity with Northern Ireland: 'It galled him that houses only two miles away should have full blackout regulations while Glaslough village could blaze with light'.[41]

Back in 1916, Shane had worked with Sir Cecil Spring-Rice, the British ambassador in Washington in an attempt to persuade America to join the war.[42] At the same time, he looked to Ireland, to its mythology and its history for inspiration for his writing and edited a literary magazine embellished with Irish verse. He became a supporter of the ideals of Sinn Féin although not of its militant policy. However, what his daughter termed his 'conflicting loyalties' only led to a sense of bewilderment and hurt when, after the war, he 'found himself unwanted in the new Free State' and given no thanks by Britain.[43]

Following Norman's death in 1914, Sir John II had made Shane's eldest son, Jack, his heir. Sir John did not die until 1944, having survived his wife, Leonie, by only a few months. Sir Shane lived until 1971 and spent his time divided between Glaslough and London. Jack did not have the same interest in Glaslough and spent many years in Rome after the war. Glaslough eventually passed to his brother Desmond who barely managed to keep it afloat, an appropriate phrase considering he once compared the house to an old ship: 'You can't crew it anymore but as long as you keep the hull watertight it is not going to come to much harm'.[44] He managed to keep Glaslough watertight long enough for his daughter Samantha to use her initiative and resilience to float the ancestral home once again, not as a private home but as a restaurant and accommodation centre, now known as Castle Leslie. In 1992, following her decision to open it to the public, Samantha claimed: 'There is much ill feeling about the landed gentry but the house has to be preserved. It is sad to see the big houses vanish but I am determined this one will survive'.[45] The rise in big house visiting from the 1980s suggests that Samantha's comments regarding the 'ill feeling' towards the old landed class were somewhat misplaced in 1992. However, they were indicative of the apprehensions that big house owners continued to hold in Ireland until quite recent times regarding the opening of their homes to the public. Fortunately for the Leslies their venture has proved to be an extremely successful one and the future of Glaslough (or Castle Leslie) is assured for the time being.[46]

THE STRUGGLE TO RETAIN ANCESTRAL HOMES

It was a small minority of families like the Leslies who managed to retain their ancestral homes. (As pointed out earlier, Mark Bence-Jones has recently estimated that only about 10 per cent of the 2,000 or so big houses catalogued by him are presently in the ownership of the original families.) Only thirty-seven of the 100 sample houses remained with the original families up to the 1960s. It is difficult to generalise why these families were successful or to ascertain the reasons for their success. Just as there was no typical Irish big house (or estate) neither was there a typical reason why some houses survived longer than most. However, a number of reasons can be put forward.

Because of the unavailability of relevant source material, one can only assume that many houses that survived did so because the levels of indebtedness of owners prior to the sale of their estates was such that much of the capital secured was available to them and then wisely invested. Some of the landowners, whose houses survived beyond 1950, had received astronomical sums under the various land acts, particularly the Wyndham Land Act: from 1885 to 1889, the Beresfords of Curraghmore had received over £263,000 for the sale of 14,000 acres under the terms of the 1885 Land Act (and £45,000 under the 1891 Land Act); under the Wyndham Act the King-Harmans of Rockingham received at least £495,000 (and £130,000 under the 1891 Land Act); the Shirleys of Lough Fea at least £310,000; the Kavanaghs of Borris, £183,000 and the Conynghams of Slane, £170,000 which cumulatively in today's terms would amount to around £80 million.[47] Amongst these, the heaviest encumbranced was the King-Harmans who had received a mortgage of £195,000 from the RCB in the 1870s.[48] Even given that the entire principal had to be repaid, they were still left with £430,000 to invest. Wills or abstracts of wills show that those owners who died in the period from the 1930s to the 1950s and who left assets in excess of £20,000 were more likely to have retained their houses, at least in the short term. J.C.W. Madden, for example, who died in 1936, left £7,000 in ordinary stock, £500 in debenture stock, and £100 in 4 per cent preference shares to pay estate and other duties while his personal estate was valued at almost £85,000 and his real estate at £10,300. The eighth Viscount Powerscourt, Mervyn Wingfield, left assets of almost

£50,000 when he died in 1949, while Arthur MacMurrough Kavanagh left assets of £23,000 in 1953.[49] Further-more, there were many smaller landlords who slipped into the farming class and who managed to retain more modest houses on an agricultural income. (A glance through a Bord Fáilte brochure will show that many of these houses, including Clohamon, are now being run as country house or farm house bed and breakfasts, though, of course, not necessarily by the original family who owned them.)

Irish landlords had, in the past, usually married with a certain amount of 'business' in mind. As wealth passed from the landed class to the business community, this inevitably led to a dilution of the social base from which landowners had traditionally sought their wives. Now it became more usual, especially for those who had been large landowners or peers (and both were often one and the same), to extend their range of potential marriage suitors to include American heiresses.[50] Of course, not all who went in search of heiresses were successful. Edward Fitzgerald, seventh Duke of Leinster, married Rafael Davidson-Kennedy, only child of an American tycoon, but Rafael later admitted that she 'hadn't a bean when they met'. Creditors and money lenders 'dogged their steps from the beginning' and their marriage ended in failure in 1946.[51] And not all Irish landowners, especially those of the 'old school' favoured this dilution of society. Lord Dunraven, for example, regretted that the post-First World War London scene was being invaded by those who 'before the war, would not have formed part of what the press is pleased to term society'.[52] Nonetheless, there were houses, such as Castleforbes, that survived largely because of fortuitous marriages that brought new wealth to an estate.[53] The present Knight of Glin has admitted that his widowed mother's marriage to Ray Milner, a wealthy Canadian industrialist, in the 1950s helped save Glin Castle at that time.[54]

Back in 1922, the *Estates Gazette* had claimed that the future of houses in Britain lay in outside income, such as fortuitous marriage settlements: 'These are the days in which the greater residential properties of the country can only be owned and kept up by those whose income is from sources apart from the property itself, and then of a very substantial character'.[55] The successful transition of some owners from landed proprietors to City businessmen probably helped supplement the upkeep of their houses in Ireland, providing they *wanted* to retain them. Sir John Keane of Cappoquin was a director and governor of the Bank of Ireland for years. Barry Maxwell, twelfth Baron Farnham, became a director of Brown, Shipley and Co. Ltd in the late 1950s and in the 1970s, he was appointed chairman of Brown Shipley Holdings Ltd and a director of Avon Rubber Co. Maxwell continued to reside for part of the year at Farnham until his death in 2001. Francis Pakenham, seventh Earl of Longford had successful academic, political and City careers as a lecturer in politics at Oxford in 1932; Minister for Civil Aviation 1948–51; chairman of National Bank Ltd from 1955 to 1963 and a director of Sidgwick and Jackson throughout the 1970s. Sir Terence Langrishe was a Lloyd's 'name' and continued to reside at Knocktopher until the 1980s.

OPENING BIG HOUSES TO THE PUBLIC

In Britain, country house owners opened their residences to the public from the 1940s. (This was not a novel idea in Britain as country houses had been opened to the public during the nineteenth century, but the difference from the 1940s was that it was now very much a money making expedient to help their owners maintain and retain them.[56]) This was never an option available to big house owners in Ireland. While in the 1880s, the seventh Duke of Devonshire opened Chatsworth to the public, he could not dream of doing likewise with Lismore in Ireland. This was not only because there was not the industrial middle class to pay to see its interior grandeur but more importantly because of the socio-political climate of Ireland at the time.[57] From the 1880s whatever kindly perception the tenantry might have had of big houses in the past was completely wiped away and replaced by a much more virulent sense of resentment towards what they represented. While in Britain the stripping of the political power and economic might of the landed class during the late nineteenth and early twentieth centuries may have led to a diminishing of 'great public enmity or suspicion' towards country houses, such was not the case in Ireland.[58] Here, old enmities and suspicions were harder to kill, particularly when they were symbolic of anything that was anti-Nationalist. Few people in Ireland shared the view that big houses were part of a shared heritage or that that heritage was worth preserving. Possibly a more recent expression of this was the burning of a number of surviving big houses in the border counties during the hunger-strike days of the early 1980s. In May 1981, the house built by Lord Rossmore in Monaghan to replace the abandoned Rossmore Park was burned by a group calling themselves the 'Republican Action Group' warning that if Bobby Sands died 'every realm of colonialism in the Republic and the North would be attacked'.[59]

Indeed the same applied to government policy towards big houses from the establishment of the Free State. Unlike in Britain, Irish governments were slow to acknowledge their cultural significance or heritage value. (The wealth tax of 1974 was to prove as detrimental

to big houses in Ireland as any legislation that had preceded it.)
While efforts were made to preserve round towers or ancient monas-
teries eight hundred years of architecture was ignored and indeed
the demolition of it was encouraged. Desmond Guinness has claimed
that when Castletown was put up for sale in 1965, it was indicative
of the attitude of the Irish government that:

> ... no official concern was expressed in spite of the international
> importance of the house with its wonderful interior. The demesne was
> split up by developers and the original contents dispersed to the four
> corners of the world.... The house was left to the mercy of vandals and
> scrap merchants.[60]

The Irish Georgian Society, formed in 1958 with the aim to restore
buildings or give grants to maintain others, bought Castletown in
1967. By the late 1970s, the Castletown Foundation had taken over
the ownership, administration and restoration work at the house and
many of its original contents were recovered and put on display when
Castletown became the first big house in Leinster to open its doors to
the public.[61]

Similarly, at the turn of the century, Muckross was sold by Henry
Herbert to Lord Ardilaun, a member of the Guinness family, who, in
turn, sold it in 1910 to William Bourne, a rich American gold miner.
Bourne gave Muckross as a wedding present to his daughter, Maud,
and her husband, Arthur Vincent. In 1929, Maud died of pneumonia
and in 1932 Vincent gave Muckross and its 11,000 acres to the state
claiming that he wished 'to see not only the youth of Ireland, but
young people from all parts of the world, come to Muckross. I want it
to be a playground for youth'.[62] For eighteen years successive governments did nothing. Then in 1950, the secretary of the Killarney Tourist
Association, acting upon a resolution passed by Killarney UDC that
year, wrote to the Taoiseach, suggesting that the house should be
used as a summer residence for the President.[63] Nothing came of this.
Then in 1954, it was reported that the Kerry County Committee of
Agriculture were to have talks with the Minister for Agriculture to
discuss the use of Muckross as an agricultural college.[64] *The Irish
Times* was despondent about the house's future: 'Muckross House
remains a silent and lonely sentinel on the shore of the Middle lake.
As successive governments have failed to find a use for it, it seems it
will eventually fall into decay'.[65] It was not until the 1960s that the
government finally decided to open it to the public.

Around the same time, Jeremy Browne, thirteenth Marquis of
Sligo, went to England to visit Lord Montague's Beaulieu (which he

described as 'a nice little house, nothing special') and the Duke of
Bedford's Woburn Abbey. He was seeking advice with regard to opening
his own house at Westport which was in danger of being demolished
because of 'the crippling burden of rates'.[66] He was one of the first
Irish big house owners to realise that the abandonment of its privacy
might be the only solution to financial difficulties. His venture has
been largely successful ensuring that Westport remains the only
house by Richard Castle to have remained in the possession of the
family who built it.

In 1975, Bord Fáilte acknowledged the fact that 'as a holiday
activity, visiting great houses and gardens ranks very highly among
both foreign and domestic visitors'.[67] That year, the cumulative number
of people who had visited big houses in Ireland was approximately
750,000, of whom almost 300,000 were foreign tourists.[68] Despite the
possible potential most owners remained reluctant to open their
houses to the public. In April, 1976, An Taisce, an organisation
formed in the 1970s on much the same lines as the National Trust in
Britain but without the financial backing, appointed a working party
to establish the importance of historic houses and gardens for the
benefit of the country. The intention was 'thus to establish the
responsibilities of government for their survival and welfare'.[69] Its
report, published in 1977, found that the annual average cost of
maintaining the eighty-one big houses surveyed was £10,000 per
annum. Forty-one owners said that major repairs were overdue on
their houses including such things as the treating of facades, renovating out-offices, repairing roofs and eradicating dry-rot. Thirteen
owners said this would cost them in excess of £20,000. The report
also claimed that owners had become anxious about the rise of costs
such as heating and the virtual disappearance of resident craftsmen
as contributory factors towards dilapidation.[70] Most of these owners
were reluctant to open their houses to the public as they were worried
about the increase in staff required. They were also concerned at the
security risk; deterred by the amount of work or investment needed
before the property could be opened, and fearful that their houses
were 'too remote, small or uninteresting'.[71] While one should not
doubt the sincerity of these replies, placing emphasis on economics,
it is probably fair to state that these owners were still sceptical of
the reaction from the public if they were seen to be 'profiteering' from
their houses.

It was not for another decade or so that big houses became a
major tourist attraction in Ireland, attractive to the indigenous population as well as to foreign tourists. For the three years from 1992 to
1994, the cumulative number of visitors to the fifty or so big houses

opened to the public averaged around 1.48 million per year, almost twice as many as in 1975 (see Table 9.1, p. 288).[72] It was a long time after the big house had been stripped of its landed estates and political power, that their symbolic nature was put to one side and their owners no longer regarded with the degree of enmity and suspicion that had been inherited from their ancestors.

In something of a variation on the same theme, Lord Henry Mountcharles opened Slane Castle as a bistro and night club. However, from the 1980s he found it financially more rewarding to use the natural amphitheatre of his demesne to host concerts of The Rolling Stones, Bruce Springsteen, Bob Dylan and Queen to name but a few.

THE THINNING OF LANDLORD SOCIETY

Inevitably, the transformation of the economic position of Irish landlords from the 1880s inaugurated dramatic changes in the lifestyles of those who lived in them. The dilution of landed society, the movement of former landlords into the business world, and the search for wealthy heiresses were symptomatic of these changes. Sons and daughters were forced into the world to make their living in what the Earl of Desart called 'other spheres of occupation'.[73] They could no longer depend on the type of allowances once paid to them from landed estates. Shane Leslie effectively became an author. One of his sons, Seymour became an electrical engineer; the eighth Earl of Mayo became a civil engineer; the Earl of Bessborough became chairman of various companies at different stages and the seventh Earl of Drogheda sat on a number of boards as director. However varied changes were from one family to another, they bore witness to the diminished circumstances of Irish landlords as a whole from the 1880s.

Socially, the land war, the War of Independence and the Civil War all contributed to the thinning of landlord society by acting as socio-political catalysts in the emigration process. The long land war and the bitterness that it engendered greatly changes the relationship between landlords and tenants, even where it had once been amicable. As R.V. Comerford rightly concludes:

> The crisis of the late 1870s gave rise to a form of civil war that incorporated, but went far beyond conventional politics and poisoned both social and political relationships. This was no inevitable progress, but rather the result of initiatives by elites and individuals endeavouring to use the crisis for their own purposes.[74]

Irish landlords had not been oblivious to changing attitudes during the land war. When Col James Crosbie was asked at a sitting of the Cowper Commission in 1887 if he had 'any reason to hope that if that malign influence was withdrawn those good feelings would again return', he replied: 'It is very hard to say. I am afraid that the foundation is so broken down that in many cases it would not'.[75] The landed class was even more shocked by the severity of the outrages directed against them as a class from 1919 to 1923. Maurice Headlam related a story regarding an elderly landlord and his wife with whom he had shared a train journey the night after their house had been burned. The old lady told him:

> When we went down the avenue and into the village, every door was shut and barred. No one would take us in. I knew every one of them, their fathers and mothers, their grandparents, all their children, and I thought they were my friends.[76]

Similarly, Lady Fingall summed up the general feeling amongst her class in the aftermath of the troubles. 'People whose families had lived in the country for three or four hundred years, realised suddenly that they were still strangers and that the mystery of it [Ireland] was never to be revealed to them'.[77] Whereas the likes of Tom Barry might have served under British army officers drawn from Irish landed families during the course of the First World War, they were very much on opposing sides from 1919 onwards. Continuing as army officers — most notably Field Marshal Sir Henry Wilson — sons of Irish landlords represented what Sinn Féin and the IRA wanted to destroy.

From an early stage, the alienation of landlords was seen to be their own doing by contemporary critics. After the Act of Union they did not attach themselves to Ireland as such but continued to look beyond its shores to Britain, remaining aloof from the majority. Their continued Loyalism beyond the 1880s and through the formative years of the Free State completed their isolation. In 1909 the Rev S.O. Hannay attacked Irish landlords for their poor foresight:

> [Ireland] remained — it still remains — for them a strange country, a place of sojourn only, where the people are strange. Like all exiles, they look wistfully away from their land of exile; but they look back to no home, forward to no home coming, for in all the wide world they have no home. The word upon their lips about the Irish people has never been 'we', always 'they'. Of late years, feeling the contempt of the English democracy, they have realised what was plain to everyone else a century ago, that they are not Englishmen.

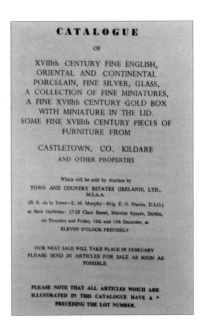

CATALOGUE

OF

XVIIIth CENTURY FINE ENGLISH,
ORIENTAL AND CONTINENTAL
PORCELAIN, FINE SILVER, GLASS,
A COLLECTION OF FINE MINIATURES,
A FINE XVIIIth CENTURY GOLD BOX
WITH MINIATURE IN THE LID,
SOME FINE XVIIIth CENTURY PIECES OF
FURNITURE FROM

CASTLETOWN, CO. KILDARE
AND OTHER PROPERTIES

Which will be sold by Auction by
TOWN AND COUNTRY ESTATES (IRELAND), LTD.,
M.I.A.A.
(B. E. de la Torre—E. M. Murphy—Brig. E. O. Martin, D.S.O.)
at their Galleries: 27-28 Clare Street, Merrion Square, Dublin,
on Thursday and Friday, 12th and 13th December, at
ELEVEN O'CLOCK PRECISELY.

OUR NEXT SALE WILL TAKE PLACE IN FEBRUARY
PLEASE SEND IN ARTICLES FOR SALE AS SOON AS
POSSIBLE.

PLEASE NOTE THAT ALL ARTICLES WHICH ARE
ILLUSTRATED IN THIS CATALOGUE HAVE A *
PRECEDING THE LOT NUMBER.

Above: Tubberdaly, King's County,
prior to its burning.
Courtesy Dermot P. Beaumont-
Nesbitt

Above: Auction Catalogue of
Castletown, County Kildare,
December 1957

Below: Carriage and new team of horses at Rathrobin, 21 May 1904.
Magan Collection, courtesy Offaly Historical and Archaeological Society

Above: *Castletown House, 2001.*
Courtesy Jim Campion

The Irish gentleman has not understood that an empire is a quickly passing thing, nailed together by force, varnished by diplomacy, waiting the inevitable dissolution of all such structures. In taking Imperialism to his heart and scorning patriotism he has mistaken the transitory for the permanent.... Men do not make their homes in empires but in countries.... Here is the last great mistake of the Irish gentry. They have taken the empire for their country, which is the same as if a man should set himself down in some great *caravanserai* and say that he had found a home.[78]

Amongst the large exodus of Protestants from the twenty-six counties during and after the troubles were a significant number of big house owners. Intimidation drove away the Desarts, Bandons, E.J. Beaumont-Nesbitt and J.M. Wilson. When Lady Alice Howard heard of the burning of Convamore in May 1920, she thought it all 'too dreadful'. It was not just the burning of a house; it was the very disappearance of landlord culture before her eyes that disturbed her as much. The following month she learned that the Probys were selling Glenart and in September shediscovered that Lord Meath was also moving to England.[79] The thinning of landlord society that happened around Lady Alice in Wicklow happened all over the country. In early 1920, Lady Gregory wrote in her journal:

An exodus from the county [Galway]. The Goughs leave the weekend and Lough Cutra is to be shut up till they see how things are.... Lord Killanin has had trouble at Spiddal and has dismissed all his men and gone to London. The Lodells, because of their motor having been searched or put out of action the night they were going to Roxboro dance, are going to live in England. Amy has left Castle Taylor and lives in England.[80]

Those who left had little desire to return. Sir Christopher Lynch-Robinson left Athavillie after it was raided during the Civil War as he 'longed for a little security and peace, and to get out of the atmosphere of killing'.[81] In 1946, he returned on a visit to his former home, which by then had been taken over by a religious order and converted into a school. After a tour of the house, Lynch-Robinson wrote:

The dear old home was unrecognisable and looked quite awful ... I must confess to a bad shock when I was shown our old drawing-room. It had been converted into a chapel ... I am no bigot ... and yet when I thought of my grandfather, that rugged old heretic ... lying out there in his grave but a few hundred yards away, I felt as if some terrible outrage had been perpetrated on his memory.[82]

Most of those who moved permanently from Ireland moved away from landownership and into business and the professions. Sir Christopher Coote, who lived in Wiltshire, was a coffee and tea merchant. Arthur Eveleigh-De Moleyns, seventh Baron Ventry, lived in Dorset, and was a certified aeronaut. Peter Evans-Freke, eleventh Baron Carbery, who lived in Sussex, was a member of the London stock exchange from 1955 to 1968. Charles Ponsonby Moore K.G., the Marquis of Drogheda, was managing director of Financial Times Ltd from 1945 to 1970, later becoming chairman from 1971 to 1975 as well as being chairman of the Royal Opera House Covent Gardens Ltd and deputy chairman of Economist Newspapers Ltd from the late 1950s to the early 1970s. James Hubert Butler, seventh Marquis of Ormonde, lived in Illinois, and had various business connections in the USA .

It was difficult for those who remained in Ireland to integrate into the political, social or cultural mainstream of Irish life. Most families attempted to keep a foot in both Ireland and Britain. They continued to look to British public schools, Oxbridge and military colleges for their education. They continued to serve Britain as soldiers and in Britain as politicians. Some of those who served in the Second World War had survived the First World War, including the four-teenth Baron Louth, the twelfth Earl of Fingall and Major-General Eric Dorman O'Gowan who was deputy chief of staff in the Middle East. The eleventh Baron Farnham was killed at El Alamein in 1942. Lord Longford continued an active political career in Britain, return-ing regularly to Tullynally. However, attempting to keep a foot in both countries did not help these families to become fully integrated in either Ireland or Britain. In Ireland, they were generally perceived as being British; in Britain they were generally perceived as being Irish. Until the 1950s, when she sold Bowen's Court, Elizabeth Bowen divided her time between both countries. She used to say that 'the Anglo-Irish were really only at home in mid-crossing between Holyhead and Dún Laoghaire'.[83]

'ALAS! THOSE JOLLY DAYS ARE OVER'

In 1923, Lord Castletown, in his memoirs, wrote of shooting parties in Ireland in the late nineteenth and early twentieth centuries:

> We used in those days have the most cheery shooting parties at home, and go a round of visits in the autumn to Moore Abbey and other places. Lord and Lady Drogheda were a most delightful couple.... Straffan with its lovely gardens we often went to, where Hugh Barton and charming Mrs Barton gave one the best of sport and the best of

claret; Castle Bernard, one of the cheeriest houses in Ireland, where many a practical joke was played; Glenart with its two kind hosts, great woodcock, shooting and high pheasants ... in one's own county at Abbeyleix, a glorious place and splendid sport; ... and sometimes my dear old friend Ormonde used to ask me to the lodge on Slievenamon, where we had all to get up an hour before the usual time, for the days were short and the woods extensive.[84]

Castletown's memoirs were a lamentation for the passing of such an era. In the same breath that he described the above social calendar, he said, 'Alas! those jolly days are over, and many of those kind hosts have gone west, never to be replaced, and the lovely old houses are sold or shut up or burnt'.[85] By the early 1920s, Moore Abbey was leased to Count John McCormack; Castlebernard and Glenart had both been burned; and the Ormondes had more or less left Kilkenny Castle for good. It was the same throughout the country. In 1921, only two guests signed the visitors' book at Dromoland compared to twenty-four in 1913. This was explained by the note: 'No shoot, no guns allowed'.[86] Constant raids during 1919 to 1923, and the fear, which generally pervaded landlord circles, made travelling from house to house virtually impossible. In 1921 Duc De Stacpoole wrote of that year: 'I saw little or nothing of my neighbours, having no near ones, and English friends were afraid to come to Ireland, so that, mostly alone in my County Galway home, I had little to do but sit before the fire, reading my books or newspapers and ponder'.[87]

Until the First World War shoots had continued on as grand a scale as ever before.[88] The Land Acts of 1903 and 1909 had had no baleful influence on sporting rights as demesne land was exempt from their provisions. Within their demesnes landlords continued to rear game and develop coverts. The war years interrupted the sport as they did all other aspects of big house social life. The revolutionary period virtually ended it for landlords who, even if they were allowed, were unlikely to tempt fate by organising a shoot in the open of their demesne when IRA gangs were actually raiding their houses for much needed arms. (Captain J.B. Drought wrote in his sporting memoirs, 'But then came war and worse — the subsequent period of civil strife, nine troublous years in all — during which only gunmen and vermin got a look in'.[89]) The compulsory acquisition of demesne lands (or even the threat of acquisition) under the Free State Land Acts led to a dramatic decline in shooting as a pastime with the landed class. Even if landlords retained the sporting rights it was argued that they were of no use to them: 'Of what use are they ... if parks and coverts are liable to splitting up and cutting down

with scarcely any notice'.[90] Perhaps more importantly, the rearing of
game in the past had been a very expensive business, one that few
could afford from the 1920s onwards. Comparing the 1890s to the
1930s, Captain J.B. Drought wrote in his Irish sporting memoirs:

> ... the novice of the nineties had a definite advantage over the
> apprentice of to-day. *Paterfamilias* could afford to be generous, when
> income tax was 9d in the £, when cartridges cost 7s 6d a hundred and
> beaters anything from 1s to 2s 6d a day. Besides, every incidental to
> game preservation was 40 per cent to 60 per cent cheaper than it is in
> these days. Above all, he had the leisure to devote to the sporting
> education of his offspring.[91]

From the 1920s, shooting parties were restricted to a very few
estates such as Glaslough, Castleforbes, Westport or Adare and they
were attended by considerably fewer people.[92]

In the main coffee mornings, dinner parties, house balls, and theatri-
cal evenings likewise became a nostalgic memory for most. If such events
did take place, they were much less extravagant, attended by fewer
people, and confined to a minority of big houses. It is a scenario
captured by John McGahern in his short story 'Eddie Mac'. As a boy,
Eddie could recall the local landlords, the Kirkwoods, getting married after which:

> ... the parties began — bridge parties, tea parties on the lawn. There
> was a big party every year when the strawberries were ripe. Every
> Sunday night there was either a dinner party in the house or they
> went out to some other house for dinner.

About twenty years later the parties had stopped, the local
Protestant community had all but disappeared.[93]

LANDOWNERS AND FOX-HUNTING, 1880–1950

It was to be expected that a class slipping towards penury was not
going to be able to maintain the high sporting and leisure life that it
had enjoyed in the eighteenth and nineteenth centuries. Furthermore, the resentment that was focused upon landowners from the
land war onwards sporadically resulted in leisure pursuits, most
notably fox-hunting, being interrupted by agrarian agitators.

Fox-hunting had been the most popular of the landed class's outdoor pastimes. The sport transcended any social divide that existed
within the landed class providing the perfect opportunity for the lesser
gentry to mix with the more opulent and socially superior larger
landowners. In 1881, there were around twenty organised packs of

foxhounds in Ireland; five packs of staghounds; and around fifty harrier clubs.[94] Fox-hunting depended largely on the tacit agreement of tenant farmers to allow the hunt to cross their lands.[95] This rural alliance was, however, severely strained from the late 1870s coinciding with the rise of the Land League. By the end of 1881, hunts throughout the country had been stopped.[96] In December of that year, the editor of *The Irish Times* wrote: 'Hunting is today practically extinct in a country which for well nigh a century stood in the very front rank in all matters appertaining to the chase'.[97] The pretext for stopping hunts was a Nationalist means of condemning the imprisonment of prominent land leaguers.[98] As hunting was so closely associated with the landlord class and with local magistrates, who were often one and the same, the stopping of hunts was regarded as a new weapon which the Land League could use against those who were perceived to be in opposition to its ideals.[99]

However, there was no nationally co-ordinated plan to disrupt the sport; it was all rather sporadic and localised. In some areas, the grievances of local farmers with their landlords overshadowed their concern for imprisoned Land League leaders. In September 1881, Lord Waterford, master of the Curraghmores, found himself in conflict with five of his tenants. When he sold the chattel interest of their farms, a meeting of an estimated 500 men proposed to stop Waterford hunting that season. The disruption to the Curraghmores, which ensued, led Waterford to resign from the mastership and in October he sold the pack of hounds which was then taken to England.[100] Towards the end of September 1881, the Kilkenny Hunt was also attacked because Sir John Blunden was accused of the 'tyrannical act' of selling the interest of several of his tenants in their holdings.[101] During the autumn of 1882, evictions by Lord Cloncurry, Lord Mayo and Arthur MacMurrough Kavanagh led to a spate of letters to newspapers calling on local farmers to stop the Kildare Hunt.[102]

While the anti-hunting campaign had all but died out by the end of 1882, it set a precedent for future agitators. By the mid-1880s, when the plan of campaign was at its height, opposition to hunting in Limerick became characterised by greater violence.[103] In January 1886, a meeting of the Limerick Hunt was held. There, 'it was unanimously decided that in view of the opposition and insults they had met with, and there being no prospect of any improvement in the near future, that hunting should be altogether stopped as far as Limerick was concerned'.[104] In December 1887, a meeting of the local branch of the National League at Navan, County Meath, dismissed the argument of landlords that the stopping of the local hunt was injurious to employment:

If they imagine that behind the protection of some unfortunate stable-men and dogboys they can conquer the national spirit of the country, they are very much astray in their calculations. What is more intoler-able is their arrogant assumption of a right to hunt in defiance of the people.[105]

In early 1888 hunts were stopped in counties Cork, Longford and Westmeath.[106]

When agitation was re-ignited with the growth of the United Irish League in the early twentieth century, hunts became the targets of agitators once again. In December 1900, the Westmeath Hunt was stopped because it included 'an obnoxious landlord' by the name of Greene who had recently carried out an eviction.[107] In November 1901, John Dillon told those present at a UIL meeting in Roscommon to stop landlords from hunting and at least one pack of hounds was subsequently attacked.[108] Much later in 1915, at a time when land purchase had slowed down, a UIL meeting at Kanturk passed a resolution that no landlord or agent 'should be allowed to hunt over the lands of unpurchased tenants'. The resolution was primarily aimed at Sir Eustace Beecher who was refusing to sell his estate at what the tenants offered.[109]

With the outbreak of the War of Independence, the stopping of hunting once again got entwined with the wider political issues. The fact that so many hunts included army officers and RIC officers in their membership, made them objects of Nationalist scorn. In January 1919, efforts were made in Kildare, Kilkenny, Meath, Westmeath and Galway to stop hunting as a protest against the internment of political prisoners, the same pretext that had been used at the height of the land war.[110] When some officers stationed at Cahir attended a meeting of the Tipperary Hunt in January 1921, the hunt was held up and shots fired at them, leading to its abandonment.[111] At the end of that month, Major-General Strickland issued an order prohibiting the meet of this hunt as well as the United, Muskerry and South Union hunts in Cork 'on the grounds that the meets are liable to cause disorder and lead to breaches of the peace'.[112] As with the burning of some big houses, the attacks on hunts were facilitated at this time by the nature of them being soft targets. And the overall prevailing terrorism of the revolutionary years kept landowners, fearful of their lives, out of the field; this explains, for example, the 'small field' which assembled for the Meath Hunt on 31 January 1922, a hunt that had been famous in the past for its large attendance.[113]

The anti-hunting campaigns compounded the growing tensions between landlords and their representatives and other sectors of society from the 1880s to the 1920s. However, it would be difficult to argue that anti-hunting campaigns were the sole reason for the decline in fox-hunting as a popular landlord pursuit. Compared to the apprehensions landlords felt from the 1880s regarding their loss of rental income, or the fear they harboured from 1919 to 1923 of more serious crimes that might be directed against them, anti-hunting campaigns were merely regarded as a nuisance to their social lives. Disruption was perhaps even welcomed by some who could save money by not having to take to the field, and who could save face at the same time by claiming social conditions, rather than their own financial state, as their reason for this.[114] In 1881, it was estimated that landlords spent £476,000 annually on hunting. It cost up to £39,000 per annum to keep a pack of hounds; horses cost about £60 per animal. Lord Waterford alone was said to be spending £6,000 per annum at this time on the sport. The £900 guaranteed to the master of the Kilkenny hounds from subscriptions was said to be 'merely a drop in the ocean of his expenses' which could be anything up to £2,000 per annum.[115] Certainly, being master of hounds was a financial burden which could shoulder with comfort from the 1880s. Lord Fingall was master of the Meath hounds 1888–91 and 1908–11, which his wife claimed 'nearly ruined him'. She later wrote: 'It was no wonder that our fortunes — or what was left of them — went blazing up the chimney cheerfully ... as cheerfully as they were eaten by the horses in the stables, and by the endless grooms and retainers outside.'[116]

The break up of landed estates in Ireland made it inevitable that the territorial basis of the sport would disappear while the shift of wealth from the landed class to the business community also made it inevitable that the social composition of hunts would change. By the 1930s, hunting in Ireland had become increasingly middle class in composition. David Cannadine quotes one observer, who in 1936, remarked of hunting in Ireland:

> The aristocracy and squirearchy who foregathered at the meet a century ago would be surprised if they could do so today, and see the change in personnel in the field. The new rich are greatly in evidence, self-made people for the most part.[117]

However, there was still room for 'survivors'. In the 1930s, Anita Leslie visited County Meath for the fox-hunting where maids still carried trays to the riders, 'stirrup cup to be quaffed in the saddle'. But she was aware that such aspects of Irish country life, although at that stage continuing 'in unawareness', were on a 'slide towards Armageddon'.[118]

In 1949, *Bailey's Hunting Directory* claimed that the re-organisation of hunting in post-war Ireland was by then due mainly to the 'increased practical interest of the farmers, who are contributing so much to the life, wealth and sport of the country today'.[119] In the 1970s, C.A. Lewis published an historical and geographical analysis of hunting in Ireland. He found that fox-hunting, at least with the recognised packs, appeared to be, 'the preserve of the larger farmers, the business and professional men, the leisured ladies, and, greatly, the more economically successful members of the community'.[120] Those former landlords who managed to farm successfully after the sale of their estates, or who successfully made the transition from country life to the business world of the city, ensured that the old landed class had some representation on the hunting field. By the 1970s, the main difference from a century before was that the organisation and administration of the sport was no longer their sole preserve; that had passed into the hands of those from the business and professional communities, as indeed, had the wealth.

LANDOWNERS AND THE ADMINISTRATION OF HORSE-RACING, 1880–1950

As regards landlords and horse-racing, similar conclusions to those on hunting can be drawn. Landlords failed to retain a monopoly of all aspects of the sport in the early twentieth century as they had done in the previous century, but they did not disappear from the racing world completely.

The economic depression and the land war of the early 1880s led to a marked decline in the number of race meetings held in Ireland and a similar decline in the amount of prize money on offer.[121] Landlords' declining rental income and rising indebtedness meant they had much less disposable income to sponsor race meetings as they had done in the past. At the same time, the prevailing agrarian agitation disrupted meetings at various venues, some of which were to find it difficult to re-establish themselves in the better years ahead. The Heath meeting at Maryboro (Portlaoise) collapsed in the early 1880s and while it was revived in 1887, it proved unsuccessful in the long term and was finally abandoned in 1890; there were no races at Laytown from 1878 to 1885; similarly, Baldoyle, Dublin's only racecourse at the time, was poorly attended.[122] The First World War led to a decline in the number of functional racecourses from fifty-four in 1913 to twenty-four in 1918, the number of race meetings from eighty-nine to fifty-six, and the number of racing days from 122 to eighty-five.[123] During the revolutionary period Punchestown race-course was singled out because of its association with landlords and the British army and its stands were burned down while the race meetings there were abandoned in 1919 and 1920 due to the stopping of hunting in Kildare. In total, seventeen meetings were abandoned throughout the country in 1921 and a further thirty-nine in 1922.[124]

While Irish racing was to become a major industry post independence, the role of landlords in various aspects of it diminished. In the nineteenth century, landlords had been instrumental in the establishment of the major racecourses in the country as well as the provincial ones. As racing became more commercial (and their own finances declined), they became less involved in this area. In July 1922, Thomas Whelan, a local merchant, founded the Naas Racecourse Company. He encouraged local businessmen and farmers to subscribe around £16,000 to the venture. Two years later, the racecourse at Naas was opened.[125] In 1945, the passing of the Racing Board and Racecourses Act brought more government control to racing, establishing the Irish Racing Board to develop, equip and maintain racecourses and to increase stake money at authorised meetings in order to encourage breeders and trainers to retain their horses in Ireland.[126] In the past it had been the patronage of landlords that had guaranteed money prizes at most meetings. The Racing Board reduced entrance fees to racecourses; racing was no longer to be the sport of an elite.

Those who continued to breed horses in Ireland were either those (former) landlords who now regarded it as a business rather than a leisure pursuit, or those from outside that class who had accumulated enough wealth to compete. Having sold most of his estate, Lord Dunraven established the Fort Union Stud at Adare, which by the late 1920s, was regarded as, 'one of the most famous establishments in Ireland'.[127] In the early part of the century, Major Eustace bought Eyrefield Lodge near the Curragh, where Pretty Polly was dropped in 1901, a filly that was to win the 'One Thousand Guineas', 'The Oaks', 'St. Leger', 'Coronation Stakes' at Ascot, and two 'Coronation Cups' at Epsom.[128] In 1902, Col W. Hall Walker, later Lord Wavertree, established Tully Stud. It was to produce ten winners of fourteen British classics. By the late 1920s, Captain Charles Moore's stud at Mooresfort in Tipperary was said to have been 'well to the fore as a high class nursery of the thoroughbred in recent years'.[129] The Marchioness Conyngham established a stud at Slane; and Sir Gilbert Greenall's stud at Kilmallock in Limerick was 'possibly ... the most palatial establishment of its kind in the country and as well as horse breeding, pedigree cattle breeding [was] carried on there'.[130]

However, many more studs and training lodges passed out of land-lord hands. Lord Rossmore, the Marquis Conyngham, and Mervyn Pratt all sold or leased out their training lodges on the Curragh in the late nineteenth century, presumably because they could no longer afford their upkeep. By 1950, Lord Mayo's extensive stud farm at Palmerstown had been taken over by W.J. Kelly. From the 1920s, professional trainers such as J.J. Parkinson and Michael Dawson assumed prominence. The new type of breeder included 'Boss' Croker, a New York politician, who purchased Glencairn estate in 1905, the Aga Khan who bought Gleshoon and later Ballymany and Joseph McGrath who bought Brownstown Stud near the Curragh. Similarly, the rise of licensed jockeys meant landlords became obsolete in this capacity, especially as racing became more commercialised post-First World War. At Punchestown, for example, races for gentlemen riders, or confined to horses belonging to members of the Kildare Hunt, had long ceased to be by the 1950s. Any aspirations former landlords now had of riding winners were confined to point to point meetings organ-ised by hunt clubs throughout the country.[131]

It was in their capacity as administrators that former landlords continued to play a key role in racing after independence. From 1914 to 1945, the background of stewards of the Irish Turf Club remained essentially the same as it had been in the pre-war era. Of the seventeen men who were stewards over this period, all were peers, officers in the British army or former landlords or their rep-resentatives.[132] The stewards of the INHSC were men of the same social class, while Sir Walter Nugent, Sir Bryan Mahon, Major Evelyn Shirley, Lt-Col Stephen Hill-Dillon were amongst the select few who served as stewards with both the Turf Club and INHSC.[133]

In 1945, the Minister for Finance, Seán T. Ó Ceallaigh, intro-duced a bill for the improvement of Irish racing (which was to become the Racing Board and Racecourses Act of 1945.) One of the aims of the bill was to replace the old governing bodies with the Irish Racing Board. During the debates on the bill, it became clear that there was an underlying resentment amongst many TDs regarding the composition of the old bodies. William Norton of Labour (Carlow–Kildare) was adamant that the new board should reflect the socio-political changes of the previous decades:

> If this bill widens the control of Irish racing, puts it into more demo-cratic hands, and gives power of control to people who are nearer to the soil, and nearer the tempo and pulse of the mass of the people, it will do one very useful thing as far as racing is concerned.[134]

Robert Briscoe of Fianna Fáil (Dublin-South) claimed that the Turf Club and the INHSC were 'controlled mainly by persons who, from a national point of view, are very far away from us, some of them actually living outside the state'.[135] He pointed to the fact that the Turf Club and the INHSC between them included twenty-nine British army officers: 'The gentlemen with military titles,' he said, 'are gentlemen who hold these titles from a foreign army.... I think the minister ought to leave these gentlemen where they are.'[136] Patrick J. Fogarty's bitterness regarding the composition of both bodies was even more perceptible. He denounced them as bodies: 'composed of a number of West Britons whose names are sufficient to stink in the nostrils of the Irish people.... They are a body of men suffering from senile decay'.[137]

However, the government had to be, and was, more far-sighted; it realised that those who sat on the old administrative bodies would have the experience to nurture Irish racing as an industry. Furthermore, any radical changes in the administrative personnel would meet with great opposition from the existing authorities, so they had to tread carefully. To overcome this opposition six out of the eleven members of the proposed new Irish Racing Board would be members of the Turf Club or INHSC, thereby giving the old governing bodies majority control. Meanwhile, the Turf Club continued to be dominated by former landlords or officers of the British army. While Joseph McGrath, Michael Osborne, Michael Dargan, Séamus McGrath and Denis McCarthy were stewards in the 1970s and the 1980s, the old order continued to be represented by the likes of Lord Donoughmore, Major Victor McCalmont, Christopher Gaisford St Lawrence and Major George Ponsonby.

The Irish Horseracing Industry Act 1994 had greater repercussions for the involvement of the old landed class in the administration of racing.[138] This act dissolved the Irish Racing Board, replacing it with the Irish Horseracing Authority. This body con-sisted of a chairman and fifteen members appointed by the Minister for Agriculture. Only two of these members were to be stewards of the Turf Club and one a steward of the INHSC. The other members were to be made up of two representatives of authorised racecourses, one representative each from the horsebreeders, horseowners, trainers, bookmakers, racing industry, racegoers, national hunt interests and four chosen by the minister, at least one of whom was to be representative of horse-racing in Northern Ireland.

CLUB LIFE, 1914–50

Club life was greatly transformed in the years after the First World War. In an altogether changing society, clubs largely became obsolete.

This was particularly true of the county clubs, which had depended almost exclusively for their membership on landlords. When this class disappeared, clubs went with them. In the 1930s, the Clare Club, for example, had to close because it was claimed that political independence had 'removed the mantle of the ascendancy'.[141] By the mid-1920s, the second of Dublin's major clubs, the Sackville Street, was also gone. Its downfall began in 1922 when it was badly damaged as a result of fighting in the city during the Civil War. Although the club was awarded £6,000 in compensation, it was not enough to keep it viable. A short time later a meeting of its administrative committee decided that an already dwindling membership would be further adversely affected by partition and the decision was taken to wind up the club which had been in existence for 130 years.[140]

It was the changing aspect of the old landlord way of life that contributed most to their fall off in numbers as club members. We have seen that in the 1870s, club membership was an essential part of landlord social status but at that time membership was affordable and the social exclusivity of rural Ireland could be easily transferred to urban-based clubs. The First World War brought great changes. Club life and social life in general, took a back seat as landlords involved themselves at the front or in domestic activities to promote the war effort. After 1918 businessmen began to join clubs in greater numbers; clubs could no longer afford to keep them out if they wished to survive.[141] By 1925, the changing circumstances of Irish landlords were reflected in the membership of the Kildare Street Club, which had fallen by 30 per cent from its pre-war level.[142] By the 1950s, much of what the club had stood for had disappeared. At a political level, Unionism had no role to play in politics in the twenty-six counties and the Kildare Street was, therefore, no longer a meeting place for those who had shared in that political ideology.

CONCLUSION

From the 1920s, rural Ireland was deserted by (former) landlords as they migrated to areas such as South County Dublin or emigrated to Britain or even further afield. Some left for economic reasons, some for political reasons, some for social reasons and perhaps many of them for a combination of all three. For those who remained, rural Ireland became a lonely, isolated place of residence. Power in their respective localities had slipped away from them; deference towards them, except from the loyal few, had disappeared. The new judicial order in the Free State completely destroyed whatever remnants of authority landed families once had as administrators of justice and took away one of the keystones of their social prestige.

Their feelings of not belonging to mainstream Irish life were linked to the growth of a new Nationalism that made them question their position and identity in Ireland. Elizabeth, Countess Fingall, saw this symbolised in her own house:

> The front of the house seems to have had a blank look, the windows staring across the country like blind eyes. It is a look that the windows of Irish country houses often have, as though indeed that was the spirit inside them, the spirit of the colonist and conqueror, looking out across the country which they possessed but never owned.[143]

They became very much turned in upon themselves and subsequently often became regarded as eccentrics in local communities quite often simply because they spoke differently from the locals or they dressed differently or they had different cultural tastes and values. John McGahern, in two of his short stories — 'Eddie Mac' and 'The Conversion of William Kirkwood' — vividly portrays their predicament. Both are set in the rural heartland of County Roscommon where the GAA has long since superseded the popular landlord pastime of hunting. In 'Eddie Mac', the Kirkwood family is portrayed as an isolated, impoverished family, their Protestant neighbours and their family fortune long since gone. Their sole servant, Annie May, pointed out:

> The parties had stopped by the time I came. There weren't enough Protestants left by that time for parties. Once the church in Ardcarne had to be closed, it was the beginning of the end. The money Mrs Kirkwood brought was running out too.[144]

Old William Kirkwood tries to integrate with the local community by bringing his son to the county GAA final but 'they barely understood the game and were not touched by the wild fever that emptied the country side on that late August Sunday'.[145] By the time young William inherited the estate in the 1940s, signs of penury were even more perceptible as was the family's continued social decline and William was unaware that he had become 'a mild figure of fun'.[146] But McGahern refuses to dwell on this perception of William; instead he points out that this perception was 'based on no knowledge of the man. It came from casual observation, complacent ignorance, simple prejudice, that simple judgement that comes more easily than any sympathy'.[147] The Emergency and William's marshalling of the Local Defence Force changes local attitudes towards him. Soon he becomes an integral part of the local community, the local sergeant assuring him that 'Only for you being a Protestant, there'd not be the slightest difference between you and the rest of us'.[148]

Yet, while this work of fiction represents that perceptions towards one big house family changed in the 1940s, in reality it was to be a while longer before they changed towards a whole class.

CONCLUSION

The big house has much to learn — and it must learn if it is to survive at all. But it also has much to give. The young people who are taking on these big houses, who accept the burden and continue the struggle are not content, now, to live for themselves only; they will not be content, either, to live 'just for the house'. The young cannot afford to be stupid — they expect the houses they keep alive to inherit, in a changed world and under changed conditions, the good life for which they were first built. The good in the new can add to, not destroy, the good in the old. From inside many big houses (and these will be the survivors) barriers are being impatiently attacked. But it must be seen that a barrier has two sides.

ELIZABETH BOWEN, 'THE BIG HOUSE' (1941), P. 30

As late as the 1870s, Irish landlords continued to be the wealthy elite of the country. Their houses had been the homes of succeeding generations of the one family and throughout the 1850s and 1860s they had continued to spend lavishly on their upkeep. They sometimes renovated or remodelled them at great expense or embellished gardens to bring them in line with current fashionable trends. Art collections were added to; furniture was imported from the continent, often bought from continental grandees whose position had been threatened long before their own. Their collections of family portraits to which they attached great importance and displayed openly to their social equals symbolised the importance attached to preserving the family lineage. Opulent reception rooms, ubiquitous libraries, grand dining-rooms formed the showpieces of grandeur aimed at impressing guests. Plentiful servants ensured a leisured lifestyle for families and provided for the comfort of guests. These servants were usually 'imported' from England where they had been professionally trained. Land was entailed to keep estates intact; heirlooms were settled to prevent heirs selling them off. Provision continued to be made for dowagers,

younger brothers and younger sisters. It was all part of maintaining
social position.

The big house in any given local community continued to represent landlord dominance. The hand of an aristocratic landlord was to
be seen in all aspects of community life. He exerted strong economic
influence over his tenants; effectively he could make or break them
by raising rents or granting abatements during periods of crisis. He
dispensed justice in legal matters and, indeed, himself or his agent
often acted as arbitrators in family disputes. He controlled local public
services, patterned local infrastructure, donated lands to churches
and schools and contributed to their upkeep, provided for the poor
and other local charities. On his demesnes and farms he employed
local people offering regular income and steady employment for
which in return retainers devoted their lives (and during periods of
agitation sometimes sacrificed them.) Between the Famine and the
1880s he or his family were not treated with open hostility (except in
isolated incidents during the early 1850s when ribbonism flourished
in certain areas.) He occasionally provided dinners or luncheons for
his tenants, usually to celebrate the birth of a child, the coming of
age of an heir, an heir's marriage or homecoming from his honeymoon, or provided picnics for the children of his tenantry on the
demesne. In return he was presented with illuminated and decorative addresses praising his paternalistic role in the local community
and expressing the desire of the tenantry that this role continue in
the future. He sat on local government bodies and he or one of his
fellow landowners was MP for the county constituency. His involvement or that of his son(s) or son(s)-in-law in the service of the empire
in a military, civil service or diplomatic role helped to strengthen
ties and loyalty to Britain. Along with the higher echelons of the
church, the legal or medical professions, such political and administrative areas provided occupational outlets for younger sons allowing
them to perpetuate their social position.

Over a relatively short period of time, about half a century, the
whole fabric of Irish landed society was totally transformed by economic,
social and political developments. Most of these were outside the control
of landlords and thus there was very little they could do to prevent
revolutionary change irrevocably altering their lives. Political and
economic decline coincided from the 1880s with the rise of the Land
League and the Home Rule movements. Landlords now provided
obvious scapegoats for aspiring Nationalist politicians at local and
national level who could expose the foul deeds of one landlord and
then transpose them to taint all others. As one witness informed the
Bessborough Commission:

It is marvellous how the unjust treatment of one landlord creates a ferment in an entire county or province.... Whenever I went west of the Shannon if a tenant grumbled or growled, his remarks was [sic] 'Oh he is as bad a landlord as so and so', a man named ****. I found the action of one unwise or bad landlord brings disfavour on the whole class in the county or province, and actually drives terror into the minds of people for miles and miles.[1]

Falling rents and growing arrears put them in a precarious financial position. By the mid-1880s the typical Irish landlord was heavily in debt. He could not extricate himself from indebtedness by recourse to borrowing or mortgaging his lands for those channels of escape from financial difficulties had been completely closed by the plummeting value of agricultural land. The cutbacks in big house expenditure, retrenchment and the sale of fixed assets such as paintings, furniture and silver that characterised the 1880s and 1890s were both symptomatic and symbolic of their changing economic position. But they did not sell their houses. They were after all their homes, the symbols of continuity in a world of change.

Yet even when the bitter agrarian struggle of the 1880s diminished their incomes, most landlords continued to cling on to the landed tradition of preserving the land for future generations for land was still a prerequisite to position. The Settled Land Act of 1882 acknowledged their need to sell heirlooms. The sale of paintings and silver was less detrimental to social position than the sale of land. At a later stage works of fine art could be replaced, land could not. Probably more importantly the land legislation of the 1880s and 1890s provided few incentives for landowners to sell (or, indeed, for tenants to purchase.) Few large landowners sold their core estates in the 1880s, but they did sell outlying estates in an attempt to remain solvent. Those who did sell large portions of their estates, such as the Duke of Leinster and the Marquis of Waterford, were able to meet immediate debts or supplement dwindling income that allowed them to continue their traditional lifestyles into the twentieth century.

The prolonged economic crisis did, however, destroy the economic (and political) confidence of the landed class; at the same time that it ironically increased the confidence of the tenant class. By the turn of the century, in the face of continued financial deterioration and with no sign of an agricultural revival, most landlords were seriously considering the option of selling their tenanted estates if the right opportunity arose. Sir Stephen De Vere may have been suffering from an attack of hyperbole in 1891 but there was still more than a grain of truth in what he wrote when he claimed:

The new land code has deprived them of a very considerable portion of their incomes.... With a courage but little appreciated they reduced their establishments, sacrificed all the luxuries and many of what are called the luxuries of life, and have borne to see without a complaint their social intercourse destroyed, their homes desolate, old friendships decayed as old friends ceased to meet ... their waste lands undrained and unplanted, their fields half stocked, their labourers unemployed, their pleasant houses and gardens crumbling to ruin — their ancient woods felled, the fair face of the land disfigured. They have seen their sons uneducated and their daughters portionless, widows entitled to large jointures struggling with abject poverty, tenderly reared ladies working for their bread.[2]

It is hardly surprising that the Wyndham Land Act of 1903 promoted the sale of estates on a revolutionary scale. The 12 per cent bonus offered to landlords proved to be the long awaited carrot. While there were those who tenaciously clung on to their tenanted estates for a variety of reasons there were many more who sold theirs off in return for huge capital sums. At the same time they retained enough demesne and untenanted land, not only to continue farming but most likely to maintain their privacy and allow the big house an air of respectability in its setting.

This work has shown that two important consequences of the 1903 Land Act need to be considered. Firstly, the act did not end landlordism in Ireland contrary to often-repeated assertions. Secondly, the huge capital sums received by landlords actually rejuvenated big house life. Having invested their capital at 3.5 to 4 per cent and divested themselves of a myriad of estate expenses landlords found themselves at least as well off as they had been prior to sales. By now land was no longer a prerequisite to social position. It had long come to be regarded as a liability. (As Lady Bracknell said in Oscar Wilde's, *The Importance of being Earnest*: 'What between the duties expected of one during one's lifetime and the duties exacted of one after one's death, land has ceased to be either a profit or a pleasure. It gives one position and prevents one keeping it up'.) Ridding themselves of their acres was not emotionally painful once generous financial incentives had been put into place. Big house social life continued on a comfortable and in many cases a grand scale until the outbreak of the First World War. The number of servants returned in big houses and on demesnes in the 1911 census is a solid indicator of this. Thus while at various stages from the early 1880s big house cutbacks had been gradual and uneven, the Wyndham Land Act provided an escape route and allowed many families to continue their former lifestyles for the best part of a generation at least.

The First World War proved an important watershed in big house life. The casualty rate amongst the landed class, the loss of sons, relatives or friends, may not have had severe socio-economic consequences but it did have a psychological effect. Big house social life was thrown into disarray. Unionist politics in the three Ulster counties reached a crisis point that eventually resulted in the demise of Unionism there and the Protestant population being 'thrown to the wolves' by the UUC and eventually abandoned to the Free State after the establishment of Northern Ireland. Further south Unionist sentiment and organisation fell asunder. The growth of Sinn Féin and the terror of the revolutionary period from 1919 to 1923 forced southern landlords to accept that a form of Home Rule was inevitable. In the twenty-six counties as a whole, landlords became a politically alienated and impotent community. The Senate became the only political body that they could realistically hope to have any influence upon, but its functions were too limited to allow (former) landlords any significant say in the running of the country and even before its dissolution they had lost interest in it.

In the aftermath of the First World War big house social life never got a chance to rejuvenate itself. During the revolutionary period, the old landed class was subjected to a degree of terrorism beyond the comprehension of those forced to live through it. The most obvious manifestation of this terrorism was the burning of almost 300 big houses. The compensation paid to victims was never going to be enough to allow them to rebuild their houses in their former splendour. After the Troubles, the old landed class became psychologically more insular than ever before. Their political connection to Britain was severed but most found it difficult to sever their old emotional ties and they therefore found themselves in a state of limbo floating between Britain and Ireland but belonging to neither.

More importantly, the period of the First World War and the revolutionary period coincided with a dramatic rise in taxation and death duties. The subsequent worldwide depression depleted their investment portfolios and the passing of Free State land legislation was aimed at the compulsory acquisition of whatever lands remained in their hands. In 1903 the dangers inherent in worldwide investments were not obvious to potential investors. By the time landlords began to sell off the bulk of their estates from 1903, the interest rates on securities which the Irish Land Conference was advising vendors to invest in yielded 3 to 3.25 per cent interest. The conference maintained that the investment of capital sums secured from sales at these rates would be enough to provide landlords with a net income equivalent to their former net rental incomes.[3] There were more enticing if more dangerous investments available which some at least must have been tempted by.[4] In 1909, even the RCB (to which landlord mortgagors were now repaying their principal after selling their estates) invested £99,250 in Russian bonds at 4.5 per cent. From 1917 they received no dividends and by 1924 their investment had been written down to £39,300.[5] Further depreciation of the RCB's investment portfolio grew out of the insecurity of the financial situation in post-war Europe. The economic depression of the 1920s knocked over £800,000 off the market value of its general fund investment of £8.79 million (or roughly 9 per cent) from 1925 to 1926 alone.[6] It was these developments that became crucial to the economic decline of the big house in Ireland for estate papers reveal that from the 1920s onwards income from investments diminished rapidly, stocks and shares were continuously sold off to meet short-term debts thereby depleting future income. At the same time farming remained unprofitable. In the end it seems that nothing was as necessary for the upkeep of big houses in Ireland as the regular rental income that had sustained them for generations.

For the houses that remained with their original owners, much had changed by the 1930s. Lavish dinners, balls and hunting parties were a thing of the past: 'we all eat and drink a good deal less, and would not find it any shame in a host not to offer what he has not got'.[7] Most of their landed friends and neighbours had emigrated (or in many cases simply died out.) Servant numbers had declined rapidly in the years after the First World War — wage rates had risen; middle class employers required more workers and were willing to pay them more and allow them more leisure time; better education became the nemesis of deference. The legal and professional classes had by now begun to regenerate themselves, severing the social links between that class and the old landed class that had existed in the past. The British army officer class was gone. While throughout the nineteenth century and up to 1921 there had been what was described as 'a dashing and sentimental intercourse ... between officers and the country house families', the treaty brought their removal and 'one mode of feeling and living came to an end'.[8] In rural Ireland, the old landed class' isolation became complete. Elizabeth Bowen claimed in 1941 that ironically, 'with grass almost up to their doors and hardly a sixpence to turn over, they continued to be resented by the rest of Ireland as being the heartless rich'. She wondered if it was 'suspicion', 'hostility' or 'irony' that kept 'so much of Ireland away from the big house door'.[9]

The more modest houses had a better chance of survival becoming the homes of large farmers. They also had the distinct advantage of remaining fashionable, being small enough to allow the family own-ers to maintain them in a servantless world, and being much more economically friendly when it came to such practical developments as the installation of electricity or central heating. However, from the 1920s to the 1950s many of the great houses, now proverbial white elephants, flooded onto the market and where a buyer could be found were more often than not sold for a fraction of what it had cost to build them more than a century before. While some remained in private ownership, others were put to a variety of new uses. Shelton became a special school. Drumcar became a hospital; Cabra became a hotel; Oak Park became an agricultural research centre; Hazlewood became the headquarters of the Italian fibre-manufacturing firm S.N.I.A.; and more recently Mount Juliet and Straffan have become country clubs. Many more such as Dartrey and Courtown were simply stripped of their lead content and demolished. Others were demol-ished because their new owners wanted the land but not the burden of the house. Members of the Irish aristocracy were now left with neither lands nor big houses, only honourable titles. In this respect, the Irish landed class was no different to landed classes throughout Europe.[10]

Today big houses continue to be sold in Ireland. However, the present market is much more favourable to vendors than it has been in the past. Indeed, the buying of Irish country houses by foreigners has become something of a phenomenon. Since the 1980s, Adare has been bought by an American and converted into a hotel; Gurteen Le Poer has been bought by a German; Knocktopher Abbey has been bought by an Englishman and is used as a time-share residence. In 1996, a newspaper report claimed that 'most of the old Anglo-Irish may have been forced to retreat from their great estates and their crumbling mansions, but a new moneyed class is moving in and taking over'.[11] Desmond Fitzgerald, Knight of Glin, and president of the Irish Georgian Society, has been quoted as saying that the rea-son for this is that 'many of the English no longer like their own countryside because it has been invaded by weekenders'.[12] Perhaps more significantly the fact remains that properties of this calibre are much more expensive in England and Germany and many of those big houses, which have fallen into decay in Ireland, can be bought quite reasonably. Mark Keenan pointed out in 1998: 'Many of these properties can now be picked up for £150,000 or so and despite a restoration cost which may run from £500,000 upwards, the option may still work out cheaper than acquiring a ready to occupy home'.[13]

Among recent buyers of well preserved big houses are composer
Andrew Lloyd-Webber who bought Kiltinan Castle and its stud near
Fethard, County Tipperary, for an estimated £1.6 million in 1995.[14]
A few months later, Sue Bramo, a Scottish horse trainer, bought
Borleagh Manor in Wexford for over £1 million.[15] Without such pur-
chasers, many more big houses in Ireland would have suffered the
same fate as those from the 1920s to the 1950s.

Indeed a lot of credit is also due to a small group of aesthetes includ-
ing people like Desmond Guinness, the Knight of Glin and Kevin B.
Nowlan. These individuals have sought to preserve big houses as
part of the Irish national heritage and they have saved houses such
as Castletown in the process. After being purchased by Desmond
Guinness in 1967, Castletown became the headquarters of the Irish
Georgian Society. As a result of a successful fund raising project in
Ireland and abroad and the voluntary work of a group of enthusiasts,
Castletown has been greatly restored. It was acquired in 1992 by the
Office of Public Works and is currently opened to the public.

Similarly, praiseworthy efforts have been made by various voluntary and public bodies to restore big houses. Having stood empty for
almost thirty years, the sixth Marquis of Ormonde decided to sell
Kilkenny Castle to a committee representing the people of the city
for the nominal sum of £50. The committee soon realised that the
restoration work was beyond their financial resources and so in 1970
the castle was handed over to the government who entrusted its
restoration to the Office of Public Works.[16] By 1976 the castle was
opened to the public and currently attracts almost 200,000 visitors
per annum. In 1976, Dublin County Council acquired Malahide from
the Talbots who had lived there for almost 800 years. Unfortunately,
the family had to sell much of the contents, including valuable works
of art, by auction in order to meet death duties. However, some of the
furniture was bought by Bord Fáilte and remains part of the house
which is also currently open to the public. In 1986, the council also
acquired Newbridge and since then has extensively restored the
house, yards and parkland.[17]

Those buying big houses are now predominantly involved in the cor-
porate sector. In April 1995, David Davies, a Welsh millionaire and
chairman of the London-based Johnson Matthey plc, paid £3.5 million
for Abbeyleix. Michael Smurfit bought and converted Straffan into
the exclusive K Club and he also owns Waterford Castle situated on
over 300 acres. Martin Naughton, executive chairman of Glen
Dimplex and one of Ireland's most successful businessmen owned
Milestown House in Louth in the early 1990s before selling it and
buying Stackallen in County Meath in 1992 for £1.65 million.[18] In the

late 1980s, Lee Mallaghan, one of the founding directors of Powerscreen Ltd., bought Carton House and demesne where he and his family have since resided. Over the years they have made efforts to restore Carton to its original splendour. There are now plans to develop the demesne as a luxurious leisure facility. While such a move will undoubtedly have its critics, it is one of the few viable alternatives to an owner in the present day to ensure the future upkeep of a mansion such as Carton. In 1996 Castlehorn Construction purchased Killeen and its 440 acres for £1.3 million with the aim of converting it into a conference centre.[19] A major restoration job has been completed at Powerscourt, which is now open to the public as a visitor centre, gallery, exhibition hall, restaurant and interpretative centre. Much of the funding came from the sale of 100 sites close to Enniskerry village. On the one hand, the diminishing of an Irish big house's estate, therefore, continues, as does the change in the house's function. On the other hand, one could also argue that the 1980s and the 1990s have in fact been decades of re-invigoration for Irish big houses, even if their role is radically different from a century ago.

APPENDIX I

TABLES

TABLE 2.1 : RENTAL OF ORMONDE ESTATE FOR THE YEARS 1850, 1870 AND 1880

Estate	1850 (£)	1870 (£)	1880 (£)	Overall Increase (%)
Kilkenny Arran	4,382	5,132	5,469	24.6
Tipperary Arran	2,090	2,576	2,587	23.7
Kilcash	5,568	5,581	5,836	4.8
Garryricken	4,856	5,764	7,460	53.6
	16,896	20,923	21,352	26.3

Source: Ormonde estate rentals and accounts, 1850, 1870, 1880 (NLI, Ormonde papers, MSS 23,798–23,800).

TABLE 2.2: RENTAL INCOME AND HOUSE AND ESTATE MAINTENANCE EXPENDITURE ON CLONBROCK ESTATE, 1860–69

Year	Rent and Arrears Received (£)	Upkeep of House (£)	House Wages (£)	Total House and Demesne Maintenance* (£)	Estate Maintenance as Percentage of Rental Income
1860	9,553	507 (5.3%)	297	3,700	38.7
1861	9,791	489 (5.0%)	298	3,634	37.1
1862	14,019	481 (3.4%)	304	3,914	27.9
1863	9,825	466 (4.7%)	317	3,383	34.4
1864	9,839	589 (6.0%)	329	3,687	36.3
1865	10,333	577 (5.6%)	360	3,544	34.3
1866	10,141	638 (6.3%)	364	3,606	35.6
1867	10,409	624 (6.0%)	357	3,806	36.6
1868	10,164	695 (6.8%)	375	3,634	35.8
1869	10,339	661 (6.4%)	393	3,891	37.6
Total	104,413	5,727 (5.5%)	3,394 (3.3%)	36,799	35.2

* Money expended on house, gardens and demesne.

TABLE 2.3: TOTAL RENTS RECEIVED ON ORMONDE ESTATE, AMOUNT EXPENDED ON CASTLE AND GARDENS AND THIS EXPENDITURE AS A PERCENTAGE OF ANNUAL RENTAL INCOME, 1870–1877

Year	Total Rent Received (£)	Amount Spent on Castle and Gardens (£)	Expenditure as Percentage of Rental Income
1870	22,122	4,757	21.5
1871	20,526	5,742	28.3
1872	19,161	6,243	32.5
1873	21,174	7,202	34.0
1874	21,145	8,283	39.2
1875	21,307	8,470	39.8
1876	20,209	12,669	62.6
1877	21,845	9,831	45.0
Total	167,489	63,139	37.7

Source: Expenditure books for Kilkenny Castle, 1870–90 (NLI, Ormonde papers, MSS 23,800–01).

TABLE 2.4: FARM INCOME AND EXPENDITURE, NET FARM PROFITS, AND LIVESTOCK BOUGHT AND SOLD ON CLONBROCK FARM, 1860–69

Year	Farm Income (£)	Farm Expend. (£)	Net Farm Profit (£)	Cattle Bought (£)	Cattle Sold (£)	Sheep Bought (£)	Sheep Sold (£)	Percentage Profit on Sale of Stock
1860	1,620	1,522	+ 98	205	684	259	874	236
1861	1,631	1,674	- 43	93	708	379	881	237
1862	1,140	1,637	- 497	292	503	271	606	97
1863	1,251	1,392	+ 141	92	400	289	843	226
1864	1,430	1,461	- 31	118	525	280	867	250
1865	1,562	1,342	+ 220	224	678	41	872	485
1866	1,060	1,341	- 281	160	578	69	436	393
1867	894	1,399	- 505	4	536	307	336	180
1868	1,116	1,262	- 146	105	553	88	522	457
1869	1,336	1,314	+ 22	175	556	183	712	254
Total	13,040	14,344	- 404	1,468	5,721	2,166	6,949	249

Source: Clonbrock estate rental and accounts, 1860–69; farm and household account books, 1834–1935 (N.L.I., Clonbrock papers, MSS 19,507–14; 19,623–32).

TABLE 4.1: THE LOWEST AND HIGHEST PRICES OF GUARANTEED LAND STOCK FOR EACH YEAR, 1893–1902, AND THE NUMBER OF LOANS APPLIED FOR UNDER THE LAND ACTS OF 1891 AND 1896

Year	Lowest Price (£)	Highest Price (£)	Number of Loans
1893	95.6	97.33	2,391
1894	97.9	98.9	2,299
1895	102.25	103.9	1,923
1896	104.75	110.0	1,501
1897	108.5	113.5	2,506
1898	111.25	114.13	6,201
1899	109.5	112.0	6,265
1900	98.4	111.4	6,382
1901	95.9	102.4	4,946
1902	91.33	96.25	3,430

Source: *A Return Showing ... the Lowest and Highest Prices ... of Guaranteed Land Stock Under the Land Purchase (Ireland) Acts 1891 and 1896.* HC, 1903, lvii.

TABLE 4.2: ESTATE DEFICIT ON CLONBROCK ESTATE, BIG HOUSE EXPENDITURE AND ESTATE EXPENDITURE, 1902–07

Year	Estate Deficit (£)	Big House Expenditure (£)		Total Estate Expenditure* (£)
1902	980	659	(67.0%)	4,454
1903	1,525	684	(44.8%)	4,307
1904	1,594	706	(44.3%)	4,804
1905	1,828	676	(36.9%)	4,548
1906	1,435	649	(45.2%)	4,379
1907	1,420	627	(44.2%)	4,649

* House, game, woods and gardens.
Source: Clonbrock estate rentals and accounts, 1902–07 (NLI Clonbrock papers, MSS 19,652–57).

TABLE 5.1: RENTS RECEIVED, ARREARS DUE AND TOTAL ESTATE EXPENDITURE ON
CLONBROCK ESTATE, 1902–15

Year	Rents Received (£)	Arrears Due (£)	Estate Expenditure (£)
1902	10,494	4,362	11,474
1903	10,586	4,195	12,111
1904	9,763	4,579	11,357
1905	9,990	4,916	11,818
1906	9,440	5,354	10,875
1907	8,726	6,370	10,146
1908	not available		
1909	9,290	5,881	11,322
1910	9,112	5,844	10,959
1911	8,670	6,357	10,014
1912	5,408	2,855	9,543
1913	5,435	3,084	7,632
1914	2,916	1,759	not available
1915	238	written off	5,457

Source: Clonbrock estate rentals and accounts, 1902–15 (NLI, Clonbrock papers, MSS (9,652–64).

TABLE 5.2: TOTAL HOUSE EXPENDITURE, WAGES EXPENDITURE, ESTATE EXPENDITURE AND FARM RECEIPTS, CLONBROCK ESTATE, 1915–35

Year	Total House Expenditure (£)	House Wages (£)	Estate Expenditure (£)	Farm Receipts (£)
1915	697	299	5,457	2,997
1916	810	284	5,318	2,672
1917	773	308	5,858	3,681
1918	774	247	6,490	3,058
1919	898	263	6,183	4,950
1920	950	263	7,791	6,118
1921	871	257	7,653	3,738
1922	729	262	6,593	3,267
1923	755	268	5,842	3,121
1924	846	273	5,869	3,550
1925	865	295	6,388	2,379
1926	776	296	5,836	2,829
1927	698	277	5,396	2,684
1928	274	295	5,539	2,774
1929	236	323	6,029	3,041
1930	250	0	4,894	2,600
1931	176	0	5,167	2,248
1932	225	0	3,642	1,507
1933	220	0	2,867	1,122
1934	0	0	2,901	1,223
1935	0	0	3,581	1,663

Source: Clonbrock farm and household account books, 1915–35 (NLI, Clonbrock papers, MSS 19510–14).

TABLE 5.3: THE AMOUNT PAID IN INCOME AND SUPER TAX BY A MARRIED PERSON WITH CHILDREN IN 1924 AND 1950

Income Level (£)	On an Earned Income 1924 (£)	On an Invested Income 1924 (£)	On an Earned Income 1950 (£)	On an Invested Income, 1950 (£)
2,000	366	416	418	515
5,000	1,478	1,528	1,818	1,925
10,000	3,828	3,878	5,043	5,140
15,000	6,328	6,378	8,668	8,765
20,000	8,828	8,879	12,293	12,390
50,000	25,078	25,728	34,793	34,890
100,000	52,578	52,628	72,293	72,390

Source: *Reports of Irish Revenue Commissioners, 1924 and 1950.*

TABLE 7.1: THE NUMBER OF BIG HOUSES REPORTED BURNED EACH MONTH
FROM JANUARY 1920 TO JULY 1921

Month (1920)	Number of Houses Burned	Month (1921)	Number of Houses Burned
January	0	January	1
February	2	February	1
March	2	March	3
April	0	April	4
May	0	May	4
June	16	June	21
July	2	July	12
August	8		
Total	30		46

Source: *The Irish Times*, all daily editions, January 1920–August 1921; *Morning Post*, 2 April 1923; CICMRs [for twenty-six counties], January 1920–July 1921 (PRO, CO 904, part iii).

TABLE 7.2: THE GEOGRAPHICAL DISTRIBUTION OF HOUSES BURNED, BY PROVINCE AND
COUNTY, JANUARY 1920–JULY 1921

Munster	Houses Burned	Leinster	Houses Burned	Connaught	Houses Burned	Ulster [three counties]	Houses Burned
Cork	26	Westmeath	6	Galway	3	Cavan	5
Tipperary	4	Meath	5	Sligo	1	Monaghan	4
Clare	7	Longford	1	Leitrim	0	Donegal	2
Kerry	3	Wexford	1	Mayo	0		
Limerick	2	Louth	1	Roscommon	0		
Waterford	0	King's Co.	1				
		Kilkenny	1				
		Dublin	1				
		Queen's Co.	1				
		Wicklow	1				
		Kildare	0				
		Carlow	0				
Total	42		19		4		11

Source: as Table 7.1.

TABLE 7.3: THE GEOGRAPHICAL DISTRIBUTION OF HOUSES BURNED,
JANUARY 1922–APRIL 1923

Munster	Houses Burned	Leinster	Houses Burned	Connaught	Houses Burned	Ulster [three counties]	Houses Burned
Tipperary	29	King's Co.	12	Galway	17	Donegal	11
Cork	19	Wexford	11	Mayo	7	Cavan	3
Kerry	9	Dublin	10	Sligo	6	Monaghan	3
Waterford	7	Louth	7	Roscommon	5		
Clare	5	Kildare	7	Leitrim	4		
Limerick	0	Meath	5				
		Longford	5				
		Carlow	5				
		Kilkenny	5				
		Wicklow	4				
		Westmeath	3				
		Queen's Co.	0				
Total	69		74		39		17

Sources: *The Irish Times*, all daily editions, January 1922–May 1923; *Morning Post*, 2 April 1923;
Damage to Property (Compensation) Act 1923: register of claims (NA, OPW files, 2D/62/60–68).

TABLE 7.4: THE NUMBER OF HOUSES BURNED EACH MONTH FROM JANUARY 1922
TO MAY 1923

Month (1922)	Number of Houses Burned	Month (1923)	Number of Houses Burned
January–April	5	January	17
May	4	February	58
June	10	March	33
July	3	April	9
August	16		
September	21		
October	16		
November	2		
December	5		
Total	82		117

Source: as Table 7.3.

TABLE 9.1: SHOWING THE NUMBER OF VISITORS TO TEN BIG HOUSES OPEN TO THE PUBLIC, 1990–94

Number of Visitors	1990	1991	1992	1993	1994
Kilkenny	127,043	141,847	151,164	146,556	140,442
Malahide	69,000	64,200	70,570	70,163	68,445
Castletown	12,708	13,574	12,903	11,652	12,602
Strokestown	8,500	12,000	12,000	11,500	13,129
Lisadell			8,800	8,000	7,152
Coole			6,695	6,192	6,735
Tullynally			5,600	7,200	6,295
Glaslough				8,000	8,500
Glin				850	2,180
Cappoquin			300	300	200
Totals	217,251	231,621	268,032	270,413	265,680

Source: Information supplied to this author by Bord Fáilte.

APPENDIX II

ALPHABETICAL LIST OF THE 100 BIG HOUSES IN THE SAMPLE, GIVING THE ACREAGE AND VALUATION OF OWNERS' ESTATES ACCORDING TO DE BURGH, *LANDOWNERS OF IRELAND*

House	County	Acreage	Valuation
Abbeyleix	Queen's County	16,307	44,568
Adare	Limerick	15,467	11,033
Ardtully	Kerry	13,192	1,374
Ballyfin	Queen's County	49,686	19,255
Barmeath	Louth	5,314	5,093
Beaulieu	Louth	1,364	1,500
Bellamont Forest	Cavan	5,321	6,504
Bishopscourt	Kildare	21,019	13,977
Borris	Carlow	29,025	15,608
Bowen's Court	Cork	6,740	3,795
Braganstown	Louth	930	825
Burnham	Kerry	93,629	17,067
Burton Hall	Carlow	5,773	3,755
Cabra	Cavan	27,064	9,471
Cappoquin	Waterford	8,909	3,327
Carton	Kildare	68,271	47,646
Castlebernard	Cork	40,941	19,215
Castlecrine	Clare	11,389	3,859
Castle Durrow	Queen's County	19,515	9,817
Castle Forward	Donegal	28,746	15,719
Castlefreke	Cork	19,859	10,755
Castleoliver	Limerick	37,257	15,918
Castleboro	Wexford	20,882	11,714
Castleffogarty	Tipperary	1,604	1,511
Castlegar	Galway	9,479	4,358
Castlesaunderson	Cavan	12,362	7,370
Castletown	Kildare	26,917	12,647
Charleville	Wicklow	14,887	10,318
Clonbrock	Galway	28,246`	11,442
Convamore	Cork	31,505	16,151
Coole Park	Galway	4,893	2,378
Coollattin	Wicklow	91,748	47,854
Courtown	Wexford	21,657	11,361
Curraghmore	Waterford	66,684	32,749
Currygrane	Longford	1,158	835
Dalyston	Galway	5,131	2,493
Dartrey	Monaghan	28,473	19,984
Derrycarne	Leitrim	32,639	10,920
Desart Court	Kilkenny	8,932	6,278

House	County	Acreage	Valuation
Doneraile Court	Cork	14,958	13,738
Drumcar	Louth	13,265	10,755
Duckett's Grove	Carlow	5,336	4,398
Dunsandle	Galway	37,057	17,393
Dunsany	Meath	5,549	4,392
Faragh	Longford	8,559	5,288
Farnham	Cavan	29,455	20,938
Ffranckfort	King's County	1,517	913
Fort Stewart	Donegal	7,547	4,486
Frenchpark	Roscommon	29,817	12,571
Garden Morris	Waterford	7,412	5,524
Geashill	King's County	30,660	13,287
Glaslough	Monaghan	49,968	21,051
Glenart	Wicklow	19,085	26,435
Glin	Limerick	5,693	3,745
Gortnamona	Kings County	1,734	834
Gowran Castle	Kilkenny	37,587	24,321
Granston Manor	Queen's County	22,241	14,151
Gurteen Le Poer	Waterford	13,524	4,982
Harristown	Kildare	15,311	10,160
Hazlewood	Sligo	28,418	14,091
Headfort	Meath	21,796	19,374
Hilton Park	Monaghan	8,193	4,867
Hollymount	Mayo	5,194	3,856
Howth	Dublin	9,438	13,310
Kilboy	Tipperary	21,081	7,162
Kilcooley	TIpperary	1,579	487
Kilkenny Castle	Kilkenny	27,804	16,359
Killeen	Meath	9,589	8,680
Knockdrin	Westmeath	5,817	3,773
Knocklofty	Tipperary	11,950	10,466
Knocktopher	Kilkenny	2,615	1,877
Lissadell	Sligo	31,774	16,774
Lissen Hall	Dublin	11,950	10,466
Lough Fea	Monaghan	26,389	20,744
Lough Rynn	Leitrim	95,006	20,292
Louth Hall	Louth	3,760	4,116
Lyons	Kildare	12,959	10,825
Malahide	Dublin	3,573	4,945
Markree	Sligo	34,120	11,548
Moore Abbey	Kildare	19,297	10,466
Moore Hall	Mayo	12,481	3,596
Mote	Roscommon	10,509	6,386
Mount Congreve	Waterford	4,311	4,264
Mount Juliet	Kilkenny	1,432	1,270
Muckross	Kerry	47,238	10,547
Newport	Mayo	7,488	2,232
Oak Park	Carlow	24,375	17,850
Palmerstown	Kildare	7,834	7,690
Portumna	Galway	52,601	20,836
Powerscourt	Wicklow	49,071	14,219

House	County	Acreage	Valuation
Rockingham	Roscommon	72,913	40,105
Slane	Meath	156,973	32,644
Springfield	Limerick	4,483	2,955
Straffan	Kildare	5,044	5,096
Summerhill	Meath	9,745	9,281
Tubberdaly	King's County	6,743	4,820
Tullynally	Westmeath	19,989	47,198
Wells	Wexford	10,855	7,552
Westport	Mayo	114,881	16,157
Woodlawn	Galway	37,257	15,918

NOTES

Chapter 1

1. In recent years those who have written about Irish landlords' houses have tended to use the term 'country house'. Mark Bence-Jones has entitled his masterful survey of these houses *A Guide to Irish Country Houses* (1978). The Knight of Glin, D.J. Griffin and N.K. Robinson have published *Vanishing Country Houses of Ireland* (1988), while more recently Peter Somerville-Large entitled his study *The Irish Country House: A Social History* (1995). While both terms are interchangeable, this author has decided to use 'big house' simply because it was the term more generally used during the period under consideration.
2. Peter Mandler, *The Fall and Rise of the Stately Home* (Yale, 1997), p. 4.
3. In 1880, there was only one duke with a big house in the twenty-six counties (Leinster); twelve earls (Fingall, Granard, Fitzwilliam, Courtown, Howth, Longford, Mayo, Desart, Wicklow, Bandon, Donoughmore and Dunraven); seven marquises (Waterford, Drogheda, Headfort, Sligo, Conyngham, Ormonde and Clonbrock); four viscounts (Powerscourt, De Vesci, Doneraile and Monck) and sixteen barons (Dunsany, Louth, Inchiquin, Digby, Farnham, Cloncurry, Langford, Ventry, Dunalley, Ashtown, Talbot De Malahide, Carew, Dunsandle, Bellew, Rathdonnell and Carbery). *Thom's Directory, 1880*, pp. 753–77.
4. Some of these aspects were suggested to this writer by Samuel Clark's and J.S. Donnelly Jr's. 'The Unreaped Harvest' in Samuel Clark and J.S. Donnelly Jr. (ed.), *Irish Peasants: Violence and Political Unrest 1780–1914* (Wisconsin, 1983), p. 429.
5. For more information on the type of sources available for the study of landed estates see Terence Dooley, *Sources for the History of Landed Estates in Ireland* (Dublin, 2000).
6. For a fuller understanding of the importance of the return of advances, see ibid. pp. 36–37.
7. Gearóid Cronin, 'John Banville and the Subversion of the Big House Novel' in Jacqueline Genet (ed.), *The Big House in Ireland: Reality and Representation* (Dingle, 1991), pp. 216–17.
8. Desmond Guinness and William Ryan, *Irish Houses and Castles* (London, 1971).
9. Mark Bence-Jones, *Twilight of the Ascendancy* (London, 1987); id., *A Guide to Irish Country Houses* (London, 1988).
10. Peter Somerville-Large, *The Irish Country House: a Social History* (London, 1995).
11. Maurice Craig, *The Architecture of Ireland from the Earliest Times to 1880* (London, 1982).
12. B.L. Solow, *The Land Question and the Irish Economy, 1870–1903* (Cambridge, Mass., 1971).
13. J.S. Donnelly Jr, *The Land and People of Nineteenth Century Cork: the Rural Economy and the Land Question* (London, 1975).
14. W.E. Vaughan, *Landlords and Tenants in mid-Victorian Ireland* (Oxford, 1994); id., *Landlords and Tenants in Ireland, 1848–1904* (Dundalk, 1984); id., 'An Assessment of the Economic Performance of Irish Landlords, 1851–81' in F.S.L. Lyons and R.A.J. Hawkins (eds.), *Ireland Under the Union: Varieties of Tension* (Oxford, 1980), pp. 173–99.
15. Vaughan, *Landlords and Tenants in mid-Victorian Ireland*, p. iv.
16. L.P. Curtis Jr, 'The Anglo-Irish Predicament' in *Twentieth Century Studies*, iv (November 1970), pp. 37–63. Bence-Jones's *Twilight of the Ascendancy*, and Somerville-Large's, *The Irish Country House* have made interesting contributions in this area.
17. K.T. Hoppen, *Elections, Politics and Society in Ireland, 1832–85* (Oxford, 1985).
18. Alvin Jackson, *Col Edward Saunderson: Land and Loyalty in Victorian Ireland* (Oxford, 1995).
19. Patrick Buckland, *Irish Unionism I: The Anglo-Irish and the New Ireland, 1885–1922* (Dublin, 1972).
20. For the decline of Unionism in County Monaghan, see Terence Dooley, *The Plight of Monaghan Protestants, 1911–26* (Dublin, 2000) and id., 'Monaghan Protestants in a Time of Crisis' in R.V. Comerford et al. (eds.), *Religion, Conflict and Co-Existence in Ireland* (Dublin, 1990), pp. 235–51.
21. Michael Hopkinson, *Green against Green: The Irish Civil War* (Dublin, 1988), p. 195.
22. Shane Leslie, *The Irish Tangle for English Readers* (London, n.d.), p. 146.
23. David Cannadine, *The Decline and Fall of the British Aristocracy* (Yale, 1990), p. 7.

Chapter 2

1   Bence-Jones, *Guide to Irish Country Houses*, p. 234.

2.   The remainder of his estate was divided between Wexford (11,729 acres); Cork (618 acres) and Armagh (31 acres). De Burgh, *Landowners of Ireland*, p. 375.

3.   Viscount Powerscourt, *A Description and History of Powerscourt* (London, 1903), p. xi.

4.   Powerscourt estate rental, 1847, 1881 (NLI, Powerscourt papers, MSS 19,202; 19,246).

5.   Powerscourt, *Powerscourt*, p. 88.

6.   Household schedule return, Powerscourt, Enniskerry, County Wicklow, 1911 census.

7.   Powerscourt, *Powerscourt*, pp. 1–16; Christies *Powerscourt, Enniskerry Co. Wicklow: Catalogue of Old Masters Pictures, French, English and Irish Furniture, Silver and a Collection of Arms and Armour to be Sold 24–25 September 1984* (in private possession).

8.   For fuller descriptions of furnishings of these rooms see Powerscourt, *Powerscourt*, pp. 25–31.

9.   Quoted in Christie's, *Catalogue*.

10.   Powerscourt, *Powerscourt*, pp. 44–50.

11.   Ibid., pp. 51–56.

12.   Ibid., p. 93.

13.   Ibid., *Powerscourt*, p. 67.

14.   Household schedule return, 1911 census.

15.   Powerscourt, *Powerscourt*, p. 71.

16.   Ibid., p. 73.

17.   According to the 1911 household schedule return for Powerscourt these out-offices were made up of five stables, three coach houses, two harness houses, three cow houses, five calf sheds, one dairy, two piggeries, six fowl houses, two barns, one turf house, two potato houses, three workshops, five sheds, two stores, one forge and one laundry.

18.   In February 1871, there were ten men employed on the demesne and ten on the farm. From June through to the end of September this number rose to a total of around fifty and there was also about twelve 'boys' employed. Powerscourt workmen's account book, 1871 (NLI, Powerscourt papers, MS 19,288).

19.   Luggala farm account book, 1898–1922; ibid. (MS 19, 296).

20.   Powerscourt, *Powerscourt*, p. 77; Bence-Jones, *Guide to Irish Country Houses*, p. 235; Guinness and Ryan, *Irish Houses and Castles*, p. 328.

21.   Powerscourt, *Powerscourt*, p. 78.

22.   Ibid.

23.   Ibid., p. 95.

24.   Edward Malins and Knight of Glin, *Irish Gardens: the Irish Heritage Series: II* (Dublin, 1977), p. 7.

25.   Ibid., p. 8.

26.   De Burgh, *Landowners of Ireland*, p. 48.

27.   Elizabeth Bowen, *Bowen's Court* (Cork, 1998 ed. (first published London, 1942)), pp. 20–21.

28.   Bence Jones, *Guide to Irish Country Houses*, p. 46.

29.   Bowen, *Bowen's Court*, p. 21.

30.   Ibid., p. 23.

31.   Ibid., p. 27.

32.   Ibid., p. 25.

33.   Ibid., p. 26.

34.   Ibid., p. 28.

35.   Ibid., p. 29.

36.   Ibid., p. 31.

37.   Bence-Jones, *Guide to Irish Country Houses*, p. vii.

38.   Ibid.

39.   *Thom's Directory, 1870*, p. 1076. This number is exclusive of magistrates who had a residential address elsewhere in Ireland, who were land agents such as William S. Trench or who were brothers or sons of landlords and not the actual owners of estates in the county.

40.   Vaughan, *Landlords and Tenants in mid-Victorian Ireland*, p. 6.

41.   Of the houses listed in Bence-Jones's *Guide to Irish Country Houses* that can be confidently assigned to a period, just over 100 were built after 1850.

42.   During this period, eighty-nine of the 100 sample houses were built.

43.   Foster, *Modern Ireland*, p. 185.

44.   A.W. Hutton (ed.), *Arthur Young's Tour in Ireland, vol. I* (London, 1892), p. 31.

45.   Bence Jones, *Guide to Irish Country Houses*, p. 75.

46.   Quoted in Guinness and Ryan, *Irish Houses and Castles*, p. 187.

47.   C.W. Ganly, A *Tribute to a Noble Life: In Memoriam of Gerald, Duke of Leinster* (privately published, n.d.), pp. 5–6.

48.   Bence Jones, *Guide to Irish Country Houses*, p. 170.

49.   Ibid. p. 277.

50.   J.P. Neale, *Views of the Seats of Noblemen and Gentlemen in England, Wales and Scotland and Ireland, vol. iii* (London, 1820), no pagination.

51.   Ibid.

52.   Shane Leslie, unpublished autobiographical sketch (NLI, Leslie papers, MS 22,884).

53.   Peter Collins, *County Monaghan Sources in the Public Record Office of Northern Ireland* (Belfast, 1998), p. 47.

54.   Lindsay Proudfoot, 'The Estate System in Mid-Nineteenth Century Waterford' in William Nolan and T.P. Power (ed.), *Waterford: History and Society* (Dublin, 1992), p. 533.

55.   Estimate of building costs of work carried out by B.T. Patterson, builders, 1860–1933 (IAA, B/09)

56.   Ibid. (B/82).

57.   Ibid. (C/39).

58.   *Sunday Tribune*, 15 February 1998.

59.   In a study of rentals of fifty estates, W.E. Vaughan found an average rental increase of just over twenty per cent; J.S. Donnelly Jr, while finding some 'extremely large' rent increases on individual estates in County Cork concluded that the more typical rent increases ranged from 20 to 30 per cent; B.L. Solow, using parliamentary papers, calculated that rents increased by just under 30 per cent from 1850–80. Vaughan, *Landlords and Tenants in mid-Victorian Ireland*, p. 48; Donnelly, *Land and People of Cork*, pp. 191–94; B.L. Solow, *The Land Question and the Irish Economy, 1870–1903* (Cambridge, Mass., 1971), pp. 66–70.

60.   Crofton estate rentals, 1852, 1880 (NLI, Crofton papers, MSS 4,089, 5,632); Butler of Castlecrine estate rentals, 1848–80 (NLI, Butler of Castlecrine papers, MSS 5,410–14, 5,422); Pratt estate rentals, 1850–97 (NLI, Pratt papers, MSS 3,122, 5,081–91); Ormonde estate rentals and accounts, 1850, 1870, 1880 (NLI, Ormonde papers, MSS 23,798–23,800); Finlay Dun, *Landlords and Tenants in Ireland* (London, 1881), p. 41.

61.   *Bess. Comm. Report*, p. 3.

62.   Quoted in Vaughan, *Landlords and Tenants in mid-Victorian Ireland*, p. 65.

63.   *Bess. Comm., Minutes of Evidence ii*, p. 1147.

64.   Cannadine, 'Aristocratic Indebtedness', p. 633.

65.   P.J. Corish, *Maynooth College, 1795–1995* (Dublin, 1995), pp. 182–83.

66.   'Instructions for counsel to advise on the title, direct searches etc.' prepared by O'Hagan solicitors for the trustees of Maynooth College, 3 November 1873 (Maynooth College Archives, 112/1) [Hereafter MCA].

67.   'Schedule of documents lodged to the Irish Land Commission by the solicitors of Maynooth College, 19 October 1908' (MCA, 107/10)

68.   Obituary of Robert Dillon, third Baron Clonbrock, in untitled newspaper clipping, 16 December 1893 (NLI, Clonbrock papers, MS 19,667).

69.   During 1849 and 1850, Clonbrock paid approximately £110 'to sundry tenants on throwing their houses and leaving the estate' — probably something akin to compensation for disturbance as existed under the Ulster custom — and continued to pay sums of up to £100 per annum during the 1860s to 'emigrants'. Clonbrock estate rentals and accounts, 1849–50, 1860–69 (NLI, Clonbrock papers, MSS 19,617–18, 19,623–32).

70.   Ibid., 1850–55 (MSS 19,617–22).

71.   Ibid., 1849, 1860–64 (MSS 19,617, 19,623–27).

72.   See Table 2.4.

73.   Clonbrock estate rentals and accounts, 1854, 1869, 1880 (MSS 19,621, 19,632–33).

74.   Ibid., 1864 (MS 19,627).

75.   Address to Hon. Luke Gerald Dillon on his marriage to Augusta Crofton, 6 April 1867 (NLI, Clonbrock papers, MS 19,665); an earlier address to Luke Gerald on reaching his majority in 1855 read: 'We look forward with the fullest confidence to your following in the footsteps of your noble father, who has at all times, with so much zeal and justice, discharged his duties as a landlord'; ibid.

76.   Crofton estate rentals, 1867–70, 1872–73, 1876–78 (NLI, Crofton papers, MSS 4,080–88).
77.   These were numerous and were categorised in estate accounts during the 1860s as: insurance, schools, head rents, county cess, income tax, poor rates, quit rents, rent charges, interest, charities, labour, mill, woods, house, gardens, improvements, salaries, emigrants, small payments, arrears cancelled, pensions, stationary and agency fees.
78.   Battersby and Co., *Kilkenny Castle: Catalogue of the Valuable Antique and Interesting Contents of this Historic Mansion to be Sold by Auction Commencing Monday 18 November 1935.*
79.   Ibid.
80.   Estimate of building costs carried out by B.T. Patterson, builders, 1860–1933 (IAA, C/7, C/49).
81.   See Table 2.3, Appendix 1.
82.   Untenanted land was land on which no formal tenancy had been created and where the landlord was, therefore the rateable occupant. It consisted of demesne and parkland, the home farm which was usually close by, out farms which could be a distance away, mountain areas used for grazing and bog areas used for turbary.
83.   These supplies are for December 1884 as similar accounts were not available for the 1860s. Clonbrock estate account book, 1880–1900 (NLI, Clonbrock papers, MS 19,511).
84.   Georgiana Bond, 'Family patchwork' [unpublished manuscript] (NLI, Bond papers, MS 18,450).
85.   Jones, *Graziers and Land Reform*, pp. 121–23.
86.   *Cowper Comm., Minutes of Evidence*, p. 645.
87.   Dun, *Landlords and Tenants in Ireland*, p. 34.
88.   *Royal Commission on Congestion in Ireland: Appendix to Tenth Report, Minutes of Evidence Taken in Counties Galway and Roscommon, 18 September to 4 October 1907 Relating Thereto,* [Cd 4007] HC 1908, xlii, p. 167.
89.   Seymour Leslie, *Of Glaslough in the Kingdom of Oriel and of the Noted Men that have Dwelt There* (Glaslough, 1913), pp. 89–90.
90.   Ibid., p. 62.
91.   Anita Leslie, *The Gilt and the Gingerbread: an Autobiography* (London, 1981), p. 15.
92.   W.B. Yeats, *The Autobiography of W.B. Yeats* (London, 1966 ed.), pp. 389–90.
93.   *Auction Catalogue of Lyons, Co. Kildare, 23 October 1962* (in private possession).
94.   *Catalogue of Paintings Sold by Trustees of Carton 4 December 1902* (PRONI, Leinster papers, D3078/2/10/6/2).
95.   *Catalogue of the Valuable Contents of Dartrey Castle to be Sold on 19 April and Three Following Days, 1937* (in author's possession).
96.   Private inventory of furniture, fixtures, fittings, linen, china and glass etc. at Ballynastragh, taken for purposes of insurance, February 1910 (NA, Esmonde papers, 981/4/2).
97.   Bennett and Sons, *Catalogue of Valuable Antique and Modern Furniture ... to be Sold at Killua Castle, Westmeath on 2 June 1920.*
98.   Shane Leslie, *The Irish Tangle*, p. 138.
99.   Seymour Leslie, *Of Glaslough*, p. 82.
100. Neale, *Seats of Noblemen, vol. ii*, no pagination.
101. *Dartrey Catalogue.*
102. Statement of Sir Thomas Esmonde on the burning of Ballynastragh, 9 March 1923 (NLI, Esmonde papers, 981/4/4/1/).
103. *Return of Untenanted Land, 1906.*
104. Copy letter H.R. Westenra to Lord Rossmore, 26 December 1824 (IAA, RPD 54.5)
105. Neale, *Seats of Noblemen, vol. iiii*, no pagination.
106. Ibid., *vol. ii.*
107. Hutton (ed.), *Arthur Young's Tour*, p. 31.
108. Seymour Leslie, *Of Glaslough*, p. 87.
109. Ormonde estate rentals and accounts, 1895–1903 (NLI, Ormonde papers, MSS 23,724–33).
110. Seymour Leslie, *Of Glaslough*, p. 88.
111. Elizabeth Bowen described a parkland as follow: 'On each side [of the avenue] lie those tree studded grass spaces we Anglo-Irish call lawns and English people puzzle us by speaking of as "the park". On these browse cattle, or there may be horses out on grass. A second gate ... keeps these away from the house in its inner circle of trees.' Bowen, 'The Big House', p. 26.
112. Malins and Glin, *Irish Gardens*, p. 1.
113. Peter McKenna, *The Emetresse* (Monaghan, 1991), p. 122.

Chapter 3

1. Bowen, 'The Big House', p. 29.
2. Quoted in Curtis, 'The Anglo-Irish Predicament', p. 42.
3. He wrote: 'With its lovely gardens and the sort of subtle influence it exerted on the whole neighbourhood [it] was, so to speak, the centre of things. Thither came from time to time much that was best in Irish and English life, soldiers, statesmen, artists.... There were boats on the lake for excursions or fishing, horses in the stable to ride or drive, shooting in the season, or fishing according to the social life of the Irish landed class, particularly the higher echelons of it to the taste of the sportsmen' C.P. Crane, *Memories of a Resident Magistrate* (Edinburgh, 1938), pp. 108, 214.
4. *Burke's Peerage and Baronetage*, pp. 1589–60.
5. Shane Leslie memoirs (NLI, Leslie papers, MS 22,885); Typescript of autobiographical sketch by Shane Leslie, ibid. (MS 22884); Castle Leslie publicity material.
6. Shane Leslie, *The End of a Chapter* (London, 1916), p. 110.
7. Seymour Leslie, *The Jerome Connexion* (London, 1964), p. 2.
8. Leslie memoirs (MS 22,885).
9. Seymour Leslie, *The Jerome Connexion*, p. 32.
10. Leslie autobiographical sketch (MS 22,884).
11. Leslie memoirs (MS 22,885).
12. Seymour Leslie, *The Jerome Connexion*, p. 88.
13. Leslie memoirs (MS 22,885).
14. Seymour Leslie, *The Jerome Connexion*, pp. 26, 35.
15. Leslie memoirs (MS 22,885).
16. Ibid.
17. Ibid.
18. Ibid.
19. Ibid.
20. Seymour Leslie, *The Jerome Connexion*, p. 5.
21. Leslie memoirs (MS 22,885).
22. Shane Leslie, *The Film of Memory* (London, 1938), p. 116.
23. Leslie memoirs (MS 22,885).
24. Anita Leslie, *The Gilt and the Gingerbread: an Autobiography* (London, 1981), p. 15.
25. Leslie memoirs (MS 22,885).
26. Anita Leslie, *The Gilt and the Gingerbread*, p. 68.
27. Leslie memoirs (MS 22,885).
28. Leslie autobiographical sketch (MS 22,884).
29. Shane Leslie, *The Film of Memory*, pp. 55–60.
30. Ibid., p. 13.
31. Anita Leslie, *The Gilt and the Gingerbread*, p. 15.
32. Leslie autobiographical sketch (MS 22,884).
33. Ibid.
34. Anita Leslie, *The Gilt and the Gingerbread*, p. 98.
35. For examples of these, see Clonbrock scrapbook (NLI, Clonbrock papers, MS 19,665).
36. *Tuam Herald*, 16 June 1855.
37. *Roscommon Journal*, 5 December 1864.
38. Earl of Meath, *Memories of the Nineteenth Century* (London, 1923), pp. 133–34.
39. Fingall, *Seventy Years Young*, p. 96.
40. Leslie autobiographical sketch (MS 22,884).
41. A directory of people to be invited to balls at Kilkenny Castle, c.1880–1912 (NLI, Ormonde papers, MS 23,552).
42. Diary of Lady Alice Howard, 21 January 1874 (NLI, Diaries of Lady Alice Howard, MS 3,600).
43. Ibid., 17–21 January 1874.
44. Ibid., March–April, 1874.
45. Ibid., 29 March–5 April, 1874.
46. Ibid., 5 September 1874.
47. Diary of Lady Crofton, 1852 (NLI, Crofton papers, MS 4,070).
48. Diary of Lord Cloncurry, 1897 (In private possession).
49. Bowen, *Bowen's Court*, p. 345.

50.   Ibid., pp. 345–6.
51.   Diary of visitors to Headfort Castle, 1887–92 (NLI, Headfort papers, MS 25,369).
52.   Bence-Jones, *Twilight of the Ascendancy*, p. 97.
53.   *Leinster Express*, 10 April 1880.
54.   Fingall, *Seventy Years Young*, p. 86.
55.   Ibid.
56.   Quoted in ibid., p. 121.
57.   List of plate in Kilkenny Castle in November 1839 and December 1848 (NLI, Ormonde papers, MS 23,809).
58.   Annie MacManus in conversation with the author.
59.   Fingall, *Seventy Years Young*, p. 300.
60.   Shooting card of hunting party at Glenart, 9–12 November 1886, enclosed in diary of Lord Cloncurry for 1886 (In private possession).
61.   Diary of Lord Cloncurry, 4 January 1887 (In private possession).
62.   Fingall, *Seventy Years Young*, p. 182.
63.   Molly Wills to Mrs Fawcett, 3 May 1904; quoted in *Journal of the Butler Society*, vol. iii, no. 2 (1988–89), pp. 202–03.
64.   Fingall, *Seventy Years Young*, p. 91.
65.   Owen Tweedy, *The Dublin Tweedys: the Story of an Irish Family, 1650–1882* (London, 1956), p. 110.
66.   *Morning Post*, 27 July 1866.
67.   Fingall, *Seventy Years Young*, p. 98.
68.   J.P. Mahaffy, 'The Irish Landlords' in *Contemporary Review*, xlii (January 1882), p. 162.
69.   For Conolly's hunting exploits see, Earl of Mayo and W.B. Boulton, *A History of the Kildare Hunt* (London, n.d.), p. 19; similarly, in Kilkenny, the Earl of Carrick hunted with his own pack at the end of the eighteenth century while in Limerick: 'Almost all the larger gentry owned a pack of some kind with which they would hunt either stag, fox or hare'; Anon, *Memoir of the Kilkenny Hunt* (Dublin, 1897), p. 9 and Col Wyndham Quin, *The Fox Hunt in Co. Limerick* (Dublin, 1919), p. 19.
70.   Muriel Bowen, *Irish Hunting* (Tralee, n.d.), pp. 5, 17, 59, 101.
71.   Ibid., pp. 40, 55, 194.
72.   Fingall, *Seventy Years Young*, pp. 98, 186, 201.
73.   In 1815, John Power of Kilfane received £600 in subscriptions from fellow landlords in Kilkenny for the upkeep of his kennels and hounds. One commentator, however, remarked: 'Considering the enormous country he hunted, the many coverts and earths which he made, and the many other contingent demands on him' it 'was not much'; Anon, *Memoir of the Kilkenny Hunt*, p. 24.
74.   Ibid., p. 95.
75.   Ibid., pp. 53,68.
76.   Lord Castletown, *Ego: Random Records of Sport, Service and Travel in Many Lands* (London, 1923), p. 17.
77.   Wyndham Quin, *The Fox Hunt in Co. Limerick*, pp. 140–41.
78.   *Return of Owners of Land of One Acre and Upwards in the Several Counties, Counties of Cities, and Counties of Towns in Ireland*, [C1492] H.C. 1876, lxxx, 61.
79.   Quoted in Gifford Lewis, *Somerville and Ross: the World of the Irish R.M.* (London, 1985), p. 126.
80.   Fingall, *Seventy Years Young*, p. 93.
81.   Desdichado (pseudonym), *Fox Hunting in Meath: an Imperfect Record of a Hunting Season in Meath, 1883–84* (Dublin, 1884), p. 35.
82.   Mayo and Boulton, *The Kildare Hunt*, pp. 267–71.
83.   Ibid., p. 271.
84.   Ibid., p. 338.
85.   Quoted in ibid., p. 303.
86.   M.G. Moore, *An Irish Gentleman: George Henry Moore* (London, n.d.), p. 92.
87.   Anon, *Memoir of the Kilkenny Hunt*, p. 65.
88.   Col S.J. Watson, *Between the Flags: A History of Irish Steeplechasing* (Dublin, 1969), p. 63.
89.   Mayo and Boulton, *The Kildare Hunt*, pp. 182–83.

90. *Irish Racing Calendar, 1872*, pp. 36, 61, 79, 106.

91. Ibid., *1880*, p. 53.

92. The stud career of the Earl of Dunraven's Desmond, for example, produced winners of races totalling £180,000 in prize money; Earl of Dunraven, *Past Times and Pastimes*, vol. *i* (London, 1922), pp. 168–69.

93. F.A. Darcy, *Horses, Lords and Racing Men* (Kildare, 1991), pp. 48–53.

94. Ibid., p. 173.

95. Moore, *An Irish Gentleman*, pp. 82–98.

96. From 1850 to 1880, fourteen men served as stewards of the Turf Club. All were landlords or army officers. They included from the 100 sample families Marquis Conyngham, Col J.C. Westenra, the Marquis of Waterford, the Earl of Howth and the Marquis of Drogheda; *Irish Racing Calendar, 1850–80*.

97. Moore, *An Irish Gentleman*, p. 104.

98. Ibid., pp. 8–9.

99. Ibid., p. 311.

100. Ibid., p. 312.

101. *Irish Racing Calendar, 1880*, p. 522.

102. Ibid.

103. Ibid.

104. Quoted in Darcy, *Horses, Lords and Racing Men*, p. 188.

105. Dunraven, *Past Times and Pastimes*, vol. *I*, pp. 168–69.

106. Leslie Memoirs (MS 22,885).

107. R.F. Brooke, *Daly's Club and Kildare Street Club, Dublin* (Dublin, 1930), p. 5.

108. Newspaper clipping, undated and untitled in scrapbook compiled by W. Walsh and titled 'Clubs and taverns of Dublin' (NLI, Walsh papers, MS 11,664).

109. Brooke, *Daly's Club and Kildare Street Club*, p. 8.

110. Walsh, 'Clubs and taverns of Dublin'.

111. Brooke, *Daly's Club and Kildare Street Club*, p. 6.

112. G.W. Maunsell, 'An Historical Note on the Kildare Street Club', August 1880 (NLI, Maunsell papers, MS 4,621).

113. Ibid.

114. Bence-Jones, *Twilight of the Ascendancy*, p. 55.

115. It was possible to establish the clubs to which ninety-five of the 100 sample landlords were affiliated in the late 1870s using works such as Bateman, *Great Landowners* (1883) and *Burke's Baronetage and Peerage* (various editions). Of the fifty-five peers, twenty-seven belonged to the Kildare Street. Another fifteen large landowners belonged to it including the likes of John Madden, Henry Bruen and Percy La Touche. The smaller landowners were not represented at all probably because they did not spend the same amount of time in Dublin.

116. Only twenty of the sample landlords, for example, belonged to the Sackville Street Club c. 1880.

117. Maunsell, 'An Historical Note on the Kildare Street Club'.

118. Bence-Jones, *Twilight of the Ascendancy*, p. 54.

119. County Club Limerick, *A Short History of a Hundred Years of Club Life* (Privately published, Dublin, n.d.), p. 6.

120. Ibid., p. 11.

121. K.T. Hoppen, *Elections, Politics and Society in Ireland, 1832–85* (Oxford, 1984), p. 119

122. Leslie memoirs (MS 22,885).

123. *Rules of the Kildare Street Club with a List of Members' Names, January 1860* (Dublin, 1860), p. 6.

124. *Rules and Regulations of the Junior United Service Club with an Alphabetical List of its Members* (London, 1855), pp. 9–10.

125. Guy Boas, *The Garrick Club, 1831–1947* (London, 1948), p. 11.

126. Diary of Lord Cloncurry, 1886 (In private possession).

127. Bence-Jones, *Twilight of the Ascendancy*, p. 54.

128. County Club Limerick, *A Short History*, p. 17.

129. Bence-Jones, *Twilight of the Ascendancy*, p. 55.

130. Ibid.

131. Edith Somerville and Martin Ross, *Irish Memories* (London and New York, 1925), p. 71.

132. Curtis, 'The Anglo-Irish Predicament', p. 40.
133. This information and what follows is based on findings regarding the 100 sample houses and is taken from a study of *Burke's Gentry* (1912 and 1958 editions), *Burke's Peerage and Baronetage* (various editions) and Bateman, *Great Landowners*.
134. Fingall, *Seventy Years Young*, p. 96
135. George Moore, *A Drama in Muslin* (London, 1886), p. 190.
136. Tweedy, *The Dublin Tweedys*, p. 107.
137. Diary of Lady Alice Howard, April–July 1874 (NLI, Diaries of Lady Alice Howard, MS 3,600).
138. Seymour Leslie, *The Jerome Connexion*, p. 46.
139. Leslie memoirs (MS 22,885).
140. Ibid.
141. Bence-Jones, *Twilight of the Ascendancy*, p. 94.
142. Quoted in Moore, *An Irish Gentleman*, p. 27.
143. Fingall, *Seventy Years Young*, p. 95.
144. Anita Leslie, *The Marlborough House Set* (New York, 1975), p. 30.
145. Fingall, *Seventy Years Young*, pp. 86–7.
146. Proposals for a settlement on the intended marriage of Charles William, Marquis of Kildare, eldest son and heir apparent of the most noble Augustus Frederick, Duke of Leinster, with the Lady Caroline Gower, one of the daughters of the most noble Duke of Sutherland (n.d., c.1847) (PRONI, Leinster papers, D3078/1/3/42).
147. Cost of settlement and deeds executed upon the marriage of Ambrose Congreve with the Hon. Alice Dillon, June–July 1866 (NA, Congreve papers, 1079/1/2/8).
148. For examples of Lady Meath's philanthropy, see Earl of Meath (ed.), *The Diaries of Mary, Countess of Meath* (London, n.d.).
149. Moore, *Drama in Muslin*, p. 328.
150. The fact that information could not be located on the formal education of a number of sons in the sample suggests they may also have remained at home under private tuition.
151. Lord Castletown, *Ego*, pp. 1, 5, 6, 8, 10, 21.
152. Dunraven, *Past Times and Pastimes, vol. i*, pp. 4–9.
153. Ibid., p. 9.
154. Jessica Gerard, *Country House Life: Families and Servants, 1815–1914* (Oxford, 1994), pp. 84–85.
155. Meath, *Memories of the Nineteenth Century*, pp. 20–21.
156. Fingall, *Seventy Years Young*, p. 79.
157. Leslie, autobiographical sketch (MS 22,884).
158. Vaughan, *Landlords and Tenants in mid-Victorian Ireland*, pp. 11–12.
159. Shane Leslie, *Doomsland*, p. 143.
160. Castletown, *Ego*, p. 1.
161. *Burke's Gentry* (1912, 1958); *Burke's Peerage and Baronetage* (various editions).
162. Meath, *Memories of the Nineteenth Century*, pp. 35, 56, 64.
163. David Cannadine, *Aspects of Aristocracy* (Yale, 1994), p. 9.
164. Ibid., p. 22.
165. Quoted in Tweedy, *The Dublin Tweedys*, pp. 111–12.
166. Quoted in ibid., p. 113.
167. Philip Magnus, *Gladstone: A Biography* (London, 1963 ed.), p. 221.
168. Cannadine, *Decline of the British Aristocracy*, p. 270.
169. Quoted in ibid., p. 275
170. Ibid., p. 280.
171. Meath, *Memories of the Nineteenth Century*, pp. 64, 146, 181, 183.
172. *Burke's Gentry* (1912 and 1958); *Burke's Peerage and Baronetage* (various editions).
173. Meath, *Memories of the Nineteenth Century*, pp. 2–3, 35.
174. Fingall, *Seventy Years Young*, p. 286.
175. Vaughan, *Landlords and Tenants in mid-Victorian Ireland*, p. 220.
176. *Burke's Gentry* (1912 and 1958); *Burke's Peerage and Baronetage* (various editions).
177. Cannadine, *Decline of the British Aristocracy*, p. 256.
178. *The Times*, 5 January 1884; quoted in ibid., p. 250.
179. Only one son from the sample was found to be a land agent. This was Arthur Bruen, son of Henry Bruen of Oak Park, who was a land agent in Ireland from 1901 to 1924. Again, if more

information was available, it is likely that this number would have been higher.

180. *Bessborough Commission, Minutes of Evidence i and ii*, pp. 481, 906, 1,297.
181. Brian Griffin, 'The Irish Police, 1836–1914: A Social History' (D. Phil. thesis, Loyola university, Chicago, 1990), p. 253.
182. *Daily Express*, 4 December 1861.
183. *Freeman's Journal*, 11 December 1888.

Chapter 4

1. As well as Granard, these included Lord Cloncurry of Kildare; R.J. Alexander of Antrim; B.R. Balfour of Louth; J.A. Stewart of Donegal and Derry; Myles O'Reilly of Galway; and Samuel Osborne of Meath.
2. Abstract of agreement for mortgage loan between Lord Granard and the trustees of Maynooth College, 8 April 1871 (MCA, 109/1).
3. P.A. Chance to Robert Browne, 15 March 1889 (MCA, 109/6)
4. Granard's father and grandfather had accumulated a huge debt burden from the late eighteenth century. Granard inherited debts of well over £100,000; Thomas Farrelly to Messrs Crozier, 23 March 1871 and 31 March 1871; Earl of Granard's estate: opinion of counsel Gerald Griffin n.d (C.1892) (MCA, 109/1–9).
5. In total the Earl owned 14,978 acres in County Longford, 4,266 in County Leitrim and 2,050 in County Wexford at this time; Bateman, *Great Landowners*, p. 185.
6. F.M. Crozier to Edward Caragher, 7 January 1881 (M.C.A, 109/6).
7. Lord Granard to president of Maynooth College, 30 February 1880 (MCA, 109/2)
8. At the time 'The poet Higgins' wrote of the Granard estate in a poem entitled 'The Land War in Drumlish, 1881':
   'Around Drumlish and Ballinamuck as you may plainly see
   The Earl of Granard owned some land — part of his property,
   And by rack-rents unjustly claimed for o'er two hundred years
   His tenants pressed were forced at last to fall into arrears.'
   Quoted in *Drumlish Land War Centenary, 1881–1981: Commemorative Booklet* (1981), pp. 39–40.
9. John Ball Greene, the man who replaced Richard Griffith at the Valuation Office, calculated that it would have been necessary to add 33 per cent to Griffith's estimates to calculate the real letting value of land in the mid 1860s. *Report of Her Majesty's Commission of Enquiry into the Working of the Landlord and Tenant (Ireland) Act 1870 and the Acts Amending the Same: Minutes of Evidence, part I* [C2779], HC 1881, xviii, 73, p. 31.
10. Quoted in An Irish Priest, *A Short History of the Land War in Drumlish in 1881* (Dublin, 1892), p. 11.
11. Ibid., p. 28.
12. The crowd was estimated at 15,000; ibid., p. 17; A.W. Percival to Fr O'Hagan, 25 February 1891 (MCA, 110/12).
13. An Irish Priest, *Land War in Drumlish*, p. 28.
14. F.M. Crozier to Edward Caragher, 7 January 1881 (MCA, 109/3).
15. Ibid.
16. An Irish Priest, *Land War in Drumlish*, p. 28.
17. *The Irish Times*, 14 January 1881.
18. An Irish Priest, *Land War in Drumlish*, pp. 29, 51.
19. Ibid., pp. 32–33.
20. F. Crozier to Rev Farrelly, 7 July 1881 (MCA, 110/16).
21. *Return of Payments Made to Landlords by the Irish Land Commission Pursuant to the First and Sixteenth Sections of the Arrears of Rent (Ireland) Act 1882*, HC 1884, lxiv.
22. From the time the sub commissioners began their operations in August 1881 to the end of the first judicial term in December 1902, they dealt with 342,019 cases in which judicial rents were fixed throughout the country. The former rents of these holdings totalled £6.93 million. The judicial rent lowered it to £5.48 million, a decrease of 20.8 per cent. *A Return Showing, According to Provinces and Counties, the Number of Cases in which Judicial Rents Have Been Fixed. All the Methods Provided by the Land Law Acts for a First and Second Statutory Term, Respectively, to 31 December 1902 with Particulars as to Acreage, Former Rents of Holdings, and Percentages of Reductions in Rents, were also Shown*, HC 1903, lvii, 91.

23.   F. Crozier to Rev Farrelly, 7 July 1881 (MCA, 110/16).
24.   *Longford Independent*, 11 December 1886.
25.   Ibid., 5 December 1887.
26.   Messrs Darley and Roe to Rev Boylan, 10 June 1886 (MCA, 110/16).
27.   'Statement of Lord Granard's interest account since May 1880'; ibid.
28.   'A Plan of Campaign: a memo for the country' in *United Ireland*, 23 October 1886. The Plan of
       Campaign was adopted on 203 estates. For a listing of these, see Laurence Geary, *The Plan of
       Campaign, 1886–91* (Cork, 1986), pp. 154–77.
29.   *Freeman's Journal*, 9 December 1886.
30.   *The Irish Times*, 8 November 1887.
31.   *President's Report, 1886*, p. 8.
32.   Lord Granard to Robert Browne, 10 October 1887 (MCA, 109/2).
33.   Copy letter, Robert Browne to Lord Granard, 28 February 1887; ibid.
34.   Messrs Darley and Roe to Rev Boylan, 16 February 1887; ibid.
35.   Lord Granard to president of Maynooth College, 13 May 1887 (MCA, 110/19).
36.   F. Crozier to president of Maynooth College, 30 January 1888 (MCA, 110/16).
37.   Corish, *Maynooth College*, p. 188.
38.   Judge T. McCarthy to president of Maynooth College, 13 May 1887 (MCA, 110/19).
39.   *President's Report, 1887–88*, pp. 12–13.
40.   Ibid., p. 13.
41.   Copy letter Lord Granard to Laurence Gillooly, Bishop of Elphin, 13 March 1888 (MCA, 109/2).
42.   *President's Report, 1887–88*, p. 14. For reactions to these events, see P.A. Chance to president
       of Maynooth College, 23 April 1888; ibid.
43.   Cardinal Logue to Robert Browne, 25 April, 1888; ibid.
44.   *President's Report, 1887–88*, p. 13.
45.   Certainly in April 1888, Granard served 'a large number' of eviction notices upon his tenants
       and was said to be 'generally engaged in carrying on war'; P.A. Chance to Robert Browne, 14
       April 1888 (MCA, 109/3). A year later it transpired that Granard had paid 'a couple of hundred'
       pounds to the Property Defence Association for the services of special bailiffs, P.A. Chance to
       Robert Browne, 15 March 1889 (MCA, 109/6).
46.   *President's Report, 1887–88*, p. 14.
47.   Further statement of solicitors to board of trustees, 22 June 1888. See also, P.A. Chance to
       Robert Browne, 23 April 1888 (MCA, 109/2–3).
48.   P.A. Chance to Robert Browne, 15 March 1889 (MCA, 109/6).
49.   Case for counsel to advise trustees of Maynooth College, 19 March 1889; ibid.
50.   Memo by P.A. Chance for trustees of Maynooth College regarding sale of Granard estate, 25
       June 1888 (MCA, 109/2). [Hereafter cited as Chance memo, 25 June 1888].
51.   Ibid.
52.   Report entitled 'Observations', n.d. (MCA, 110/17).
53.   Messrs Crozier to P.A. Chance, 12 March 1889 (MCA, 109/6).
54.   Messrs Crozier to P.A. Chance, 15 March 1889; ibid.
55.   *President's Report, 1889–90*, p. 8.
56.   P.A. Chance to Robert Browne, 15 December 1887 (MCA, 109/3).
57.   Report of C. Friery on visit to the Drumlish portion of the estate of the Earl of Granard,
       December 1887; ibid.
58.   Chance memo., 25 June 1888; *President's Report, 1888–89*, p. 8.
59.   Statement of solicitors to college trustees, 23 June 1890 (MCA, 109/6).
60.   Case for counsel to advise trustees with reference to realisation of mortgages upon the estates
       of Lord Granard, 13 November 1890; ibid.
61.   Ibid.
62.   Messrs Crozier to P.A. Chance, 17 January, 10 February 1891; ibid.
63.   T. McCarthy to president of Maynooth College, 8 February 1892 (MCA, 110/12).
64.   P.A. Chance to Robert Browne, 8 February 1892 (MCA, 109/9).
65.   Canon Thomas Conefry to president of Maynooth College, 15 April 1891 (MCA, 111/26).
66.   R.D. Cochrane's report on Castleforbes demesne, February 1892 (MCA, 109/9).
67.   Quoted in Corish, *Maynooth College*, p. 184.
68.   *Roscommon Herald*, 30 April 1892.
69.   An Irish Priest, *Land War in Drumlish*, p. 55.

70. Bence-Jones, *Twilight of the Ascendancy*, p. 69; id., *A Guide to Irish Country Houses*, p. 67.

71. Statement regarding the Earl of Granard's estate laid before the trustees of Maynooth College, June 1906 (MCA, 110/14).

72. Ibid.

73. Corish, *Maynooth College*, p. 184.

74. Vaughan, *Landlords and Tenants in mid-Victorian Ireland*, p. 172.

75. Ibid., p. 227.

76. It has been argued by J.S. Donnelly Jr that this economic crisis brought about a 'revolution of rising expectations' as tenants farmers, used to a degree of prosperity from the 1850s, were motivated by a strong desire to maintain the economic gains made; Donnelly, *Land and People of Cork*, pp. 249–52.

77. See, Vaughan, *Landlords and Tenants in mid-Victorian Ireland*, pp. 208–16; Donnelly, *Land and People of Cork*, pp. 249 ff; Samuel Clark, *Social Origins of the Irish Land War* (Princeton, NJ, 1979); idem., 'The Social Composition of the Land League' in *I.H.S.* xvii: 68 (September 1971), pp. 447–79; A.W. Orridge, 'Who Supported the Land War? An Aggregate-data Analysis of Irish Agrarian Discontent, 1879–82' in *Economic and Social Review*, xii: 3 (April, 1981), pp. 203–33; Paul Bew, *Land and the National Question in Ireland, 1858–82* (Dublin, 1978).

78. Donnelly, *Land and People of Cork*, p. 265.

79. In 1881, John Ball Greene, the man who replaced Griffith at the valuation office, claimed that it would have been necessary to add 33 per cent to Griffith's estimates to calculate the real letting value of Irish land by that time. *Bess. Comm., Minutes of Evidence, vol. i.*, p. 31.

80. As the *Bessborough Commission Report* concluded in 1881, the feeling of resentment was 'contagious and has spread far and wide. Even a single case, very likely misapprehended in which a landlord, of previously good reputation in this respect, is thought to have acted unfairly, may largely affect the condition and the good feeling of an entire neighbourhood', *Bess. Comm. Report*, p. 8.

81. De Burgh, *Landowners in Ireland*, p. 163; Dun, *Landlords and Tenants*, p. 41.

82. De Burgh, *Landowners in Ireland*, p. 357; Ormonde estate rentals, 1879–90 (NLI, Ormonde papers, MS 23,800–01).

83. *Bessborough Commission, Minutes of Evidence vol. i*, p. 453.

84. *King's County Chronicle*, 6 November 1879.

85. *Leinster Express*, 1 November 1879.

86. *Weekly Freeman's Journal*, 27 December 1880; 14, 22 January 1881.

87. Landed estates, particularly larger ones, were usually divided into administrative units to facilitate the collection of rents. The Ormonde estate, for example, was divided into the administrative units of Arran (Kilkenny), Arran (Tipperary), Kilcash and Garryricken.

88. *King's County Chronicle*, 30 October 1879.

89. Ibid.

90. Clonbrock estate rentals, 1865–69, 1880–82 (NLI, Clonbrock papers, MSS 19,920–34).

91. Ibid., 1880–89 (MS 19,631–40).

92. *Weekly Freeman's Journal*, 24 December 1880.

93. Ibid., I January 1881.

94. Ormonde estate rental, 1870–90 (NLI, Ormonde papers, MSS 23,800–01, 23,724–33).

95. Ibid.

96. Summary of rentals of Pratt estate, 1880–82 (NLI, Pratt papers, MS 5,090).

97. These figures are based on calculations of Matthew Franks, agent to Lord Castletown, in correspondence to Lord Castletown (NLI, Fitzpatrick papers, MS 13,752 (10)).

98. Irish Land Committee, *The Land Question in Ireland, vol. xiv: The Working of the Land Act* (London, 1882), p. 35.

99. *A Return Showing According to Provinces and Counties the Number of Cases in which Judicial Rents Have Been Fixed by All the Matters Provided by the Land Law Acts for a First and Second Statutory Term Respectively to 31 December 1902 with Particulars as to Acreage, Former Rents of Holdings, and Percentage of Reductions in Rents*, HC 1903, lvii, 91.

100. In its early years the Land Commission found itself inundated with appeals from landlords, such as Shirley, who questioned the level of rent reductions on their estates. By August 1882, the number of appeals to be dealt with was 2,611; within a year this number had risen to 7,215. However, it was rare that a landlord's appeal against new rents was successful and even where he might have been successful in having the judicial rent raised, it invariably remained

below the old rent. In the appeals heard up to August 1883, the aggregate old rent of all cases was £35,556. The rent fixed by the commissioners lowered the aggregate to £28,360. The appeals were only nominally successful raising the new rents to £29,075, but still keeping them around 20 per cent below the old rents; *Weekly Freeman's Journal*, 19 March 1887; *Report of the Irish Land Commissioners for the period from 22 August 1882 to 22 August 1883*, HC, 1884, lxiv.

101.   *Weekly Freeman's Journal*, 7 December 1887, 18 February 1888.

102.   For growing financial difficulties see below pp. 100–104.

103.   DCMCR, Northern Division, August and September 1896.

104.   *Cowper Commission, Minutes of Evidence*, p. 150.

105.   Marquis of Dufferin to Edward Carson, 24 April 1897; quoted in Buckland, *Documentary History*, p. 48.

106.   *An Act to Make Provision Respecting Certain Arrears of Rent in Ireland (45 and 46 Vict., c. xlix (18 August 1882))* and *Return of Payments Made to Landlords by the Irish land Commission Pursuant to the First and Sixteenth Sections of the Arrears of Rent (Ireland) Act 1882*, HC 1884, lxiv.

107.   Ibid.

108.   Geary, *The Plan of Campaign*, p. 180.

109.   Crofton estate rentals, 1876–78, 1886–90 (NLI, Crofton papers, MSS 4086–88, 4,100)

110.   Cloncurry estate rentals, 1875–89 (NLI, Cloncurry papers, MSS 12,893–12,907).

111.   Lord Cloncurry to his Newport tenantry, 15 April 1881; quoted in *The Irish Times*, 2 May 1881.

112.   Ibid.

113.   Clonbrock estate rentals and accounts, 1882–1887 (NLI, Clonbrock papers, MSS 19,633–38).

114.   Butler of Castlecrine estate rentals and accounts, 1895–1903 (NLI, Butler of Castlecrine papers, MS 5,426).

115.   Ormonde estate rental, 1896 (NLI, Ormonde papers, MS 23,725).

116.   Ibid., 1897 (MS 23,726).

117.   Ibid., 1897–1903 (MSS 23,726–32).

118.   Shane Leslie, *Doomsland*, pp. 361–62.

119.   Quoted in W.E. Vaughan, 'An Assessment of the Economic Performance of Irish Landlords, 1851–81' in F.S.L. Lyons and R.A.J. Hawkins (eds.), *Ireland Under the Union: Varieties of Tension* (Oxford, 1980), p. 185.

120.   Crofton estate rental and accounts, 1880 (NLI, Crofton papers, MS 4,090).

121.   This does not include 1885 for which no accounts were available. Crofton estate rentals and accounts, 1880–84, 1886–90 (NLI, Crofton papers, MSS 4,090–94, 4,100).

122.   Summary of income and expenditure on Mahon of Castlegar estate, 1881–86 (NLI, Mahon of Castlegar papers, MS 23,348).

123.   Fourteen of the 100 sample landlords had loans from the RCB in the 1880s. Their average debt burden was 18.4 per cent although there was a very wide range in burden from 2.1 per cent on the Farnham estate to 55.8 per cent on the Howth estate; RCB mortgage ledgers, D1–D3, Y (Church House, Rathmines); L.P. Curtis Jr has estimated that 120 landlords who had loans from the RCB had an average annual interest burden of 27.4 per cent of tenement valuation; W.E. Vaughan contends that 22 per cent of rent receipts is probably a more realistic average of annual interest repayments; Curtis, 'Encumbered Wealth', p. 343; Vaughan, *Landlords and Tenants in mid-Victorian Ireland*, p. 131.

124.   *Bess. Comm., Minutes of Evidence, vol. i*, p. 16.

125.   The Convention was a landlord organisation set up in 1886 because landlords felt they needed to protect their interests and property from the threat posed by the National League, the plan of campaign and government legislation which they perceived to be infringing upon their tenurial rights,

126.   *Irish Landowners' Convention Report, 1893–84*, pp. 28–29.

127.   *RCB report, 1886*, pp. 11,44; ibid., *1890*, p. 12; ibid., *1901*, p. 14.

128.   E. Murphy to Rev Farrelly, 29 December 1880 (MCA, 107/7).

129.   Rev. Andrew Boylan to Sir A.J.R. Stewart, 28 September 1882 (MCA, 107/7).

130.   Quoted in Donnelly, *Land and People of Cork*, p. 305.

131.   *The Times*, 9 December 1882

132.   *Cowper Commission, Minutes of Evidence*, p. 16.

133. *RCB report, 1886*, pp. 9–10.
134. Cannadine, *Decline and Fall of the British Aristocracy*, p. 95.
135. *Cork Examiner*, 1 August 1883.
136. *Irish Landowners' Convention Report*, 1886, p. 21.
137. Quoted in Cannadine, *Decline of the British Aristocracy*, p. 62.
138. *An Act to Further Amend the Law Relating to the Occupation and Ownership of Land in Ireland and for Other Relating Purposes Thereto* (33 and 34 Vict., c. xlvi (22 August 1881)).
139. Lord Cloncurry to his Newport tenantry, 15 April 1881; quoted in *The Irish Times*, 2 May 1881.
140. *Return of Proceedings under the Land Law (Ireland) Act up to 31 July 1884*, HC, 1884, lxiv, 144.
141. Ibid.
142. Commissioner Lynch, *Land Purchase in Ireland: a Retrospect and a Forecast* (Dublin, 1912), p. 1.
143. Quoted in L.P. Curtis Jr, *Coercion and Conciliation in Ireland, 1880–1892: A Study in Conservative Unionism* (Princeton, N.J., 1963), p. 347.
144. *Cowper Commission, Minutes of Evidence*, p. 473.
145. Ibid., p. 647.
146. *Cowper Commission, Minutes of Evidence*, p. 170.
147. *An Act to Provide Greater Facilities for the Sale of Land to Occupying Tenants in Ireland* (44 and 45 Vict., c. cxlviii (22 August 1885)).
148. J.T. Trench, Lord Lansdowne's agent, told the Cowper commission: 'I cannot see at all the logic of impounding some of the landlord's money to secure the debt of a third party over whom he has lost all control', *Cowper Commission, Minutes of Evidence*, p. 481.
149. These figures have been culled from *Returns of Advances*, a full list of which appears in the bibliography.
150. From 1885 to 1905, the 100 landowners in the sample sold a total of 152,100 acres (for £1.5 million) representing about 7 per cent of the 2.2 million acres they owned in the 1870s.
151. *Return Showing, as Far as Practicable, for Each Year (or Other Stated Period) the Lowest and Highest Prices (in Each Calendar Year) of Guaranteed Land Stock; and the Number and Amount of Loans under the Land Purchase Acts with the Total Amount of the Acreage Purchased*, HC 1903, lvii, 313.
152. Ibid.
153. *Report of the Estates' Commissioners for the Year from 1 April 1920 to 31 March 1921 and for the Period from 1 November 1903 to 31 March 1921*, HC, 1921, xiv, p. iv.
154. List of encumbrances on Leinster estate, n.d. (NLI, Leinster papers, MS 19,692).
155. Ibid.
156. Statement of application of sums received upon sale of Leinster estate, 1887–88 (PRONI, Leinster papers, D3078/2/15/8).
157. Ibid.
158. *Freeman's Journal*, 2 December 1893.
159. J.R. Mahon to G.C. Mahon, 25 April 1887 (NLI, Mahon papers, MS 22,231).
160. See Table 4.2.
161. Fingall, *Seventy Years Young*, pp. 116–17, 186.
162. Ibid., p. 138.
163. Headfort estate rentals and accounts, 1901–03 (NLI, Headfort papers, MSS 25,341 (5–8), 26,697 (5–8)).
164. Hone, *The Moores of Moore Hall*, p. 231.
165. See p.89.
166. Fingall, *Seventy Years Young*, p. 22.
167. Seymour Leslie, *The Jerome Connexion*, p. 34.
168. For this 'American craze' see David Littlejohn, *The Fate of the English Country House* (Oxford, 1997), p. 134.
169. Ibid.
170. Copy of letter from Dr Browne to P.A. Chance, enclosed in letter from P.A. Chance to Dr Browne, 7 June 1889 (MCA, 107/8).
171. Valuation of Diamonds and Jewellery for his Grace, the Duke of Leinster, 1883 (PRONI, Leinster papers, D3078/2/10/2); *Catalogue of Pictures, Plate, Antiquities etc. at Carton, Kilkea Castle, 13 Dominick Street, Dublin and 6 Carlton House Terrace, London* (privately published, Dublin, n.d.).

172. *Catalogue of Old Irish Silver Plate Sold by Order of Trustees of Late Lord Fitzgerald at Christie's, 4 December 1902* and *Catalogue of Ancient and Modern Pictures Sold at Christie's, 6 December 1902* (PRONI, Leinster papers (D3078/2/10/6/2–3).
173. Leslie memoirs (MS 22,885).
174. Powerscourt, *Powerscourt*, p. 74.
175. Mahaffy, 'The Irish Landlords', p. 171.
176. Quoted in Lennox Robinson, *Bryan Cooper* (London, 1931), pp. 25–26.
177. *Westminster Gazette*, 23 January 1909.
178. Battersby & Co., *Catalogue of Contents of Salterbridge, Cappoquin to be Sold 5 December 1916 by Direction of Col. G.R. Hamilton; Catalogue of Valuable Antique and Modern Furniture, Silver Plate, Old Sheffield Plate, Library and 200 Oil Paintings to be Sold at Killua Castle, Westmeath, by Direction of General R.S. Fetherstonhaugh, 2 June 1920* (NLI)

Chapter 5

1.   *Return of the Resolution and Statement Adopted by the Irish Landowners Convention on 10 October 1902; and Report of the Irish Land Conference Dated 3 January 1903; and Minute on the Land Conference Report Adopted on 7 January 1903 by the Executive Committee of the Irish Landowners Convention*, HC 1903, lvii, 321.
2.   For his own version of his role in the conference, see Dunraven, *Past Times and Pastimes, vol. ii*, pp. 3–11.
3.   Ibid.
4.   Ibid.
5.   *Irish Landowners Convention Report, 1904*, p. 11.
6.   *Return Showing the Average Number of Years' Purchase Under the Land Purchase (Ireland) Acts 1891–96 for the Years 1901 and 1902 and Under the Act of 1903 to 31 July 1908 in the Different Counties of Ireland*, HC 1908, xc, 356.
7.   *Land Purchase (Ireland) Act, 1903* (3 Ed., c. xxxvii (1 November 1903)); for an excellent study of the 1923 Land Act (and earlier land acts) see J.T. Sheehan, 'Land Purchase Policy in Ireland 1917–23: From the Irish Convention to the 1923 Land Act (unpublished MA thesis, Maynooth, 1993).
8.   Information regarding sales is drawn from these advances, a full list of which appears in the bibliography.
9.   Alvin Jackson, *Col Edward Saunderson: Land and Loyalty in Victorian Ireland* (Oxford, 1995), p. 202.
10.   Ibid.
11.   Returns of Advances, 1907, 1908.
12.   Jackson, *Saunderson*, p. 204.
13.   C.H. Maude to secretary of estates commissioners, 15 January 1909; quoted in T.H. Maxwell, *Irish Land Purchase Cases: Being a Verbatim Reprint of All the Cases Dealing with Land Purchase Recorded in the Irish Report and the Irish Law Times During the Years 1904–11 Inclusive* (Dublin, 1912), p. 219.
14.   Ibid.
15.   *Irish Landowners Convention Report, 1905*, pp. 9–10.
16.   Ibid., p. 10.
17.   Ibid., p. 12.
18.   *Irish Landowners' Convention Report, 1910*, p. 61.
19.   Messrs Guinness and Mahon to W.H. Mahon, 18 October 1910 (NLI, Mahon papers, MS 23,373).
20.   *Irish Land Commission Report, 1923–28*, p. 14.
21.   *Irish Landowners Convention Report, 1910*, p. 13.
22.   Sir Henry Doran to Congested Districts Board, 1917 (NA, Childers papers, Box 2).
23.   Confidential report of the Irish Committee on Land Purchase on the Amendments Referred to them by the Irish Convention, 9–10 January 1918 (NA, Childers papers, Box 1).
24.   Doran to Congested District Board, 1917.
25.   *Morning Post*, 17 February 1903.
26.   Ibid.
27.   *Connaught Leader*, 2 July 1904.
28.   See for example, *Roscommon Messenger*, January–December 1907; *Western News*, 2 November 1907.

29. See David Seth Jones, 'The Cleavage Between Graziers and Peasants in the Land Struggle, 1890–1910' in Clark and Donnelly, *Irish Peasants*, pp. 374–413; id., *Graziers, Land Reform and Political Conflict in Ireland* (Washington, 1995).

30. *Royal Commission on Congestion in Ireland: Appendix to the Tenth Report, Minutes of Evidence Taken in Counties Galway and Roscommon, 18 September to 4 October 1907 and Documents Relating Thereto*, [Cd 4007], HC 1908, xliii, p. 177.

31. Ibid., p. 178.

32. *Report of Estates Commissioners ... to 31 March 1921*.

33. *Return of Advances Under the Irish Land Act 1903 During the Month of November 1909* [C 5488], HC 1909, lxxiii; *Return of Advances Under the Irish Land Act During January to December 1913*, [Cd 3531], HC 1914, lxvi.

34. Dunraven, *Crisis in Ireland*, p. 21.

35. Ibid.

36. *Irish Land Commission Report, 1923–28*, p. 14; *Return of Untenanted Land and Demesnes, 1906*.

37. *Royal Commission of Enquiry on Congestion in Ireland: Appendix to Tenth Report, Minutes of Evidence*, [Cd 4007], HC 1908, xlii, 5, p. 182.

38. Jackson, *Saunderson*, p. 208.

39. Clonbrock investment books, 1914–35 (NLI, Clonbrock papers, MSS 19,572–73).

40. Ormonde investment books, 1914–17 (NLI, Ormonde papers, MSS 19,572–73); Statement of application of sums received on sale of Leinster estate, 1904 (PRONI, Leinster papers, D3078/2/15/10).

41. *The Irish Times*, 18 May 1917.

42. Clonbrock investment books, 1914–35 (NLI, Clonbrock papers, MSS 19,572–73).

43. In 1910, for example, the Ahascragh estate yielded £3,489 per annum in rents but only a net income of £1,449. When it was sold that year £48,900 was available for investment at 3.5 per cent after expenses were met. Clonbrock's agent informed him that this investment would yield £176 more per annum than rental income had; E.G. Armstrong to Lord Clonbrock, 13 January 1910, enclosed in Clonbrock estate rental and account ledger, 1910; ibid., MS 19,659.

44. Clonbrock farm and household account books, 1834–1935; ibid. (MSS 19,507–14).

45. Bence-Jones, *Twilight of the Ascendancy*, p. 296.

46. Shane Leslie, *The Film of Memory*, p. 106.

47. *Weekly Irish Times*, 13 January 1923.

48. *Evening Herald*, 9 March 1976.

49. Leslie memoirs (MS 22,885).

50. Quoted in Robinson, *Bryan Cooper*, p. 80.

51. Fingall, *Seventy Years Young*, p. 386.

52. Bowen, *The Last September*, p. 71.

53. Arthur Maxwell to Aileen Coote, 31 December 1916 (NLI, Farnham papers, MS 18,616).

54. Buckland, *Irish Unionism I*, p. 32

55. For reasons of tradition, see ibid., pp. 32–33.

56. Charles Monck to J.E. MacDermott, 8 October 1914 (NLI, Monck papers, MS 26,867).

57. *House of Lords War Memorial* (London, n.d.).

58. Anita Leslie, *The Gilt and the Gingerbread*, p. 26.

59. Frank Pakenham, *Born to Believe* (London, 1953), p. 18.

60. De Stacpoole, *Irish and other Memories*, p. 192.

61. *Burke's Landed Gentry of Ireland* (London, 1958 ed.), p. xviii.

62. Bence-Jones, *Twilight of the Ascendancy*, p. 187.

63. Robinson, *Bryan Cooper*, p. 131.

64. Amongst the peers who fought and survived were the fifth and sixth Marquises of Ormonde; Arthur Maxwell, eleventh Baron Farnham; Richard Granville, fourth Earl of Listowel; Thomas McClintock, third Baron Rathdonnell. Amongst the untitled landowners who survived were Bryan Cooper of Markree; Robert Doyne of Wells; John Congreve of Mount Congreve; and William Burton, eldest son of William F. Burton of Burton Hall. In total of forty-seven fathers or eldest sons from the sample families who were actively involved, ten were killed.

65. Of the others, the eldest son of the eighth Earl of Mayo was killed in 1915, but the Earl himself lived until 1939 when he was succeeded by another son, Ulick, who had survived the war and lived until 1962; the eldest son of Viscount Clifden was also killed in 1915 but the Viscount

lived another thirty years ; the fifth Baron De Freyne was killed in 1915, but his brother, who succeeded him lived until 1935; the fifth Earl of Longford was killed at Gallipoli the same year but his brother, Edward, who succeeded him lived until 1961.

66.   In the sample, the total number who succeeded to houses and estates in the period under study was 324. Of these forty-six died unmarried while a further seventy-three died leaving no children. This means that 36 per cent of owners did not have direct lineal heirs to succeed them.

67.   Court of Irish Land Commissioners' record on Monck estate, Charleville, numbers S2,319, S2,374 (NLI, Monck papers, MS 26,859).

68.   Ibid.

69.   Mr [?] Blair to Charles Monck, 21 October 1912 (NLI, Monck papers, MS 22,865).

70.   The previous February he had received personal loans of £3,000 from Clarebell Investments Co. and £1,000 in other amounts 'borrowed from time to time from money lenders'; Monck to MacDermott, 8 October 1914 (MS 26,867)

71.   Copy letter J.E. MacDermott to Charles Monck, 19 October 1914 (NLI, Monck papers, MS 26,867).

72.   Receipt of encumbrances on Monck estate, n.d, c.1922; ibid.

73.   Agreement signed between Viscount Monck and J.E. MacDermott, 1925; ibid. (MS 26,870)

74.   Executors' account of Viscountess Monck drawn up by J.E. MacDermott, 1930; ibid. (MS 26,879).

75.   Case for counsel: to advise and settle draft deed of release proposed by J.E. MacDermott, 14 March 1933; ibid. (MS 26,880).

76.   *Catalogue of Sale of the Contents of Charleville House by Private Auction* (Dublin, 1932); ibid. (MS 26,969).

77.   Kolbert and O'Brien, *Land Reform in Ireland*, p. 46.

78.   *Twenty-Sixth Report of the Congested Districts Board for Ireland, 1918*, [Cd 9139], HC 1918, vii, 769; Return of Advances from 1914 to 1918 (see bibliography).

79.   W.L. Micks, *An Account of the Congested Districts Board for Ireland, 1891–1923* (Dublin, 1925); a congested district was defined as one where 'more than twenty per cent of the population of a county, or in the case of County Cork, either riding thereof, live in electoral divisions of which the total rateable value, when divided by the number of the population, gives a sum of less than £1.10s.0d for each individual, these divisions shall for the purpose of this [1891 Land Act] be separated from the county in which they are geographically situated, and form a separate county....'

80.   *Irish Land Commission Report for the Period from 1 April 1923 to 31 March 1928*, p. 20.

81.   Confidential memo by Sir Henry Doran to Congested Districts Board, 1917 (NA, Childers papers, Box 2).

82.   Fitzpatrick, *Politics and Irish Life*, p. 72.

83.   IGCMR, February 1918.

84.   Ibid.

85.   Ibid.

86.   Ibid., February 1918.

87.   Ibid., January 1918.

88.   Ibid., May 1920.

89.   Ibid., October 1920.

90.   *The Irish Times*, 1 June 1920.

91.   Ibid.

92.   Ibid., 2 June 1920.

93.   Ibid.

94.   Diary of Lord Mahon of Castlegar, 1920 (NLI, Mahon of Castlegar papers, MS 19,940).

95.   Quoted in Bence-Jones, *Twilight of the Ascendancy*, p. 193.

96.   Return of outrages made to the inspector general of the RIC, May 1919–November 1920 (PRO, CO 904, police reports, part vi).

97.   Ibid.

98.   Art O'Connor, 'A Brief Survey of the Work Done by the Agricultural Department from April 1919 to August 1921' presented to Dáil Éireann (UCD Archives, Mulcahy papers, P7A/63).

99.   Duc De Stacpoole, *Irish and other Memories* (London, 1922), p. 255.

100.   H. and W. Stanley solicitors to Minister for Home Affairs, 11 January 1922; Commissioner of guards to Minister for Home Affairs, 15 November 1922 (NA, Dept. of Justice files, H5/538).

101.   Lord Castletown to W.T. Cosgrave, 1 May 1922; ibid. (H5/174)

102. Lord Powerscourt to Minister for Home Affairs, 17 June 1922. ibid. (H5/389).
103. H.P. Maxwell to Minister for Home Affairs, 23 May 1922. ibid. (H5/135).
104. Secretary of Minister for Home Affairs to adjutant general, 13 June 1922; ibid.
105. It was not until December 1922 that new civic guard barracks were opened in Kerry at Tralee and Listowel; Secretary of Minister for Home Affairs to W. Rochfort [agent who replaced H.P. Maxwell], 22 November 1922; ibid.
106. Patrick Hogan to W.T. Cosgrave, 7 April 1923 (NA, Dept. of Taoiseach files, S3192).
107. Ibid.
108. Memo. by Patrick Hogan on land bill of 1920, 14 December 1922; ibid. (S1995).
109. Hogan to Cosgrave, 7 April 1923.
110. *An Act to Amend the Law Relating to the Occupation and Ownership of Land and for Other Purposes Relating Thereto* (No. 42 of 1923).
111. Ibid., sect. 24(1).
112. A home farm was defined as a farm 'used for the convenience of the owner's residence and ... not merely as an ordinary farm for the purpose of profit'.
113. *Iris Oifigiúil*, 14 April, 13 June, 1925.
114. Ibid., and 12 October, 5 November 1926.
115. *Irish Land Act, 1931* (no. 11 of 1931).
116. *Dáil debates*, xlviii, 13 July 1933, 2378.
117. Ibid., 2380.
118. *Irish Land Act, 1933*, (no. 38 of 1933).
119. Kolbert and O'Brien, *Land Reform in Ireland*, p. 55.
120. See below, pp. 136–39.
121. 'Western landowner' to editor of *The Irish Times*, 18 July 1922; *The Irish Times*, 21 July 1922.
122. D. Johnson, *The Inter-War Economy in Ireland: Studies in Irish Economic and Social History 4* (Dundalk, 1985), p. 5.
123. Ibid., pp. 16–17.
124. Summary of receipts and payments on Lord Wicklow's estate, 1934–36 (NLI, Wicklow papers, unsorted P.C. 225 (5)).
125. Summary of receipts of payments for the year ending 31 December 1937 on Lord Wicklow's estate; ibid.
126. Butler of Castlecrine estate cattle book, 1896–1930 (NLI, Butler of Castlecrine papers, MS 4,524).
127. *Sixty-Fourth Report of the Commissioners of Inland Revenue for the Year Ended 31 March 1921*, [Cmd 1436], HC 1921, xiv, p. 11.
128. Ibid.
129. There was a much less noticeable rise on smaller estates of £1,000 to £20,000 in valuation. The rate on estates valued at over £1,000 remained at 3 per cent from 1894 to 1919; on estates valued at over £5,000 they rose from 3 per cent to 4 per cent in 1909; and on estates valued at over £10,000 they rose from 4 per cent in 1894 to 5 per cent in 1909; ibid.
130. In 1923 an agreement was reached between the Irish and British governments that to avoid double taxation a sum equal to the amount payable in Britain would be deducted from the amount of duty due in Ireland. *Report of Irish Revenue Commissioners, 1926*, p. 55; *1950*, p. 72.
131. *Report of Irish Revenue Commissioners, 1930*, p. 57; *1950*, p. 72.
132. *Reports of Irish Revenue Commissioners, 1924–50*.
133. This was carried out by using the valuation lists in the Valuation Office, Middle Abbey Street.
134. *Department of Local Government and Public Health Report, 1948–49*, p. 3.
135. Ibid., *1939–40*, p. 2
136. Ibid., *1934–35*, p. 3.
137. Diary of Sir Shane Leslie, 30 September 1939 (NLI, Leslie papers, MS 22,863).
138. McKenna, *The Emetresse*, p. 123.
139. Ibid.
140. Headfort estate ledgers, 1897, 1916, 1920 (NLI, Headfort papers, MSS 26,697 (2,43,47)).
141. Ormonde estate ledgers and accounts, 1903–40 (NLI, Ormonde papers, MSS 23,731–69).
142. This information was gleaned from a study of return of advances, 1903–15 (see bibliography); the Ormonde retained 120 acres of demesne land around Kilkenny, 1,100 acres in Garryricken and 3,500 acres in Kilcash.
143. Investment account of Lord Ormonde, 1915–57 (NLI, Ormonde papers, MSS 23,991–92).

144. Ormonde estate ledger, 1919 (NLI, Ormonde papers, MS 23,749).
145. Ibid., 1920–21 (MSS 23,750–51).
146. Ormonde estate ledgers and accounts, 1917–19, 1925 (NLI, Omonde papers, MSS 23,727–9, 23,735).
147. Ibid. (MS 23,750).
148. *The Irish Times*, 13 September 1921.
149. Ibid., 7 January 1922.
150. Statement of estate duties and charges on Lord Courtown's estate, n.d. (C. 1917) (NLI, Wicklow papers, unsorted PC 225).
151. *Catalogue of Library of J.R. Garstin of Irish Literature to be Sold by Auction 1918* (in private possession).
152. Executor's account of the personal estate of Hon. H.M, Howard, 1919 (NLI, Wicklow papers, unsorted, PC225).
153. *Catalogue of Valuable Antiques and Modern Furniture ... and 200 Oil Paintings at Killua Castle, 2 June 1920* (NLI)
154. *The Irish Times*, 9 January 1923; *Weekly Irish Times*, 13 January 1923.
155. *Catalogue of an Important and Valuable Collection of Works of Art Removed from Carton with the Consent of the Trustees of His Grace, the Duke of Leinster, to be Sold ... on 2 December 1925 and Two Following Days... (*IAA, RP. D 28.4).
156. Fingall, *Seventy Years Young*, p. 180; Library: *Catalogue of a Collection of Important Books Selected from the Library at Carton with the Consent of the Trustees of the Duke of Leinster to be sold by Auction by Bennett and Sons* (Dublin, 1925).
157. Messrs. Jackson, Stops and Joyce to Edward MacDermott, 16 September 1931 (NLI, Monck papers, MS 26,909).
158. *Catalogue of the Valuable Contents of Dartrey Castle, Cootehill, Co. Cavan* which Will be Sold by Auction on the Premises on Monday 19 April 1937 and Three Following Days* (in author's possession).
      * Although cited as being situated in Cootehil, County Cavan, the castle was actually located in Rockcorry, County Monaghan. Cootehill is the nearest large town.
159. Bowen, *Bowen's Court*, pp. 26–27.
160. Thomson, *Woodbrook*, p. 13.
161. Ibid., p. 186.
162. Robinson, *Bryan Cooper*, p. 164.
163. Barton later sold the house in 1949 to Patrick Gallagher who restored the main block to its original size; Bence Jones, *Irish Country Houses*, pp. 124, 266.
164. *Irish Independent*, 6 April 1996.
165. Sophia Trench to Mrs Henry Bruen, 11 September 1880 (NLI, Bruen papers, MS 29,775).
166. Edward McParland and Nicholas Robinson (eds.), *Heritage at Risk: A Digest of An Taisce's Report on the Future of Historic Houses, Gardens and Collections in the Republic of Ireland* (Dublin, 1977), p. 17.
167. W.G. Jones, *The Wynnes of Sligo and Leitrim* (Manorhamilton, 1994), p. 91.
168. Quoted in ibid., p. 92.
169. See below, pp. 256–69.
170. Desmond Guinness, 'The Irish Georgian Society: The First Thirty Years' in *Bulletin of the Irish Georgian Society*, vol. xxxi, (1998), p. 23.
171. Anita Leslie, *The Gilt and the Gingerbread*, p. 40.
172. Jackson, *Saunderson*, p. 210.
173. *Report of the Estates' Commissioners for the Year from 1 April 1920 to 31 March 1921 and for the Period from 1 November 1903 to 31 March 1921*, HC, 1921, xiv, p. 4.
174. Ibid.
175. Headfort estate account books, 1921–50 (NLI, Headfort papers, MSS 26,697 (22–50)).
176. Of the 100 sample houses, thirty-seven were still in the ownership of the original families by the 1960s; eighteen had been burned (five were rebuilt and two of these later demolished); ten were demolished or vacated and let fall into ruins by their owners and thirty-five were sold. Of the thirty-five sold, fourteen passed into private or state ownership; eleven were demolished; four became educational institutions; five became medical or industrial institutions and one became a hotel.

Chapter 6

1. Elizabeth Bowen, 'The Most Unforgettable Character I've Met' in Lee, *The Mulberry Tree*, pp. 254–65.
2. Ibid., p. 254.
3. Ibid., p. 255.
4. Ibid., p. 256.
5. Ibid.
6. Ibid., p. 257; Bowen, *Bowen's Court*, pp. 291–65.
7. Bowen, 'The Most Unforgettable Character', p. 257.
8. Ibid.
9. Ibid., pp. 258–59.
10. Ibid., p. 265.
11. *The Servant's Practical Guide, 1880*, p. 2.
12. David Thomson, *Woodbrook* (London, 1974 ed.), p. 29.
13. Fingall, *Seventy Years Young*, pp. 96, 113.
14. Former maidservant at Louth Hall to the author, 9 June 1993.
15. Mary MacMahon, 'Servants', in *The Celt*, vol. xvi (November 1857), p. 255.
16. Anita Leslie, *The Gilt and the Gingerbread*, pp. 11–12.
17. Thomson, *Woodbrook*, pp. 77–78.
18. *Catalogue of Auction Sale of Furniture at Straffan* (in private possession).
19. Fingall, *Seventy Years Young*, p. 115.
20. Ibid., p. 337.
21. Signed agreement between Thomas Burke and Walter Blake, 3 May 1861 (NLI, Blake of Ballyglunin papers, MS 27,001).
22. Signed agreement between J. Carroll and Walter Blake, 3 May 1861; ibid.
23. 'Rules to be observed by the lodge-keeper at Kilkenny castle' May 1913 (NLI, Ormonde papers, MS 24,951).
24. One must be careful about drawing conclusions regarding information on servant numbers in big houses from these household schedule returns. This obviously would not be the total number of servants employed. It is possible that some servants may have lived outside the big house, although this number would have been quite small. Estate papers suggest that most servants lived in. The advertisement columns of newspapers suggest that employers preferred domestics to be unattached. When servants got married they tended to leave the employment of the big house. The most usual reason for servants being absent on the night is the absence of their employers (for example, a note on the return for Coolattin, County Wicklow, reads: 'Earl Fitzwilliam and retinue in England on night of 2 April 1911'.)
25. Fingall, *Seventy Years Young*, p. 208.
26. Mary Carbery, *The Farm by Lough Gur* (Dublin, 1973 ed.), p. 22.
27. Thomson, *Woodbrook*, p. 25.
28. Fingall, *Seventy Years Young*, p. 30.
29. Leslie memoirs (MS 22,885).
30. Thomson, *Woodbrook*, p. 64.
31. Household account book for Carton, 1884 (PRONI, Leinster papers, D3078/2/13).
32. Workmens' account books of Kilkenny Castle, 1880–85 (NLI, Ormonde papers, MSS 23,891–93).
33. A study of the advertisement columns of *The Irish Times* for 1885 shows that butlers in other households were paid between £40–45 per annum.
34. T.R. Blackley to Lord Farnham, 1 January 1898 (NLI, Farnham papers, MS 18,617 (2)).
35. Book of labourers' agreements on Ballyglunin estate, 1879–90 (NLI, Blake of Ballyglunin papers, MS 27,000).
36. There is no record of perks, although these most likely also existed.
37. Garden account book of Powerscourt estate, 1878 (NLI, Powerscourt papers, MS 19,253); Workmen's account books of Kilkenny Castle, 1885 (NLI, Ormonde papers, MS, 28,893).
38. Wages account books of Powerscourt, 1906–12 (NLI, Powerscourt papers, MS 19,292).
39. Former servant employed at Louth Hall to author, 9 June 1993.
40. *Report by Miss Collet on the Money Wages of Indoor Domestic Servants in Great Britain*, [Cd 9346], HC 1899, xcii, 22. [Hereafter cited as *Collet Report*].
41. Clonbrock wages account books, 1904–05 (NLI, Clonbrock papers, MS 19,567).
42. Fingall, *Seventy Years Young*, p. 30.

43.   Thomson, *Woodbrook*, p. 292.
44.   Quoted in Horne, *The Rise and Fall of the Victorian Servant*, p. 164.
45.   *Collet Report*.
46.   Leslie memoirs (MS 22,885).
47.   Fingall, *Seventy Years Young*, p. 96.
48.   Anita Leslie, *The Gilt and the Gingerbread*, p. 83.
49.   R. O'Brien to Lord Inchiquin, 12 December 1871 (NLI, Inchiquin papers, MS 3,593).
50.   M. Crawford to Lady Farnham, n.d. (1893) (NLI, Farnham papers, MS 18,616).
51.   Mrs Woods to Lady Farnham, n.d. (1893); ibid.
52.   *The Irish Times*, 2, 4 January 1911.
53.   Fingall, *Seventy Years Young*, p. 78.
54.   J. Dutton to Lord Inchiquin, 1 November 1871 (NLI, Inchiquin papers, MS 3,593).
55.   In England, upper servants were usually children of artisans, tradesmen, farmers and shop-
      keepers who could afford to educate their children and train them in 'the graces and steady
      habits' employers required; Gerrard, *Country House Life*, p. 167.
56.   Horne, *The Rise and Fall of the Victorian Servant*, p. 35.
57.   *66th Annual Report of the Dublin Providence Home*, 1904 (Dublin, 1904), p. 2.
58.   Ibid., p. 4.
59.   R. O'Brien to Lord Inchiquin, 12 December 1871 (NLI, Inchiquin papers, MS 3,593).
60.   *The Irish Times*, 22 September 1882.
61.   Ibid., 19 September 1882.
62.   Quoted in ILPU, *Ireland under the League: Illustrated by Extracts from the Evidence Given
      Before the Cowper Commission* (London, 1887), pp. 45–46.
63.   IGCMR, February 1898.
64.   Ibid., February 1898, June 1902; February, March 1909; February 1913.
65.   *Galway Express*, 25 March 1893.
66.   T.R. Blackley to Lord Farnham, 17 December 1896 (NLI, Farnham papers, MS 18,616).
67.   Blackley to Farnham, 18 February 1896: ibid.
68.   Blackley to Farnham, 10 February 1897; bid.
69.   CICMR, Galway E.R., November 1901.
70.   IGCMR, June 1901.
71.   A. Waterfield to J. Brennan, 11 September 1922 (NA, Dept. of Finance files, F302/13)
72.   *Saorstát Éireann: Census of Population, vol. x, General Report, 1926*, pp. 154, 165; *Censuses of
      Population of Ireland 1946 and 1951, General Report* (1958), p. 98.
73.   J.R. Mahon to G.C. Mahon, 25 April 1887 (NLI, Mahon papers, MS 22,231).
74.   T. Morrow to Lord Farnham, 5 February 1897 (NLI, Farnham papers, MS 18,618).
75.   *Annual report of Domestic Training Institute, Charlemont Street, 1911*, p. 4.
76.   *The Irish Times*, 13 September 1921.
77.   Ibid., 7 January 1922.
78.   Agreement signed by Viscount Monck and Edward MacDermott, n.d. (1925) (NLI, Monck
      papers, MS 26,870).
79.   In 1911, there were fourteen servants returned for the castle alone. Augustine Compton, the
      butler, was married and lived outside the castle and it is possible there were other servants in
      the castle who did likewise.
80.   Thomson, *Woodbrook*, p. 294.
81.   Bowen, 'The Most Unforgettable Character', p. 255.
82.   Ibid., pp. 257, 263,
83.   IGCMR, September 1918, January 1919.
84.   *Ministry of Reconstruction: Report of the Women's Advisory Committee on the Domestic Service
      Problem together with Reports by Sub-committees on Training, Machinery of Distribution,
      Organisation and Conditions*, [Cmd 67], HC 1919, xxix.
85.   Ibid.
86.   *Weekly Irish Times*, 14 January 1920.
87.   Leonora Davidoff and R. Hawthorn, *A Day in the Life of a Victorian Domestic Servant* (London,
      1976), p. 88.
88.   'Pater Familia' to editor, 7 March 1922; *The Irish Times*, 8 March 1922.
89.   See Helena Maloney to editor in *The Irish Times*, 14 March 1923. Maloney, who was secretary
      of the Domestic Workers' Union called for a twelve-hour working day, including meal times,

but was aware that 'it is an up hill work getting even this humble standard conceded'. Maloney claimed that 'the living in system is at the root of the evil'. He said that it was unacceptable that servants should be continuously at the beck and call of employers: 'The time has long gone when they can condemn a whole class of their fellow creatures to a state of semi-slavery'.

90. See chapter 7.

91. Diary of William Mahon of Castlegar, 1 November, 27 December 1923 (NLI, Mahon of Castlegar papers, MS 19,992).

92. *The Irish Times*, 20 April 1921.

93. Ibid., 12 November 1921.

94. Ibid., 15 November 1921.

95. IGCMR, February 1919.

96. Ibid., November 1919.

97. Memo by J. Kelly addressed to Minister for Agriculture, 'The lands of Tubberdaly Co. Westmeath [*sic*]', 4 July 1923 (NA, Dept. of Justice files, H5/888).

98. In 1913, it cost £1,300 to install electricity at Kilkenny Castle; Ormonde estate ledger and accounts, 1913 (NLI, Ormonde papers, MS 23,743).

99. Bowen, 'The Big House', p. 27.

100. Bence-Jones, *Twilight of the Ascendancy*, pp. 93–94.

101. In 1945, a *Report on the Organisation of Private Domestic Employment in Britain* claimed that: 'The younger generation in the years between the two world wars was inclined more and more to think that the domestic worker held an inferior place in the labour market and to despise her accordingly. To live at home, to be a free agent in the evening after factory, shop and office had closed, became increasingly desirable'; quoted in Horne, *The Rise and Fall of the Victorian Servant*, p. 166.

102. Quoted in Bence-Jones, *Twilight of the Ascendancy*, p. 301.

Chapter 7

1.   As was pointed out in the introduction to this work, Hopkinson's authoritative *Green Aagainst Green* devotes only just over two pages to the plight of southern Protestants at this time. Nor does Dónal O'Sullivan's, *The Irish Free State and its Senate*, nor Bence-Jones', *The Twilight of the Ascendancy* adequately deal with the intimidation landowners were subjected to.

2.   In order to estimate the number of big houses burned a study of every daily edition of *The Irish Times* from January 1919 to the end of April 1923 was undertaken by the present writer. This was further supplemented by a further study of county inspectors' police reports from January 1919 to December 1921, a study of the Office of Public Work's files in the National Archives which deal with compensation for persons and property injured during the revolutionary period, and a study of similar files belonging to the Irish Compensation Commission of 1922–30 in the Public Record Office, London.

3.   CICMR, County Meath, February 1920.

4.   Ibid.

5.   *The Irish Times*, 7 February 1920; *Meath Chronicle*, 24 September 1921.

6.   *The Irish Times*, 7 February 1920.

7.   Ibid.

8.   *The Irish Times*, 7 February 1920.

9.   Lady Fingall, *Seventy Years Young*, p. 453.

10. Quoted in Oliver Coogan, *Politics and War in Meath 1913–23* (Dublin, 1983), pp. 150–51.

11. *Westmeath Guardian*, 24 June 1921.

12. IGCMR, June 1921; CICMR, County Westmeath, June 1921.

13. Quoted in *Westmeath Guardian*, 1 July 1921.

14. *Westmeath Examiner*, 9 July 1921.

15. Ibid.

16. Ibid.

17. Ibid.

18. Quoted in *Westmeath Guardian*, 8 July 1921.

19. Based on research carried out by this author for forthcoming publication entitled 'IRA Activity in Co. Kildare During the War of Independence'.

20. *Kildare Observer*, 3 February 1923.

21. Ibid.

22. Ibid.
23. Seven men had been executed at the Curragh on 19 December 1922, six of whom were from Kildare while the seventh was from County Tipperary; National Graves Association, *The Last Post: The Details and Stories of Republican Dead, 1913–75* (Dublin, 2nd ed., 1976).
24. Ibid.
25. See below pp. 190–92.
26. *Kildare Observer*, 3 February 1923.
27. Ibid.; *Leinster Leader*, 3 February 1923.
28. *Offaly County Chronicle*, 19 March 1923.
29. Ibid.
30. *Iris Oifigiúil*, 21 July, 9 October 1925.
21. Memo prepared for Minister for Agriculture, 'The lands of Tubberdaly Co. Westmeath (*sic*)' 4 July 1923 (NA, Department of Justice files, H5/888).
32. Ibid.
33. Ibid.
34. Ibid.
35. Copy letter from Christopher Jones to E.J. Beaumont-Nesbitt, 10 July 1923; ibid.
36. Memo of Patrick Hogan re. Beaumont-Nesbitt estate, 14 July 1923; S. Liddy, Garda Commissioner, 28 July 1923; Deputy commissioner of Guards to secretary of Minister for Home Affairs, 20 January 1924; ibid.
37. C. O'Cugain, to secretary of Minister for Home Affairs, 30 January 1924; ibid.
38. Deputy commissioner of guards to secretary of Minister for Home Affairs, 20 January 1924; ibid.
39. Note of W.J.H. Tyrell regarding reasons for attack on Ballindoolin, 15 December 1922 (in private possession).
40. Griffin, 'The Irish police, 1836–1914; pp. 376–77.
41. Mitchell, *Revolutionary Government*, pp. 128–29.
42. IGCMR, June 1920; CICMR, County Monaghan, November 1919.
43. H.F. Hibbert to IUA, 23 April 1920; quoted in Buckland, *Documentary History*, pp. 380–81.
44. IGCMR, August 1920.
45. *The Irish Times*, 3 September 1920.
46. Police report on 'Ballyturin tragedy', May 1921 (PRO, Return of outrages 1903–21, CO904, part vi).
47. *Northern Standard*, 17 July 1920.
48. Ibid., 19 August 1921.
49. IGCMR, April 1921.
50. Ibid., June 1921.
51. R.E. Longfield to H. De F. Montgomery, 16 March 1920; quoted in Buckland, *Documentary History*, p. 381.
52. Duc De Stacpoole, *Irish and other Memories*, p. 255.
53. Lennox Robinson, *The Big House*, in Lennox Robinson, *Plays* (London, 1928), p. 306.
54. *The Irish Times*, 7 April 1920.
55. Robinson and Dorman, *Three Homes*, p. 242.
56. Quoted in ibid., p. 247.
57. IGCMR, March 1920.
58. Fitzpatrick, *Politics and Irish Life*, p. 60.
59. IGCMR, July 1920.
60. *The Irish Times*, 6 April 1921; Bence-Jones, *Twilight of the Ascendancy*, p. 204.
61. *The Irish Times*, 25 May, 1920.
62. CICMR, Galway E.R., June 1920.
63. CICMR, County Kerry, March 1921.
64. General Orders: New Series, June 1921 (UCD Archives, Mulcahy papers, P7/A/45).
65. CICMR, County Tipperary, June 1921.
66. *The Irish Times*, 30 June 1921.
67. Ibid., 7 May 1921 and quote from ibid., 29 October 1921.
68. Ibid., County Cork, May, June 1921.
69. Tom Barry, *Guerilla Days in Ireland* (Dublin, 1991 ed.), p. 116.
70. Ibid.
71. Ibid.

72. Erhard Rumpf and A.C. Hepburn, *Nationalism and Socialism in Twentieth Century Ireland* (Liverpool, 1977), pp. 39–40.
73. See Peter Hart, 'The Geography of Revolution in Ireland 1917–23' in *Past and Present* (May 1997).
74. Ibid., p. 147.
75. *The Irish Times*, 22 October 1922.
76. Ibid., 6 April 1921.
77. Bence-Jones, *Twilight of the Ascendancy*, p. 195.
78. *The Irish Times*, 12 November 1921; Bence-Jones, *Guide to Irish Country Houses*, p. 296.
79. Dorothy MacArdle, *The Irish Republic* (London, 1968 ed.), p. 170.
80. IGCMR, August 1919.
81. For success of Republican police and Dáil courts, see Mitchell, *Revolutionary Government*, pp. 150–53; for their growth in respectability amongst the Loyalist community see *The Irish Times*, 2 June, 5 July 1920.
82. CICMR, County Kildare, September 1921.
83. Ibid.
84. Ibid.
85. D.I. to C.I., County Carlow, 28 October 1921 (PRO, Police breaches of truce reports July–December 1921, CO 904 part iv).
86. Breaches of truce reports, 19–24 September 1921 (CO 904, part iv).
87. CICMR, County Kildare, September 1921.
88. A police report on Harristown claimed that the IRA presence: 'must certainly create fear in the minds of law abiding residents, restrict the privileges of the ordinary subject, and place property most unsafe'; 'IRA rebel camp at Harristown House, Kildare', n.d. Breaches of truce reports (CO 904, part iv).
89. Hopkinson, *Green against Green*, p. 35.
90. Quoted in ibid., p. 90.
91. *Church of Ireland Gazette*, 16 June 1922.
92. Rev. Sterling Berry to Minister for Home Affairs, 10 June 1922 (NA, Dept. of Justice files, H5/372).
93. Report on land agitation in Laois [Queen's County], 1922 (NA, Dept. of Taoiseach files, S5366).
94. Peter Hart, 'The Protestant Experience of Revolution in Modern Ireland' in Richard English and Graham Walker (ed.), *Unionism in Modern Ireland: New Perspectives on Politics and Culture* (Dublin, 1996), pp. 81–98; Terence Dooley, 'Protestant Migration from the Free State to Northern Ireland, 1920–25: a Private Census for County Fermanagh' in *Clogher Record*, vol. xv, no. 3, (1996), pp. 87–132; *Church of Ireland Gazette*, 16 June 1922.
95. Hart, 'The Geography of Revolution', p. 147.
96. Hopkinson, *Green against Green*, p. 158.
97. Ibid., pp. 221ff.
98. Quoted in ibid., p. 221.
99. *The Irish Times*, 31 January 1923.
100. Ibid., 31 January 1923.
101. Ibid., 2 March 1923; *Leinster Leader*, 3 February 1923.
102. See p. 193.
103. *The Irish Times*, 18 September 1922.
104. Ibid; *King's County Chronicle*, 24 August 1922.
105. *The Irish Times*, 9 January 1923.
106. *Anglo-Celt*, 20 January 1923.
107. *Kilkenny People*, 13 May 1922; *The Irish Times*, 20 January 1999; see also, Jim Maher, *The Flying Column in West Kilkenny* (Dublin, 1988).
108. Memo from Patrick Hogan to President W.T. Cosgrave, 7 April 1923 (NA, Dept. of Taoiseach files, S3192).
109. Ibid.
110. Hogan to Cosgrave, 7 April 1923.
111. Commissioner of guards to Minister for Home Affairs, 15 November 1922 (NA, Dept. of Justice files, H5/538).
112. *The Irish Times*, 18 August 1922.
113. Rev Almoner to Minister for Home Affairs, 22 October 1923; ibid. (H5/135).

114. *The Irish Times*, 31 January 1923.

115. Fingall, *Seventy Years Young*, p. 237.

116. *The Irish Times*, 12 August 1922.

117. I Would like to thank Ms Aideen Ireland of the NA for bringing this correspondence to my attention.

118. Quoted in *Freeman's Journal*, 12 March 1923.

119. Sir Thomas Esmonde to Lord Eversley, 20 June 1923 (NA, Esmonde papers, 981/4/8/2).

120. Esmonde was the first chairman of Wexford county council in 1899. He was Home Rule MP for North Wexford from 1900–18. He was also Papal Chamberlain, an honour he received in 1898.

121. Sir Thomas Esmonde to President W.T. Cosgrave, 8 May 1925 (NA, Esmonde papers, 981/4/8/5).

122. Paula Hornstein to Sir T. Esmonde, 21 May 1923; ibid. (981/4/8/3).

123. P.J. McGrath to Esmonde, 1 May 1923; ibid.

124. Fr J.J. Rossiter to Esmonde, 11 March 1923. ibid. (981/4/8/1).

125. William Stafford to Esmonde, 14 March 1923; ibid.

126. Lord Courtown to Esmonde, 14 March 1923; ibid.

127. *Leinster Leader*, 14 April 1923.

128. Ibid., 21 April 1923.

129. Hubert Butler, *Escape from the Anthill* (Mullingar, 1985), p. 67.

130. *Leinster Leader*, 7 May 1921.

131. Fingall, *Seventy Years Young*, p. 414.

132. Quoted in Bence-Jones, *Twilight of the Ascendancy*, p. 211.

133. *The Irish Times*, 7 February 1923.

134. Quoted in Hone, *The Moores of Moore Hall*, p. 264.

135. Extracts of Lord Lansdowne's agent's report sent to Lansdowne and forwarded to Winston Churchill; enclosed in Lord Lansdowne to Winston Churchill, 20 September 1922 (NA, Dept. of Taoiseach files, S1940).

136. See for example, Judgement of Mr Justice Devitt at Manorhamilton court, 8 May 1923, regarding claim no. 195/C of J. Lee and J.C. Dixon for damage to Glenfarne Hall, County Leitrim (NA, OPW files, 2D/62/76).

137. Ibid.

138. Copy of report of Mr J.C. Butler, inspecting officer of OPW, 14 August 1925, on damage to Mitchelstown Castle (NA, OPW files, 2D/62/76).

139. Saunderson, *The Saundersons of Castlesaunderson*, p. 73.

140. *Westmeath Guardian*, 8 July, 5 August 1921.

141. S. Douglas to Lord Dunalley, n.d.; J.H. Dudley to Lord Dunalley, 7 August 1922; W. Harkness to Lord Dunalley, 12 August 1922 (NLI, Dunalley papers, MS 29,810 (17)).

142. Copy letter Lord Dunalley to President W.T. Cosgrave, 10 January 1924; ibid. (MS 29,810 (19)).

143. J.H. Dudley to Lord Dunalley 20 and 26 October 1925; ibid. (MS 29,810 (20)).

144. Robinson, *Bryan Cooper*, p. 139.

145. R. Walker to Lord Dunalley, 20 May 1924 (NLI, Dunalley papers, 29,810 (19)).

146. *An Act for Amending the Law Relating to Local Government in Ireland and for Other Purposes Connected Therewith* (61 and 62 Vict., c. xxxvii (12 August 1898)).

147. *An Act to Amend the Enactments Relative to Compensation for Criminal Injuries in Ireland* (9 and 10 Geo. V, c. lxvi (16 April 1919)) and *An Act to Amend the Enactments Relative to Compensation for Criminal Injuries in Ireland* (10 and 11 Geo. V, c. lxvi (23 December 1920)).

148. County councils were accused of ignoring the awards and refusing to budget for them in their rate assessments. In October 1922 Lord Shaw of Dunfermline, who was to chair the Compensation (Ireland) Commission, pointed out that: 'county councils who, in ordinary circumstances, would have stood defendants in the issue of claims for malicious damage to property, were declining to defend the cases. The reasons for that may have been partly financial and partly owing to the state of the country.' Compensation (Ireland) Commission: interim report no. 3, 21 October 1922 (NA, Dept. of Finance files, 169/65); *The Irish Times*, 14, 22 October 1921.

149. A study of the *Northern Standard*, *Dundalk Democrat*, and *Leinster Leader* for the period January 1920 to July 1921 shows that this was certainly the case in counties such as Monaghan, Louth, Kildare, Meath and King' County.

150. R.B. McDowell, *Crisis and Decline: the Fate of Southern Unionists* (Dublin, 1997), p. 138.

151. *The Irish Times*, 22 September 1921.

152. Ibid., 8 October 1921.

153. Hone, *The Moores of Moore Hall*, p. 266.

154. *The Irish Times*, 12 November 1921, 29 January 1922.

155. *The Irish Times*, 5 December 1921.

156. Quoted in Ronan Fanning, *The Irish Department of Finance, 1922–58* (Dublin, 1978), p. 139.

157. Memo by Minister for Finance, 'Property losses compensation', 9 November 1923 (NA, Dept. of Taoiseach files, S6365).

158. Compensation commission: procedure for dealing with cases: minute sheet initialled by 'J.D.' to Mr O'Brien, 25 July 1922 (NA, Dept. of Finance files, 169/40).

159. A.H. Waterfield to Joseph Brennan, 21 October 1922; ibid.

160. Compensation (Ireland) Commission: Interim report no. 1, 6 December 1925; ibid., (169/65).

161. *The Irish Times*, 22 September 1923.

162. Bence-Jones, *Twilight of the Ascendancy*, pp. 238–39.

163. *Irish Independent*, 19 August 1922.

164. *Morning Post*, 2 April 1923.

165. Compensation (Ireland) Commission: final report, March 1926 (NA, Dept. of Finance files, 19/2/6)

166. M. Sturgis to secretary Provisional Government, 26 July 1922; quoted in *Compensation for Malicious Injuries in Ireland*, [Cmd 1736], HC 1922, xvii.

167. McDowell, *Crisis and Decline*, p. 140.

168. Quoted in Buckland, *Irish Unionism I*, p. 214.

169. R.C. Williams to OPW, 3 May 1922 (NA, Dept. of Finance files, 169/17).

170. *Damage to Property (Compensation) Act, 1823*, (No. 15 of 1923 (12 May 1923)).

171. J.J. McEligott to M.A. Corrigan (chief state solicitor), 14 May 1923 (NA, Dept. of Finance files, 746/20).

172. R. Dudley to Lord Dunalley, 27 May 1924 (NLI, Dunalley papers, 29,810 (19)).

173. *Morning Post*, 2 April 1923.

174. Lord Devonshire to T.M. Healy, 24 March 1923 (NA, Dept. of Taoiseach files, S2158).

175. Text of statement read by President W.T. Cosgrave in Dáil Éireann, 27 May 1923; ibid.

176. Draft of statement to be delivered by President W.T. Cosgrave to Dáil Éireann 26 March 1923; ibid. (S2188).

177. Ibid.

178. Sir Thomas Esmonde to Lord Eversley, 20 June 1923 (NA, Esmonde papers, 981/4/8/2).

179. Sir Thomas Esmonde to President Cosgrave, 8 May 1925; ibid., (981/4/8/5).

180. Copy transcript of stenographer's notes: compensation claim of Sir T. Esmonde versus Minister for Finance, February 1925; ibid., (981/4/9/4).

181. *Echo and South Leinster Adventurer*, 1 August 1925.

182. Myles Higgins to Sir Thomas Esmonde, 13 March 1925 (NA, Esmonde papers, 981/4/9/1).

183. Sir Thomas Esmonde to President W.T. Cosgrave, 27 July 1925; ibid., (981/4/9/9).

184. T.F. Moloney to Sir Thomas Esmonde, 12 December 1925; ibid.

185. Joseph Brennan to Sir Thomas Esmonde, 6 January 1926; ibid.; copy transcript of debate on Damage to Property (Compensation) Bill, 11 March 1926; ibid.

186. Damage to Property (Compensation) Act, 1923: register of claims (NA, OPW files, 2D/62/60–69).

187. S. and R.C. Walker to Lord Dunalley, 15 August 1924 (NLI, Dunalley papers, MS 29,810 (19)).

188. R. Dudley to Lord Dunalley, 23 June 1923; ibid., (MS 29,810 (17)).

189. Dudley to Dunalley, 24 April 1924; ibid., (MS 29,810 (19)).

190. B.E.F. Sheehy (architect) to Dunalley, 14 April 1925; ibid., (MS 29,810 (20)).

191. Lord Dunalley, *Khaki and Green* (London, 1940), p. 248.

192. Bence-Jones, *Guide to Irish Country Houses*, p. 164.

193. Desart and Lubbock, *A Page from the Past*, p. 223.

194. E.J. Beaumont-Nesbitt to Mrs M. Savage-Armstrong, 19 January 1925; quoted in Buckland, *Documentary History*, p. 382.

195. Bence-Jones, *Guide to Irish Country Houses*, p. 182.

196. Quoted in Bence-Jones, *Twilight of the Ascendancy*, p. 238.

197. Brian Beaumont-Nesbitt to Bobbie Tyrell, 27 September 1991; Bobbie Tyrell to Brian Beaumont-Nesbitt, 2 October 1991 (Beaumont-Nesbitt papers, private possession).

Chapter 8

1.   Horace Plunkett, *Noblesse Oblige: an Irish Rendering* (Dublin, 1908), p. 26.
2.   Leslie memoirs (MS 22,885).
3.   See pp. 214–18.
4.   Quoted in Cannadine, *The Decline of the British Aristocracy*, p. 36.
5.   Hoppen, *Elections, Politics and Society*, p. 336.
6.   Foster, *Modern Ireland*, p. 377.
7.   For election expenses, see Hoppen, *Elections, Politics and Society*, p. 84.
8.   Ibid., p. 335.
9.   Quoted in *Irish Landowners' Convention Report, 1897*, p. 22.
10. Ibid.
11. Marquis of Sligo, *Westport House*, p. 51.
12. Hoppen, *Elections, Politics and Society*, p. 339.
13. See Virginia Crossman, *Local Government in Nineteenth Century Ireland* (Belfast, 1994); for detailed discussion of the functions of local administrators see ILPU, *Local Government in Ireland: A Sketch of the Present System and Methods of Procedure* (Dublin, 1886) and W.F. Bailey, *Local and Centralised Government in Ireland* (London, 1888).
14. As the nineteenth century progressed and the number of government functionaries increased in each county the high sheriffs' perceptions of themselves as being central to local government were, perhaps, exaggerated, but, nevertheless, they were keen to hold on to the social position a shrievalty gave them. In County Westmeath, for example, no one could attend a grand jury assize dinner unless invited to do so by the high sheriff; J.C. Lyons, *Anecdotes for the Historical Appendix to the Grand Juries of the County of Westmeath* (Ladestown, 1852), pp. 14–15.
15. W.L. Feingold, 'Land League Power: The Tralee Poor Law Election of 1881' in Samuel Clark and J.S. Donnelly Jr (ed.), *Irish Peasants: Violence and Political Unrest 1780–1914* (Wisconsin, 1983), p. 287.
16. As K.T. Hoppen points out landlords were not slow to use punitive measures to ensure tenant loyalty at these elections in the years before the advent of the Land League; for measures taken by E.P. Shirley and his agent in Monaghan, see Hoppen, *Elections, Politics and Society*, p. 150.
17. Quoted in Feingold, 'The Tralee Poor Law Election of 1881', p. 289.
18. Quoted in *Belfast Newsletter*, 17 December 1901.
19. For the case of John Heffernan in Kildare, see Thomas Nelson, *The Land War in Co. Kildare* (Maynooth, 1985), p. 25.
20. Sir Stephen De Vere, 'Local Government in Ireland' in *Contemporary Review*, lx (November 1891), p. 733.
21. Ibid., p. 734.
22. *The Times*, 2 May 1907.
23. *Morning Post*, 11 April 1899.
24. *Freeman's Journal*, 14 November 1901.
25. Quoted in ibid., 19 December 1901.
26. Ibid., 26 July 1902.
27. *Daily Express*, 2 December 1904.
28. Ibid.
29. Buckland, *Irish Unionism I*, p. xiv.
30. For a study of this growth see Vaughan, *Landlords and Tenants in mid-Victorian Ireland*, pp. 141–50.
31. Ibid., p. 161.
32. ILPU, *Ireland Under the League*, p. 52.
33. Ibid., p. 54.
34. See *Irish Landowners' Convention Report*, 1897, p. 17.
35. Quoted in Geary, *The Plan of Campaign*, p. 52.
36. ILPU, *Union or Separation* (Dublin, 1886), p. 17.
37. Dun, *Landlords and Tenants in Ireland*, pp. 37, 42.
38. Earl of Meath (ed.), *The Diaries of Mary, Countess of Meath* (London, n.d.), p. 70.
39. Quoted in Somerville-Large, *The Irish Country House*, p. 316.
40. *Irish Landowners' Convention Report, 1894*, p. 17.
41. IGCMR, October 1900.

42. Ibid., December 1901.

43. IUA, *The New Home Rule and the Old Objections* (Dublin, 1906), pp. 13–14.

44. See ILPU, *Union or Separation*.

45. Both quoted in Geary, *Plan of Campaign*, pp. 28–29.

46. *Northern Standard*, 16 July 1910.

47. Quoted in Buckland, *Documentary History*, p. 166.

48. Quoted in *The Irish Times*, 16 October 1885.

49. It did have the support of individual Protestant clergymen (as opposed to having definite links with Protestant Churches as in Ulster) and academics such as J.H. Jellett and John Pentland Mahaffy, but it had only limited support from the Protestant business community who were too largely dependent on Catholic customers to risk injury to their trade; see Buckland, *Irish Unionism* I, p. 18.

50 The other two members were J.H. Jellett and J.P. Mahaffy; *The Irish Times*, 16 October 1885.

51. Brian Jenkins, *Sir William Gregory of Coole: The Biography of an Anglo-Irishman* (Buckinghamshire, 1986), p. 297.

52. See for example, *The Irish Times*, 9 January 1886; *List of Unionist Clubs of Ireland and List of Executive Committee of the Council for 1895* (in private possession); lists of landlords seated on platforms at anti-Home Rule demonstrations as published in IUA, *Great Demonstration in Dublin Representing the Unionism of the Provinces of Leinster, Munster and Connaught* (Dublin, 1911).

53. Lionel Pleignier to secretary IUA, 27 August 1891 (PRONI, IUA papers, D989/A/8/2).

54. Ibid.

55. ILPU, *Irish Election of 1885*, p. 5.

56. *The Irish Times*, 8 January 1886.

57. IUA, *The Intolerance of Irish Nationalism Towards Irish Unionism* (Dublin, 1908), p. 2.

58. Ibid.

59. *Notes from Ireland*, November 1912.

60. For lack of progress of IUA, see IUA, *The Irish Unionist Alliance: An Account of its Work and Organisation* (Dublin, 1893).

61. Leslie memoirs (MS 22,885).

62. Reginald Lucas, *Col Saunderson MP: A Memoir* (London, 1908), p. 66.

63. See Terence Dooley, 'Why Monaghan Protestants opposed Home Rule' in *Clogher Record*, vol. xiv (1993), pp. 42–46.

64. Leslie memoirs (MS 22,885).

65. His name appears as Moore in Walker, *Parliamentary Results*, p. 306.

66. Quoted in John Magee, 'The Monaghan Election of 1883 and the Invasion of Ulster' in *Clogher Record* (1974), p. 101.

67. Leslie, *Doomsland*, p. 53.

68. The text read as follows: 'ORANGEMEN IN MONAGHAN: The late Invincibles and Land Leaguers are afraid to enter Monaghan, but they have flooded your county with proclamations asking your attendance at Roslea on the 16th, to hear their treasonable speeches. Attend then, with Sir John Leslie, Colonel Lloyd and myself, to assist our Fermanagh brethren in supporting their rights and oppose the rebels to the utmost, showing them that Orangemen are, as heretofore, loyal to England. They declare that you are as ready to obey them as their dupes in the south, but we will show them, as did the Tyrone men, that they are liars and slanderers. Boycott and emergency men to the front, and down with Parnell and rebellion.' Quoted in J.W. Taylor (ed.), *The Rossmore Incident: An Account of the Various Nationalist and Counter-Nationalist Meetings Held in Ulster in the Autumn of 1883 together with the Correspondence Between Lord Rossmore and the Lords Commissioners* (Dublin, 1884), p. 13.

69. Hugh Shearman, *Anglo-Irish Relations* (London, 1959), p. 151; for a much fuller discussion of the 'Roslea Incident' see Magee, 'The Monaghan Election of 1883', pp. 147–66.

70. IGCMRs, May–December 1901.

71. The distilled argument of the Covenant read: 'Being convinced in our consciences that Home Rule would be disastrous to the material well-being of Ulster, as well as the whole of Ireland, subversive to our civil and religious freedom, destructive of our citizenship and perilous to the unity of the Empire, we ... do hereby pledge ourselves ... to stand by one another in defending for ourselves and our children our cherished position of equal citizenship in the United Kingdom, and in using all means which may be found necessary to set up a Home Rule parliament'. Quoted in A.C. Hepburn, *The Conflict of Nationality in Modern Ireland* (London, 1980), p. 76.

72. *Northern Standard*, 9 August 1913; CICMR, County Cavan, July 1913; CICMR, County Donegal, September 1912; and Report by inspector general of RIC to chief secretary, 'Ulster movement against Home Rule', 23 November 1913 (PRO, CO 904, part vi).

73. CICMR, County Cavan, September 1913; January 1914; 'Ulster movement against Home Rule'.

74. CICMR, County Donegal, October 1913; January, March, May 1914.

75. 'UVF county committee for Monaghan, 20 September 1912' (PRONI, UUC papers, D1327/4/18); CICMR, County Cavan, November 1913; 'Ulster movement against Home Rule'.

76. Quoted in *Irish Post*, 17 January 1914.

77. CICMR, County Donegal, January, May, June 1914.

78. CICMR, County Monaghan, July, August, 1913.

79. UVF county committee for County Monaghan, 20 September 1912 (PRONI, UUC papers, D1327/4/18).

80. CICMR, County Cavan, March 1912.

81. CICMR, County Cavan, March 1914.

82. CICMR, County Donegal, June 1914.

83. Return of arms for month ending 28 February 1917, County Cavan, County Donegal and County Monaghan (PRO, CO 904, part vi).

84. Return of arms for month ending 28 February 1917, County Monaghan (PRO, CO 904, part vi).

85. In May 1914, the county inspector of Monaghan claimed that businessmen there were reluctant to become involved because an outbreak of hostilities might lead to sectarian animosity that would be 'deep rooted' and 'long standing' and 'very injurious to trade'. From Donegal, the county inspector reported: 'The businessmen will tell you they are opposed to Home Rule, but in this county, where they are in a minority, and dependent for their trade on their Catholic customers who are in the majority, I doubt if they would participate as a body in any attempt at open hostility'; CICMR, County Monaghan, May 1914; 'Ulster movement against Home Rule'.

86. Quoted in *Northern Standard*, 1 November 1913.

.87. Shane Leslie, *The Irish Tangle for English Readers*, p. 13.

88. Gerald Madden to editor of *Northern Standard*, October 1913; *Northern Standard*, 1 November 1913.

89. See pp. 122–27.

90. Buckland, *Irish Unionism* I, p. 35.

91. Extract from J.M. Wilson's notes of conversations with anonymous or semi-anonymous informants during a tour of Irish counties, 1915–17; quoted in Buckland, *Documentary History*, p. 348.

92. See resolution of executive committee of IUA, 4 August 1914, in Buckland, *Documentary History*, p. 343; F.S.L. Lyons, *Ireland Since the Famine* (London, 1981 ed.), p. 310; Foster, *Modern Ireland*, p. 612; Woodenbridge speech, *The Irish Times*, 21 September 1914.

93. *The Irish Times*, 5,6,8, August 1914; *Freeman's Journal*, 6,7 August 1914.

94. *The Irish Times*, 6 August 1914.

95. *Freeman's Journal*, 1 July 1915.

96. Bryan Cooper, *The Tenth Irish Division in Gallipoli* (London, 1918), p. 253.

97. For a detailed picture of this conversion, see Robinson, *Bryan Cooper*, pp. 110–23.

98. IGCMR, February 1917; see also Buckland, *Irish Unionism* I, p. 110; R.B. McDowell, *The Irish Convention* (London, 1970), p. 127; Stephen Gwynn, *John Redmond's Last Years* (London, 1919), p. 313.

99. Michael Laffan, *The Partition of Ireland, 1911–25* (Dublin, 1983), pp. 33, 202

100. *Northern Standard*, 17 June 1916.

101. *UUC Yearbook, 1917* (PRONI, D972/17).

102. *Ulster and Home Rule: No partition of Ulster* [pamphlet issued by Unionists of Monaghan, Cavan and Donegal, April 1920] (PRONI, D1545/8).

103. 'Report of Major Saunderson', c.1917 (PRONI, Writings of J.M. Wilson, D989/A/8/7/1).

104. Major Somerset Saunderson to William Martin, 10 July 1916; quoted in *Northern Standard*, 22 July 1916.

105. Ibid.

106. *Northern Standard*, 22 July 1916.

107. Edward Carson to William Martin, 17 July 1916; quoted in ibid.

108. Ibid., 26 May 1917.

109. See Terence Dooley, 'County Monaghan, 1914–18: Recruitment, the Rise of Sinn Féin and the Partition Crisis' in *Clogher Record*, xvi (1998), pp. 144–58.

110. *Dundalk Democrat*, 3 October 1914.

111. What limited statistics there are available give some weight to these statements. In November 1916, there were 9,023 of military service age in the county. Of these the labour of 5,140 was considered indispensable; 1,483 were deemed physically unfit for service; leaving 2,234 possible recruits. By October 1916, only 738 men, including Catholics and Protestants, had recruited. Similarly, if casualty rates can be taken as an indicator of levels of recruitment (Protestant and Catholic), Monaghan had a much lower rate than the six counties and was only marginally behind Cavan and Donegal (1.82 per cent of eligible males as compared to 1.72 per cent in Cavan and 1.71 per cent in Donegal). It had the tenth lowest rate in the country as a whole; CICMR, March, July, October 1917; Statement giving particulars regarding men of military age, 19–41, in Ireland with an estimate of the number of men available for military service based on the National Register 1915, and the number of men who have joined H.M. Forces since the outbreak of war (NA, CSORP, 24317, 1916); Patrick Casey, 'Irish Casualties in the First World War' in *The Irish Sword*, vol. xx (summer 1997), p. 206.

112. *Northern Standard*, 11 December 1915.

113. Ibid., 30 January 1915.

114. For example, between May 1851 and December 1913, a total of 59,824 persons had emigrated from County Monaghan, an average of 965 per annum. In 1914 only 304 persons emigrated and by 1918 this figure had fallen even further to 12 persons; *Emigration Statistics of Ireland, 1914 and 1918*, [Cd 7313], lxix; [Cd 7883], lxxx.

115. Letter from Michael Knight to Monaghan county council; Minutes of Monaghan county council, 8 June 1915 (Monaghan county council offices, minute books).

116. CICMR, September 1914.

117. Ibid., September 1915.

118. Ibid., December 1920.

119. Quoted in *Northern Standard*, 13 July 1915.

120. CICMR, County Donegal, January 1917.

121. CICMR County Cavan, November 1914.

122. Charles Craig to Lord Farnham, 12 May 1919; quoted in Buckland, *Documentary History*, pp. 137–38.

123. Quoted in Laffan, *The Partition of Ireland*, p. 65.

124. *Ulster and Home Rule: No Partition of Ulster* (PRONI, D1548/8).

125. Quoted in *Northern Standard*, 13 March 1920.

126. Ibid.

127. *Anglo-Celt*, 17 April 1920.

128. Saunderson, *The Saundersons of Castlesaunderson*, p. 73.

129. Lord Farnham to Hugh Montgomery, 13 April 1920; quoted in Buckland, *Documentary History*, p. 419.

130. Ibid.

131. *Dundalk Democrat*, 17 July 1920.

132. Ibid.

133. Quoted in *Northern Standard*, 15 July 1921.

134. Quoted in Aiken McClelland, 'Orangeism in County Monaghan', *Clogher Record* (1978), p. 400.

135. Ibid.

136. Quoted in *Northern Standard*, 20 July 1923.

137. Ibid., 19 July 1924.

138. Quoted in iIbid.

139. See Terence Dooley, 'Monaghan Protestants in a Time of Crisis, 1919–22', in R.V. Comerford et al. (eds.), *Religion, Conflict and Coexistence in Ireland* (Dublin, 1990), pp. 235–51; id., *The Plight of Monagan Protestants 1911–26* (Dublin, 2000).

140. *The Irish Times*, 16 January 1920, 15 April 1921.

141. J.W. Garvey to F.H. Crawford, 21 August 1921; quoted in Buckland, *Documentary History*, p. 383.

142. Quoted in Dunraven, *Past Times and Pastimes, ii*, p. 202.

143. Diary of Lady Alice Howard, 31 December 1921 (NLI, Diaries of Lady Alice Howard, MS 3,625).

144. Quoted in *The Irish Times*, 6 March 1922.

145. Earl of Desart and Lady Sybil Lubbock, *A Page from the Past: Memories of the Earl of Desart* (London, 1936), p. 222.
146. *Parl. debates [Lords], 5th series, lii*, 4 December 1922, col. 224.
147. J.M. Wilson to Edward Carson, 14 December 1922; quoted in Buckland, *Documentary History*, p. 389.
148. *The Irish Times*, 11 August 1920.
149. Ibid., 7 October 1920.
150. For example, there were only four members of the 100 sample families who were county councillors in 1918.
151. Algernon Coote to editor of *Leinster Leader*, 1 September 1920; quoted in *Leinster Leader*, 4 September 1920.
152. *Irish Independent*, 20 January 1920.
153. Ibid.
154. Ibid.
155. *The Irish Times*, 22 January 1923.
156. Ibid.
157. *Thom's Directory, 1923*, p. 1094.
158. Vaughan, *Landlords and Tenants in mid-Victorian Ireland*, p. 227.
159. *Constitution of the Irish Free State (Saorstát Éireann) Act, 1922* (No. 1 of 1922).
160. Rumpf and Hepburn, *Nationalism and Socialism in Twentieth Century Ireland*, p. 112.
161. Donal O'Sullivan, *The Irish Free State and its Senate: A Study in Contemporary Politics* (London, 1940), p. 86.
162. *Senate Debates, i, 1922–23*, pp. 8–9.
163. Ibid., p. 14.
164. Ibid., p. 10.
165. O'Sullivan, *The Irish Free State and its Senate*, p. 514.
166. *Senate Debates, i,1922–23*, p. 4.
167. Ibid.
168. *The Irish Times*, 10 January 1923.
169. Ibid., 3, 19, 24 February 1923.
170. Ibid., 28 February, 12 March 1923.
171. *Senates Debates, iii, 1924–25*, p. 894.
172. *Senate Debates, ii, 1923–24*, pp. 966–67.
173. O'Sullivan, *The Irish Free State and its Senate*, p. 429.
174. J.L. McCracken, *Representative Government in Ireland: a Study of Dáil Éireann, 1919–48* (London, 1958), p. 137.
175. Ibid.
176. Quoted in O'Sullivan, *The Irish Free State and its Senate*, p. 374.
177. Quoted in ibid., p. 232.
178. Abolition of the Seanad: miscellaneous correspondence: the case against the present Seanad, n.d. (1934) (NA, Dept. of Taoiseach files, S 2926).
179. T.W. Westropp Bennett, *Pro Domo Sua: Being the Speech of the Chairman of the Seanad ... in Defence of the House of the Oireachtas against Mr De Valera and the Government* (Dublin, 1936), p. 41.
180. Marquis of Sligo, *Westport House*, pp. 64–65.
181. W.E.H. Lecky, *The Leaders of Public Opinion in Ireland* (New York, 1889), p. xv.
182. Ibid., p. 20.
183. *Westminster Gazette*, 23 January 1909.
184. J.P. Mahaffy, 'The Irish Landlords' in *Contemporary Review*, xli (January 1882), p. 166.
185. Stephen Gwynn, *Experiences of a Literary Man* (London, 1926), p. 11.

Chapter 9
1. See pp. 122–27.
2. Seymour Leslie, *The Jerome Connexion*, p. 89.
3. Cannadine, *Decline of the British Aristocracy*, pp. 86–87.
4. Seymour Leslie, *The Jerome Connexion*, p. 36.
5. Ibid., p. 37.
6. Ibid., p. 64.

7. Leslie Memoirs (MS 22,885).
8. Shane Leslie, *Doomsland*, p. 55.
9. Shane Leslie, *The Film of Memory*, p. 14.
10. Quoted in Anita Leslie, *The Gilt and the Gingerbread*, p. 126.
11. Shane Leslie, *The Film of Memory*, p. 361.
12. Leslie memoirs (MS 22,885).
13. Shane Leslie, *Doomsland*, p. 217; in his unpublished memoirs he claimed: 'I could never give myself or others one sweeping reason for becoming a Roman Catholic'; Leslie, autobiographical sketch (MS 22,884).
14. Leslie, autobiographical sketch (MS 22,884).
15. Leslie memoirs (MS 22,885).
16. Seymour Leslie, *The Jerome Connexion*, p. 49.
17. Anita Leslie, *The Gilt and the Gingerbread*, p. 26.
18. Leslie memoirs (MS 22,885).
19. Quoted in ibid.
20. Anita Leslie, *The Gilt and the Gingerbread*, p. 12.
21. Leslie memoirs (MS 22,885).
22. Anita Leslie, *The Gilt and the Gingerbread*, p. 11.
23. Ibid.
24. Ibid.
25. Ibid.
26. Leslie memoirs (MS 22,885).
27. Anita Leslie, *The Gilt and the Gingerbread*, p. 86.
28. Leslie memoirs (MS 22,885); id., *The Film of Memory*, pp. 110, 118–19.
29. Ibid.
30. Shane Leslie, *The Film of Memory*, p. 87.
31. Leslie memoirs (MS 22,885).
32. Seymour Leslie, *The Jerome Connexion*, pp. 34, 60.
33. Ibid., p. 34.
34. Ibid., pp. 36, 58.
35. Ibid., p. 175.
36. Ibid., p. 36; Mark Bence-Jones, *Life in an Irish Country House* (London, 1996), pp. 76, 79.
37. Ibid.
38. Anita Leslie, *The Gilt and the Gingerbread*, p. 81.
39. Seymour Leslie, *The Jerome Connexion*, p. 37.
40. Ibid.
41. Anita Leslie, *The Gilt and the Gingerbread*, p. 194.
42. See Shane Leslie, *The Irish Issue in its American Aspect* (London, 1919).
43. Anita Leslie, *The Gilt and the Gingerbread*, p. 143.
44. Quoted in Anne Morrow, *Picnic in a Foreign Land* (London, 1989), p. 237.
45. *Sunday Press*, 7 May 1995.
46. See recent article in *Northern Standard*, 5 August 1999.
47. *Returns of advances, 1881–1921.*
48. RCB mortgage ledgers, D1–D3 (Church House, Rathmines).
49. NA wills 1948/132; 1955/1670; 1931/Dn; 1936/294.
50. Just as significant in this respect was the fact that more spouses were sought outside of Ireland and Britain. Over one quarter of the spouses of eighty-six heirs to the 100 estates who married in the post war period were born outside Ireland or Britain.
51. *Sunday Press*, 9 January 1914; Estorick, *Heirs and Graces*, p. 14.
52. Quoted in Cannadine, *Decline of the British Aristocracy*, p. 352.
53. G.R. Searle has written of British landlords in the post-war period: 'Agricultural land by itself could no longer sustain landed society in the social role which had become traditional. So, to secure an adequate income, other strategies needed to be adopted — including the making of advantageous marriages with social outsiders, including Americans, and becoming involved in unprecedented ways, in the world of business and finance; quoted in Cannadine, *Decline of the British Aristocracy*, p. 392.
54. Morrow, *Picnic in a Foreign Land*, p. 40.
55. Quoted in ibid., p. 369.

56. See Peter Mandler, *The Fall and Rise of the Stately Home* (London, 1997).

57. Ibid., p. 190.

58. Ibid., p. 4.

59. Untitled newspaper clipping dated 5 May 1981 (IAA, RWC 596); Rossmore claimed £500,000 in compensation and was awarded £330,000, levied on County Monaghan at large.

60. Guinness, 'The First Thirty Years', p. 12.

61. Ibid., pp. 10, 12.

62. Quoted in *The Irish Times*, 29 June 1954.

63. Secretary of Killarney Tourist Association to an Taoiseach, 17 May 1950 (NA, Dept. of Taoiseach files, S6355).

64. *The Irish Times*, 18 January 1954.

65. Ibid., 29 June 1954.

66. Bence-Jones, *Irish Country Houses*, p. 284; Morrow, *Picnic in a Foreign Land*, p. 108.

67. McParland and Robinson, *Heritage at Risk*, p. 11.

68. Quoted in ibid.

69. Ibid., p. 6.

70. Ibid., pp. 17–21.

71. Ibid., p. 13.

72. Information supplied to this writer by Bord Fáilte.

73. Desart and Lubbock (ed.), *A Page from the Past*, p. 222.

74. Comerford, *Fenians in Context*, p. 224.

75. *Cowper Commission, Minutes of Evidence*, p. 506.

76. Headlam, *Irish Reminiscences*, pp. 222–23.

77. Fingall, *Seventy Years Young*, p. 414.

78. *Westminster Gazette*, 23 January 1909.

79. Diary of Lady Alice Howard, 13 May, 21 June and 12 September 1920 (NLI, Diaries of Lady Alice Howard, MS 3,624).

80. Robinson (ed.), *Lady Gregory's Journals*, pp. 13–14.

81. Christopher Lynch-Robinson, *The Last of the Irish R.M.s* (London, 1951), p. 175.

82. Ibid., p. 176.

83. Quoted in Gearóid Cronin, 'The Big House and the Irish Landscape in the Work of Elizabeth Bowen', in Genet, *The Big House*, p. 143.

84. Castletown, *Ego*, pp. 67–68.

85. Ibid., p. 68.

86. Quoted in Fitzpatrick, *Politics and Irish Life*, p. 79.

87. De Stacpoole, *Irish and other Memories*, p. v.

88. For example, from 1900 to 1914 inclusive, 13,184 birds had been shot on the Marquis of Westport's demesne; J.B. Drought, *A Sportsman Looks at Éire* (London, n.d.), p. 10.

89. Ibid.

90. Ibid., p. 11.

91. Ibid., p. 14.

92. See Bence-Jones, *Life in an Irish Country House*, pp. 18, 62, 76.

93. McGahern, 'Eddie Mac', pp. 285, 286.

94. *The Irish Times*, 15 October 1881.

95. In 1881, Lord Curraghmore pointed out that 'it is almost impossible to carry on this sport unless it is supported and carried on with enthusiasm by every class'. Similarly, Viscount Galway, who had been Master of Foxhounds for thirty-one years, advised his fellow landowners that 'it is a good policy while thus exercising the hounds for the huntsman to call at several farms. The farmer and his wife will like the act of courtesy, and occasionally, perhaps, some hitherto unknown grievance may be brought to light which a little tactful conversation may smooth over and remove'; Curraghmore quoted in ibid; Galway, *A Pack of Foxhounds*, p. 11.

96. L.P. Curtis Jr has found that, by the end of 1881, practically every hunt in the country had been subjected to an attack of one form or another; Curtis, 'Stopping the Hunt', p. 356.

97. *The Irish Times*, 27 December 1881.

98. See ibid., 3 September 1881.

99. In Queen's County, for example, thirty-three members of the hunt were magistrates in the late 1870s; twenty-seven were members of the grand jury; and between them they owned 44 per cent of the land there; J.W.H. Carter, *The Land War and its Leaders in Queen's County*,

1879–82 (Portlaoise, 1994), p. 224; see also letter from 'One who does not like to injure you' to Burton Persse, master of the Galway Blazers, quoted in *The Irish Times*, 2 January 1882

100. *Freeman's Journal*, 26 September 1881; *The Irish Times*, 12 October 1881.
101. *Freeman's Journal*, 21 September 1881.
102. Curtis, *Stopping the Hunt*, p. 374.
103. Wyndham Quin, *The Limerick Hunt*, p. 150.
104. Ibid.
105. *Weekly Freeman's Journal*, 31 October 1887.
106. Ibid., 7 January 1888.
107. IGCMR, December 1900.
108. Ibid., November 1901 and CICMR., County Roscommon, November 1901.
109. IGCMR, February 1915.
110. IGCMR, January 1919.
111. *The Irish Times*, 21 January 1921.
112. Ibid., 31 January 1921.
113. Ibid., 2 February 1922.
114. As R.V. Comerford has rightly concluded the gentry 'were no doubt annoyed' by the stopping of hunting at this time 'but they were also saved much expenditure and unnecessary consumption which most of them could ill afford'; Comerford, *Fenians in Context*, p. 236; for examples of financial difficulties of various hunt clubs at this time see, Anon, *Kilkenny Hunt*, pp. 83–92; *Freeman's Journal*, 31 October 1881; Mayo and Boulton, *Kildare Hunt*, pp. 356–7.
115. *The Irish Times*, 15 October 1881.
116. Fingall, *Seventy Years Young*, pp. 117, 186.
117. Quoted in Cannadine, *Decline of the British Aristocracy*, p. 363.
118. Anita Leslie, *The Gilt and the Gingerbread*, p. 131.
119. *Bailey's Hunting Directory, 1939–49*, p. 1; it is probably fair to conclude that many of these farmers were former landlords who, following the sale of their estates, remained farming.
120. C.A. Lewis, *Hunting in Ireland: An Historical and Geographical Analysis* (London, 1975), p. 139.
121. *Irish Racing Calendar*, 1890, p. 137.
122. D'Arcy, *Horses, Lords and Racing Men*, p. 197.
123. *Irish Racing Calendar, 1913, 1918.*
124. Ibid., *1919–22.*
125. D'Arcy, *Horses, Lords and Racing Men*, p. 263.
126. *An Act to Provide for the Improvement and Development of Horse Breeding and Horse Racing and for the Better Control of Racecourses, and for This and Other Purposes to Establish a Board to be Called the Racing Board....* (No. 16 of 1945).
127. F.F. MacCabe and T.E. Healey, 'Racing, Steeplechasing and Breeding in Ireland', in Charles Richardson (ed.), *British Steeplechasing* (London, 1927), p. 295.
128. Ibid., p. 252.
129. Ibid., p. 294.
130. Ibid., p. 296.
131. For examples of this type of participation, see INHSC, *Irish Point to Point Handbook* (1945).
132. These seventeen men were: Lord Decies, Lord Enniskillen, Percy La Touche, Frank Brooke, Sir William Goulding, J.K. Laidlaw, Sir Bryan Mahon, Sir Walter Nugent, Colonel Charteris, Captain Charles Moore, Major Evelyn Shirley, Captain Gerald Dunne, Isodore Blake, Captain Boyd-Rochfort, Cecil Stafford-King-Harman, Lieutenant Colonel Stephen Hill-Dillon, Major Dermot McCalmont; *Irish Racing Calendar*, (various editions, 1914–45).
133. From 1925 to 1945, this administrative board was dominated by Sir Walter Nugent, Sir Bryan Mahon, A.D. Comyn, Colonel G.W. Stacpoole, Major Evelyn Shirley, the Earl of Fingall, Lieutenant Colonel Stephen, Hill-Dillon, Captain Boyd-Rochfort, J.K. Laidlaw, Major A.H. Watt, Duc de Stacpoole, Sir James Nelson, A.L. Moore, and F.W. Wise; ibid.
134. *Dáil debates, 14 February–25 April, 1945*, 96, col. 832.
135. Into this category, he put the likes of Lord Dunraven, Lord Talbot De Malahide, Lord Fingall, Lord Drogheda, Lord Granard and Evelyn Shirley; ibid., col. 929.
136. Ibid., col. 930.
137. Ibid., 8 March, col. 1086.
138. *An Act to Provide for the Improvement and Development of the Horse Racing Industry and for the Better Control of Racecourses and for this and Other Purposes to Establish a Body to be*

Called the Irish Horseracing Authority.... (No. 18 of 1994).

139. Quoted in R.B. MacDowell, *Land and Learning: Two Irish Clubs* (Dublin, 1993), p. 38 from C. Curtis and T.M. Wilson, *Ireland from Below: Social Change and Local Communities* (Galway, 1982).

140. McDowell, *Land and Learning*, p. 38.

141. Even by 1914, eighty businessmen had joined the Kildare Street Club; ibid., p. 89.

142. Ibid., p. 99.

143. Fingall, *Seventy Years Young*, p. 29.

144. John McGahern, 'Eddie Mac' in id., *High Ground* (London, 1985), p. 73.

145. Ibid., p. 68.

146. See opening quotation of this chapter, p. 242.

147. John McGahern, 'The Conversion of William Kirkwood' in id., *High Ground*, p. 123.

148. Ibid., p. 127.

Chapter 10

1. *Bess. Comm., Minutes of Evidence I*, p. 67.

2. Sir Stephen De Vere, 'Local Government in Ireland' in *Contemporary Review*, lx (November 1891), p. 735.

3. See for example, G. De L. Willis to editor of *Freeman's Journal*, 9 September 1903; *Freeman's Journal*, 10 September 1903.

4. *Final Report of the Royal Commission Appointed to Inquire into and Report upon the Operation of the Acts Dealing with Congestion in Ireland*, [Cd 4097], HC 1908, xliii, 1, pp. 69–70.

5. *RCB Report, 1924*, p. 10.

6. *RCB Report, 1926*, p. 9.

7. Bowen, 'The Big House', p. 29.

8. Bowen, *Bowen's Court*, pp. 10–11.

9. Bowen, 'The Big House', pp. 28, 29.

10. M.L. Bush, *The English Aristocracy: a Comparative Synthesis* (London, 1984), p. 151.

11. *Irish Independent*, 6 April 1996.

12. Ibid.

13. *Sunday Tribune*, 15 February 1998.

14. *Irish Independent*, 6 April 1996.

15. Ibid.

16. Katherine Lanigan, 'The Castle is Open Again' in *Old Kilkenny Review*, no. 4, (1977), p. 248.

17. Reeves-Smyth, *Irish Country Houses*, pp. 33, 36.

18. *The Irish Times*, 19 January 1992.

19. Ibid., 25 January 1996

Bibliography

PRIMARY SOURCES: I MANUSCRIPTS

National Library of Ireland

Sorted Collections [Estate Papers]

Ashtown Papers; Bellingham Papers; Blake of Ballyglunin Papers; Bond Papers; Bruen Papers; Butler of Castlecrine Papers; Castletown Papers; Clonbrock Papers; Crofton Papers; Diaries of Lady Alice Howard; Dunalley Papers; Farnham Papers; Fitzwilliam Papers; Granard Papers; Headfort Papers; Inchiquin Papers; Leitrim Papers; Leslie Papers; Mahon of Castlegar Papers; Monck Papers; O'Donnell of Newport Papers; Ormonde Papers; Powerscourt Papers; Pratt Papers

Unsorted Collections [Estate Papers]

Bernard Papers; Bowen Papers; Conyngham Papers; Dartrey Papers; De Freyne Papers; Doneraile Papers; Dunsandle Papers; Garstin Papers; Louth Papers; Wicklow Papers

Other Collections

Bencke Papers; Collins Papers; Maunsell Papers; John Redmond Papers; Shane Leslie Papers.

National Archives

Estate Papers

Bellew of Barmeath Papers; Blake of Ballyglunin Papers; Congreve Papers; Esmonde of Ballynastragh Papers; Guinness Mahon Papers

Other Papers

1911 Census: household schedule returns of 100 sample houses; Chief Secretary's Office: Irish Crime Records, Registered Papers, Official Papers, Outrage Papers; Childers Papers; Dáil Éireann Files, 1922–24; Dáil Éireann: Minutes of Proceedings of First Dáil, 1919–21; Dáil Éireann: Private Sessions of Second Dáil: Minutes of Proceedings 18 August 1921–14 September 1921; Department of Finance Files; Department of Justice Files; Department of Taoiseach Files; Government and Cabinet Files, 1922–51; Irish Convention 1917–18 Papers; Office of Public Works Files; Individual Wills and Abstracts of Wills.

Public Record Office, Northern Ireland

Carson Papers; Dunraven Papers; In-correspondence of the Irish Loyal and Patriotic Union (later Irish Unionist Alliance); Leinster Papers [consulted on microfilm, John Paul II Library, NUI, Maynooth]; Memo on Southern Unionists in war of independence and civil war; Minutes Book of the Executive Committee of the Irish Unionist Alliance; Minutes Book of the General Council of the Irish Unionist Alliance; Papers of the Joint Committee of the Unionist Associations of Ireland; Southern Irish Loyalist Relief Association Papers; The Plight of Southern Irish Unionists; UUC Yearbooks, 1913–20; UVF Papers Relating to Counties Monaghan, Cavan and Donegal; J.M. Wilson's Tour of Ireland; J.M. Wilson: Miscellaneous Writings.

Public Record Office, London

Colonial office Papers, Class CO 904 (Dublin Castle Records): Anti-government Organisations, 1882–1921 (CO 904 part I); Police Reports, January 1892–December 1897 (CO 904 part ii); Police Reports, February 1898–December 1913 (CO 904 part iii); Police Reports, 1914–21 (CO 904 part iv); Judicial Proceedings, Enquiries and Miscellaneous Records, 1872–1926 (CO 904, part vi); Irish Compensation Claims Registers and Indexes (CO 905) 1992–30.

Minutes, Papers and Correspondence of the Irish Boundary Commission and Records of Oral and Written Evidence Submitted to Commission.

(Consulted on microfilm, NLI)

The Library of Trinity College, Dublin
Bond of Faragh Papers; Courtown Papers; Crofton Papers (County Monaghan estate)

University College Dublin Archives
Collins Papers; Mulcahy Papers; O'Malley Papers; O'Callaghan Westropp Papers; Aiken Papers.

Monaghan County Museum
Marron Papers; Thomas Toal Papers; Minutes of Clones Urban District Council, 1911–25;
Miscellaneous Estate Records and Maps.

Monaghan County Council offices
Minute Books of Monaghan County Council 1899–1930

The Registry of Deeds Office, Dublin
Transcripts of Leases, Mortgages and Releases

The Valuation Office, Dublin
Cancelled Books of the Tenement Valuation

Church House, Rathmines
Representative Body of Church of Ireland Mortgage Ledgers

St Patrick's College Maynooth
Mortgage Papers; President's Reports, 1880–1930.

Irish Architectural Archives, Dublin
Files on individual houses

Private Possession
Beaumont-Nesbitt Papers; Denis Carolan-Rushe Papers; Cloncurry Papers; Dartrey Papers.

PRIMARY SOURCES: II PARLIAMENTARY PAPERS

Returns of Advances under Land Acts 1881–1909
*Return of Proceedings Under the Land Law (Ireland) Act 1881 as to Advances to Occupiers up to
    31 March 1883*, [C 2674], HC 1883, lvii; to 30 June 1883, [C 3680], HC 1883, lvii; to 31 July 1883,
    [C 3744], HC 1883, lvii; to 31 January 1884, [C 3888], HC 1884, lxiv; to 31 March 1884, [C 3993],
    HC 1884, lxiv; to 30 June 1884, [C 4114], HC 1884, lxiv; to 30 September 1884,[C 4232], HC
    1884–85, lxv; to 31 December 1884, [C 4295], HC 1884–85, lxv; to 31 March 1885,[C 4408], HC
    1884–85, lxv; to 30 June 1885, [C 4510], HC 1884–85, lxv.
*Return Giving the Name of Landowners the Purchase of Whose Properties under the Land Purchase
    (Ireland) Act 1885 has been Sanctioned by the Irish Land Commission, Showing Area of the
    Property; County; Rental; Valuation; Purchase Money; and Number of Holdings on the Estate*, HC
    1889, lxi, 685; to 31 January 1889, HC, 1890, lx, 115.
*Return of Advances under the Purchase of Land (Ireland) Act 1891 up to 31 March 1891 Specifying the
    Situation, Size, Rateable Value, Rent, Vendor, Purchaser, Purchase-money, Advance and
    Guarantee Deposit of each Holding ...*, HC 1892, lxv; to 1893, HC 1893–94, lxxv, 25; to 1894, HC
    1894, lxxii, 75; to 1895, HC 1895, lxxxii, 161; to 1896, HC 1896, lxix, 689; to 1897, HC 1898, lxxiv,
    195; to 1898, HC 1899, lxxix, 743; to 1899, HC 1899, lxxix, 851; to 1900, HC 1900, lxix, 757; to
    1901, HC 1901, lxi, 563; to 1902, HC 1903, lxxxiv, 929; to 1903, HC 1903, lvii, 31; to 1904, HC
    1904, lxxx, 529; to 1905, HC 1905, lxv, 599.
*Return Giving the Names of the Landowners the Purchase of Whose Properties under the Land Purchase
    (Ireland) Act 1885, has been Sanctioned by the Irish Land Commission Since 1 January 1889
    Showing Area of Property, Where Situate, Rental, Valuation, Purchase Money, Holdings on Estate*,
    HC 1890, lx, 171.
*Return of Advances Made under the Irish Land Act 1903 and Irish Land Act 1909, During the Period
    from 1 November 1903 to 31 March 1920*: during 1906, [Cd 2988], [Cd 3039], [Cd 3153], [Cd 3206],
    HC 1906, C, 917; [Cd 3310], [Cd 3434], [Cd 3531], [Cd 3532], [Cd 3535], [Cd 3557],HC 1907, lxx,

549; during 1907, [Cd 3815], [Cd 3921], [Cd 4012], [Cd 4035], [Cd 4048], [Cd 4113], [Cd 4172], [Cd 4273], [Cd 4296], HC 1908, xc, 131; during 1908, [Cd 4359], [Cd 4375], [Cd 4394], [Cd 4410], HC 1908, xc, 701; [Cd 4453], [Cd 4463], [Cd 4490], [Cd 4601], [Cd 4665], [Cd 4851], HC 1909, lxxiii, 135; January–October 1909, [Cd 5059], [Cd 5129], [Cd 5178], [Cd 5195], [Cd 5342], [Cd 5348], [Cd 5387], [Cd 5402], HC 1910, lxxvi, 195; November 1909 to October 1910, [Cd 5488], [Cd 5489], [Cd 5490], [Cd 5624], [Cd 5639], [Cd 5750], [Cd 5758], [Cd 5887], [Cd 5890], [Cd 5952], HC 1911, lxvi, 29; November 1910 to December 1911, [Cd 6028], [Cd 6029], [Cd 6096], [Cd 6137], [Cd 6187], [Cd 6263], [Cd 6330], [Cd 6393], [Cd 6403], [Cd 6420], [Cd 6424], [Cd 6443], HC 1912–13, lxix, 747; during 1912, [Cd 6507], [Cd 6592], [Cd 6648], HC 1912–13, lxxi, 1; [Cd 6728], [Cd 6744], [Cd 6768], [Cd 6812], [Cd 6850], [Cd 7004], [Cd 7026], HC 1913, liii, 55; during 1913, [Cd 7114], [Cd 7143], [Cd 7162], [Cd 7222], [Cd 7231], [Cd 7288], [Cd 7411], [Cd 7414], [Cd 7489], [Cd 7577], HC 1914, lxvi, 1; January–February 1914, [Cd 7586], [Cd 7606], HC 1914, lxvi, 849; March 1914–May 1915, [Cd 7664], [Cd 7665], [Cd 7761], [Cd 7762], [Cd 7864], [Cd 7925], [Cd 8007], [Cd 8064], [Cd 8093], [Cd 8159], [Cd 8164], HC 1914–16, liii, 167; July 1915 to March 1916 [Cd 8562], [Cd 8646], [Cd 8753], HC 1917–18, xxv, 539; April–December 1916 [Cd 9063], [Cd 9209], HC 1918, xx, 617; during 1917 [Cmd 57], [Cmd 68], [Cmd 370], HC 1919, xlii, 31; during 1918 [Cmd 582], [Cmd 767], [Cmd 785], [Cmd 934], HC 1920, xl, 29; during 1919, [Cmd 1030], HC 1920, xl, 389; [Cmd 1142], [Cmd 1247], [Cmd 1298], [Cmd 1357], HC 1921, xxviii, 473; January–March 1920 [Cmd 1460], HC 1921, xxviii, 869.

Reports from Select Committees and Royal Commissions

Report from the Select Committee on Irish Land Act, 1870; Together with the Proceedings of the Committee, Minutes of Evidence, Appendix and Index, HC 1877 (388), xii, 1 (George Shaw LeFevre, Chairman).
Report from the Select Committee on Irish Land Act, 1870, Together with the Proceedings of the Committee, Minutes of Evidence, Appendix and Index, HC 1878 (249), xv, 1 (George Shaw LeFevre, Chairman).
Report of Her Majesty's Commission of Enquiry into the Working of the Landlord and Tenant (Ireland) Act, 1870 and the Acts Amending the Same, [C 2779], HC 1881, xviii, 1 (Earl of Bessborough, Chairman); *Minutes of Evidence*, pt. i [C 2779], HC 1881, xviii, 73. *Minutes of Evidence and Appendices*, pt. ii, [C 2779], HC 1881, xix, 1; *Index to Minutes of Evidence and Appendices* [C 2779], HC 1881, xix, 825.
Report of the Royal Commission on the Land Law (Ireland) Act, 1881, and the Purchase of Land (Ireland) Act, 1885, [C 4969], HC 1887, xxvi, 1 (Earl Cowper, Chairman); *Minutes of Evidence and Appendices* [C 4969], HC 1887, xxvi, 25; *Index to Evidence and Appendices* [C 4969], HC 1887, xxvi, 1109.
Report from the Select Committee of the House of Lords on the Landlord and Tenant (Ireland) Act 1870; with the Proceedings, Minutes of Evidence, Appendix and Index, 1872 (403) xi.
Report of the Royal Commission on the Land Law (Ireland) Act, 1881, and the Purchase of Land (Ireland) Act 1885, with Evidence, Appendices and Index, [C 4969], HC 1887, xxvi.
Report of Mr. R. Bourke, the Treasury Representative in Ireland, Under the Arrears of Rent Act, [C 3685], HC 1883, lvi, 73.
Report of the Irish Land Purchase Commissioners with Respect to Sales Completed During January to June 1889, [C 5879], HC 1889, xxvii, 493.
Report from the Select Committee on Land Acts (Ireland); with the Proceedings, Evidence and Index, HC 1894, xiii, 1.

Other Reports

First report of the Royal Commission Appointed to Enquire into and Report upon the Operation of the Acts Dealing with Congestion in Ireland, [Cd 3266], HC 1906, xxxii, 617;
Evidence and Documents [Cd 3267], HC 1906, xxii, 621; *Second Report* …,[Cd 3318] HC 1907, xxv, 1; *Evidence and Documents*, [Cd 3319], HC 1907, xxxv, 5; *Third Report* …, [Cd 3413], HC 1907, xxxv, 333; *Evidence and Documents*, [Cd 3413], HC 1907, xxxv, 337; *Eighth Report* …, [Cd 3838], HC 1908, xli, 1; *Evidence and Documents*, [Cd 3845], HC 1908, xli, 487; *Tenth Report* …, [Cd 4006], HC 1908, xlii, 1; *Evidence and Documents* [Cd 4007], HC 1908, xlii, 5; *Final Report* …, [Cd 4097], HC 1908, xliii, 729; *Index to Evidence*, [Cd 4098], HC 1908, xliii, 1; *Digest of Evidence*, [Cd 4099], HC 1908, xliii, 369.
Annual Reports of the Congested Districts Board for Ireland: [Cd 6908] HC 1893–94, lxxi, 525; [C 7266], HC 1893–94, lxxxi, 583; [C 7522], HC 1894, lxviii, 681; [C 7791], HC 1895, lxxix, 517; [C 8191], HC 1896, lxviii, 52; [C 8622], HC 1897, lxxii, 439; [C 9003], HC 1898, lxxii, 481; [C 9375], HC 1899, lxxvii, 755; [Cd 239], HC 1900, lxviii, 183; [Cd 681], HC 1901, lx, 1; [Cd 1192], HC 1902, lxxxiii, 71;

[Cd 1622], HC 1903, lv, 99; [Cd 2275], HC 1905, lxiii, 229; [Cd 2757], HC 1906, xcvii, 355; [Cd 3161], HC 1906, xcvii, 493; [Cd 3767], HC 1908, xxiii, 287; [Cd 4340], HC 1908, xxiii, 443; [Cd 4927], HC 1909, xvi, 1; [Cd 5712], HC 1911, xiii, 397; [Cd 6553], HC 1912–13, xvii, 1097; [Cd 7312], HC 1914, xvi, 6, 1097; [Cd 7865], HC 1914–16, xxiv, 621; [Cd 8076], HC 1914–16, xxiv, 693; [Cd 8356], HC 1916, vi, 525; [Cd 8853], HC 1917–18, xv, 199; [Cd 9139], HC 1918, vii, 769; [Cmd 759], HC 1920, xix, 889;[Cmd 1409], HC 1921, xiv, 613.

Report of the Irish Land Commissioners for the Period from 1 April to 31 March 1900, [Cd 294], HC 1900, xvii, 143; for 1903–04, [Cd 2168], HC 1904, xvii, 1; for 1907–08, [Cd 4242], HC 1908, xxiii, 1; for 1908–09, [Cd 4809], HC 1909, xxiii, 579; for 1914–15 [Cd 8042], HC 1914–16, xxiv, 225; for 1917–18 [Cmd 19], HC 1919, xxiv, 219; for 1919–20 [Cmd 1064], HC 1920 xix, 1149.

Sixty-fourth Report of the Commissioners of Inland Revenue for the Year 31 March 1921, [Cmd 1436], HC 1921, xiv, 439.

Board of Trade: Report by Miss Collet on the Money Wages of Indoor Domestic Servants in Great Britain, [Cd 9346], HC 1899, xvii, 22.

An Interim Report of the Estates Commissioners for the Period from 1 November 1903 to 31 December 1904 with Appendices, [Cd 2471], HC 1905, xxiii, 177.

Report of the Estates Commissioners for the Year Ending 31 March 1910 and for the Period from 1 November 1903 to 31 March 1910 with Appendices, [Cd 5423], HC 1910, xxi, 847; for 1917–18, [Cd 8766], HC 1919, xxiv, 137; for 1919–20, [Cmd 1150], HC 1921, xiv, 661.

Ministry of Reconstruction: Report of the Women's Advisory Committee on the Domestic Service Problem Together with Reports by Sub-committees on Training, Machinery of Distribution, Organisation and Conditions, [Cmd 67], HC 1919, xxix.

Special Returns

Return of the Amount Awarded to Tenants at Land Sessions in Ireland, Exclusive of Costs, under the Landlord and Tenant (Ireland) Act 1870 up to 31 December 1875, HC 1877, (194), lxix, 593.

Return for 1870 of Number of Landed Proprietors in each County, Classed According to Residence, Showing Extent and Value of Property Held by Each Class - and, Similar Return of Number of Landed Proprietors in each Province, HC 1872, (167), xlvii.

Return of Owners of Land, of One Acre and Upwards, in the Several Counties, Counties of Cities, and Counties of Towns in Ireland, [C 1492], HC 1876, lxxx, 61.

Return Showing, for Each County in Ireland, for the Year Ending 22 August 1882, and for Each Month from September 1882 to April 1883, the Number of Applications for Fair Rents Lodged in the Land Commission Court, those Fixed, Dismissed, Struck Out and Withdrawn, the Number of Agreements out of Court, and of Appeals Lodged, Heard and Withdrawn, HC 1883, lvii, 977.

Return of the Disposition of the Sum of £5,000,000 Granted under the Land Purchase Act 1885 up to 31 March 1888, Showing: Number of Applications, the Amounts of the Whole, of Those Accepted and Rejected; of Advances Issued, Sanctioned, and Under Consideration; of Instalments Repayable up to 1 November 1887, and Those Remaining Unpaid; and Amount of Disposal of Commissioners Should Applications Under Consideration be Sanctioned; also Details of Estates for Sale in Court Under Receivers, HC 1888, lxxxiii, 649.

Return of the Number of Estates for Sale in the Land Court Which on 31 December 1881 and 1886, Were Under Receivers, Their Rental, the Number of Receivers, Their Receipts During 1887, Sales During 1883–87, Amounts Realised, Number of Officials in the Land Judges Branch and Their Salaries in 1887, HC 1888, lxxxiii, 649.

Return Showing for Each Union in Ireland to 31 March 1897, the Name of Each, the Number of Holdings in Each, for Which Judicial Rents Have Been Fixed for a Second Statutory Term, the Aggregate Former (Non-judicial) Rents, Those Fixed for a First Statutory Term and for a Second, and the Average Percentages by Which the First Term Judicial Rents Were Less than the Former (Non-judicial Rents), and the Second Term Rents than the First, HC 1897, lxxiii, 617.

Return Showing, According to Provinces and Counties the Number of Loans Issued under the Purchase of Land (Ireland) Acts 1891 and 1896, During 1898, and the Total Rental of the Holdings in Respect of such Loans; also the Total Purchase Money, the Amount of the Loans so Issued and the Average Number of Years' Purchase Calculated on the Rent, HC 1899, lxxix, 1067.

Return Showing the Number of Properties in the Land Courts of Ireland, Dates When Each Came Under Their Control, Number of Tenants, Gross Rental of Each Estate, Where Receivers Have Been Appointed; and Showing Also When Each Estate was Last Put up for Sale by the Court, HC 1890, lx, 135.

Return of Estates Sold to Persons Other than the Land Commission; of Applications for Advances Lodged Where Sales Have Not Yet Been Completed; of Proceedings Under Various Sectors of the Irish Land Act 1903 ... in Respect of the Period of Six Months Ended 30 April 1904, HC 1904, lxxx, 515.

Return of Estates Purchased by the Congested Districts Board for Ireland in Respect of the Period of Six Months Ended 30 April 1904, for the Purpose of Resale to Tenants and the Enlargement of Holdings..., HC 1904, lxxx, 525.

Return Showing, as far as Practicable, for Each Year (or Other Stated Period) the Lowest and Highest Prices (in Each Calendar Year) of Guaranteed Land Stock; and the Number and Amount of Loans Under the Land Purchase Acts with the Total Amount of the Acreage Purchased, HC 1903, lvii, 313.

Return Showing, According to Provinces and Counties, the Number of Cases in Which Judicial Rents Have Been Fixed by All the Methods Provided by the Land Law Acts for a First and Second Statutory Term Respectively to 31 December 1902, with Particulars as to Acreage, Former Rents of Holdings, and Percentage of Reduction in Rents, HC 1903, lvii, 373.

Return Giving by Counties and Provinces, the Area, the Poor Law Valuation, and Purchase Money of Lands Sold, and Lands in Respect of Which Proceedings have been Instituted and are Pending for Sale Under the Irish Land Purchase Acts; also the Estimated Area, Poor Law Valuation, and the Purchase-Money of Lands in Respect of Which Proceedings for Sale Have Not Been Instituted Under the Said Acts, [Cd 4412], HC 1908, xc, 1401; [Cd 6130], HC 1912–13, lxxi, 761; [Cd 6930], HC 1913, liii, 767.

Return Showing the Average Number of Years Purchase Under the Ashbourne Act for the Years 1901 and 1902, and Under the Act of 1903 to 31 July 1908, in the Different Counties of Ireland, HC 1908, xc, 1411.

Return Showing by Counties the Average Number of Years' Purchase Under the Different Land Purchase Acts or Clauses from 1870 to 1903, With the Average Percentage of Reductions, the Number and Acreage of Holdings Purchased Under Each Act and the Amount of Interest and Sinking Fund Payable by the Tenant-Purchasers ... up to 1 November 1908., HC 1908, xc, 1413.

Return of the Resolution and Statement Adopted by the Irish Landowners' Convention on 10 October 1902; and Report of the Irish Land Conference Dated 3 January 1903; and Minute on the Land Conference Report Adopted on 7 January 1903 by the Executive Committee of the Irish Landowners' Convention, HC 1903, lvii, 321.

Return of Untenanted Lands in Rural Districts, Distinguishing Demesnes on Which There is a Mansion, Showing: Rural District and Electoral Divisions; Townland; Area in Statute Acres; Poor Law Valuation; Names of Occupiers as in Valuation Lists, HC 1906, c, 177.

Return Showing for Each Year Since 1823 the Taxes in Force in England and Wales, Scotland, and Ireland, Separately, in Cases Where the Taxes were not Common to all Three Countries, or, Where the Same Duties Were in Force in all Three Countries but the Rate of Tax was Different, Specifying the Principal Rates, and Showing Where Available the Amounts Raised Thereunder in Each Country, HC 1912–13, xlix, 675.

PRIMARY SOURCES: III ACTS

An Act to Further Amend the Law Relating to the Occupation and Ownership of Land in Ireland or for Other Relating Purposes Thereto (33 and 34 Vict., c.xlvi (22 August 1881)).

An Act to Make Provisions Respecting Certain Arrears of Rent in Ireland (45 and 46 Vict., c.xlix, (18 August 1882)).

An Act to Provide Greater Facilities for the Sale of Land to Occupying Tenants in Ireland (44 and 45 Vict., c.xlviiii (22 August 1885)).

An Act to Provide Funds for the Purchase of Land in Ireland and to Make Permanent the Land Commission and to Provide for the Improvement of the Congested Districts in Ireland (51 and 52 Vict., c.cii (5 August 1891)).

An Act for Amending the Law Relating to Local Government in Ireland and for Other Purposes Connected Therewith (61 and 62 Vict., c.xxxvii (12 August 1898)).

Land Purchase (Ireland) Act 1903 (3 Ed., cxxxvii (1 November 1903).

An Act to Amend the Enactments Relative to Compensation for Criminal Injuries in Ireland (9 and 10 Geo. V., c.xiv (16 April 1919)).

An Act to Amend the Enactments Relative to Compensation for Criminal Injuries in Ireland (10 and 11 Geo. V., c.lxvi (23 December 1920)).

Damage to Property (Compensation) Act, Irish Acts, Number 15 of 1923.

An Act to Amend the Law Relating to the Occupation and Ownership of Land and for Other Purposes Relating Thereto, Irish Acts Number 42 of 1923.

Irish Land Act 1931, Irish Acts Number 11 of 1931.

Irish Land Act 1933, Irish Acts Number 38 of 1933.

An Act to Provide for the Improvement and Development of Horse Breeding and Horse Racing and for the Better Control of Race Courses, and For This and Other Purposes to Establish a Board to be Called the Racing Board ..., Irish Acts, Number 16 of 1945.

An Act to Provide for the Improvement and Development of the Horse Racing Industry and for the Better Control of Race Courses and for This and Other Purposes to Establish a Body to be Called the Irish Horseracing Authority ..., Irish Acts, Number 18 of 1994.

PRIMARY SOURCES: IV BRITISH AND IRISH GOVERNMENT PUBLICATIONS

Annual Reports of the Revenue Commissioners of Saorstát Éireann, 1924–50; Annual Reports of the Irish Land Commissioners, 1921–50; Saorstát Éireann: Census of Population, vol x, General Report 1926; Censuses of Population of Ireland 1946 and 1951: General Report (1958); Dáil debates; Iris Oifigiúil, 1923–50; Senate debates; Terms of Reference of the Property Compensation Commission Set Up by Agreement Between the British Government and the Irish Provisional Government (1922).

PRIMARY SOURCES: V PUBLISHED REPORTS, ANNUALS, CALENDARS AND CATALOGUES

Annual Reports of Irish Loyal and Patriotic Union (later Irish Unionist Alliance) 1885–1920; Annual reports of Ulster Unionist Council, 1913–20; Bailey's Hunting Directory, 1939–49; Battersby and Co., Kilkenny Castle: Catalogue of the Valuable Antique and Interesting Contents of this Historic Mansion to be Sold by Auction Commencing Monday 18 November 1935 (NLI); Battersby and Co., Catalogue of Contents of Salterbridge, Cappoquin, to be Sold 5 December 1916 by Direction of Col. G.R. Hamilton (NLI); Bennett and Sons, Catalogue of Valuable Antique and Modern Furniture, Silver Plate, Old Sheffield Plate, Library and 200 Oil Paintings to be Sold at Killua Castle Westmeath, by Direction of General R.S. Fetherstonhaugh, 2 June 1920 (NLI); Catalogue of a Collection of Important Books Selected from the Library at Carton with the Consent of the Trustees of the Duke of Leinster to be Sold by Auction by Bennett and Sons, 1925 (NLI);Catalogue of an Important and Valuable Collection of Works of Art Removed From Carton with the Consent of the Trustees of His Grace the Duke of Leinster to be sold on 2 December 1925 and Two Following Days by Bennett and Sons (IAA); Catalogue of Pictures, Plates and Antiquities at Carton, Kilkea Castle and 13 Dominick St. Dublin and 6 Carlton House Terrace, London (Privately published, 1885); Catalogue of Old Irish Silver Plate Sold by Order of Trustees of Late Lord Fitzgerald as Christie's, 4 December 1902 (PRONI); Catalogue of Ancient and Modern Pictures Sold by Order of Trustees of Late Lord Fitzgerald at Christie's, 6 December 1902 (PRONI); Catalogue of Library of J.R. Garstin of Irish Literature to be Sold by Private Auction, 1918 (Private possession); Catalogue of the Entire Library from Doneraile Court ... to be Sold by Auction ... on 17 and 18 December 1969 (NLI); Catalogue of the Valuable Contents of Dartrey Castle, Cootehill, Co. Cavan Which Will be Sold by Auction on the Premises on Monday 19 April 1937 and Three Following Days (Private possession); Catalogue, Powerscourt, Enniskerry, Co. Wicklow: Catalogue of Old Masters' Pictures, French, English and Irish Furniture, Silver and a Collection of Arms and Armour to be Sold 24–25 September 1984 (Private possession); Catalogue of the Sale of the Contents of Charleville House by Private Auction, 1932 (NLI); House of Lords War Memorial (London, n.d.); Irish Landowners' Convention Annual Reports, 1887–1919; Irish Racing Annual, 1940–50; Irish Racing Board Annual Reports, 1946–50; Irish Racing Calendar, 1865–1950; Protestant Defence Association of Ireland Annual Reports, 1880–89; Representative Body of Church of Ireland: Annual Reports Presented to the General Synod, 1871–1950; Sixty-sixth Annual Report of the Dublin Providence Home, 1904 (Dublin, 1904); The Annual Report of the Domestic Training Institute, 1910 (Dublin, 1911).

PRIMARY SOURCES: VI NEWSPAPERS, JOURNALS, PERIODICALS

An Taisce; Belfast Newsletter; Cavan Weekly News; Church of Ireland Gazette; Connaught Leader; Cork Examiner; Country Life; Daily Express; Daily Telegraph; Dublin Daily Express; Dundalk Democrat; Echo and South Leinster Adventurer; Freeman's Journal; Galway Express; Iris Oifigiúil; Irish Ancestor;

Irish Georgian Society Bulletin; Irish Independent; Irish Press; Irish Tatler and Sketch; Kildare Observer; Kilkenny People; King's County Chronicle; Leinster Leader; Leinster Express; Longford Independent; Morning Post; Northern Standard; Notes from Ireland; Offaly County Chronicle; Roscommon Journal; Roscommon Messenger; Sunday Independent; Sunday Press; Sunday Tribune; The Irish Times; The Times; Tuam Herald; Weekly Freeman's Journal; Weekly Irish Times; Western People; Westmeath Examiner; Westmeath Guardian; Westminster Gazette.

PRIMARY SOURCES: VII PUBLISHED CONTEMPORARY WORKS

[This is a select list of published contemporary works; others which were consulted during the research of this work are referenced
in the endnotes.]

An Irish Priest, *A Short History of the Land War in Drumlish in 1881* (Dublin, 1892).

Anon., *Memoir of the Kilkenny Hunt: Compiled by One of its Members in the Year of its Centenary, 1897* (Dublin, 1897).

Breen, Dan, *My Fight for Irish Freedom* (Dublin, 1981 ed.).

Bowen, Elizabeth, *Bowen's Court* (New York, 1942).

Bowen, 'The Big House' in Hermione Lee (ed.), *The Mulberry Tree: Writings on Elizabeth Bowen* (London, 1986) pp. 25–29.

Bowen, 'The Most Unforgettable Character' in Hermione Lee (ed.), *The Mulberry Tree* (London, 1986) pp. 254–64.

Brooke, R.F., *Daly's Club and Kildare Street Club*, Dublin (Dublin, 1930).

Carbery, Mary, *The Farm by Lough Gur* (Dublin, 1973 ed.)

Castletown, Lord, *Ego: Random Records of Sport, Service and Travel in Many Lands* (London, 1923).

County Club, Limerick, *A Short History of a Hundred Years of Club Life* (Privately published, Dublin, n.d.)

Crane, C.P., *Memoirs of a Resident Magistrate* (Edinburgh ,1938).

Desdichado (pseudonym), *Fox Hunting in Meath: An Imperfect Record of a Hunting Season in Meath, 1883–4* (Dublin, 1884).

De Stacpoole, Duc, *Irish and Other Memories* (London, 1922).

Drought, J.B., *A Sportsman Looks at Eire* (London, n.d.).

Dunraven, Earl of, *Past Times and Pastimes vol. 1* (London, 1922).

Drumlish Land War Centenary, 1881–1981: Commemorative Booklet (1981)

Dun, Finlay, *Landlords and Tenants in Ireland* (Ireland, 1881).

Fingall, Elizabeth Countess, *Seventy Years Young* (London, 1937).

Ganly, C.W., *A Tribute to a Noble Life: In Memoriam of Gerald, Duke of Leinster* (Dublin, n.d.)

Gwynn, Stephen, *Experiences of a Literary Man* (London, 1926).

Headlam, Maurice, *Irish Reminiscences* (London, 1947).

Hone, Joseph, *The Life of George Moore* (London, 1936).

Hone, Joseph, *The Moores of Moore Hall* (Cape, 1939).

Hutton, A.W. (ed.), *Arthur Young's Tour in Ireland, vol. 1* (London, 1892).

ILPU, *Ireland Under the League: Illustrated by Extracts From the Evidence Given Before the Cowper Commission* (London, 1887).

ILPU, *Statement Presented to the Prime Minister by the ILPU, Part III: the Union Vindicated Ireland's Progress 1782–1800–1886* (Dublin, 1886).

ILPU, *Union or Separation* (Dublin, 1886).

INHSC, *Irish Point to Point Handbook* (Dublin, 1945).

Irish Land Committee, *The Land Question in Ireland, Volume XIV: The Working of the Land Act* (London, 1882).

IUA, *The Intolerance of Irish Nationalism Towards Irish Unionism* (Dublin, 1908).

IUA, *The Irish Unionist Alliance: An Account of its Work and Organisation* (Dublin, 1893).

IUA, *The New Home Rule and the Old Objections* (Dublin, 1906).

Leslie, Anita, *The Gilt and the Gingerbread: An Autobiography* (London, 1931).

Leslie, Anita, *The Marlborough House Set* (New York, 1975).

Leslie, Seymour, *Of Glaslough in the Kingdom of Oriel and of the Noted Men Who have Dwelt There* (Privately Published, Glaslough, 1913).

Leslie, Seymour, *The Jerome Connexion* (London, 1964)

Leslie, Shane, *The Irish Tangle for English Readers* (London, 1946).

Leslie, Shane, *The Irish Issue in its American Aspect* (London, 1919).

Leslie, Shane, *The End of a Chapter* (London, 1916).

Leslie, Shane, *The Film of Memory* (London, 1938).

Lucas, Reginald, *Col. Saunderson M.P.: A Memoir* (London, 1908).

Lynch, Comm., *Land Purchase in Ireland: A Retrospect and a Forecast* (Dublin, 1912).

Lynch-Robinson, Christopher, *The Last of the Irish R.M.s* (London, 1951).

MacCabe, F.F., and T.E. Healey, 'Racing, Steeplechasing and Breeding in Ireland' in Charles Richardson (ed.), *British Steeplechasing* (London, 1927).

Mahaffy, J.P., 'The Irish Landlords' in *Contemporary Review*, xli, 1882.

Mayo, Earl of and Boulton, W.B., *A History of the Kildare Hunt* (London, n.d.).

Meath, Earl of (ed.), *The Diaries of Mary, Countess of Meath* (London, n.d.).

Meath, Earl of, *Memories of the Nineteenth Century* (London, 1923).

Moore, M.G., *An Irish Gentleman: George Henry Moore* (London, n.d.).

Neale, J.P., *Views of the Seats of Noblemen and Gentlemen in England, Wales and Scotland and Ireland vol. iii* (London, 1820).

Ormonde, Marquis of, 'Address by Marquis of Ormonde on Handing Over of Kilkenny Castle' in *Journal of the Butler Society* (1968), pp. 14–15.

Ossory, Earl of, 'The Attack on Kilkenny Castle' in *Journal of Butler Society*, Vol. i, no. 4 (1972), pp. 259–74.

Pakenham, Frank, *Born to Believe* (London, 1953).

Probyn, J.W. (ed.), *Systems of Land Tenure in Various Countries* (London, 1881).

Robinson, Lennox (ed.), *Lady Gregory's Journals* (New York, 1947).

Robinson, Lennox, *Bryan Cooper* (London, 1931).

Robinson, Lennox, Tom Robinson, and Nora Dorman, *Three Homes* (London, 1938).

Rules of the Kildare Street Club with a List of Members Names, January 1860, (Privately Published, Dublin, 1860).

Rules of the Sackville Street Club and a List of Members, 1860 (Privately Published., Dublin, 1860).

Taylor, J.W. (ed.), *The Rossmore Incident* (Dublin, 1884).

Thomson, David, *Woodbrook* (London, 1974).

Wyndham Quin, Col., *The Fox Hunt in Co. Limerick* (Dublin, 1919).

Yeats, W.B., *The Autobiography of W.B. Yeats* (London, 1966).

PRIMARY SOURCES: VIII WORKS OF REFERENCE, GUIDES AND DIRECTORIES

Bailey's Hunting Directory, 1939–49.

Bateman, John, *The Great Landowners of Great Britain and Ireland* (London, 1883).

Bence-Jones, Mark, *A Guide to Irish Country Houses* (London, 1988, revised ed.)

Burke's Landed Gentry of Ireland (various eds.)

Burke's Peerage, Baronetage and Knightage (various eds.)

Collins, Peter, *County Monaghan Sources in the Public Record Office of Northern Ireland* (Belfast, 1998)

Corkayne, G.E., *Complete Peerage of England, Scotland, Ireland etc., Extant, Extinct or Dormant* (Exeter, 1887–98). 8 volumes.

Dooley, Terence, *Sources for the History of Landed Estates in Ireland* (Dublin, 2000)

Hayes, R.T. (ed.), *Manuscript Sources for the History of Irish Civilisations* (Boston, 1965). 11 vols.

Hussey De Burgh, U.H., *The Landowners of Ireland: An Alphabetical List of the Owners of Estates of 500 Acres or £500 Valuation and Upwards in Ireland* (Dublin, 1878).

The Servant's Practical Guide, 1880 (London, 1880).

Thom's Almanac and Official Directory of the United Kingdom and Ireland (Dublin, 1845–1950).

Walker, B.M., *Parliamentary Election Results in Ireland, 1801–1922* (Dublin, 1978).

SECONDARY SOURCES

[This is a select list of secondary works; others which were consulted in the research of this work are referenced in the endnotes.]

Somerville, Edith and Ross, Martin, *The Big House of Inver* (London, 1978 ed.).

Banville, John, *The Newton Letter* (London, 1982).

Bence-Jones, Mark, *Twilight of the Ascendancy* (London, 1987).

Bew, Paul, *Land and the National Question in Ireland 1858–82* (Dublin, 1978).

Boas, Guy, *The Garrick Club, 1831–1947* (London, 1948).

Bowen, Elizabeth, *A World of Love* (London, 1967 ed.).

Bowen, Elizabeth, *The Last September* (London, 1987 ed.).

Bowen, Muriel, *Irish Hunting* (Tralee, n.d.)

Buckland, Patrick, *Irish Unionism 1885–1923: A Documentary History* (Belfast, 1973).

Buckland, Patrick, *Irish Unionism I: the Anglo-Irish and the New Ireland 1885–1922* (Dublin, 1972).

Buckland, Patrick, *Irish Unionism II: Ulster Unionism and the Origins of Northern Ireland 1885–1922* (Dublin, 1973).

Cannadine, David, *The Decline and Fall of the British Aristocracy* (Yale, 1990).

Cannadine, David, *Aspects of Aristocracy* (Yale, 1994).

Carey, Joyce, *Castle Corner* (London, 1950).

Carter, J.W.H., *The Land War and its Leaders in Queen's County, 1879–82* (Portlaoise, 1994).

Clark, Samuel and J.S. Donnelly, *Irish Peasants: Violence and Political Unrest 1780–1914* (Wisconsin, 1983).

Clark, Samuel, *The Social Origins of the Irish Land War* (Princeton, 1979).

Comerford, R.V, *The Fenians in Context: Irish Politics and Society 1848–82* (Dublin, 1985).

Comerford, R.V. et al (eds.), *Religion, Conflict and Co-existence in Ireland* (Dublin, 1990).

Corish, P.J., *Maynooth College, 1795–1995* (Dublin, 1995).

Craig, Maurice, *The Architecture of Ireland from the Earliest Times to 1880* (London, and Dublin 1982).

Cronin, Gearóid, 'John Banville and the Subversion of the Big House Novel' in Genet, Jacqueline (ed.), *The Big House in Ireland: Reality and Representation* (Dingle, 1991), pp. 215–32.

Curtis, L.P., Jr., 'Encumbered Wealth: Landlord Indebtedness in Post-Famine Ireland' in *American Historical Review*, 85: 2 (April 1980), pp. 332–67.

Curtis, L.P., Jr., 'Stopping the Hunt, 1881–2: An aspect of the Irish Land War' in C.H.E. Philpin (ed.), *Nationalism and Popular Protest in Ireland* (Cambridge, 1987), pp. 349–401.

Curtis, L.P., Jr., 'The Anglo-Irish Predicament' in *Twentieth Century Studies*, no. 4 (November 1970), pp. 37–63.

Curtis, L.P., Jr., *Coercion and Conciliation in Ireland, 1880–1892: A Study in Conservative Unionism* (Princeton, NJ, 1963).

Darcy, F.A., *Horses, Lords and Racing Men* (Kildare, 1991).

Dawes, F.V., *Not in Front of the Servants* (London, 1973).

Donnelly, J.S. Jr., *The Land and People of Nineteenth-Century Cork: The Rural Economy and the Land Question* (London, 1975).

Dooley, Terence, *The Plight of Monaghan Protestants, 1911–26* (Dublin, 2000)

Edgeworth, Maria, *Castle Rackrent* (London, 1976 ed.).

Estorick, Michael, *Heirs and Graces: The Claim to the Dukedom of Leinster* (London, 1981).

Fanning., Ronan, T*he Irish Department of Finance, 1922–58* (Dublin, 1978).

Farrell, T.J., *Troubles* (London, 1975).

Feingold, W.L., 'Land League Power: The Tralee Poor-Law Election of 1881', in Samuel Clark and James S. Donnelly Jr. (eds.), *Irish Peasants: Violence and Critical Unrest 1780–1914* (Manchester, 1983), pp. 285–310.

Fitzpatrick, David, *Politics and Irish Life 1913–21* (Dublin, 1977).

Foster, R.F., *Modern Ireland, 1600–1972* (London, 1989 ed.)

Garvin, Tom, *The Evolution of Irish Nationalist Politics* (Dublin, 1981).

Geary, Laurence, *The Plan of Campaign 1886–11* (Cork, 1985).

Genet, Jacqueline, *The Big House in Ireland: Reality and Representation* (Dingle, 1991).

Gerard, Jessica, *Country House Life: Families and Servants, 1815–1914* (Oxford, 1994).

Glin, Knight of, Griffin, D.J. and Robinson, N.K., *Vanishing Country Houses of Ireland* (1988).

Griffin, Brian, 'The Irish Police, 1836–1914: A Social History', (Unpubl. D.Phil Thesis, Loyola University, Chicago, 1990).

Guinness, Desmond and William Ryan, *Irish Houses and Castles* (London, 1971).

Guinness, Desmond, 'The Irish Georgian Society: The First Thirty Years' in *Bulletin of the Irish Georgian Society*, vol. xxxi, 1988, pp. 3–28.

Hart, Peter, 'The Protestant Experience of Revolution in Modern Ireland' in Richard English and Graham Walker (eds.), *Unionism in Modern Ireland: New Perspectives on Politics and Culture* (Dublin, 1996), pp. 81–98.

Hopkinson, Michael, *Green against Green: The Irish Civil War* (Dublin, 1988).

Hoppen, K.T., *Election, Politics and Society in Ireland, 1832–85* (Oxford ,1984).

Horn, Pamela, *The Rise and Fall of the Victorian Servant* (Dublin and New York, 1975).

Jackson, Alvin, *Col. Edward Saunderson: Land and Loyalty in Victorian Ireland* (Oxford, 1995).

Jenkins, Brian, *Sir William Gregory of Coole: The Biography of an Anglo-Irishman* (Buckinghamshire, 1986).

Jones, David Seth, *Graziers, Land Reform and Political Conflict in Ireland* (Washington, 1995).

Jones, W.G., *The Wynnes of Sligo and Leitrim: The Powerful Family of Hazlewood and Lurganboy* (Manorhamilton, 1994).

Keane, Molly, *Mad Puppetstown* (London, 1985 ed.).

Keane, Molly, *Two Days in Aragon* (London, 1985 ed.).

Kolbert, C.F. and T. O'Brien, *Land Reform in Ireland: A Legal History of the Irish Land Problem and its Settlement* (Cambridge, 1975).

Laffan, Michael, *The Partition of Ireland 1911–25* (Dublin ,1983).

Leslie, Shane, *Doomsland* (London, n.d.).

Lewis, C.S., *Hunting in Ireland: An Historical and Geographical Analysis* (London, 1975).

Lewis, Gifford, *Somerville and Ross: The World of the Irish R.M.* (London, 1985).

Littlejohn, David, *The Fate of the English Country House* (Oxford, 1997).

Lyons, F.S.L., 'The Twilight of the Big House', in *Ariel*, vol. I, no. 3, (July 1970), pp. 3–14.

Malins, Edward, and Glin, Knight of, *Irish Gardens: The Heritage Series II* (Dublin, 1977).

McDowell, R.B., *Land and Learning: Two Irish Clubs* (Dublin, 1993).

McDowell, R.B., *The Irish Convention*, (London 1970).

McGahern, John, 'Eddie Mac' in John McGahern, *High Ground* (London, 1985).

McGahern, John, 'The Conversion of William Kirkwood' in John McGahern, *High Ground* (London, 1985).

McKenna, Peter, The *Emetresse*, (Monaghan 1991).

McNiffe, Liam, *A History of the Garda Síochána: A Social History of the Force, 1922–52 with an Overview of the years 1952–97* (Dublin, 1997)

McParland, Edward and Robinson, N.K. (eds.), *Heritage at Risk: A Digest of An Taisce's Report on the Future of Historic Houses, Gardens and Collections in the Republic of Ireland* (Dublin ,1977).

Mandler, Peter, *The Fall and Rise of the Stately Home* (Yale, 1997).

Mitchell, Arthur, *Revolutionary Government in Ireland: Dáil Éireann 1919–22* (Dublin, 1995).

Moore, George, *A Drama in Muslin* (Paris, 1886).

Morrow, Ann, *Picnic in a Foreign Land: The Eccentric Lives of the Anglo-Irish* (London, 1989).

O'Grada, Cormac, 'The Investment Behaviour of Irish Landlords, 1850–75: Some Preliminary Findings' in *Agricultural History Review*, xxiii, (1975), pp. 139–55.

Philpin, C.H.E. (ed.), *Nationalism and Popular Protest in Ireland* (Cambridge, 1987).

Pomfret, John E., *The Struggle for Land in Ireland, 1800–1923* (Princeton, NJ, 1930).

Proudfoot, Lindsay, 'The Management of a Great Estate: Patronage, Income and Expenditure on the Duke of Devonshire's Irish Property, c. 1816–1891', *Ir. Econ. & Soc. Hist.* xiii, (1986), pp. 32–55.

Robinson, Lennox, *The Big House* in Lennox Robinson, *Plays* (London, 1928).

Robinson, Olive, 'The London Companies as Progressive Landlords in Nineteenth-Century Ireland', *Econ. Hist. Rev.* 2nd ser., 15:1 (August 1962), pp. 103–18.

Rumpf, Erhard and Hepburn, A.C., *Nationalism and Socialism in Twentieth Century Ireland* (Liverpool, 1977).

Sheehan, J.T., 'Land Purchase Policy in Ireland 1917–23: From the Irish Convention to the 1923 Land Act, (Unpubld. MA thesis, Maynooth, 1993).

Sligo, Marquis of, *Westport House and the Brownes* (Mayo, 1981).

Solow, B.L., *The Land Question and the Irish Economy, 1870–1903* (Cambridge, Mass., 1971).

Somerville-Large, Peter, *The Irish Country House: A Social History* (London, 1995).

Tweedy, Owen, *The Dublin Tweedys: The Story of an Irish Family, 1650–1882* (London, 1956).

Vaughan, W.E., *Landlords and Tenants in mid-Victorian Ireland* (Oxford, 1994).

Watson, Col. S.J., *Between the Flags: A History of Irish Steeplechasing* (Dublin, 1969).

ABBREVIATIONS

APL   (Unionist) Anti-Partition League
BC papers Irish Boundary Commission papers
CICMR   County Inspector's confidential monthly report
CO   Colonial Office, Dublin Castle records
CSORP   Chief Secretary for Ireland's office, registered papers
GHQ   General head quarters (IRA)
IAA   Irish Architectural Archives
IGCMR   Inspector General's confidential monthly report
ILPU   Irish Loyal and Patriotic Union
INHSC   Irish National Hunt and Steeplechase committee
INV   Irish National Volunteers
IRA   Irish Republican Army
IUA   Irish Unionist Alliance
MCM   Monaghan County Museum
MMP   St Patrick's College, Maynooth, mortgage papers
MP   Member of Parliament
NA   National Archives, Dublin
NLI   National Library of Ireland, Dublin
PDA   Protestant Defence Association
PRO   Public Record Office, London
PRONI   Public Record Office of Northern Ireland
RCB   Representative Church Body (Representative Body of the Church of
           Ireland)
RIC   Royal Irish Constabulary
TD   Teachta Dála (a member of Dáil Éireann)
TCD   Trinity College Dublin
UCD   University College Dublin
UIL   United Irish League
UUC   Ulster Unionist Council
UVF   Ulster Volunteer Force

INDEX